The Electoral Challenge

The Electoral Challenge

Theory Meets Practice

Edited by

Stephen C. Craig
University of Florida

A Division of Congressional Quarterly Inc.
Washington, D.C.

CQ Press
1255 22nd Street, NW, Suite 400
Washington, DC 20037

Phone: 202-729-1900; toll-free, 1-866-427-7737 (1-866-4CQ-PRESS)

Web: www.cqpress.com

Copyright © 2006 by CQ Press, a division of Congressional Quarterly Inc.

All rights reserved. No part of this publication may be reproduced or transmitted in any form or by any means, electronic or mechanical, including photocopy, recording, or any information storage and retrieval system, without permission in writing from the publisher.

Cover design by Lorraine Doneker

⊚ The paper used in this publication exceeds the requirements of the American National Standard for Information Sciences—Permanence of Paper for Printed Library Materials, ANSI Z39.48-1992.

Printed and bound in the United States of America

10 09 08 07 06   1 2 3 4 5

Library of Congress Cataloging-in-Publication Data

The electoral challenge : theory meets practice / edited by Stephen C. Craig.
   p. cm.
  Includes bibliographical references.
  ISBN 1-933116-61-7 (pbk. : alk. paper)
  1. Presidents—United States—Election. 2. Political campaigns—United States. 3. Voting—United States. I. Craig, Stephen C. II. Title.

JK524.E366 2006
324.70973—dc22
                                            2005037105

For

Jane, Jon, Michelle A., Alison, David B., Page, Neal, Frank,

Aaron, Justin, Elizabeth C., Jamie C., Michael C., Carla, Lee, Heather C., Kris,

Diane, Ani, Tad, Slade, Charles, Tom E., Jeremy F., Carmen, Nicole F.,

Travis, Ralph, Brian, Sarah, Catrine, Michael G., Melinda,

Kim H., Gavin, T. J., Mary, Nicole J., Craig, Lyndsay, Adam, Seth, Heather K.,

Alex, Barda, Michelle M., Shannon, David K., Scott L., Ed, Jackie,

Michael L., Ramon, Jen, Wally, Catherine, Elizabeth M., Norma, Paul, Tim, Jay,

Kolby, Joe P., Bill, David R., Ian, Tom R., Kimberly S., Nick,

Elicia, Joe S., Debbie, Corey, Paul, Scott S., Gary, Ted, Tracey, Keith, Jeremy T.,

John, Mari, Ashley, Chris, Justin, Donna, Dana, Jamie W., Susie, Andrew,

and, it is hoped, many generations of students to come

in the University of Florida's

Graduate Program in Political Campaigning

Contents

	Tables, Figures, and Boxes	viii
	Preface	ix
	Contributors	xiii
1.	Do Campaigns Really Matter? Thomas M. Holbrook	1
2.	Campaign Strategy Michael John Burton and Daniel M. Shea	22
3.	Voter Competence Thomas E. Patterson	39
4.	Money and Elections John C. Green	58
5.	Political Advertising Lynda Lee Kaid	79
6.	Free Media in Campaigns Erika Franklin Fowler and Kenneth M. Goldstein	97
7.	Campaigning on the Internet Dennis W. Johnson	121
8.	Direct Democracy and Candidate Elections Daniel A. Smith	143
9.	Grassroots Mobilization Peter W. Wielhouwer	163
10.	The Effects of Political Consultants David A. Dulio	183
11.	Perspectives on Campaign Ethics R. Sam Garrett, Paul S. Herrnson, and James A. Thurber	203
12.	Two Views From the Trenches: Looking At Versus Looking Along David B. Hill	226
	Connecting the Study and Practice of Politics David Beattie and Sheryl Lovelady	231
	References	239

Tables, Figures, and Boxes

Tables

4.1 Congressional Campaign Spending and Open-Seat Victories, 1986–1998	59
4.2 Congressional Campaign Spending and Challenger Victories, 1986–1998	61
6.1 Breakdown of Typical Hour of News Coverage in 2004	112
11.1 Reported Frequency of Unethical Campaigning	210
11.2 Candidates' Characterizations of Latest Campaign	210
11.3 Acceptability of Making Factually True Statements Taken Out of Context	211
11.4 Acceptability of Focusing on Opponents' Negative Personal Characteristics	213
11.5 Acceptability of Using Push-Polls	213

Figures

6.1 Cable Television News Audience Growth, 1989–2003	107
6.2 U.S. Daily Newspaper Circulation Versus Number of Households, 1940–2000	108
6.3 Evening News Viewership, All Networks, 1980–2004	109
9.1 Personal Contacting Rates, 1956–2004	173

Boxes

5.1 General Effects of Exposure to Political Advertising	82
5.2 Factors That Condition the Effects of Exposure to Political Advertising	84
5.3 Effects of Exposure to Negative Advertising	90

Boxes: "The Consultants Respond About..."

Do Campaigns Really Matter?	18
Campaign Strategy	36
Voter Competence	54
Campaign Spending	74
Paid and Free Media	116
Campaign Technology	136
Campaign Ethics	218

Preface

Do campaigns really matter? A good bit of academic literature suggests that they do not—or at least not as much as politicians and the media tend to think they do. It has now been more than half a century since James Farley, President Franklin Roosevelt's campaign manager, offered what is known as Farley's Law: most elections are decided before the campaign even begins. More recently, in an analysis of the 1984, 1988, and 1992 presidential elections, Holbrook (1996) concluded that the *general* level of support for candidates during a campaign season is a function of national conditions (which vary primarily from one election to the next), whereas *fluctuations* in candidate support over the course of a single election year are in response to campaign-specific events. Although Holbrook acknowledged that these events (for example, the so-called convention bump, candidate debates, and blunders by one of the candidates) do have an impact, national conditions—measured in terms of *consumer sentiment* and *presidential job approval,* both factors that are in place before the general election campaign begins in earnest—ultimately matter a great deal more in determining who wins and who loses.

Similarly, J. Campbell (2000) conceded that *nonsystematic* campaign events, or those that are idiosyncratic to a particular election—for example, Truman's relentless attacks on the "do-nothing" Republican Congress in 1948, Kennedy's strong performance in the first-ever televised presidential debates in 1960, the violent clashes between police and anti-Vietnam protesters during the 1968 Democratic National Convention in Chicago, and Ford's apparent misstatement about the Soviet domination of Eastern Europe in a 1976 debate—can have significant, and even decisive, effects on the outcome of an extremely close contest. Yet he argued that these events were important precisely *because* the elections in question were close. In most instances (according to Campbell and others), nothing that happens during the campaign is likely to have more than a marginal impact, with the great majority of votes falling into place very early (because of the effects of partisan attachments, incumbent evaluations, the national economy, incumbency, and selective perception and overall indifference on the part of voters) and one candidate often running clearly ahead of the other(s).

Analyses such as those provided by Holbrook and Campbell apply specifically to the top of the ticket, but there are reasons to suspect that short-term forces such as issues, candidate traits, and campaign events may have even less impact on lower-level races in which voter attention is typically even more limited and in which factors such as partisanship and incumbency often appear to be overwhelmingly decisive, regardless of what does or does not happen over the course of the campaign (Jacobson 2004). Overall, then, the conventional wisdom within the academic community is that campaign events and the decisions made by candidates and their advisors matter relatively little, except under the most unusual of circumstances. That wisdom may be changing, especially after the spectacular failure of forecasting models to predict accurately the outcome of the 2000 presidential election (see the symposium in *PS: Political Science and Politics,* March 2001). Nevertheless, the weight of the evidence seems to indicate that most campaigns at all levels are over, or almost over, before they even begin.

Candidates and political operatives would, of course, disagree. Indeed, industry journals (most notably, *Campaigns and Elections*) and a number of trade books (for example, Bailey et al. 2000; Watson and Campbell 2003; also see Thurber and Nelson 2004) seek to illustrate the importance of the various strategic and tactical decisions made both in advance of the campaign and during the heat of battle. Unfortunately these accounts provide little more than anecdotal evidence bearing on the larger question: Do campaigns matter? Candidate A is said to have won because of an effective communications strategy, including just the right mix of positive and negative advertising (and of communications media, electronic versus direct mail). Candidate B's winning edge is thought to have resulted from an effective targeting of potential supporters and a strong get-out-the-vote effort on election day. Candidates C, D, and E were able to defeat their opponents because of newspaper endorsements, innovative use of the Internet, and better money management, respectively, and so on. The problem is not that the conclusions drawn from case studies such as these are wrong. The problem is that one cannot draw broad conclusions from case studies, period. What works for one candidate in one type of situation may not (and often does not) work for another candidate who faces a different opponent and an entirely different set of circumstances.

At the same time, a considerable amount of academic research has been produced in recent years that bears directly on many of the claims made by political practitioners. Scholars have, for example, tried to determine whether

- negative ads drive turnout rates up or down and whether they are more effective than positive ads at shaping voter preferences
- party and candidate mobilization efforts have a significant impact on turnout
- personal appearances by a candidate in a state or local area help to generate support for that candidate on election day
- increased spending by a candidate results in higher vote totals
- the Internet is more effective than other communications channels
- elections are shaped by factors such as candidate debates, scandals, external events, or the hiring of professional consultants

The literature has not yet provided definitive answers to these (and many other) questions, but there is little doubt that we are better informed today about the factors shaping election outcomes than was the case fifteen or twenty years ago.

On February 25, 2005, the Graduate Program in Political Campaigning at the University of Florida hosted a conference to assess the state of knowledge about several of these factors. Our approach was to bring together two groups of individuals that do not interact with (or, for that matter, trust) each other very much: academics and campaign consultants. Most professionals seem to believe that the academic literature on campaigns and elections is either obvious (it tells you what everyone already knows anyway) or wrong—though they are generally too busy with their work to follow that literature closely. For their part, many academics take the position that campaign consultants operate mainly by the seat of their pants, that is, promoting the latest folk wisdom about which strategies and tactics work and which ones do not, without knowing one way or the other until it is too late. A problem here, at least in the past, has been that too many academics study campaigns and elections without ever talking directly to those on the front lines, getting involved in a campaign, or otherwise taking the time to learn about the latest developments in the increasingly professionalized field of campaign management.

Without necessarily resolving these issues, the workshop at the University of Florida provided a unique opportunity for the two sides to get together and hear what the other had to say. The structure of the event was fairly simple: A number of outstanding scholars prepared review essays outlining what we know (or think we know) in a number of areas relevant to the world of practical politics. After each participant presented his or her conclusions, a group of invited consultants had the chance to present their views. This book is the product of that exchange. There are twelve chapters, the first eleven of which provide a broad overview of existing research on topics such as campaign strategy, campaign spending, political advertising, voter mobilization, and the Internet (with some new data concerning campaign ethics thrown in for good measure). In the final chapter, some noted practitioners provide their perspective regarding the strengths and weaknesses of the academic approach, and suggest avenues for future work that might provide valuable insights into the nature of campaign decision-making and the ways in which campaigns can help to shape electoral outcomes. In addition, comments from consultants who attended the UF conference are provided in boxes that follow several of the chapters. As will be apparent to readers, these political professionals do not always see the world of campaigns and elections the same way their academic counterparts do, although the level of outright disagreement between the two groups is not nearly as high as some might expect.

The Graduate Program in Political Campaigning was created in 1985 in response to complaints from students that the political science department did not offer enough classes dealing with the nuts and bolts of everyday politics. It was then, and is still today, one of the few practical politics programs in the country (especially at the graduate level), not because young people are not interested in such studies, but, in large measure, because of the difficulty of blending two worlds that do not always see eye to eye. Although this book, and the conference on which it is based, will not change that, we at the University of Florida hope that it represents a step in the right direction. Academics and political consultants have much to learn from one another, and for that to happen the lines of communication must remain open.

Let me close by expressing my thanks to Dana Rubenstein, Debbie Wallen, and Nick Runyan, without whose heroic efforts the Political Campaigning conference would never have gotten off the ground; to those who participated in that conference, especially the consultants who took time away from their day jobs to talk politics in a setting new and unfamiliar to most of them; to Roger Austin, Jim Kane, Susan MacManus, and David Wolfson for their contributions as discussion facilitators; and to my colleague Michael Martinez for his helpful comments on early drafts of several chapters in this book.

Contributors

About the Editor

STEPHEN C. CRAIG is professor of political science at the University of Florida, as well as director of the university's Graduate Program in Political Campaigning. He is the author of *The Malevolent Leaders: Popular Discontent in America* (1993); editor of *Broken Contract? Changing Relationships Between Americans and Their Government* (1996); and coeditor of *After the Boom: The Politics of Generation X* (1997), *Ambivalence and the Structure of Political Opinion* (2005), and *Ambivalence, Politics, and Public Policy* (2005). Craig has worked extensively with academic and political surveys and has conducted polling and focus-group research for clients in Florida and elsewhere.

About the Contributors

DAVID BEATTIE is president of Hamilton Beattie & Staff, a political consulting firm providing strategic research for members of Congress, private companies, and interest groups. In 2000 he was named Pollster of the Year by the American Association of Political Consultants, and he has been identified as a "Mover and Shaker" by *Campaigns and Elections* magazine. Beattie received a B.A. in political communication from George Washington University and an M.A. in political science from the University of Florida, where he serves as an adjunct professor with the Graduate Program in Political Campaigning.

MICHAEL JOHN BURTON is assistant professor of political science at Ohio University. He received his Ph.D. in political science in 1995 from the State University of New York at Albany and has worked as an analyst for the Congressional Research Service and as a political aide on Capitol Hill and in the White House. He is the coauthor of *Campaign Craft: The Strategies, Tactics, and Art of Political Campaign Management* (2001) and *Campaign Mode: Strategic Vision in Congressional Elections* (2003). In addition to researching campaign strategy, Burton is also studying the development of bureaucratic structures within the White House.

DAVID A. DULIO is assistant professor of political science at Oakland University. He is the author of *For Better or Worse? How Political Consultants Are Changing Elections in the United States* (2004) and the coeditor of *Crowded Airwaves: Campaign Advertising in Elections* (2000) and *Shades of Gray: Perspectives on Campaign Ethics* (2002). He also has written numerous articles and book chapters dealing with campaigns and elections in the United States. During the 2001–2002 academic year, Dulio served as an American Political Science Association congressional fellow in the office of former U.S. representative J. C. Watts Jr.

ERIKA FRANKLIN FOWLER is a Ph.D. candidate in the Department of Political Science at the University of Wisconsin-Madison. A summa cum laude graduate of St. Olaf College with a B.A. in political science and mathematics, Fowler also is research director of the University of Wisconsin NewsLab, the largest and most comprehensive local news tracking project in the country. Her primary research interests include political communication, political behavior, and research methodology.

R. SAM GARRETT received his Ph.D. in political science from American University's School of Public Affairs in 2005 and serves as an analyst in U.S. national government at the Congressional Research Service. He completed his essay while assistant director for research at American University's Center for Congressional and Presidential Studies and instructor in the Department of Government, where he continues as a research fellow and adjunct professor.

KENNETH M. GOLDSTEIN is professor of political science at the University of Wisconsin-Madison and the director of the University of Wisconsin Advertising Project (www.polisci.wisc.edu/tvadvertising) and the University of Wisconsin NewsLab. He is the author of *Interest Groups, Lobbying, and Participation in America* (1999) and *Paid Media in American Elections* (forthcoming from Princeton University Press) and coeditor of *The Medium and the Message: Television Advertising and American Elections* (2004). His research on political advertising, voter turnout, survey methodology, Israeli politics, and presidential elections has appeared in numerous journal articles and book chapters. Goldstein is a consultant for the ABC News elections unit and has worked on network election night coverage since 1988.

JOHN C. GREEN is Distinguished Professor of Political Science and director of the Ray C. Bliss Institute of Applied Politics at the University of Akron. He is a coauthor of *The Financiers of Congressional Elections: Investors, Ideologues, and Intimates* (2003) and coeditor of *The State of the Parties* (2003) and *The Christian Right in America* (2003). He has written numerous journal articles and book chapters on campaign finance, political parties, and religion and politics.

PAUL S. HERRNSON is director of the Center for American Politics and Citizenship and professor of government and politics at the University of Maryland. He is the author of *Party Campaigning in the 1980s* (1988) and *Congressional Elections: Campaigning at Home and in Washington*, 4th ed. (2004) and is a coauthor or coeditor of several other books, including *The Financiers of Congressional Elections: Investors, Ideologues, and Intimates* (2003), *Responsible Partisanship? The Evolution of American Political Parties in the Post-War Era* (2003), and *War Stories from Capitol Hill* (2004). Herrnson also has written extensively on Congress, campaign finance, political parties, and elections; served as an American Political Science Association congressional fellow; and received several teaching awards, including a Distinguished Scholar-Teacher Award from the University of Maryland.

DAVID B. HILL is president of Hill Research Consultants, a public opinion and marketing research firm located in The Woodlands, Texas. He became a political pollster and consultant in 1984 after working as a university professor for ten years, including in a tenured position at Texas A&M University. He has advised more than a dozen U.S. senators and governors (among them Mel Martinez and Bob Martinez, Florida's first Hispanic senator and governor, respectively). Hill also consults with numerous national advocacy groups and has polled for almost twenty successful initiatives for constitutional amendments in a half-dozen states. Since 2003, he has written a weekly column on polls and polling for *The Hill,* a newspaper for and about Congress.

THOMAS M. HOLBROOK is professor of political science at the University of Wisconsin-Milwaukee. He is a former editor of *American Politics Research* and the author of *Do Campaigns Matter?* (1996). In addition, he has written several scholarly articles on the role of presidential campaigns in U.S. politics and is a sometimes-accurate forecaster of presidential elections.

DENNIS W. JOHNSON is professor of political management and associate dean of the Graduate School of Political Management at George Washington University. He has written widely on politics, campaigns, and political consultants. Among his publications are *No Place for Amateurs: How Political Consultants Are Reshaping American Democracy* (2001) and *Congress Online: Bridging the Gap between Citizens and Their Representatives* (2004).

LYNDA LEE KAID is professor of telecommunication in the College of Journalism and Communications at the University of Florida. She previously served as director of the Political Communication Center and supervised the Political Commercial Archive at the University of Oklahoma. Her research specialties include political advertising and news coverage of political events. She is the author or editor of more than twenty books, including *New Perspectives on Political Advertising* (1986), *Political Advertising in Western Democracies* (1995), *The Electronic Election* (1999), *Civic Dialogue in the 1996 Presidential Campaign* (2000), *Videostyle in Presidential Campaigns* (2001), and *Handbook of Political Communication Research* (2004).

SHERYL LOVELADY is a political strategist with the consulting firm of Hamilton Beattie & Staff. She has fifteen years of experience advising candidates and working on issue campaigns at the local, county, legislative, and statewide levels. As executive director of an Oklahoma state legislative caucus, she directed the campaigns of more than thirty candidates, including four consecutive successful special elections. Lovelady received a B.A. in history from the University of Oklahoma and has served as an adjunct faculty member at Seminole State College.

THOMAS E. PATTERSON is Bradlee Professor of Government and the Press at Harvard University's John F. Kennedy School of Government. His most recent book, *The Vanishing Voter* (2003), looks at the causes and consequences of declining electoral participation. *Out of Order* (1993), his book on the media's political role, received the American Political Science Association's Graber Award for best book in political communication of the last decade, and an earlier book, *The Unseeing Eye* (1976), was named by the American Association for Public Opinion Research as one of the fifty most influential books on public opinion in the past half-century. Patterson also is the author of *Mass Media Election* (1980) and two general American government texts, *The American Democracy* (now in its seventh edition) and *We the People* (now in its sixth edition). His research has been funded by the Carnegie, Ford, Markle, Knight, Smith-Richardson, Pew, and National Science foundations.

DANIEL M. SHEA received his Ph.D. from the State University of New York at Albany in 1993 and is associate professor of political science and director of the

Center for Political Participation at Allegheny College. His research interests include political parties, elections, voter behavior, and congressional dynamics. He is the coauthor of *New Party Politics: From Jefferson and Hamilton to the Information Age* (2000), *Campaign Mode: Strategic Vision in Congressional Elections* (2003), and *The Fountain of Youth: Political Parties and the Mobilization of America's Youth* (2005). He is currently working with a team of scholars on *The Pathways of American Government* (a text with Prentice Hall).

DANIEL A. SMITH is associate professor of political science at the University of Florida. He is the author of *Tax Crusaders and the Politics of Direct Democracy* (1998) and coauthor of *Educated by Initiative: The Effects of Direct Democracy on Citizens and Political Organizations in the American States* (2004). He has written numerous scholarly articles and chapters on the politics and process of direct democracy, including campaign financing and the role of political parties and interest groups involved in ballot measures. Smith was a Senior Fulbright Scholar in Ghana during 2000–2001. He serves on the board of directors of the Ballot Initiative Strategy Center Foundation and is a member of the board of scholars of the Initiative and Referendum Institute.

JAMES A. THURBER is professor of government and director of the Center for Congressional and Presidential Studies at American University. He is the author, coauthor, or coeditor of several books, including *Rivals for Power: Presidential-Congressional Relations* (1996), *Congress and the Internet* (2002), *Campaign Consultants, Political Parties, Interest Groups, and Voters in American Elections* (2004), and *Campaigns and Elections, American Style*, 2d ed. (2004), and has written numerous articles and chapters on topics such as congressional budgeting and reform, interest groups and lobbying, and campaigns and elections. Thurber was an American Political Science Association congressional fellow and served as principal investigator of a seven-year project funded by Pew Charitable Trusts to study campaign conduct.

PETER W. WIELHOUWER is assistant professor of political science at Western Michigan University. After earning his Ph.D. from the University of Georgia in 1994, he served on the faculties of Spelman College and Regent University, where he directed the School of Government's graduate program in political management. Before joining the faculty at Western Michigan, he was speechwriter to the general in charge of coordinating operational experiments for the military at the United States Joint Forces Command's Joint Experimentation directorate. His teaching and research areas include campaigns and elections, political behavior, faith and politics, and racial politics. He has consulted for several Virginia campaigns and has spoken on campaign ethics for (among others) American University's Campaign Management Institute, the American Association of Political Consultants, and the Leadership Institute. Wielhouwer's research has appeared in the *American Journal of Political Science, Journal of Politics,* and *American Politics Research,* among others.

The Electoral Challenge

1 Do Campaigns Really Matter?

Thomas M. Holbrook

It has been almost ten years since the publication of *Do Campaigns Matter?* (Holbrook 1996), in which I argued against the general sentiment among scholars that presidential campaigns have, at best, "minimal" effects on election outcomes. Three additional presidential elections have occurred during that time, and the number of scholarly articles and books on campaign effects has grown accordingly. In this chapter, which serves as a backdrop for the more narrowly focused essays that follow, I return to the question of whether campaigns matter by reviewing recent developments in the academic literature, and by revisiting as well as broadening the way in which the question itself is conceived. First, I examine early research that helped to define the "minimal-effects" perspective. Second, I briefly review my own arguments and findings from *Do Campaigns Matter?*, along with a number of other studies that have dealt primarily with the persuasive effects of presidential campaigns. Third, I discuss the unnecessarily narrow framework used by most scholars working in this area and then review research on nonpersuasion effects that appear to be associated with political campaigns. Finally, I suggest that the presidential arena might not be the best place to look for evidence of campaign effects at all.

Setting the Stage: Early Work and Minimal Effects

Modern election research originated with two studies conducted by members of the so-called Columbia school (reflecting the authors' institutional affiliation). The first of these was Lazarsfeld, Berelson, and Gaudet's *The People's Choice* (1944), which looked at residents of Erie County, Ohio, over the course of the 1940 presidential race between Franklin Roosevelt and Wendell Willkie; this was followed by Berelson, Lazarsfeld, and McPhee's *Voting* (1954), a study of Elmira, New York, during the 1948 contest between Harry Truman and Thomas Dewey. Even by contemporary standards, the design of the Columbia studies was quite sophisticated in that both used panel surveys, interviewing the same group of voters throughout the summer and fall of the election year. This approach was particularly well-suited for detecting campaign effects and, indeed, the authors anticipated that what people experienced during the campaign season would influence how they voted—a seemingly plausible expectation.

Lazarsfeld and his colleagues (1944) focused mainly on the influence of media exposure (radio and newspaper) during the campaign and, in the end, concluded that what voters read or heard about the candidates had surprisingly little impact on how they voted. Instead, it appeared that there was a strong social dimension to the vote, specifically, that various groups in society were predisposed to supporting one party or the other; to the extent that there was any movement in candidate preferences during the campaign, it usually resulted from wayward voters returning to their group's historical voting pattern.[1] This phenomenon led to the creation of something called the "index of political predisposition" (a precursor to the concept of party identification, discussed later in this chapter), which emphasized the group-based aspects of voting.

Looking at changes that took place during the time period covered by their surveys, Lazarsfeld et al. (1944, 102) found that a mere 8 percent of all voters could be described as having been "converted" by the campaign. The rest either exhibited no change from their original vote intention (69 percent), initially planned to cross over or were undecided but ended up voting in a manner consistent with their social group characteristics (17 percent), or changed from expressing a vote preference to "undecided" (6 percent).[2] This, to the authors, was evidence of the relative inefficacy of the campaign. In a separate essay that summarized many of the findings from *The People's Choice,* Lazarsfeld (1944) made a pointed assessment of the importance of campaigns, concluding that "[i]n an important sense, modern Presidential campaigns are over before they begin" (317), and that "elections are decided by the events occurring in the entire period between two Presidential elections and not by the campaign" (330).

The Elmira study followed up on many of the key findings from *The People's Choice* but also placed a greater emphasis on the degree to which issues and interpersonal communications can affect vote choice (Berelson, Lazarsfeld, and McPhee 1954). As before, Berelson and colleagues learned that a relatively modest share of the electorate changed their minds during the campaign—and that those who did usually returned to the predictable voting pattern of their social group(s). The authors concluded that the principal effect of campaigns is to pressure people toward consistency and that "as time goes on . . . we find that people abandon deviant opinions on specific issues to agree with the position taken by their party" (285). In other words, even voters who initially take issue positions contrary to those of their preferred party are more likely to change those positions than to use them as grounds for supporting the other party's candidate.

Although some scholars took exception (for example, see Gosnell 1950), the results of these early studies stood essentially unchallenged for many years. With the conventional wisdom being that campaigns didn't count for very much, the academic study of presidential campaigns lay largely dormant and untouched until the 1990s. In the 1960s the *American Voter* model (Campbell, Converse, Miller, and Stokes 1960) gained currency among scholars. This model identified party identification—an orientation typically learned during childhood, from one's parents—as the decisive factor shaping vote choice. Later, as various examinations of issue-based voting gained prominence,[3] and especially as the literature on economic voting took off,[4] little attention was paid to the potential importance of campaigns in shaping election outcomes. If anything, the predictability of individuals' votes based on their partisan loyalties and a handful of retrospective evaluations, and of election outcomes based on macroeconomic conditions and presidential approval scores, contributed to a general sense in the academic community that if campaigns did matter, they mattered only at the margins.[5]

Renewed Interest in Campaigns

After several decades of relative neglect, political campaigns began to draw increased scholarly attention in the late 1980s and early 1990s. A few studies began to focus on changes in public opinion that took place during campaigns, and on the impact of specific campaign events on both partisanship (Allsop and Weisberg 1988) and candidate preference (J. Campbell, Cherry, and Wink 1992; Geer 1988). This line of research signaled a renewed interest in campaigns that was fueled further by several articles that appeared in print almost simultaneously (Bartels 1993; Finkel 1993; Gelman and King 1993). Finkel (1993), which harkened back to earlier work done by the Columbia group, examined changes in vote intention over the course of the 1980 campaign season. Finkel's main finding was that very few people (less than 5 percent) changed their minds during the campaign, and that vote intention in the early summer was a very strong predictor of how one voted on election day. Given such results, Finkel (1993, 19) argued that campaign effects would have to be much more substantial to be considered nonminimal.

Bartels (1993) also focused on changes in vote intention during the 1980 presidential campaign and found that, although candidate support was highly stable over time, exposure to the campaign via mass media was an important predictor of the changes that occurred. Among Bartels's conclusions was that exposure to the media is likely to be most important when people have relatively weak ties to the candidates, and when one of the candidates is relatively unknown. Finally, Gelman and King (1993) provided an innovative and provocative analysis of more than 67,000 survey respondents from dozens of surveys that were conducted during the summer and fall of the 1988 presidential contest. The authors maintained, among other things, that campaigns (and the media's coverage of them) tend to make elections more predictable by helping bring voters to "enlightened" decisions based on "fundamentals" such as performance evaluations and party cues.

Do Campaigns Matter?

These studies helped to form my own ideas about whether and how campaigns might matter (Holbrook 1994, 1996). One particularly troublesome aspect of the earlier work was the implication that, in order to "matter," campaigns had to be not just *a* determinant of election outcomes but *the* determinant. Take the estimates from Lazarsfeld, Berelson, and Gaudet (1944) and from Finkel (1993), for example, that roughly 8 percent and 5 percent of voters were converted by the campaigns in 1940 and 1980, respectively. Although effects of this magnitude may not have been decisive to the outcomes of those two elections, they could be consequential in years when the final result is much closer. More to the point, when researchers examine changes in vote intention among respondents who have already made up their minds, it is not too surprising to find that the rates of conversion are fairly low. In fact, when Finkel's "conversion" category is expanded to include those who were undecided in June and ultimately voted contrary to their predispositions in November, it grows to almost 16 percent of the electorate. Moreover, the proportion of voters who were "activated" (that is, moving from the undecided column to voting in line with their predispositions) is substantial in both the Lazarsfeld et al. and Finkel studies (14 percent and 44 percent, respectively).[6] Surely these findings represent campaign effects of some consequence. I argue elsewhere (Holbrook and McClurg, 2005) that the ability of parties to activate (or reactivate) their partisans is an important asset that may well be determinative in some cases. In fairness, Finkel (1993, 19) acknowledged that activation and other sources of indirect influence can also be an important function of campaigns. But because the judgment of what constitutes minimal versus nonminimal effects seems to be made on the basis of changing voters' minds, there is a tendency to dismiss these effects as being trivial.

In *Do Campaigns Matter?* (Holbrook 1996), I developed a model of campaign effects and tested it using trial-heat polling data from the 1984, 1988, and 1992 presidential elections. I tried to acknowledge that the ability of campaigns to influence public opinion was constrained by such things as voters' long-term partisan predispositions and the political and economic context of the election, while showing that, given those constraints, campaign events could nevertheless exert considerable sway over people's preferences. The model was based on several different propositions, three of which I see as most important:

- First, there exists for each election cycle an equilibrium level of support for the candidates, and that equilibrium reflects the political and economic context of the election.
- Second, public support for the candidates during the campaign season fluctuates, sometimes widely, around the equilibrium, and those fluctuations are in response to campaign events.
- Third, the magnitude of the impact of campaign events depends partly on the disparity between relative candidate support in the polls and the expected (equilibrium) level of support. In other words, candidates running far behind their expected level of support can expect greater increases in support in response to favorable campaign events, compared with candidates running ahead of their expected level.

Among my major empirical findings were that (1) economic conditions and presidential approval determine the equilibrium level of support during a campaign, (2) campaign events do a fair job of explaining fluctuations around that equilibrium level, and (3) among these events, nominating conventions are particularly important (though their impact is stronger for the challenging party candidate and is constrained by the equilibrium level of support for the candidates), presidential debates are usually associated with relatively small shifts in candidate support, and day-to-day campaign events also have a modest impact.

Overall, my analysis indicated that what went on during the campaign generally was not as important to the ultimate outcome as was the context of the campaign. By far the most important determinant of the outcomes of the three elections I examined were the national economy and presidential approval. In this sense, my results were consistent with Lazarsfeld's (1944) conclusion that what goes on between elections is more important than what goes on during the campaign. This is not to say that the campaigns didn't matter, however. Indeed, a set of "counter-factuals" showed that switching net campaign effects from one election to another could easily have changed two of the three outcomes (nothing, it seems, could have produced a different result in 1984).[7] In the end, I took the influence of campaign events on fluctuations in candidate support to represent meaningful and theoretically interesting campaign effects, even if those effects cannot be said to have "caused" the outcome.

There have been two notable book-length treatments of the impact of campaigns since the publication of *Do Campaigns Matter?* J. Campbell's *The American Campaign* (2000) used a number of different types of data to examine presidential elections from 1952 to 1996. Campbell's main findings were that campaigns usually follow certain predictable patterns, chief among them a "narrowing" effect in which the trailing candidate draws closer to the front-runner as the race nears its climax.[8] In Campbell's model, which focuses on the general election, the predictability of *campaigns* helps to make *elections* predictable. In some ways, his research supports the view of Gelman and King (1993), specifically, that campaigns help bring voters the information they need to make "enlightened" decisions—the latter reflecting the fundamental aspects of the political and economic context, which are the things that make elections predictable in the first place. While Campbell's approach differs from mine on many of the particulars, his point about the role of information is consistent with the underlying logic of my own model of campaign effects. In terms of actual vote changes, Campbell estimated that fall campaigns account for shifts of about four percentage points on average. A more recent analysis that considered elections from 1948 to 2000 directly addressed the question of whether campaigns mattered enough to determine the final outcome (Campbell 2001). Campbell concluded that they had a major impact in 1948 and 1960, and probably affected the outcomes in 1976, 1980, and 2000 as well. This interpretation, of course, defines *impact* in terms of potential to change the election result, which is a pretty tough standard.

A second major treatment of campaign effects is *The 2000 Presidential Election and the Foundations of Party Politics* (R. Johnston, Hagen, and Jamieson 2004). This innovative study builds on existing work on campaigns from the perspective of both political science and communications. What makes the book most exciting, and what allowed for a detailed analysis of many different aspects of the 2000 campaign, is the design of the National Annenberg Election

Study (NAES) that year. The NAES was a massive rolling cross-sectional public opinion survey (N = 37,000) that went into the field in December 1999 and continued until mid-January 2001. Using data collected from July through election day, R. Johnston and colleagues were able to capture campaign dynamics in a way that had previously not been possible. Also, in addition to the NAES, the authors incorporated data from the Campaign Media Analysis Group regarding the tone and volume of campaign advertising in specific media markets, as well as the content of network news and newspaper coverage of the campaign. By attaching media and advertising information to individual respondents' survey records, Johnston and colleagues could see how voters reacted to specific campaign information as that information was produced. This approach represented real progress over analyses such as my own that have gauged the impact of campaign events based on the assumption that those events produce certain types of information.[9]

Findings from R. Johnston et al. (2004) are far too numerous to detail here, but a few speak most directly to the issue of the campaign's overall impact. First, regarding major campaign events, the authors found convention bumps similar to the ones that Campbell and I identified; they pinpointed the beginning of the bumps as coinciding with the announcement of vice presidential candidates just days prior to the major parties' respective conventions. Second, the final two debates had important, offsetting effects that influenced the tenor of the campaign, whereas the first and last debates had significant short-term priming effects that resulted in increased salience for Social Security as an issue in the presidential race.[10] Third, media coverage of the campaign was influential; it appears, for example, that the media were responsible for Democratic nominee Al Gore's decline in the polls during late September and early October, as well as his recovery in the last couple of weeks prior to election day. Of particular interest here, at least from the standpoint of the efficacy of campaigns, is that media content was influenced by the activities and strategies of the candidates. For instance, R. Johnston et al. (2004) attributed Gore's media advantage in the late stages of the campaign to his decision to emphasize the importance of Social Security. Fourth, the impact of advertising was decidedly one-sided: support for Gore was very susceptible to influence from advertising whereas support for Bush was relatively immune to such effects. This asymmetry enabled the Republicans to use advertising as a means of overcoming Gore's advantage in media coverage during the closing days. Finally, and this runs counter to some prior research (J. Jones 1998; Daron Shaw 1999b), the authors found no discernible, theoretically plausible influence from campaign appearances by the candidates. In fact, the only statistically significant influence from such appearances was a rather implausible negative effect of Bush-Cheney visits on Bush's standing in the polls.

A number of other scholars have examined the impact of presidential campaigns on votes and election outcomes. These inquiries can be classified broadly into one of three categories: (1) aggregate-level national events models, (2) individual-level events models, or (3) aggregate-level, state campaign activities models.[11] Daron Shaw's work in the first category focused on the same types of events that I considered in *Do Campaigns Matter?*, though his measures were in many ways much more refined. The principal contribution of Shaw's approach was in distinguishing among categories of events, and incorporating measures of media coverage as a conditioning influence on the impact of events. The argument here is twofold: First, although efforts to measure the impact of campaign events have detected some interesting influences, those models are likely to be misspecified because they usually employ measures that combine seemingly dissimilar events into single variables. In an analysis of campaign events from 1952 to 1992, Shaw (1999a) demonstrated that some types of events (national conventions, candidate blunders, party unity activities, presidential debates) have stronger and more lasting effects on candidate support than do others (most speeches, external events not related to the campaign). A more detailed study of the 1992 and 1996 campaigns (Shaw 1999c) found that the influence of events (this time measured using broader, catch-all variables) was conditioned by media coverage at the time of the event; that is, the impact of an event expected to favor one party tended to be exacerbated by positive media coverage and dampened by negative coverage for that party at the time of the event.

Two other national aggregate-level studies have looked at how events influence the contours of candidate support during campaigns. Wlezien and Erikson (2002) was perhaps the most exhaustive analysis of trial-heat results, with data amassed from over 1,400 polls conducted during fifteen presidential campaigns from 1944 to 2000. In an elegant essay, the authors examined the statistical properties of what they called the "bump and wiggle" of public opinion during these campaigns. Essentially, their interest was in how voter preferences evolve over time and the degree to which observed changes in candidate support that might be attributed to campaign effects represent real, sustained opinion shifts rather than transient effects that dissipate quickly over time. They found that, while changes occurring early in the campaign (the hundred days prior to the conventions) are sometimes quite substantial, they are generally transitory and do not represent genuine changes in candidate support. In contrast, the relatively smaller shifts that take place during the last hundred days of the campaign are usually real, permanent changes. Somewhat ironically, then, the wider swings in public opinion that one might normally assume are most important turn out to be considerably less meaningful than are the smaller bumps and wiggles occurring later in the campaign.

Stimson's *Tides of Consent* (2004), which is a broader treatise on macroopinion in the United States, includes an interesting analysis of the impact of presidential campaigns from 1960 to 2000 (see chapter 4). Like a number of others, Stimson examined changes in trial-heat polls during the campaign season with a specific emphasis on the impact of party nominating conventions and candidate debates.[12] His findings for both were similar to those reported in *Do Campaigns Matter?* First, he found that conventions create substantial and durable shifts in opinion. The latter point appears to be at odds with the conclusion in Campbell (2000) that about 50 percent of the effect of the convention bump dissipates by election day. In fairness, though, the focus in this instance was just on the second convention because the bump from the first would no doubt be affected by the occurrence of the second. Stimson estimated that the average effect of the second convention is a bump of five percentage points in the convening party's favor, an amount that could have an important impact on the eventual outcome. Regarding debates, he found that they have relatively slight effects and are probably of little consequence to the ultimate outcome—except, of course, for extremely close contests when almost any event is potentially decisive.

Hillygus and Jackman (2003) also focused on the role played by conventions and debates, but this study differs from the others in a couple of important respects. For one thing, although the authors addressed aggregate shifts, most of their analysis attempted to gauge the impact of conventions and debates on individual voters (cf. R. Johnston, Hagen, and Jamieson 2004). In addition, they used panel data from a survey conducted by Knowledge Networks during the 2000 presidential campaign; this enabled them to control for prior predispositions when measuring the impact of events—an extremely important advantage.[13] Absent panel data, the interpretation of observed changes in public opinion following campaign events must be limited to statements like the following: "The level of support for a candidate was higher (or lower) after an event than before the event." The implication here is that the event changed people's minds, or perhaps activated some predisposition, and yet such a conclusion can be reached with confidence only if one knows what each individual's opinion was prior to the event. Due to the large size of the overall sample (29,000), Hillygus and Jackman were able to use 2,588 panel respondents for their convention analysis and 3,102 panel respondents for their debate analysis.

Hillygus and Jackman introduced their study (2003) by saying that they assumed the question of "do campaigns matter?" had been answered in the affirmative by prior research, and that they were more interested in determining how and for whom campaigns matter. The ensuing analysis was quite sophisticated and provided a detailed account of the process by which conventions and debates influence the public. First, the results indicated that conventions and debates do influence how people intend to vote, though the former tends to have a decidedly larger impact. Second (and this is where the panel design really bears fruit), Hillygus and Jackman concluded that the effects are strongest among mismatched partisans (those who initially favored the other party's candidate), undecided voters, and independents. Although the observed pattern was somewhat different for Democrats and Republicans, overall it appears that individuals with these characteristics are most likely to *change* their vote intention in response to the conventions and debates.

The third major group of studies dealing with campaign effects considers the impact of activities below the national level, which seems appropriate given that presidential races are all about putting together the right combination of states in the quest for an electoral college majority.[14] Research in this area is mixed but generally points to the existence of some important effects. Daron Shaw's analysis of the 1988–1996 campaigns in the states (1999b) is perhaps the most comprehensive effort, examining the impact of both candidate visits and campaign media expenditures. Results showed that each variable has a significant effect on state-level vote distributions, especially in places where higher numbers of citizens are undecided about which candidate they will support. Examining the impact of candidate visits on turnout (more on this later) and vote percentages (within media markets rather than states), Jeffrey Jones (1998) also found interesting conditional effects: candidate visits had a significant impact on voting, though the magnitude of that impact was much greater for visits occurring late in the campaign than for those that occurred earlier.

In an analysis of campaign appearances in the 1996 election, Herr (2002) reported mixed results, with only appearances by President Clinton in the month of October shaping the ultimate distribution of votes. Finally, my own work in this area also has been somewhat inconsistent. An examination of Harry Truman's whistle-stop campaign in 1948 indicated that Truman's state-level campaign strategy, along with Dewey's lack of the same,[15] played a key role in the president's successful bid for reelection (Holbrook 2002a). My work with Scott McClurg, however, suggests that although candidate visits and media expenditures did not affect state-level results in presidential campaigns from 1992 to 2000, national party monetary transfers to the state parties had a significant impact (Holbrook and McClurg, 2005).

Presidential Campaigns Matter

Although the "modern" study of political campaigns began over sixty years ago with Lazarsfeld, Berelson, and Gaudet (1944), almost all of the studies cited in the preceding section have been published since 1990. This reflects a renewed interest in campaigns that was, to a large degree, sparked by the emerging academic consensus that campaigns didn't matter. The newer threads of research clearly suggest otherwise, at least at the presidential level. To summarize: National nominating conventions are prime opportunities to get one's message out in a relatively uncontested format, something that is particularly important for the lesser-known (challenging-party) candidate; the public's response is usually a substantial shift in support toward the convening party,[16] though some disagreement exists among scholars over the extent to which the convention bump dissipates. And although presidential debates generally lead to fairly small shifts in candidate support,[17] some evidence indicates that specific debates can alter the tenor of the campaign in a more substantial way (R. Johnston, Hagen, and Jamieson 2004).

Moreover, day-to-day campaign events appear to have a cumulative effect on the candidates' relative standing in the polls (Holbrook 1996; Shaw 1999a), depending on the content of media coverage of the campaign at the time of the event (Shaw 1999c). Evidence also indicates that campaign activities in the states play an important role in shaping state-level results,[18] though some activities weigh more heavily than others and their overall impact may be influenced to some degree by when they occur. Finally, Johnston et al. (2004) presented evidence that illustrates the role played by campaign advertising and media coverage of the campaign (also see chapters 5 and 6 in this volume), not just in terms of changing minds but also in priming voters to place more emphasis on some criteria than on others (see note 10).

There can be little doubt, then, that campaign activities influence the levels of candidate support exhibited by voters. In this sense, campaigns clearly matter, and they matter quite a lot. But do campaigns *determine* election outcomes? This is a tricky, and perhaps unfair, question. In any given election, any number of factors *influenced* the outcome but could not necessarily be said to have *determined* the outcome. Certainly, in close races such as occurred in 1960, 1968, 1976, 2000, and 2004, the outcomes might have been different had the respective campaigns been waged differently. In contrast, the contexts surrounding the elections in 1972 and 1984 were such that it likely would have taken a Herculean effort by the challengers, McGovern and Mondale (combined with a total collapse by the incumbents, Nixon and Reagan, respectively), to alter the final result. But this argument misses an important point: campaigns don't need to be the primary determinant of election outcomes in order to matter. They matter by being among the factors that shape the public's overall evaluations of the candidates and that ultimately, in combination, help to explain election outcomes.

A Broader View of How Campaigns Matter

In the remainder of this chapter, I propose that scholars may underestimate the extent to which campaigns matter by focusing too narrowly on their role in shaping presidential election outcomes. First, I argue that the entire discussion has been distorted by an overemphasis on the competitive, horse-race aspect of elections. Second, I suggest that the presidential perspective is unnecessarily restrictive and probably biases our findings in a manner that prevents us from seeing the full impact that campaigns often have.

The Civic Functions of Campaigns

It is easy to comprehend why most academic research, as well as most casual discussions of whether campaigns matter, tend to focus on election outcomes. It is the final outcome, and the relentless march toward it, that most people care about and that usually dominates coverage in the media. Yet campaigns serve other important functions—civic functions—that, while less glamorous and certainly less visible than the head-on competition between candidates, are still important and might help to shape the eventual outcome in any event. Broadly speaking, these civic functions of campaigns are *voter education* and *voter mobilization*.

Voter Education. In my earlier work (see Holbrook 1996), I have maintained that campaigns are nothing if not large-scale efforts to generate information with the express purpose of persuading voters. That is, campaigns seek to "educate" voters about why they should support one candidate rather than others. The assumption put forth in Gelman and King (1993) was probably correct—that the information generated by campaigns serves to "enlighten" voters concerning the issues of the day, while also reinforcing the importance of fundamental considerations such as partisanship, ideology, and presidential performance. Yet even if this account isn't exactly right, we should not underestimate the potential importance of information acquisition during the campaign and the consequences it can have for both voters and the election outcome.

The existing literature on voter learning during presidential campaigns suggests that even though voters may not live up to the civic ideal of being fully informed, learning nevertheless does take place—with the nature of that learning varying with different types of campaign events. Thomas Patterson, in *The Vanishing Voter* (2002, 125), reported that just prior to election day in 2000, "On the average issue, 38 percent correctly identified the candidate's position, 16 percent incorrectly identified it . . . and 46 percent said they did not know it." Although this may be taken as a sign that the campaigns that year did not do a good job of educating voters, Patterson pointed to distinct periods of intense voter learning: the contested primary season, the convention period, and the debates. During these times, voters learned about 80 percent of what they learned during the 2000 campaign as a whole (127). What went on during the remainder of the campaign appears to have accomplished relatively little by way of conveying information about the candidates' policy stands.

Although little academic research has been done on the role of conventions in voter education (a topic ripe for future investigation), numerous scholars have examined the role of debates as sources of information.[19] Most recently, a meta-analysis of the literature on presidential debates indicated that they tend to increase citizens' issue knowledge while also influencing the salience of some of the issues discussed by the candidates (Benoit, Hansen, and Verser 2003).[20] Some evidence indicates that debates may be of particular benefit to those who possess relatively low levels of preexisting information. Along these lines, my analysis of trends in six elections (1976–1996) revealed that the gap in candidate information between low- and high-education respondents generally widened over the course of the general election campaign but was sometimes reduced in size by the presidential debates (Holbrook 2002b).

Some studies suggest that campaign advertising also contributes to voter education. Brians and Wattenberg (1996), for example, found that voter recall of campaign ads in the 1992 presidential contest was positively associated with knowledge of candidate issue stands, and that this relationship was stronger among respondents who were interviewed in October as opposed to September (that is, later in the campaign rather than earlier). Freedman, Franz, and Goldstein (2004) provided an interesting take on this topic, with an innovative look at the 2000 presidential election. Unlike Brians and Wattenberg, who relied on people's (not always reliable) recollection of what they had seen during the campaign, Freedman and colleagues used data from a satellite tracking system to calibrate the level of advertising in the media market in which a voter resided. Integrating this information with data from the National Election Study survey,[21] the authors showed that exposure to advertising had a significant, if modest, effect on knowledge of candidates' issue positions—but a much more pronounced impact on respondents' ability to articulate reasons for voting for or (especially) against George W. Bush and Al Gore. In addition, some evidence indicated that the individuals who benefited most from campaign advertising were those who needed information the most, specifically, voters with relatively low levels of preexisting information.

As mentioned earlier, one of the biggest holes in our understanding of how campaigns affect citizen competence stems from the lack of research on the impact of conventions. I tend to agree with Stimson (2004) that the convention period is probably a period of very intense learning, a period that can help to frame and establish the parameters of the fall campaign. At the same time, however, we know very little about how much and what kind of learning takes place during the nominating conventions. Given that these are the only occasions when parties and candidates are able to control the flow of information, thereby ensuring that the information stream is clearly biased in their favor, relatively rapid learning might be expected.

Voter Mobilization and Turnout. The other civic function of campaigns is that of mobilizing the electorate to turn out on election day. Of course, similar to voter education, campaigns perform this function in their selfish pursuit of votes. But the end result, still, is voter mobilization. One group of academic studies has examined the impact of party contacting on participation in elections.[22] Most of these analyses focus on party contacting during both presidential *and* congressional election cycles, and the general conclusion is that contacting motivates people to get out and vote. This effect is fairly robust even when researchers take into account the increasing tendency for campaigns to target voters who are already predisposed toward voting.[23] The first read on the impact of personal contacting in 2004 was provided by *The Vanishing Voter* project, the results of which suggested that get-out-the-vote efforts by organized groups, along with encouragement from friends and family, played an important role in convincing young people to participate.[24]

A handful of studies have looked exclusively at the impact of presidential campaign activities on mobilization and turnout, producing decidedly mixed results. Both Jeffrey Jones (1998) and Herr (2002) assessed the impact of campaign appearances on turnout, the latter in 1996 and the former in presidential elections from 1980 to 1992. Using media markets as his unit of analysis, Jones observed a significant influence from candidate visits, with the impact of visits relatively proximate to the election having a much stronger effect than did those occurring earlier in the campaign. The Herr study, however, found no connection between candidate appearances and turnout in the 1996 election. To be fair, though, Herr considered only the thirty-seven states that candidates visited in 1996, thus limiting variation on the primary independent variable in his analysis. McClurg and I examined the relative mobilization effects of campaign appearances, candidate media expenditures, and national party monetary transfers to the states in the 1992, 1996, and 2000 elections (Holbrook and McClurg, 2005). We discovered that campaign appearances and media expenditures had no discernible impact on turnout in these races. We did, however, find a significant and robust impact from national party transfers to the states; even when controlling for previous levels of turnout, more party money led to higher levels of turnout. We attributed these effects to party money being used to target core constituency groups to make it to the polls on election day. Finally, the general impact of campaign activities in the states emerged as an important determinant of voter engagement in Patterson's study of the 2000 election. Results indicated that residents of so-called battleground states (where the race was competitive and the candidates invested the bulk of their resources) were more likely than others to report having thought and talked about the campaign, to be able to recall campaign news stories, and, ultimately (though very slightly), to have voted (T. Patterson 2002, 143).

A heated and seemingly endless debate is ongoing among political scientists concerning the potential for negative advertising to demobilize the electorate.[25] Given the extensive literature on this topic, it is not surprising that different studies have occasionally produced conflicting results. In a meta-analysis of fifty-two empirical studies (Lau et al. 1999; also see Lau, Sigelman, and Brown 2005), the authors concluded that there simply was no consistent pattern of findings concerning the mobilizing or demobilizing effects of negative advertising.[26] However, more recent scholarship suggests that negative ads may actually have a positive impact. Djupe and Peterson (2002), for example, found that negative campaigning leads to increased turnout in U.S. Senate primaries, while Lau and Pomper (2001) observed a positive relationship between overall negativity and turnout in Senate general elections—but only among strong partisans, with a demobilizing effect being evident among independents. Goldstein and Freedman's study (2002a) took advantage of the new technology that enabled the authors to match respondents with the ads to which they could have been exposed during the 1996 presidential election (see note 21); they found strong evidence indicating that negative ads stimulated turnout. Clinton and Lapinski's analysis (2004) of a Knowledge Networks sample (see note 13) four years later provided at least modest support for the proposition that negative ads can stimulate turnout among targeted populations toward whom the ads are directed. Finally, Freedman, Franz, and Goldstein (2004) examined the impact of advertising in general (regardless of tone) in the 2000 presidential race and found that exposure to ads had a positive influence on both political interest (especially among low-information voters) and turnout.

Looking for Campaign Effects in the Least Likely Place

Although the academic research cited in this chapter illustrates clearly that presidential campaigns do indeed "matter," our perspective is nonetheless distorted by the fact that scholars have tended to look for campaign effects in many of the wrong places. Certain characteristics of presidential campaigns make them, on the one hand, the most obvious place to look for campaign effects but, on the other hand, an arena that is particularly inhospitable to such effects. Given that such campaigns usually involve two extremely well-known (at least by the fall) candidates possessing relatively equal levels of resources, and given that both sides are staffed with experienced professionals who can be counted on to do their jobs effectively, it may be somewhat surprising to find presidential campaign effects of the magnitude reported in prior research. The ideal electoral contexts for detecting campaign effects are those in which voters' preexisting levels of information are relatively low and in which an asymmetry exists in the competing streams of information (Zaller 1996). This is not an accurate description of modern presidential elections.

In fact, the information environment most likely to produce strong campaign effects is found in elections for state and local offices. Notwithstanding the fact that our empirical work has sometimes uncovered impressive effects, we are unnecessarily biasing our estimate of the impact of campaigns by focusing so much of our attention on the race for the presidency. Although presidential elections, and especially presidential election outcomes, are higher profile and no doubt of greater interest to most observers, they represent only one level at which campaigns can be evaluated. If we are interested in answering the question "Do campaigns matter?", then the influence of contests taking place elsewhere on the ballot surely warrant scrutiny, because that is where effects are likely to be most pronounced.

One consistent message from research on nonpresidential elections has been the importance of two key elements in any campaign: the candidates themselves and campaign resources. The literature on congressional campaigns points to a huge information advantage for most incumbents—an advantage that can usually be overcome only by experienced, well-funded challengers; in open-seat contests the political experience of the candidates and the amount of money they can raise become even more important.[27] Similar effects are found in state-legislative, gubernatorial, local, and initiative elections.[28] Research at these different levels of government has also contributed to a better understanding of how campaigns act to mobilize and inform voters.[29]

Together, the studies cited in the notes to this section identify a host of important and interesting campaign effects, most of which cannot be examined at the presidential level due to the relative parity of candidate exposure and campaign resources that is characteristic of national elections. Thus, if we broaden the scope of our inquiry when we ask, "Do campaigns matter?", the answer—which is already in the affirmative—becomes a resounding YES! This point has been made elsewhere (Finkel 1993; Holbrook 1996), of course, but the time has come to take it more seriously when assessing how campaigns influence voters.

Moving Beyond the Candidates' Campaigns

Finally, I would argue that the study of presidential campaigns needs to be a bit more holistic in its approach. Although this is beginning to change, most research on the topic has looked mainly at the effect of actors associated with the formal campaign. Yet surely the electorate is influenced by other actors as well. Indeed, some recent work has incorporated the impact of media coverage.[30] What I'm thinking about, however, are the "extra-campaign groups" acting with the intent to influence the election outcome. McClurg and I have unearthed some interesting effects from party spending patterns (Holbrook and McClurg, 2005), and party activities undoubtedly are important in other ways as well. The activities of groups—including, for example, political action committees, so-called 527s (see chapter 4 in this volume), religious organizations, labor unions, and the like—certainly need to be explored to a greater extent than has been the case thus far. And this exploration should include attention not just to persuasion and contribution to the outcome but also to mobilization and voter education effects. A focus on extra-campaign organizations seems especially relevant today, given the explosion in advertising and mobilization efforts in recent election cycles. Looking closely at these sort of effects should help to broaden our understand of how campaigns matter.

Conclusion

My goal in this chapter has been to provide a broad overview of the academic literature on the impact of political campaigns. Do campaigns really matter? The answer, I think, is unequivocally yes. Numerous studies indicate that campaign events can produce changes in the distribution of candidate preferences, and others highlight the important civic functions of campaigns, that is, voter education and mobilization. The evidence on campaign effects is in some ways even stronger when our attention shifts from the presidency to congressional, state, and local elections. Campaigns matter, and sometimes they matter quite a lot. Are they *the* determining factor in who wins and who loses? At the presidential level, it is likely that in most cases they are not. Yet even here, campaigns do not have to be the most important factor in an election for them to matter. As I noted earlier, many factors—including the campaign—come together to produce election outcomes, and all of those factors *matter* because each contributes in its own way to shaping those outcomes.

The Consultants Respond About

DO CAMPAIGNS REALLY MATTER?

It is understandably insulting to consultants when academics suggest that their efforts have only a limited impact in determining who wins and loses on election day. As much of the research cited in this book clearly shows, such an assertion also happens to be untrue—though the *degree* to which campaigns matter, and the particular *aspects* of campaigns (strategy, message, images versus issues, negative ads, grassroots mobilization, and so on) that matter the most, are not always obvious even to political professionals. Nevertheless, at the end of the day, most consultants have little doubt that what they do counts for quite a lot. And they're probably right, if not always for the reasons they think.

DEMOCRATIC POLLSTER. Do campaigns matter? It depends how you define "matter." All that matters to me is what happens on that Tuesday in November. Academics, though, are concerned about how informed voters are and all that

continues...

other stuff, but that's not necessarily important for what we do.

REPUBLICAN MEDIA CONSULTANT. Campaigns do matter, but academics and journalists may not always know why. And that's because there is so much that goes on internally in a campaign that never gets recorded. There are moments of truth in every campaign when you make very large decisions based on all your research, all of your data. . . . There is so much folklore in campaigns. I've been involved with several campaigns when a particular negative ad runs one or two times and it becomes the reason the guy won or lost. More often than not that's simply not true, but it becomes conventional wisdom anyway.

DEMOCRATIC MEDIA CONSULTANT. How do you go about isolating one means of communication and determining whether it's the most effective? I think a [winning] campaign has to have all of them.

DEMOCRATIC POLLSTER. It's tough to see campaigns mattering much in congressional races, because redistricting by computer has made so many of the districts a foregone conclusion. But you also have the fact that voters are more polarized than in the past. It used to be that a competitive race started out with 40 percent Republican, 40 percent Democratic, and 20 percent undecided. Increasingly, initial polls are showing more that start out 45–45 with 10 percent in the middle. So on the one hand, there are fewer people to talk to [and to be influenced by the campaign]. But on the other hand, maybe campaigns actually matter more today *because* you have fewer and fewer people to effect change on [and winning a majority of that small number can be decisive].

Notes

1. For example, working-class and Catholic voters generally ended up supporting the Democratic ticket (as they had in the past), whereas most of their middle-class and Protestant counterparts sided with the Republicans.

2. The percentages reported here reflect changes that occurred between May and October; some people in this latter group reached a final decision during the closing days of the campaign (Lazarsfeld 1944, 325–326).

3. See Fiorina (1981); Key (1966); Markus and Converse (1979); Nie, Verba, and Petrocik (1976); Page and Jones (1979).

4. See Kiewiet (1983); Kramer (1971); Lewis-Beck (1988); Markus (1988); Tufte (1978).

5. See J. Campbell and Garand (2000); Lewis-Beck and Rice (1992).

6. These two figures differ partly because only 36 percent were undecided in the spring wave of the 1940 panel, compared with 55 percent at approximately the same point in 1984; hence, there were more opportunities for activation in the latter case. Another possible explanation is that Finkel's estimate was based on actual votes, whereas Lazarsfeld and his colleagues looked at October vote intention.

7. The term *counter-factuals* refers to the use of different scenarios to simulate how the results might have changed under each. For instance, my analysis showed that if the cumulative effects of the 1988 and 1992 campaigns had been switched, the election outcomes would have changed as well (Holbrook 1996, 148).

8. This happens for a number of reasons, including, for example, the tendency for front-runners (1) to wage relatively "safe" campaigns (trying to protect their lead rather than expand it) and (2) to be subjected to closer scrutiny by both voters and media (see J. Campbell 2000, 43–44).

9. For instance, in *Do Campaigns Matter?* I listed a series of positive and negative events for each candidate without measuring the actual content of media coverage. Although most of those events probably generated the expected *tone* of coverage, there could have been exceptions, and considerable variation probably occurred in the *amount* of information generated.

10. By *priming* I mean that the increased attention paid to Social Security by the media and the candidates elevated its importance and increased its accessibility in the minds of voters, leading them to assign more weight to Social Security when deciding whom to support. For a more complete discussion of priming effects, see Iyengar and Kinder (1987) and Jacobs and Shapiro (1994).

11. See Herr (2002); Holbrook (2002a); Hillygus and Jackman (2003); Holbrook and McClurg (2005); J. Jones (1998); Shaw (1999a, 1999b, 1999c); Stimson (2004); Wlezien and Erikson (2002).

12. See Holbrook (1994, 1996); Shaw (1999a, 1999c); Wlezien and Erikson (2002).

13. Knowledge Networks is a private firm that conducts surveys via the Internet, selecting respondents through random digit dialing in such a way that they represent a random probability sample of the entire U.S. population falling within the Microsoft WebTV network. For additional details, see Hillygus and Jackman (2003, 584); Iyengar, Norpoth, and Hahn (2004, 162–163); Clinton and Lapinski (2004, 75); and Knowledge Network's own Web site at www.knowledgenetworks.com/index2.html.

14. See Herr (2002); Holbrook (2002a); Holbrook and McClurg (2005); J. Jones (1998).

15. Truman generally campaigned in states that were competitive or had a large number of electoral votes, whereas Dewey's appearances followed a less predictable pattern. Truman also used the campaign stops to make localized appeals, whereas Dewey frequently chose to deliver speeches aimed at the national radio audience (Karabell 2000).

16. See J. Campbell (2000); Hillygus and Jackman (2003); Holbrook (1994, 1996); R. Johnston, Hagen, and Jamieson (2004); Stimson (2004).

17. See Hillygus and Jackman (2003); Holbrook (1994, 1996); Stimson (2004).

18. See Herr (2002); Holbrook (2002a); Holbrook and McClurg (2005); J. Jones (1998); Shaw (1999b).

19. See Bishop, Oldendick, and Tuchfarber (1978); Chaffee and Dennis (1979); Holbrook (1999, 2002b); Lemert (1993); A. Miller and MacKuen (1979).

20. Meta-analysis is an approach that uses statistical techniques to combine the results of several different studies in order to provide a quantitative evaluation or summary of the effects of variables common to the studies.

21. See Freedman, Franz, and Goldstein (2004, 726–727) for additional details about the satellite data provided by the Campaign Media Analysis Group. This information was combined with survey respondents' self-reports of their television viewing habits

to create a measure of maximum possible exposure (what the authors call an "upper bound on the number of spots" someone might have seen; Freedman and Goldstein 1999, 1198).

22. See Abramson and Claggett (2001); A. Gerber and Green (2000a, 2000b); Goldstein and Ridout (2002); Huckfeldt and Sprague (1992); Kramer (1970); McClurg (2004); Rosenstone and Hansen (1993); Wielhouwer (1999, 2003); Wielhouwer and Lockerbie (1994); also see chapter 9 in this volume.

23. See Abramson and Claggett (2001); Goldstein and Ridout (2002); Wielhouwer (1999).

24. See www.vanishingvoter.org/releases/release111104.shtml.

25. See Ansolabehere and Iyengar (1995); Ansolabehere, Iyengar, and Simon (1999); Ansolabehere et al. (1994); Clinton and Lapinski (2004); Djupe and Peterson (2002); Finkel and Geer (1998); Freedman and Goldstein (1999); Kahn and Kenney (1999); Lau et al. (1999); Sigelman and Kugler (2003); Wattenberg and Brians (1999); also see chapter 5 in this volume.

26. One explanation for such inconsistency is that a disconnect appears to exist between how academic researchers define negativity and what voters perceive to be negative (Sigelman and Kugler 2003).

27. See Herrnson (2004); Jacobson (2004).

28. On state-legislative elections, see Abbe et al. (2003); Carey, Niemi, and Powell (2000); Gierzynski and Breaux (1993); Hogan (2004); Van Dunk (1997). On gubernatorial elections, see Carsey (2000); King (2001); Partin (2002); Squire (1992). On local elections, see Gierzynski, Kleppner, and Lewis (1998); Krebs (1998). On initiatives, see Bowler, Donovan, and Happ (1992); Hadwiger (1992).

29. See Hogan (1999); Jackson (1997, 2002); Nicholson (2003); Niven (2001); Partin (2001); S. Patterson and Caldeira (1983).

30. See R. Johnston, Hagen, and Jamieson (2004); Shaw (1999c).

2 Campaign Strategy

Michael John Burton and Daniel M. Shea

More than sixty years ago, a team of scholars from Columbia University tried to measure the effects of presidential campaign activities on the final vote tally. They found that the vast majority of voters in Erie County, Ohio, chose their candidate in the 1940 election well before the campaign even began in earnest (Lazarsfeld, Berelson, and Gaudet 1944). In fact, a person's religion, socioeconomic status, and place of residence (urban versus rural) provided the basis for what was called an "index of political predisposition" (16–27) that predicted, in advance and with a reasonably high degree of accuracy, how that person was likely to vote. For example, "Of all rich Protestant farmers almost 75 [percent] voted Republican, whereas 90 [percent] of the Catholic laborers living in [the city] voted Democratic" (26). Campaign flyers, political events, and news stories had scant impact on the election outcome. Indeed, in the contest between Republican Wendell Willkie and Democrat Franklin Roosevelt, only 8 percent of those who had backed Roosevelt in 1936 withdrew their support four years later in the midst of the 1940 campaign (102).

Today the notion that a political campaign may have caused one in twelve voters to switch sides might be greeted with skepticism, as much of the academic community has come to believe that structural factors inherent in the political environment all but predetermine the outcome of American elections (see chapter 1 in this volume). At that time, though, the finding seemed to show that the effects of campaigning were quite limited. During the 1930s and 1940s, in a world that lived in fear of demagogic dictators, the notion that only a fraction of the population was open to campaign rhetoric reassured people who wanted to believe that American Exceptionalism was securing the home front.[1] Framed in terms of a wartime outlook, the conclusions of the Erie County study spoke to the virtues of stability induced by a deep social structure. However, looking at the same issue from the scholarship of a new millennium, conversions by 8 percent of the population suggest great volatility in the electorate.

We understand the world around us by the way we frame it: what we believe to be important, what we consider irrelevant, what we understand as the natural state of affairs. If we assume that voters are eminently persuadable, then a finding of 8 percent volatility reflects the stability of the electorate; if, on the other hand, we assume that the electorate is stable, then 8 percent might seem like a surprisingly high number of people converted. Yet the idea of perceptual framing involves more than merely setting a standard; it refers to what catches our attention and how we mold our understanding of our world. Even simple matters of fact and cause are subject to interpretation, as anyone who has served as a juror knows. Did the airline crash victims die because the pilot failed to control the plane? Or was the airframe inherently unstable? Or did the wickedness of the world bring the wrath of God? A grieving spouse, an engineer, and a radical theologian can frame the same event in fundamentally different ways, and each can find support in differing lines of evidence.

At a certain level, we "create" the world we inhabit by constructing storylines that we can understand. It is not necessarily an issue of who is right and who is wrong, and it is not simply a matter of partial information (for example, the blind scientists who make faulty generalizations about elephants because each has examined a different part of the animal); rather, it is a matter of approaching the subject with unrelated purposes. We learn about the things we look for, and we all look for different things.

Campaigns and elections are this way. What you are looking for influences what you find. A political scientist who is interested in the big picture of American elections, and whose discipline encourages the study of campaigns through the examination of large data sets, will tend to find that, in most elections, most of the time, campaigns just do not matter very much. A political journalist, on the other hand, looks for "news" (dramatic stories, sensational events) and will therefore seek out the hot campaign, complete with attention-grabbing characters and tragic ironies that emphasize the volatility of elections. A political practitioner, by contrast, is intimately familiar with the details of campaigns, the assumption being that the quality of the campaign is the most important factor in the outcome of the election—and so she *must*, because if she throws her hands up in the air and waits for divine intervention then surely the battle will be lost. Few consultants have ever picked up a lucrative contract by telling a prospective client that campaign effects are minimal.

In this chapter we explore various understandings of strategy in American elections, looking at strategic effects from the perspective of scholars, journalists, and practitioners. Scholars seek the role of strategy in the big picture; journalists look for it in the crucible of impassioned politics; and practitioners are on a ceaseless quest for strategic advantage in the electoral warfare that is their trade. None of these experts is ultimately right or wrong. Each seeks a type of truth that serves a different professional purpose.

Scholars

Political science, as we now know the institution, developed from the notion that power and knowledge should be sharply distinguished from one another. Although persuasive rhetoric cannot truly be removed from discussions of public policy—even the most conscientious political scientist has a point of view—we can, if we try, at least spell out our biases and offer politicians and the public a better view of social problems. Truth *should* speak to power. In a world where a well-chosen anecdote can back up any political position, and where opinions can be pressed on all sides, scholars have sought to widen their analyses and to discover solid factual grounding. They ask pointed questions: What do we know about the empirical world? What is generally true? While water-cooler conversations about politics commonly revolve around funny stories and urban legends, academic political scientists try to assemble an understanding of the world that looks not at outlier cases, but at more typical situations—not passing trends, but enduring regularities.

From the scholars' perspective, then, the problem with our conventional understanding of politics lies precisely with our everyday frames of reference. Ordinary voters watch a campaign performance that appears to be dominated by famous (at least at the highest level) political actors; in fact, it is not a single show at all but rather an assortment of individual campaigns, each connected to the others by only the barest thread. Lacking a disciplined effort, we cannot grasp the *general* nature of elections because we are confronted with a broad onslaught of *discrete* elections. To solve this problem, scholars develop highly structured frameworks to help map the forest without becoming spellbound by the trees.

Empirical analysis of political campaigns is an effort to reproduce within the precepts of social science what traditional scientists have done for the natural world. Debates over the applicability of the scientific method developed for the natural world to the study of human behavior (which often seems utterly unpredictable) have raged for years. But even if political scientists concede that people are more unpredictable than the rotation of planets and the forces of a magnetic field, there is some value in looking for the regularities of political life. To find them, scholars of politics, like their natural science counterparts, will try to work out theories of political action, derive testable hypotheses from these theories, gather evidence that will test the theories, and then compare theoretical expectations with the evidence gathered.

That was the approach used in the study of Erie County voters in the 1940 presidential campaign. Lazarsfeld, Berelson, and Gaudet surveyed a large number of people over the course of the election to see how many of them changed sides. They found that most had made an early choice and stuck with it until the end:

> There is a familiar adage in American folklore to the effect that a person is only what he thinks he is, an adage which reflects the typically American notion of unlimited opportunity, the tendency toward self-betterment, etc. Now we find that the reverse of the adage is true: a person thinks, politically, as he is, socially. Social characteristics determine political preference. (Lazarsfeld, Berelson, and Gaudet 1944, 27)

The view that elections are largely predetermined by structural social factors was reinforced by much of the scholarly literature that followed. In their classic study of the 1956 presidential election, Angus Campbell and colleagues (1960) introduced the so-called funnel of causality, in which long-term forces, and especially one's partisan attachments, create a perceptual lens through which short-term events are interpreted. The typical voter may take issues, character, candidate messages, and other campaign developments into account, they argued, but partisanship nevertheless tends to shape the meaning of those factors for most people. A decade and a half later, Nie, Verba, and Petrocik (1976) challenged this view, maintaining that short-term issues had become more important than they had been in the recent past; at the same time, however, it was clear that many voters were still guided by their partisan loyalties.

Contemporary political scientists continue trying to piece together complex models of electoral behavior. Tufte (1975), for instance, was able to explain roughly 98 percent of the variance in the two-party distribution of the popular vote in midterm congressional elections by taking into account two factors largely outside the control of candidates: national economic conditions and presidential job approval. Lewis-Beck and Rice (1992) showed that a handful of variables can be combined to predict the number of congressional seats that each party will hold after an election: rate of growth (or decline) in personal disposable income, presidential job approval, the number of seats a party has exposed (that is, how many it currently holds), and the length of time the president has been in the White House.

Following recent presidential elections, scholars have attempted to gauge the accuracy of various statistical models that were used to predict the outcome in advance. A number of different approaches exist, but for presidential contests the same two factors identified by Tufte (economic conditions and presidential approval ratings) generally drive the forecasts, which often are very accurate. One assessment of the forecasts offered in 2004 reviewed the calculations of seven teams of scholars, finding that they missed the final vote tally by an average of just 2.6 percentage points. Four of these teams were within two points of perfection—a remarkable feat given that the predictions were made nearly a year in advance. Some models were off the mark by three or four percentage points, an error margin that was attributed to "unexpected developments" such as the war in Iraq, or to measurement error and the failure to consider all significant variables.[2] Overall, though, campaign effects in the race between George W. Bush and John Kerry seemed to be minimal (see American Political Science Association 2005).

Studies such as those just described are motivated, in part, by the desire among scholars to develop and test broad theories, many of which stem from fundamental assumptions about human behavior. We may posit, for example, that the typical voter is "rational" in the sense that he or she will try to reach certain goals as efficiently as possible, using resources strategically. One goal might be to vote for candidates who will press for agreeable policies; another might be to spend free time with loved ones. The two goals clash insofar as more time spent researching candidates means less time with family (and vice versa). Some researchers therefore suggest that voters often use "cognitive shortcuts"—that is, simple ideas (or cues) that boil down complicated scenarios—in order to figure out who will get their vote. Such ideas might include, for example, the state of the economy, partisanship, peace and war, and incumbency.[3]

Looking at the mental processes of individual voters might seem to emphasize the importance of a campaign's message, but the shortcuts identified by political scientists often tie electoral outcomes to structural elements of society rather than the personal whims of voters. In 1966 V. O. Key suggested that voters are inclined to use past events as a guide to their behavior on election day; in other words, they are even willing to vote against their own party if the party has not performed well in office. According to Key (1966, 9), "As voters mark their ballots they may have in their minds impressions of the last TV political spectacular of the campaign, but, more important, they have in their minds recollections of their experiences of the past four years." Fiorina (1981, 106–129) built on Key's argument, maintaining that voters typically compile a "running tally of retrospective evaluations" and that this calculation directly shapes their partisan orientation, which, in turn, plays a powerful role in determining future voting decisions. Alternatively, perhaps the strongest voting cue is simple incumbency. Mayhew (1974a, 1974b) suggested that because members of Congress want to be reelected, they spend a great deal of time working toward that end—and that, as public officials, these same incumbents have a disproportionate ability to make their views heard and to claim credit for the good things that government does (including casework on behalf of constituents and programs that provide benefits to the district or state), thereby promoting their standing with voters. Thus the "electoral connection," as described by Mayhew, emphasizes the power of incumbency over the noise and fanfare of the time-honored American campaign.

A strength of the scholarly perspective lies in its capacity to deflate one of the great myths that exist about elections: that political campaigns are colossal battles between well-armed adversaries. The truth of the matter, when viewed from on high, is that most elections, most of the time, are decided long before the race begins. Incumbents usually win. Candidates allied with the president in times of prosperity—they win, too. So do those with experience, and who fit with the demographic, partisan, and basic attitudinal makeup of their constituency. It is a rare campaign strategy that can elect candidates whose background, ideology, and partisanship are at odds with the people they are seeking to represent. There are half a million elective offices in the United States, and scholars familiar with the literature can predict the outcome of races for the vast majority of them.

But not quite all. Some races—not many, but some—are genuine cliffhangers, or they steadfastly manage in some way to defy conventional wisdom. These elections are the province of political journalists, and they provide the kind of drama that readers and viewers demand.

Journalists

Journalists are, by definition, interested in reporting *news*. News can be defined in terms of "who, what, when, where, why, and how," but a relatively well-defined set of people, events, places, and developments qualify as news. In politics, reporters mostly cover "serious" candidates in important elections, especially those in which local voters will be casting ballots, and the reporting generally strives to be even-handed toward the two major parties while maintaining a focus on great "stories." This familiar definition of news, it should be said, is a contemporary notion with roots in a completely different kind of reporting than exists today. To understand what *is,* we should consider what *was.*

In the early days of the republic, news reporting (if we may call it that) was little more than storytelling, with yarns woven to entertain rather than inform. This "news" was produced by local printers, who saw the publication of broadsheets containing the day's events as a gainful sideline to the production of other printed materials, for example, playing cards, invitations, and the like. On occasion, a printer would obtain government contracts for their wares and, in partial repayment, the news reported in that printer's broadsheet would reflect the views of the party in power. Building a readership, therefore, meant inflaming public passion—and with politics a key source of public argumentation, printers who wanted to sell papers would align themselves either with the incumbent party or its major opposition.

With the invention of the telegraph, publishers found economic benefit in combining their reporting efforts. In 1850 the New York Associated Press began an effort to coordinate a news-sharing system that would soon enforce new discipline on reporters; specifically, the news they gathered was expected to meet the needs of readers across the country and across party lines (Blondheim 1994). Indeed, with the rising popularity of the so-called penny press earlier in the century, strict party alignment had been on the wane anyway. In the second half of the 1800s, publishers found that the real money was not in hawking papers so much as in selling advertisements. And advertising, it was thought, would be most profitable if newspapers focused on sensational stories of crime, death, and political corruption. The resulting spate of yellow journalism, though frowned upon by intellectuals, was enthusiastically consumed by the public, and it was highly profitable.

The landscape shifted again after the turn of the twentieth century with the rise of the Progressive Movement, a middle-class revolt against corruption and especially the sleaze associated with party machines.[4] Openly partisan newspapers found themselves at odds with the prevailing public mood, while many journalists were driven as much by social rage as by career ambition. The muckrakers, as they were called, wanted to clean up government, and much of their passion was directed against party politics; but they also wanted to make a name for themselves—and perhaps, finally, a comfortable living wage. Big stories made big reporters. In the 1970s, reporters like Carl Bernstein and Bob Woodward (1974) of the *Washington Post,* who uncovered criminal wrongdoing in Richard Nixon's 1972 presidential reelection campaign, set a new standard for investigative journalism. After Nixon's resignation, journalism came to be seen as a noble profession, and journalists were viewed by some as a new, powerful engine of social reform that represented, in a sense, a revived progressive movement.

Even in a world where anyone with a computer and an Internet connection has the ability to influence uncounted readers, professional journalism remains the primary gatekeeper of campaign information (which explains why even the most iconoclastic Internet bloggers claim to be "journalists"). Reporters, of course, frequently say they try to avoid bias, but the very notion is wrongheaded. Every perspective begins with a point of view, and even a casual reading of mainstream reportage—including print, radio, and television—reveals a bias toward "fairness" and "good stories," two principles that (along with commercial considerations, as noted earlier) inevitably draw reporters to the most exciting campaigns. They are attracted to hard-fought political games, and this means they generally report on competitive elections.

Reporters give the bulk of their attention to so-called horse-race stories: Who is ahead, who is behind, and by how much? Does the challenger stand a chance? Has he or she peaked too soon? Internal dynamics are also deemed important: Who is working for the candidates? Who has endorsed them? How much money have they raised? The strategic twists and turns of each campaign, the moves that seem to reshape the probability of success, are considered hot news. "By comparison," according to media scholar Doris Graber (2005, 234), "reporters slight political, social, and economic problems . . . unless these issues can be made exciting and visually dynamic." For scholars the important point is the outcome of the election (and the factors that cause people to vote the way they do), but for a journalist the real story is the process, the *way* one candidate defeats another. Journalists focus on the details of the game—the ups, downs, twists, and turns of a year-long contest. It is grand sport, a twelve-month Super Bowl, the best reality show on television! Little wonder that an average of roughly 15 percent of television news during election years is about political campaigning (Graber 2005, 231). News is big business, and campaigns are big news.

Strategy has become the preeminent fixation of political journalism in the United States,[5] with reporters usually zeroing in on each new charge, unflattering revelation, fundraising downturn, lost endorsement, and sagging poll number. Failure, in particular, gives the news media something to talk about. In the waning days of the 2004 presidential election, the discussion of strategy once again took center stage (Project for Excellence in Journalism 2005). Each candidate's policy positions had been laid out in the debates, or well before, and each new poll said essentially the same thing—that the race was exceedingly close. So what was left to report? The candidates' closing strategy, of course: What was the end-game plan? How might John Kerry go about trying to finish off President Bush, and what steps was the president's team planning to take to ensure that voters sent Kerry back to the Senate?

After it was all over, postelection assessments once again underscored the apparent importance of strategy. It was often assumed, for example, that the brilliance of Bush advisor Karl Rove had won the day. It was his decision to play hard to the president's conservative base, and to conserve resources so as to be in a position to "out-mobilize" the Democrats on election day. Presidential elections are especially good opportunities for media analysis, as the electoral college provides state-by-state battles and a multitude of strategic decisions concerning the allocation of time and money by each campaign. Journalists, kibitzing with each other during a year of campaign travel, end up locked in an ongoing competitive search for the next strategic factor, always looking for the next silver bullet that will prove (or appear to prove) decisive in shaping the election outcome.

The parallel between electoral analysis and sports analysis on television is uncanny. On one channel Terry Bradshaw tells us why the Redskins will lose their next game, while on another George Will waxes philosophical about the limits of American liberalism. Journalists and news editors understand that their focus on "the game" will draw more readers; that is, they appreciate the business side of their reporting. Yet they also believe in what they preach: decisions by campaign operatives make a difference. They appreciate the long-term structural dimensions that shape a candidate's or party's fortunes, but they also have faith in campaign effects. Moreover, by helping voters understand the complexities of new-style political campaigns,[6] and by underscoring the most exciting parts of the process, they believe that they will encourage citizens to become engaged.

The mainstream news media are neither left nor right on a consistent basis (D'Alessio and Allen 2000); they are mainly searching for a good story. Because reporters are looking for drama, because they are looking for intriguing personalities, and because they want to be fair, reporters especially tend to seek out competitive races. And because good storytelling relies on detail, nuance, and a focus on people, reporters approach these campaigns with investigative tools frequently ignored by academics: They talk to voters. They talk to key players (including consultants) and wise observers (who have seen it all before). They watch campaign events and learn the candidate's stump speech by heart, listening for the smallest shift in emphasis, which may in turn indicate a shift in strategy or message.

The insights gained from personal observation are leveraged by the fact that reporting is part of the campaign. While scholars report their findings long after the election is over, reporters release theirs in real time—which gives them (unlike academic researchers) a certain amount of power, since what they say or write can have an impact on the outcome. They can squeeze information out of the campaign by methods reminiscent of a district attorney, or a member of the Soprano crime family. In the process, campaign operatives are given an "opportunity" to explain charges that have been leveled at their candidate; that is, reporters let the campaign know that everyone else is talking, so maybe it is best to clear the air right now. Of course, the weakness of media reporting is that it lacks the kind of big-picture viewpoint that scholars enjoy and, indeed, although reporters can become thoroughly familiar with the campaigns they cover, they do not know nearly as much about the internal functioning of the campaign organization as do the political professionals who run the show.

Campaign Professionals

The scholar looks at the big picture, and the reporter tries to find a good story. The campaign professional, in contrast, has a wholly different mission: to win the election at hand. Few other jobs draw such an absolute distinction between success and failure. If the candidate is not ahead of the pack on election day, it is all over. As a result, campaign professionals often come to believe that elections are like battles—and to prepare for engagement, they throw themselves into what is known as "campaign mode" (Burton and Shea 2003).

We can offer no formal definition of campaign mode here; it is a way of life more than a point of discussion, though its contours can be discerned from history and experience. As electoral strategies are formulated, debated, implemented, and reformulated, an intuitive sense of political strategy takes hold in the professional mind. In Washington and on the campaign trail, one will hear political professionals say, "She understands," or "He gets it," or "She knows how the game is played." A White House official once described campaign mode as the ability to "think three or four moves ahead" (Burton and Shea 2003, 4). Cold calculations must be made about the strengths and weaknesses of both the candidate and the opposition, the opportunities presented and foreclosed by one's political environment, and the perils that await the candidate once the electoral season begins. Some people get "it"; others do not.

Political advice has a long history. Thomas Jefferson, Andrew Jackson, and Abraham Lincoln, for example, all had acquaintances who offered advice—much of it unsolicited, much of it bad. The rise of campaign consulting as we know it today began with the strategic thinking of William McKinley's longtime advisor Mark Hanna, who devised a systematic approach to the Ohio Republican's 1896 presidential campaign (see Reichley 1992, 140–147). Fundraising and voter outreach were mapped along the lines of "business principles," meaning that various constituencies would be targeted and solicited according to their relative likelihood of supporting the Republicans (Troy 1996). Plenty of backroom politicking continued, to be sure, but the fundamental idea of the McKinley campaign was that the electorate needs to be viewed as a whole, analytically segmented, and then courted according to the needs and demands of specific constituency groups.[7]

As the old political party structure began to fall away in the 1960s, and as more voters began to say, "I vote for the candidate, not the party,"[8] those who sought elective office understood that they needed to find outside assistance. A growing number of campaign professionals were there to help and, of course, to make a nice living in the process. In the 1992 presidential campaign, consultants became media stars to perhaps a greater degree than had ever before been the case (but see McGinniss 1969). *The War Room,* for example, was a popular documentary film that centered less on candidate Bill Clinton than on his principal advisors, George Stephanopoulos and James Carville (both of whom have gone on to become prominent television personalities), as well as Carville's then-girlfriend (now wife) on the Republican side, Mary Matalin. More recently, one of the first battles waged among contenders for the 2004 Democratic nomination was for the services of heavyweight political consultant Robert Shrum. This competition was a reflection not only of Shrum's skills but also of his reputation, that is, landing him as an advisor would automatically enhance the credibility of any candidate, especially in the eyes of journalists covering the campaign (who, as noted earlier, tend to focus on such matters).

In the twenty-first century, political consulting is a mature industry (also see chapter 10 in this volume). Practitioners in Washington and around the country specialize in all aspects of the campaign process, from polling to letter stuffing to grassroots mobilization to video production. In the monthly magazine *Campaigns and Elections,* candidates for public office can find advertisements for all sorts of campaign-related products and services. Consultants even have their own professional organization, the American Association of Political Consultants, which gives out "Pollie" awards after every election to members for distinguished performances in a variety of areas (best television and radio ads, best direct-mail piece, best fundraising campaign, best candidate web site, and so on).

Ultimately, though, consultants are driven not by a desire for recognition but by the need to win elections. Whether motivated by business considerations or ideological conviction,[9] this imperative causes campaign professionals to view campaigns differently than either academics or journalists. To the professional, strategy can seem like *everything*. If strategy does not matter, then the consultant has lost all reason for being: Why would any candidate hire someone whose actions had little or no effect on the final outcome? Understandably, then, political professionals tend to believe in the power of strategy and tactics even to the point of self-deception. As the race winds down, front-running campaigns often fear the effects of a last-minute "October surprise,"[10] while their ill-fated opponents are telling themselves, "We can do it!" Campaign mode, in this sense, is a state of mind that combines a visceral drive to win elections with a deep-seated habit of strategic thinking. Ideally, strategic thinking in campaign mode is based on an understanding of political terrain that helps a professional choose the campaign rules most likely to produce victory.

Strategic thinking is as much an art as it is a science. Using election day as an anchor point, a political operative will survey the existing situation and then reverse-engineer a campaign victory by designating the week prior to the election for a get-out-the-vote drive, the week prior to that as an opportunity to refine the campaign's voter lists, and so forth, until the plan reaches back to the present moment in time (see C. Shaw 2000, 250). Many campaigns create wall-sized calendars that chart each significant event leading up to the election; everyone in the office can thus see what needs to be done, and when. With the immovable deadline looming, there simply is no time to discuss anything that does not relate directly to the task at hand. Backward mapping sets the goal; forward planning shows the way. Sometimes, of course, this process is overtaken by the frenzy of day-to-day events; that is, campaign decision-makers establish their strategic plan but then end up adjusting their approach to fit new developments as they occur.

Strategy is governed by perception. Political professionals of all stripes often understand a state, district, ward, or precinct in much the same way. In campaign mode, electoral victory is the axis around which the world turns. Accordingly, professionals view any voting district as a conglomeration of voters, demographic characteristics, media markets, neighborhoods, partisan and ideological preferences, long-standing political alliances (and disputes), and other electorally significant features that must be either exploited or overcome in order for their candidate to win at the polls on election day. People in the district are seen as volunteers, staffers, base voters, swing voters, and soft partisans. Segments of the electorate that are unalterably loyal to the opposition simply recede from view. Persuadable voters, on the other hand, are said to be "on the radar screen," worth keeping an eye on. Like other electorally significant features of a district, the uncommitted voters (who, as a mass, are capable of turning the election) become extremely salient aspects of the political terrain.

Looking back at the 2004 presidential election, media consultant Robert Shrum declared, "Everything mattered—everything they did, everything we did, and a series of external events all mattered" (Institute of Politics et al. 2005, 134). To make sense of such chaos, consultants need to know at least a few rules of electoral strategy. Some are drawn as simple imperatives, such as "You have to have a plan" (Grey 1999, 89). Others are statements of political fact that carry obvious strategic or tactical implications. EMILY's List, a political action committee that funds pro-choice Democratic women, named itself after the idea that "Early Money Is Like Yeast—it makes the 'dough' rise." In California, campaign operatives commonly say, "It's not real until it's on television." Former U.S. House Speaker Tip O'Neill's rule that "all politics is local" is among the most widely accepted principles of American politics. Thus, putting all of the pieces together, a California campaign organization might want to start with a plan, raise early money, get itself on the air, and address local issues whenever possible.

For political professionals, these maxims are not just hackneyed clichés, but essential bits of knowledge. While some practitioners might debate the validity, relative priority, or general application of certain presuppositions, much of the conventional wisdom about campaigning consists of some very basic and widely accepted rules. The strength of the professional viewpoint is precisely in its creative thinking, vision, and ability to see not only *what is* but *what could be,* as opposed to the journalist who talks about *what has happened* in a particular campaign, and the scholar who talks about *what usually happens* across the broad spectrum of American elections.

Conclusion

Scholars, journalists, and practitioners—each of these groups can trump the others on its own turf. Scholars understand that most electoral outcomes are utterly predictable, so they marginalize discussions of campaign operations.

Journalists, who talk to operatives and to voters on a daily basis, understand the power of structural influences but focus primarily on the campaigns where strategy matters. Consultants with a vested interest in the business of campaign strategy must assume that strategy is everything, or nearly everything, so they are acutely aware of campaign decisions and their potential consequences. Each perspective serves a specific need. Because journalists must engage voters in order to sell papers (or commercials), underscoring the drama of elections becomes critical to their professional livelihood. Because scholars seek to explore and to comprehend general social phenomena, underlying forces are brought to the fore. And because practitioners will not otherwise be successful, they must demonstrate to their clients the power of campaign strategy. In the end, consultants are correct in underscoring the weight of strategic moves, journalists are correct in reporting them, and political scientists are correct in reminding everyone that the sum total of all campaign decisions in all elections is, most of the time, something close to a strategic wash.

There is, of course, a certain amount of crossover. Some journalists are familiar with academic scholarship and know a great deal about the business of campaigning, and many consultants know exactly how reporters think. Similarly, a growing number of scholars are attempting to spell out the origins and effects of campaign decisions using a variety of traditional political science techniques For example, Skaperdas and Grofman (1995) developed a formal model that calculates the probability of a candidate "going negative" on his or her opponent(s).[11] Sellers (1998) used empirical analysis to assess the degree to which a candidate's public record makes voters likely to accept that person's campaign promises. Theilmann and Wilhite (1998) surveyed working consultants, asking how they would react to hypothetical campaign scenarios. D. Green and Gerber (2004) conducted field experiments with prospective voters to see which voter-contact methods are most likely to get people to the polls on election day (also see chapter 9 in this volume). Shaw (1999d) interviewed campaign professionals to help determine the electoral college strategies of recent presidential candidates.[12] Fenno (1996) followed numerous U.S. senators on the campaign trail using his trademark "soak and poke" approach to political science research, which bears a close resemblance to solid investigative reporting.

Each of these scholarly efforts assumes, at least implicitly, that campaigns do matter: campaign effects may be small, but they exist nonetheless. The story of the typical American campaign involves a front-runner who is trying to defend a lead, competing against a dark horse who seeks to defy the odds.

Campaign Strategy 35

There are numerous structural impediments to a challenger's bid to unseat an incumbent, a fact that is well known to scholars, journalists, and practitioners alike, just as other structural factors create inherent advantages and disadvantages on both sides. Yet no single perspective can provide a master framework for understanding electoral phenomena, and there is little use in (and little justification for) trying to persuade political consultants that most campaigning is pointless. Just as practitioners and journalists are wise to track the empirical findings of scholars, political scientists should pay careful attention to the perspectives offered by reporters and consultants. Each has wisdom to offer, and if the purpose of political science scholarship is to understand the big picture, scholars should continue their ongoing reassessment of strategic decision-making in American elections.

The Consultants Respond About

CAMPAIGN STRATEGY

Strategy is difficult for consultants (and professors, for that matter) to talk about in broad terms. Any self-respecting campaign manual will have a list of do's and don'ts that readers are urged to follow if they want to get their candidate elected, but those do's and don'ts usually have more to do with tactics than strategy. That is, they don't show you how to put all of the different pieces together into a coherent whole—least of all one that will be successful across candidates, across offices, and across time. The reason, of course, is that winning strategies are to some degree campaign specific: What works this time may not work every time. If political consultants knew with certainty how to build a winning strategy, there would be a lot more winners than there are losers, and it's hard to imagine how that might work. Nevertheless, lessons are learned (mainly from experience), internalized, and applied (with a greater or lesser degree of success) in future races. What follows here are a few of the elements that the campaign professionals who participated in our conference felt were important.

If, for example, people tend not to vote on the basis of candidates' issue stands (see "The Consultants Respond" box in chapter 3), one reason may have to do with the way in which campaigns often are framed for them:

DEMOCRATIC MEDIA CONSULTANT. We think about it as voters forming *impressions* about candidates, which is very different than absorbing *information* about candidates. Campaigns need to

continues...

be less about imparting information, and more about trying to shape voters' impressions. Academics and journalists sometimes criticize consultants for their messages as being repetitive and simple, and they're right—because we're trying to drive a message through a huge glut of information [about politics and many other things] that voters are exposed to. . . . If Coca-Cola tried to advertise all of the supposed benefits of Coca-Cola to people, I doubt it would have the brand image it has. The essence of their brand image for the last 20–25 years is that "Coke is fun to drink." They don't talk about the caffeine, they simply advertise it as fun.

Some of the most critical strategic (and tactical) choices that must be made during a campaign deal with the question of whether and how to go negative:

REPUBLICAN MEDIA CONSULTANT. Consider, for example, the decision about when to go negative. Does a candidate want to go negative? Should you go negative [at all]? Does the candidate have the stomach to go negative? From the Republican side, typically it comes down to, "Well, you're the consultant and you want to run this negative ad, but I have to live in this town when you're gone and this is all done. . . . I have to go back to my country club, and it's going to be very uncomfortable doing that after I've just attacked this guy in my community." We also battle with our candidates a lot of times about *how* to go negative. When you run a negative ad, you usually don't want them to deliver the negative message. But some candidates demand that, because they want to be the star of the show. . . . Somehow, you have to try and achieve two things at once: tear down your opponent and get the truth out, but also introduce your candidate to the voters. It can be a balancing act.

Notes

1. American Exceptionalism is the idea that the history and development of the United States renders comparison to other nations, including Western European nations, problematic. At its most optimistic (or jingoistic), the argument holds that the United States is immune to the social and political maladies that plague other parts of the world. From a strictly analytic perspective, it holds that for better or for worse, American beliefs and practices are measurably different from those belonging to citizens elsewhere. For a contemporary treatment of American Exceptionalism, see Lipset (1996).

2. Such variables might, for example, include inflation, crime rates, health care costs, gasoline prices, and a variety of other factors that influence voter sentiments toward the parties and candidates.

3. For instance, partisan voters may simply determine the candidates' party affiliations and vote accordingly, that is, by reasoning, "I'm a Democrat (Republican) and he's a Democrat (Republican). Chances are we have the same values and agree on most

issues. Why should I spend time studying each candidate's positions in detail? I'll simply vote for him."

4. See McGerr (2003); White and Shea (2004, 64–69).

5. See Cappella and Jamieson (1997); Fallows (1996).

6. See Semiatin (2004); Wattenberg (1998).

7. We refer here to the cultivation of support from local party leaders (known as bosses)—individuals who were highly influential during this period and whose support was key to delivering votes for chosen candidates on election day.

8. See White and Shea (2004, chapter 3); Wattenberg (1998). However, some political scientists (for example, Bartels 2000; Hetherington 2001; Green, Palmquist, and Schickler 2002; but see Fiorina 2002) believe that there has been a resurgence of partisanship among voters in recent years.

9. Although the popular impression of campaign consultants is that they are hired guns, not beholden to any particular cause, research has shown that most consultants work fairly closely with party operatives (Dulio 2004).

10. The term *October surprise* entered the political lexicon during the 1980 presidential contest between incumbent Jimmy Carter and challenger Ronald Reagan. Republicans feared that the administration might negotiate a last-minute release of hostages being held by radicals at the U.S. embassy in Teheran, Iran, and thereby give Carter's campaign a big boost. (It didn't happen. The hostages were released on the day Reagan was sworn in as president in January 1981.) Along the same lines, Democrats in 2004 worried that an eleventh-hour capture of terrorist leader Osama bin Laden would ensure the reelection of President Bush (it also didn't happen and Bush won anyway).

11. Also see Haynes and Rhine (1998); Damore (2002).

12. Also see Sigelman and Buell (2003); Burden (2005).

3 Voter Competence

Thomas E. Patterson

Following the U.S. invasion of Iraq in 2003, opinion polls revealed that nearly half of the American public incorrectly believed that the Iraqi regime had close ties to the terrorist network al Qaeda, while nearly one in four erroneously believed that Iraq was directly involved in the terrorist attacks on the World Trade Center and the Pentagon on September 11, 2001. One-fourth also wrongly claimed that America's military actions had the backing of most of the rest of the world.[1]

When it comes to elections, Americans are usually no better informed. For example, a study of the 2000 presidential election found that Democratic contender Al Gore's stand on prescription drug benefits for the elderly was the only issue position familiar to even as many as half of American adults (T. Patterson 2002, 126). Occasionally an issue will be of sufficient magnitude to imprint itself in people's minds. For example, more than 80 percent of Americans during the 1972 presidential campaign knew that Democratic nominee George McGovern favored a rapid withdrawal of U.S. troops from Vietnam. Ordinarily, though, voters do not possess large amounts of information about issues and candidates. Such findings have led some analysts to conclude that citizens, or at least large numbers of them, are unable or unwilling to cast a thoughtful vote. Is this the case? Do America's voters lack the competence required to make a reasoned choice?

The Information Standard and Its Limits

In the closing chapter of one of the first major studies of voting behavior in the United States, Berelson, Lazarsfeld, and McPhee (1954) maintained that voters generally failed to meet a high standard of citizenship and, specifically, that most of them lacked a substantial understanding of election-related issues. This argument was affirmed two decades later by Converse (1975, 79), who noted that "the most familiar fact to arise from sample surveys is that popular levels of information about public affairs are, from the point of view of an informed observer, astonishingly low." The same conclusion was borne out in Delli Carpini and Keeter's *What Americans Know About Politics and Why It Matters* (1996), which documented the many gaps in Americans' political knowledge, including their unfamiliarity with key issues. Scholars also have examined the effects of low information and concluded that it increases the likelihood that citizens will express opinions inconsistent with their personal interests (Althaus 2003). Other research has demonstrated that less-informed citizens are more likely to respond to new information that is either inaccurate or immaterial to the issue at hand (Kinder and Sanders 1996), and that the acquisition of substantial new information increases the likelihood that voters will make choices consistent with their policy attitudes (Fishkin 1991).

An argument can be made for using the possession of factual information as the standard for judging voter competence; certainly, the equating of *informed* with the possession of *information* has an obvious logic. The information standard has roots in early twentieth-century Progressivism (McGerr 2003), when reformers sought to wrest political control from the party bosses. It was a time when public education, mass communication, and scientific knowledge were expanding rapidly. The Progressives held that citizens were rational enough to make their own decisions, that they did not need the guiding hand of partisanship. The Progressives invented new institutions—the referendum, the initiative, recall elections, and primary elections—that were intended to empower the public. They envisioned a type of politics in which informed citizens would not only choose candidates on the basis of policy positions but also, through the initiative and referendum, make some policy decisions directly.

Although the Progressive model ever since has influenced how public schools, the news media, scholars, and civic groups like the League of Women Voters tend to idealize voting, the model is not beyond challenge. For one thing, there is nothing innately natural or superior about the model, even in its origins. The Progressives were reform-minded to be sure, but their ideas and innovations had a political purpose. Most were middle-class Republicans of Protestant faith from smaller cities and towns, and their embrace of the "thinking" citizen as opposed to an "emotional" one reflected their distrust of the new immigrants, predominantly Catholic, who supplied the votes that powered Democratic Party machines in many of the nation's large cities.

A larger problem with the Progressive model is that politics is not primarily a question of information. Politics is largely about the mobilization of bias, that is, the efforts of people to promote their beliefs and interests. A thoughtful vote is rooted in core values, not bits of information. Furthermore, information is more a consequence of political inquiry than a cause of it (Lasch 1995). Although information by itself can trigger thought about a particular issue or development, the likelihood that it will do so is small. Over the course of a political campaign, voters are bombarded with hundreds of messages, nearly all of which go unheeded. Only when an item catches a voter's attention—which normally occurs only when it touches on something he or she cares about—is that individual likely to seek more information about it. In the absence of such a commitment, little information acquisition occurs.

Information is a byproduct of inquiry in another way as well. Once someone makes a judgment about a political issue or leader, much of the information that contributed to that judgment is disgorged. In other words, although the judgment is retained, most of the raw material that went into it is not. Studies of "learning without involvement" indicate that the half-life of undigested information is measured in minutes, sometimes seconds (Krugman 1965). Most information literally goes in one ear and out the other. The half-life of information that gets a person's attention is measurably longer, but much of it is also soon lost to memory. As a consequence, the amount of information that a voter can retrieve when asked about issues and candidates is substantially less than that which was taken into account when the decision was made.

The Competency Question

Although it is possible to devise tests of voter competence, including the information standard, their utility is debatable. Modern democracies do not apply such tests as a condition of suffrage, and their use in the past was motivated primarily by a desire to discriminate against particular groups—southern blacks being the clearest example in the American case. In any event, it is presumptuous to claim that ordinary people are somehow incapable of figuring out which candidate or party might better represent them. These same people routinely carry out the demanding role of consumer, sometimes under challenging financial constraints. Of course, there are always some consumers who make lousy choices, as in the case of the alcoholic who puts drink ahead of family or the spendthrift whose wild buying leads to ruin. But the consuming public as a whole navigates the complex world of product advertising and purchasing quite well.

How can such people possibly be unfit for the less-imposing task of casting a vote for candidates for public office? As Popkin (1991) argued, the skills of everyday life are more than adequate to the challenge of casting a reasoned vote. Most citizens have a range of experiences that provide a basis on which to decide whether a particular candidate meets their political expectations; they ordinarily can determine who is on their side and who is not, and during campaigns they become increasingly aware of the candidates' policy positions.[2] Voters also have an ability to distinguish between what is more and less politically important. In 1992, for example, a sagging economy prompted voters to reject President George H. W. Bush's bid for a second term even though his opponent, Bill Clinton, was dogged throughout the campaign by allegations of personal misconduct. Of course, these skills are not distributed evenly across the electorate, just as consumption skills are distributed unevenly across the buying public. For the citizen with a marginal interest in politics or whose life is consumed by more pressing concerns, the vote might at times be cast foolishly. But there is reason to assume that the large majority of voters understand their interests well enough to make a reasoned choice, even though they may rely on party, group, polling, and media cues as well as other shortcuts to compensate for their inability to bring to mind more substantial information about candidates and issues.[3]

We should not assume, however, that voters are equipped to handle every possible situation that comes their way. In this context, the critical question is not whether voters are competent but whether election campaigns foster or frustrate their effort to cast a thoughtful vote. Campaigns can be run in ways that make it easier for voters to render a thoughtful judgment about the candidates, or they can be run in ways that make the task considerably more complicated. In this chapter, I argue that political campaigns in the United States are not especially "voter friendly." To the contrary, they have many features that can easily confound or frustrate voters.

Party Platforms

Electoral choice in America is simplified by the country's two-party system, which reduces the decision that must be made by voters to yes or no, that is, where a vote for one party is automatically a vote against the other. Voters in a multiparty system have a more difficult calculus. They must decide among several alternatives and might even have to decide whether to cast a "strategic" ballot (backing a second choice if their preferred party seems unlikely to get enough votes to qualify for a share of the legislative seats being contested).

Two-party systems also are relatively stable by comparison with multiparty systems, where it is not unusual for a new party to arise or an older party to wither, thus requiring voters to learn anew the alternatives. In a two-party system, the choices are ordinarily the same from one election to the next. And if the parties' platforms remain stable as well, voters begin each election with a fairly clear understanding of the differences between them. Moreover, because one of the parties will have been the party in control of government, voters can act retrospectively by supporting or opposing that party depending on their level of satisfaction with its performance (Fiorina 1981).

For a long period in American history, the U.S. party system did function in ways that eased the voter's choice. Elections were waged primarily on economic issues that consistently divided the two parties, with Republicans being unabashed proponents of free markets and Democrats seeking to protect the economically disadvantaged. Except in the South, where race was the decisive issue, this alignment closely matched the policy concerns of ordinary Americans, cementing their party loyalties. The Democratic Party was the choice of lower-income workers, while the GOP was the preferred party of business interests and the middle class. That era ended with the triumph of Franklin Roosevelt's New Deal, which, along with Lyndon Johnson's Great Society, created a safety net for the economically vulnerable and policy mechanisms for stabilizing the economy. An electoral majority that could routinely be rallied by economic appeals no longer existed.

As the economic issue weakened, a large set of less comprehensive issues emerged. Civil rights, street crime, school prayer, and welfare dependency were among the earliest of these issues, followed later by abortion, the environment, education, global trade, and others. All were important, but none had the scope of the economic issue. As a result, the issues of one election were often different from the issues that had dominated the previous election or that would come to the forefront in the next one. Moreover, the new issues intersected the older economic issue in confounding ways. Opposition to antiwar demonstrations united working-class whites and blacks, but civil rights demonstrations divided them. No one supported crime, but conservative Republicans and blue-collar Democrats more frequently considered jail the answer than did moderate Republicans and middle-class Democrats. Few said godlessness was good for society, but Protestant fundamentalists of both parties were opposed to the ban on prayer in the public schools and to abortion rights. Political, economic, and reproductive rights for women created divisions even among women. And so it went, issue after issue (see Burnham 1970).

These changes complicated the choice facing voters because the past was now less of a guide to the present and the future. As a result, voters needed more information on the issues of the moment and had to weigh more factors in deciding which party to support; there also was a greater likelihood that voters would both like and dislike some of what each party was proposing. The choice offered by America's two major parties had become harder to evaluate.

It was a period of drift and shifting alliances, which some analysts took as a sign that voters were floundering. For the most part, however, voters were behaving in astute ways. An increasing number of working-class whites stopped participating in elections; their traditional party was now less attractive, but the opposing party was still unacceptable. Other voters responded to overriding issues, rejecting their traditional party if its position was opposite their own. Examples are the southern whites who abandoned the Democratic Party because of its stance on civil rights, and black Americans who embraced it for the same reason. Some voters stayed with their party, either because they supported its initiatives or were at a loss as to what the other side truly represented. (The percentage of Americans unable to express a clear image of either party increased threefold in the period between the 1950s and the 1970s; see Wattenberg 1998.) And then there were the many voters—nearly double the proportion as compared with the 1950s and early 1960s—who called themselves "independents" and split their ballots, believing that neither party was the full answer to their needs.

A prominent feature of this new electoral system was single-issue interest groups. More numerous and more powerful than in the past, they flourished because of the emergence of new controversies and because computer-based mass mailings had made it easier for them to attract members and raise money. These groups sank their teeth into candidates for office, who could not do without their money and who dared not alienate their hard-core members. Group demands gradually lured ambitious politicians toward the extremes of their respective parties. The conservative pull of the Christian right on Republican candidates is but one of many examples. The gap in the policy positions of Democratic and Republican leaders widened accordingly. Most citizens, however, remained closer to the political center, taking relatively moderate positions on issues of public policy.[4]

Party systems are not supposed to operate in this way. Theory holds that in a two-party system, when the public is concentrated in the center, the parties will converge on the middle as a vote-maximizing strategy (Downs 1957). What the theory fails to anticipate, however, is the capacity of interest groups in a money-driven electoral process to pull candidates away from the center and thus away from where most voters are, thereby making it harder for them to determine which party better represents their interests.

Today's campaigns are also characterized by promises—seemingly endless promises. Unlike in the age of the economic issue, today's candidates find it harder to run on broad statements of principle; instead, they build their followings by catering to interest groups. After his successful 1976 presidential campaign, Jimmy Carter asked his staff to compile a record of his policy promises; they assembled a list that contained more than 150 proposed initiatives (T. Patterson 1993, 13). Of course, by virtue of their alliances and limits on the federal treasury, candidates are not free to make any promise they might wish. Nevertheless, policy promises are the stepping stones to victory, especially at the presidential level. One consequence is a public that is wary of taking candidates at their word. Most Americans believe that politicians will say almost anything to get themselves elected, which raises a question in some voters' minds about the weight to place on candidates' policy stands (T. Patterson 2002, 52–55).

A century ago, British historian and statesman James Bryce worried that the growing complexity of American society threatened the parties' ability to forge and mobilize cohesive majorities. Social complexity is now orders of magnitude greater than it was then, and it clearly has overtaken the parties. The consequences include an electorate that must work harder than ever to determine which party is the better choice.

Negative Campaigns

In the 1950s and 1960s, control of election campaigns shifted rapidly from the political parties to individual candidates, largely as a consequence of television and refinements in techniques of mass persuasion. While Americans were initially thrilled by the chance for a close-up look at the candidates and their campaigns, they no longer feel so positive about the process. The new style has brought out aspects of politics that were once largely out of sight. Ambition, manipulation, and deception have become as prominent as issues of policy and leadership, and U.S. campaigns have become decidedly negative in character.

No exact date marks the point at which campaigns turned sour, but plenty of examples can be cited to illustrate the tendency—perhaps none more clearly than the 1988 presidential campaign of George H. W. Bush. When *Time* magazine did a cover story that year on "The Year of the Handlers," heralding consultants who bring "hot-button" issues like abortion and flag burning into play, the Bush campaign was the prototype. Its symbol became Willie Horton, a felon who not by chance was also an African American male. A television ad by a conservative political action group, Americans for Bush, explained that Horton had brutally raped a white woman while on weekend furlough from a Massachusetts prison during the tenure of Governor Michael Dukakis, who was Bush's opponent in the presidential race (see Diamond and Bates 1992). The Bush campaign then produced its own attack ad based on the Massachusetts furlough program in an effort to portray Dukakis as too soft on crime and (some alleged) too liberal on race.

Negative advertising has become a defining feature of U.S. campaigns, as candidates have discovered that it is easier in many situations to attract swing voters by tearing down one's opponent than by talking about one's own platform. Hart (2000; also see West 2001), for example, reported that "reactive ads," which are attacks on an opponent or defenses against such attacks, increased fourfold in presidential elections between 1960 and 1996. Although negative campaigns are as old as the Jefferson-Adams race of 1800, the contemporary version has no historical equal. "You can't compare a nasty quote about Thomas Jefferson," says one-time presidential speechwriter Richard Goodwin (quoted in Shaw 1996), "with the intensity and penetration [of today's attacks]."

Journalists have contributed to the negative tone of campaign politics. The Vietnam War and the Watergate scandal poisoned the relationship between journalists and politicians during the late 1960s and early 1970s, and reporters have been zeroing in on political candidates ever since. Although the press is often accused of having a liberal bias, its real bias is a preference for controversy. Whereas news coverage of presidential candidates during the 1960s was largely positive, by the 1980s such coverage had reached a point where more than half of it was negative—and it has basically remained at that level ever since (Farnsworth and Lichter 2005; T. Patterson 1993).

According to the norms of American journalism, reporters are not supposed to take sides on policy issues and, by and large, they do stay out of policy debates. However, there is no norm that limits what journalists can say about a candidate's personality or skills. Rarely do journalists ignore a chance to exploit what they see as a personal failing. On the network evening newscasts during the 2000 general election, for example, a good deal of George W. Bush's coverage implied that he was not particularly intelligent; nine such claims were made in the news for every assertion to the contrary. Al Gore fared no better; his coverage was dotted with suggestions that he was not very truthful. Such claims outpaced rebuttals by a margin of seventeen to one (Lichter 2001).

Journalists usually seek dramatic stories. As a result, they are drawn to political conflict (Fallows 1996), which tends to further highlight the negative aspects of campaign politics. News coverage of the 1996 Republican nominating race illustrates the point. Although nearly two-thirds (66 percent) of assertions made in the candidates' speeches were positive statements about what they hoped to accomplish if elected, these statements only infrequently made it into the news. Instead, journalists generally reported the parts of candidates' speeches where they attacked one another, embedding these snippets in news commentary suggesting that the Republican contenders had virtually nothing constructive to say (*Media Monitor* 1996).

Conflict can draw people to politics: a good fight attracts a crowd. But a sharp and meaningful encounter is different from the steady negativity that pervades contemporary campaigns. Although a negative campaign can boost voter interest in a particular contest, relentlessly negative politics—one campaign after another, election year after election year—wears down some citizens to the point where they begin to lose interest in the electoral process as a whole.[5] The negative tone of campaigns also diminishes the public's opinion of those who run for office. A study of the 1960–1992 presidential elections found that negative impressions of the candidates rose step by step with the increase in negative advertising and negative news coverage (T. Patterson 1993). Gallup polls provide further evidence of this pattern. Between 1936 and 1968, Barry Goldwater was the only major-party presidential nominee who had an overall unfavorable public image at the end of the campaign. Since 1968 more than one-third of the presidential nominees have been perceived unfavorably or nearly so. When citizens believe that candidates are not fit for the office they seek, their interest in election politics is diminished.[6]

News Coverage

The news media are voters' window on the campaign. The media are not their sole source of information, of course, but it is no exaggeration to say that what citizens see through that window will affect much of what they think about candidates and issues. Ideally, the media would clarify the choice facing voters by bringing to light critical differences between the candidates. In practice, however, the news media are more likely to cloud and submerge the issues than to illuminate them.

For most journalists, an election campaign is less a choice over leadership and policy than it is a competitive struggle between power-driven leaders. As Paul Weaver (1973, 69) observed some years ago, journalists tend to see policy issues as "noteworthy only insofar as they affect, or are used by, players in pursuit of the game's rewards." As a result, election coverage is mostly a story of strategy, tactics, and maneuvering. The central theme is the horse race—who is ahead and who is behind, and the strategies and tactics that put them there. Issues are part of the coverage, to be sure, but they matter a great deal less than the question of who's winning and why.[7] Further, when issues *are* covered, they frequently involve controversies rather than substantive policies. During a long period of the 2004 presidential campaign, for example, the news media focused on personal events that took place three decades earlier—whether George W. Bush had fulfilled his duties as a member of the National Guard, and whether John Kerry's service in Vietnam was as honorable as he and his supporters claimed. These issues were not irrelevant, but they were hardly those that were uppermost in people's minds. Voters were concerned primarily with economic conditions and the conflict in Iraq. Nevertheless, day after day, journalists pursued Bush's and Kerry's military records, stopping only after CBS News embarrassed itself by getting duped into reporting a fraudulent document that claimed Bush had deliberately disobeyed a military order while in the National Guard (see chapter 7).

Such controversies have been a large part of election coverage since the 1970s. A short list would include the media frenzies that erupted around Jimmy Carter's statement in 1976 to *Playboy* magazine that he had experienced "lust in his heart," Ronald Reagan's fanciful claims in 1980 (for instance, his assertion that trees and plants caused 80 percent of the country's air pollution), vice presidential nominee Geraldine Ferraro's tax returns in 1984, Gary Hart's affair with Donna Rice in 1988, Bill Clinton's affair with Gennifer Flowers in 1992, Al Gore's fundraising appearance at a Buddhist temple in 1996, George W. Bush's drunken-driving record in 2000, and John Kerry's war record in 2004. Research has shown that such issues receive nearly as much coverage as substantive policy issues and in some cases even more. For example, the revelation in 2000 that Bush had been arrested a quarter-century earlier for drunken driving got more coverage on the evening newscasts during the final days of the campaign than did all of Bush's and Gore's foreign policy statements during the entire general election (T. Patterson 2002, 57).

Gaffes and indiscretions can give reporters an opportunity to unmask a candidate by exploiting the disparity between the impression the candidate has been trying to create and what the incident seems to suggest. More often than not, however, they divert attention from larger issues and, in some cases, merely feed the media's appetite for titillating stories. They fit Republican media guru Roger Ailes's "orchestra-pit theory" of election news: "If you have two guys on a stage and one guy says, 'I have a solution to the Middle East problem,' and the other guy falls in the orchestra pit, who do you think is going to be on the evening news?" (Fouhy 1995, 1). Ailes's good story–versus–important issue theory was confirmed in 1996 when GOP presidential nominee Bob Dole fell off a speaking platform in Chico, California, and landed, sure enough, at the top of the evening's news programs.

At the end of nearly every recent campaign, the candidates have complained that their policy appeals were largely ignored by the news media. Although journalists can rightly argue that candidates often duck tough issues, the evidence suggests that it is journalists more than candidates who set the news agenda. In the 1960s, presidential candidates and the reporters covering them had almost equal speaking time on the network evening news shows. That ratio began to change in the 1970s and, today, journalists dominate. Research shows that in recent campaigns, journalists covering the candidates have talked six minutes on the evening newscasts for each minute the candidates spoke (Lichter 2001, 16).

Given the limited capacity that most voters have for acquiring and storing information about candidates and issues, the news media's failure to highlight the more significant aspects of an election might not be a huge problem. However, the news, as voters' window on the campaign, does affect people's beliefs about whether an election deserves their attention. Polls indicate, for example, that most Americans feel that political campaigns today seem more like theater or entertainment than like something to be taken seriously (T. Patterson 2002, 56).

The Election Framework

Elections take place within a framework of structures and laws that affect how campaigns are conducted and that shape the electoral environment to which voters respond. The framework for elections in the United States is one of the most elaborate in the world, reflecting the nation's systems of federalism and divided power. Most European democracies are unitary governments with parliamentary systems. In some European countries, voters are called to the polls only every few years to select their national legislators. America's voters bear a heavier burden. They choose separately among candidates for state *and* local office and for legislative *and* executive office. Moreover, unlike European democracies that entrust party organizations with the task of selecting party nominees, the United States assigns this task to voters in primary elections.

Primary elections can present a tough challenge because they prevent voters from relying on party labels to make their choice: the candidates are all Democrats or all Republicans. Nominating races also sometimes attract large fields of contenders, all or most of whom (even in the case of presidential primaries) are relative unknowns. Of the eight Republican contenders in 1996, for example, only Senate majority leader Bob Dole and television personality Pat Buchanan had national reputations of any magnitude. In 1988 each of the Democratic contenders had a low recognition level—so much so that the press dubbed them "the seven dwarfs." In 2004 all nine Democratic contenders were relative unknowns.

Multi-candidate races place imposing demands on voters. A poll of New Hampshire voters in 1976, for example, indicated that when the six Democratic candidates were evaluated in pairs, Jimmy Carter fared poorly; that is, one-on-one, voters seemed to prefer his rivals (T. Patterson 2002, 151). Yet Carter ended up winning the New Hampshire primary because voters divided their support among his more liberal opponents, thereby enabling the centrist former governor of Georgia to finish in first place with 28 percent of the total. His victory was trumpeted by the news media, providing him a publicity bonanza that gave him the momentum to win additional primaries, which further fueled the media flurry. Later, liberal Democrats rallied around a late entrant to the race, California's Governor Jerry Brown, who beat Carter in each of their four head-to-head primaries. By then, however, Carter had a big enough delegate lead to assure his nomination at the Democratic convention (T. Patterson 1980, 10–13).

Primary elections turn U.S. campaigns into marathon events that last for months. In Europe, because party organizations choose nominees, the active campaign lasts for only a month or two. Not so in the United States. In fact, in the case of presidential elections, the active campaign now begins more than a year before election day. At first glance, a long campaign would seem to offer exactly what citizens need to cast a thoughtful vote, specifically, a lengthy period in which to assess the candidates. Yet time by itself does not create an informed electorate. Too much time can numb voters, which is precisely what often happens. On occasion, as in 2004 (T. Patterson 2005), a presidential campaign will capture and hold the public's attention almost from beginning to end. Typically, however, the race chugs along month after month toward the finish line, dulling the voters' interest and taxing their attention.

Because the campaign lasts so long, it inevitably affects voters' perceptions of what is at stake. In Europe's relatively short election cycles, voters tend from beginning to end to focus on whether the majority party has governed well or poorly. In America's longer campaigns, people's thoughts about the performance of the governing party may dominate at the beginning but, by the end, are sometimes eclipsed by their beliefs about whether the candidates have campaigned well or poorly (T. Patterson 1980, 102). And over the course of the long campaign, even though considerable learning takes place, voters are sure to forget some of what they had learned earlier. In 2000, for example, fewer Americans were able to identify George W. Bush's position on gun control in October than could do so in February (T. Patterson 2002, 113).[8]

Of course, an exciting presidential primary race can draw people to the campaign and heighten their awareness of the contending candidates and what they stand for. However, these primaries provide the electorate with an unequal experience because of how they unfold. As a practical matter, the nominating races are almost always effectively over several months before the last contests in early June. Front-loading of the nominating schedule (placement of a large number of state primaries near the front end of the process) has led presidential hopefuls to raise and spend tens of millions of dollars on these early races in an effort to secure the nomination with a decisive victory on Super Tuesday (the day in early March when, traditionally, a large number of states hold their contests simultaneously). Such a victory is ordinarily sufficient to make the winner's nomination a virtual certainty, which leads other contenders to quit the race or at least to scale back their efforts dramatically. As a result, millions of citizens—namely, those living in states that have yet to hold their primaries—are deprived of the opportunity to get a close look at the candidates. It is not simply that residents of these states vote at a lower rate; they also are less informed about the candidates and issues (T. Patterson 2002, 112).

In the presidential general election, Americans' opportunity to be part of the action is determined largely by the electoral college. The popular-vote winner in each state gets all of that state's electoral votes (save for Maine and Nebraska, which allocate their electoral votes by congressional district). Not surprisingly, candidates concentrate their efforts on the so-called battleground states, where polls show the contest to be relatively close. During the 2000 general election campaign, for example, there were no ad buys and no candidate visits in Kansas, which is a lopsidedly Republican state. In neighboring Missouri, which was a battleground state, there were eighteen candidate visits and millions of dollars spent on televised political advertising. According to Kathleen Hall

Jamieson (quoted in Marks 2000), "The process effectively takes half the country and says, 'you're just spectators.' " Residents of non–battleground states typically exhibit a lower turnout rate than residents of the battleground states and are also less likely to discuss the campaign and to pay attention to it (T. Patterson 2002, 111). Knowing their vote is meaningless in the sense that the electoral vote outcome in their state is a foregone conclusion, they simply do not engage the campaign as fully as do battleground-state voters.

A lack of competition also distorts congressional races. Most U.S. House districts so lopsidedly favor one party over the other that the campaign in these districts is more of a ritual than a reality. The margin of victory in House races today is roughly two-to-one, and incumbents almost always win. More than 98 percent of House incumbents seeking another term were reelected in 2002 and 2004. Of the 435 House districts nationwide, in fewer than three dozen do both parties have a realistic chance of winning.

Incumbents now possess so many advantages over their opponents that the process nearly mocks the principle of fair elections. When national campaign finance laws were changed during the 1970s in reaction to the Watergate scandal, political action committees (PACs) suddenly sprouted—their number increasing from approximately 600 to 4,000 within a decade. This new source of money turned out to be a bonanza for incumbents because many PACs are reluctant to oppose politicians who are already in power. During the 2003–2004 campaign cycle, according to the Federal Election Commission, PACs contributed $246.8 million to House and Senate incumbents and a mere $22.3 million to their challengers. Congressional incumbents also operate what amounts to year-round reelection campaigns at taxpayer expense. When members of Congress in the 1960s voted to greatly enlarge their personal staffs, they argued that additional employees were needed to offset the executive branch's domination of policy information. However, most of these staff members concentrate primarily on public relations, constituency service, and other activities that serve to keep their bosses in office (Cain, Ferejohn, and Fiorina 1987).

Finally, when the state legislatures draw up the boundaries of House districts after each ten-year census, they usually shape them in ways that protect incumbents of both parties. For example, the boundaries of California's fifty-three U.S. House districts were drawn in such a way that all of them gave one party or the other a decided advantage.[9] In many such districts, there is no campaign to speak of and the news media provide little or no coverage. Because no competition exists, there simply is no incentive for the candidates to mount a full-scale campaign or for news organizations to cover the race. For their part, voters in these districts have little reason to make an effort to understand what the opposing candidates represent.

Electoral competition is the lifeblood of democracy, and the American electorate is in a sense being bled to death. Voters have little reason to invest time and energy in races where the ballots they cast (if they bother to cast them at all) are a rubber stamp of decisions made earlier by state legislators. The U.S. House of Representatives has the lowest membership turnover of any national legislative body in a Western democracy. That might not be a cause for concern if Americans were generally pleased with the performance of Congress, but ample evidence suggests they are not (Hibbing and Theiss-Morse 1995; Kimball and Patterson 1997).

A Concluding Observation

Voters, on balance, have the competence required to make electoral democracy work effectively. Whether they are able to do so in every situation is a different question. The political scientist V. O. Key (1966, 2) once compared the "voice of the people" to an echo, and pointed out that "[t]he output of an echo chamber bears an inevitable and invariable relationship to the input." Elections in the United States are waged within a framework and in a manner that can baffle even well-intended citizens. Some analysts might conclude that the voters' shortcoming is therefore somehow their own failing and an indication of incompetence or irresponsibility. A more reasonable assessment would shift the failing to the political elites that operate American campaigns. As E. E. Schattschneider (1960) argued, the challenge of democracy is not to make citizens conform to its demands, but rather to shape it so that it is fit for them.

The developments that have weakened Americans' ability to inform themselves about candidates for office are deeply rooted and unlikely to be reversed easily or soon. The cacophonous frenzy of the modern professionally run and heavily mediated campaign challenges the attentiveness and clear thinking of even the conscientious citizen. Elections in the United States are marathon spectacles filled with images and rituals, many of them empty of any substance or meaning. As a result, campaigns have become less a test of voters' foresight than of their forbearance.

THE CONSULTANTS RESPOND ABOUT

VOTER COMPETENCE

Our consultants had varying opinions regarding voter competence. Most agreed that people are generally ill informed but potentially educable (at least up to a point) via information provided by the campaigns, while a few insisted that the problem is mainly a matter of the understandably low priority given to politics by the average citizen.

Emphasizing the electorate's basic shortcomings:

REPUBLICAN GENERAL CONSULTANT. No, voters are not very competent. The reason I feel this way is based on my belief that voters are more swayed, not by policies or programs but by personalities.

Of course, sometimes campaigns can help:

REPUBLICAN POLLSTER. It's true, we frequently assume that voters don't know enough—that they aren't competent. And that's just the way it is, certainly at the beginning. Sometimes it takes the course of the campaign for voters to learn and [for us] to make the public informed.

But not always:

DEMOCRATIC MEDIA CONSULTANT. One thing I like about focus groups is that you get a very stark reminder of how little the voters you are trying to communicate with know about your candidates, and about the general terrain of the election. Some of the arguments that campaigns become absorbed in haven't even reached the people sitting in the room. Because you talk about these issues every day on four or five conference calls, you think that they're out there but they're not. Focus groups also give you a sense of the language voters use to describe the problems and challenges in their lives, and the thin impressions they do have about the candidates. You rarely hear a voter say in a focus group, "I *know* such and such a candidate is for this," but you often hear them say, "I think he's this or that kind of person."

In a focus group I attended a while back, one voter said, "Look, I just think the governor should be a CEO and [candidate] seems like a better CEO." The moderator probed to try and figure out what information went into that, but the voter couldn't pinpoint it. He just said, "I get a better impression of him as a CEO than I do of his opponent. He seems like he can do the job and [the other candidate] can't." This was about all the information that was going to go into the person's decision. He recorded himself as a solid supporter of [candidate] but didn't know anything about where he stood. His im-

continues...

pression of [candidate] was very thin, but his preference for him was very strong.

REPUBLICAN GENERAL CONSULTANT. Several years ago, we were looking at some survey results and I saw a group of men who had already told us that they were pro-choice on abortion—and yet in the models we gave them to select attributes of the candidates they preferred, they were choosing the pro-life candidate. I said this can't be right, there has to be a flaw here. So they called them all back and what happened was that there were all these Republican men who said they chose the pro-life candidate because it's probably going to be a Republican who will be better on tax issues. They were using that information [based on party stereotypes] to come up with an entirely different conclusion than what we expected.

DEMOCRATIC POLLSTER. We did a focus group in one congressional race where there was a woman who mentioned that the Democratic candidate was pro-choice. It's a common perception among voters that Democrats are pro-choice and Republicans are pro-life—except that in one of the television ads we showed, this particular Democrat stated clearly that he was pro-life. The woman just sat there shaking her head. She wouldn't let go of the [stereotype] even though we told her directly that it wasn't true here.

In contrast, representing a somewhat more charitable view:

DEMOCRATIC MEDIA CONSULTANT. Consultants are often accused of looking at voters as incompetent or stupid or not [able to understand] complicated messages. Our firm tends to look at them as *busy*. They are extraordinarily busy people, and politics is only one thing that is competing for their attention and for their time. We do what we do with a healthy respect for the demands on voters' time and attention during campaigns.

DEMOCRATIC POLLSTER. There are varying degrees of incompetence. Voters are not always willing to change their minds, partly because they don't trust politicians or the media—the places where they're getting their information sources from. We look for evidence of voter competence on polling questionnaires, and sometimes the comments just have nothing to do with the questions; it makes you wonder, what was this person asked? I listen to the calls whenever this sort of thing happens. The interviewer thoroughly asks the question and it seems like the voter understands, but there are other things going on in that person's mind that determines how they interpret the information you're giving them and how they spit it back to you.

You have to engage voters before you can persuade them. We're just now getting to the point where we are starting to see some creative advertising on the political side that is able to get people engaged in the process. . . . In fact, sometimes consultants are the ones who are incompetent. Just because a consultant thinks an ad is good, that doesn't mean a voter does. About a month or so after the last election, I showed my wife three ads that I thought worked pretty well—but the one I liked best, she hated it because to her it was just another typical political ad like you see in every campaign.

REPUBLICAN GENERAL CONSULTANT. We tend to look at the electorate as a whole, rather than every voter individually. Individual voters look at a lot of different things to make their decision. . . . In the end, elections are less about opinions than they are about choices.

DEMOCRATIC POLLSTER. In 2004, voters were anxious. In focus groups, we saw that some of them may have disagreed with the president on policy points but they knew where he stood. This provided a comfort level. In other words, voters knew who President Bush was even if they didn't agree with him 100 percent of the time. On the other side, Senator Kerry wasn't comfortable enough to tell the voters who he really was and what he was about.

DEMOCRATIC POLLSTER. The Democrats mistakenly try to explain policy nuances, but voters lose the big picture.

A lot of times we fall into the trap of saying, "Well, if we could just make everyone more competent they'll agree with our way of thinking." We need to let go of that and realize that in reality, voters *are* competent. Candidates need to accept that . . . they need to find where they agree with people at the outset, or they won't be able to talk to them at all in the limited amount of time available.

And finally, going back to the importance of candidate impressions:

INDEPENDENT POLITICAL ANALYST: A good sense of who's on their side is much more important than anything having to do with the specific issues in defining a campaign. People say that a race was decided by abortion or by [where to locate] the new airport. More likely than not, though, it's defined by voters going to the polls and making their decision on much more of a gut level than actually putting the candidates' issue papers next to each other. . . . It's interesting to watch the Democrats and Republicans in action, especially on the congressional level. The Democrats come out of the box talking about issues, while the Republicans define themselves based on character early on. This undercuts the Democrats' efforts and, as a result, Republicans win more elections.

DEMOCRATIC MEDIA CONSULTANT. There are two types of [candidate] competence that voters care about. One is rational competence, which is the ability to sort out issues and take positions. Second has to do with emotional competence. Really good ads use enough rational competence to be credible, but they also try to play into voters' beliefs about emotional competence or character—telling them, "This is a bad guy," or "I'm a good guy," or "I'm just like you, and the other guy isn't like you." At the end of the day, those are the frames that voters use to condense their choices, and the frames that consultants use to present them.

Notes

1. These figures are based on nationwide polls conducted from June through September 2003 by the Program on International Policy Attitudes (PIPA) at the University of Maryland and Knowledge Networks, a private firm that conducts surveys via the Internet. See PIPA/Knowledge Networks Poll, "Misperceptions, the Media and the Iraq War," www.pipa.org/OnlineReports/Iraq/IraqMedia_Oct03/IraqMedia_Oct03_rpt.pdf.

2. See chapter 1 in this volume for a discussion of campaign learning.

3. See Lupia and McCubbins (1998); Sniderman, Brody, and Tetlock (1991).

4. See Fiorina (2005); but also Abramowitz and Saunders (2005).

5. See Cappella and Jamieson (1997); T. Patterson (2002).

6. For a different perspective, see chapters 1 and 5 in this volume. At least some evidence suggests that negative ads associated with the campaign itself (as opposed to news coverage by the media) may stimulate both voter turnout and the learning of candidates' issue stands by voters (on the latter, see Craig, Kane, and Gainous 2005).

7. See Fallows (1996); Farnsworth and Lichter (2005); T. Patterson (1993).

8. But see note 6, as well as a recent special issue of the journal *Political Communication* (October–December 2005) that deals in depth with the topic of campaign learning.

9. One recent response to this situation has been an effort, in California and elsewhere, to use initiative elections (where voters can directly adopt either new legislation or amendments to their state constitution) to take redistricting authority away from the legislature and give it to a nonpartisan or bipartisan commission that would presumably be motivated by something other than a desire for electoral self-preservation (see www.iandrinstitute.org).

4 Money and Elections

John C. Green

Almost everyone believes that money matters in winning elections. After all, money pays for the many ways that citizens are contacted and persuaded to vote for a candidate—including paying salaries of the political professionals who increasingly direct such efforts. So firm is this conviction that the impact of money is regularly described, with only a trace of cynicism, as "buying" votes on election day. Although the direct purchase of votes is strictly illegal, highly inefficient (that is, not affordable in terms of the dollar amounts that would be needed to ensure victory), and rarely pursued in contemporary campaigns, use of such shorthand terminology reveals much about the public's understanding of money and elections.[1]

Rhetoric aside, this understanding can be summarized in terms of three popular claims or assumptions: First, that money matters in campaigns the same way it does in the marketplace, namely, the more candidates spend, the more votes they receive. Second, building on the market analogy, that the candidate who spends the most in a campaign is most likely to win the election. And third, that the level of spending is equally important for gaining and then subsequently maintaining control of elective public office.[2]

Since the late 1970s political scientists have systematically investigated these claims using statistical analysis, drawing three roughly parallel conclusions about the role of money in elections:

- Money is a *dynamic factor* in campaigns, with the capacity to change the behavior of voters. All else being equal, money has a market-like impact on the number of votes candidates receive.
- The impact of money *varies with the context* of the campaign, because all else is rarely equal and other factors influence voting besides money. Money matters more for some kinds of candidates than for others, and its impact varies with electoral circumstances.
- Money is most valuable in *gaining* control of elected office and less valuable (but still important) in *maintaining* such control.

In this chapter I review the academic literature on money and elections, summarizing its findings in a mostly nontechnical fashion. I begin with an illustration of the relationship that appears to exist between campaign spending and winning elections, and conclude with a list of research questions that have yet to be answered.

Money and Winning Elections: An Illustration

Tables 4.1 and 4.2 provide a simple picture of the relationship between spending and winning elections, adapted from the work of Gary Jacobson (2001, 44–45). The cases cover seven congressional elections between 1986 and 1998. Table 4.1 cross-tabulates the levels of spending for Democratic and Republican U.S. House candidates running in open seats, that is, in contests in which no incumbent member of Congress sought reelection. The left-most column categorizes Democratic candidates by the level of spending in their campaigns in 1998 constant dollars. The same breakdown occurs across the top of the table for the Republican candidates. Each entry represents the percentage of the time that the Democratic candidate won (the percentage of Republican victories can be calculated by subtracting the entries from 100 percent).

The second column from the left in Table 4.1 (in bold) summarizes the impact of Democratic candidate spending overall. The average percentage of Democratic wins rises from just 14 percent (among candidates who spent less than $200,000) to 60 percent (among those who spent more than $600,000).

Table 4.1 Congressional Campaign Spending and Open-Seat Victories, 1986–1998

Democratic Spending		Republican Spending			
		Less than $200,000	$200,000 to $400,000	$400,000 to $600,000	More than $600,000
	Average percent won	95%	56%	44%	30%
Less than $200,000	**14%**	67	33	0	0
$200,000 to $400,000	**40%**	100	67	22	0
$400,000 to $600,000	**55%**	95	53	40	28
More than $600,000	**60%**	100	64	69	45

Source: Adapted from Jacobson (2001, 45). Table entries are the percentage of Democratic wins in open-seat races.
Note: Spending values are in 1998 constant dollars.

A similar pattern appears for Republican candidate spending (top row, also in bold), with the percentage of Democratic wins falling from 95 percent (that is, only 5 percent of Republican candidates who spent less than $200,000 won) to 30 percent (or 70 percent Republican victories among those who spent over $600,000). These patterns generally hold within the table as well. For example, when the Democrat spent over $600,000 and the Republican less than $200,000, the Democrat won 100 percent of the time. But when both candidates spent more than $600,000, the results were nearly even (the Democrat won 45 percent of the time).

The results in Table 4.1 tend to confirm the second popular assumption noted earlier, about the impact of money on elections: the more candidates spend, the more likely they are to win. These data also imply, but do not confirm, the first assumption (that more money produces more votes) while providing partial support for the third assumption (that spending helps candidates gain control of public office). Because incumbents are not included, however, the patterns are not relevant to the question of whether money is critical for *maintaining office* once a politician has been elected. In fact, open-seat House races are unusual events, rarely accounting for as much as one-sixth of congressional races, and typically less than that.

What about the more common type of election, in which an incumbent member of Congress faces a challenger? Table 4.2 presents this situation in a fashion analogous to Table 4.1, with two differences: the spending categories have a wider range (the top category for spending is over $800,000), and each entry is the percentage of victories by challengers regardless of their party affiliation. The top row in the table (in bold) follows a familiar pattern, as the percentage of challenger victories increases from 0 percent among those who spent less than $200,000 (again calculated in 1998 constant dollars) to 37 percent among challengers spending more than $800,000. Thus, the more the challenger spends against an incumbent, the more likely that challenger is to win the election. Even under the best circumstances, high-spending challengers do not win as often as their counterparts in open-seat races (as a glance back at Table 4.1 reveals). Nevertheless, the results here provide further support for popular assumptions about the importance of money in electoral politics.

However, a very different pattern emerges for incumbents in Table 4.2. As the second column from the left (in bold) shows, the proportion of challenger wins actually increases from 0 percent in races where incumbents spent less than $200,000 to 14 percent when the incumbent spent over $800,000. Put an-

Table 4.2 Congressional Campaign Spending and Challenger Victories, 1986–1998

Incumbent Spending		Challenger Spending				
		Less than $200,000	$200,000 to $400,000	$400,000 to $600,000	$600,000 to $800,000	More than $800,000
	Average percent won	0%	6%	13%	22%	37%
Less than $200,000	0%	0	0	0	0	0
$200,000 to $400,000	0%	0	3	0	0	0
$400,000 to $600,000	2%	0	4	12	40	50
$600,000 to $800,000	6%	0	7	13	36	25
More than $800,000	14%	0	9	15	17	39

Source: Adapted from Jacobson (2001, 44). Table entries are the percentage of wins by challengers running against incumbents of either party.
Note: Spending values are in 1998 constant dollars.

other way, none of the incumbent candidates lost reelection when their spending was at the *lowest* level—but roughly one-sixth lost when they spent at the *highest* level! Unlike open-seat and challenging candidates, then, it appears that the more incumbents spend, the less likely they are to win. This pattern runs counter to all three of the popular claims about the impact of money on elections.

This contrary evidence is especially interesting because incumbent candidates generally play a dominant role in congressional elections. After all, they already hold office, enjoy numerous advantages, and typically raise the lion's share of money spent in House races. For instance, in the 2004 congressional elections, major-party incumbents spent more than $311 million, compared to approximately $69 million by challengers and $51 million by candidates in open seats (Currinder 2005, 125).

The reader will want to keep these patterns in mind as I review the literature on campaign spending in the sections that follow. Tables 4.1 and 4.2 present a very simple (one might say too simple) picture of a complicated subject. The fact is that many factors other than money influence victory or defeat at the polls, and political scientists need to take into account these other factors when they systematically assess the impact of money on winning elections.

Assessing the Impact of Campaign Spending

Most of the academic literature on money and elections concerns campaigns for the U.S. House of Representatives. Research on this topic moved into high gear once reliable information on campaign spending became available in federal elections; in this regard, a signal event was passage of the Federal Election Campaign Act in 1971 and its amendments in 1974 (Corrado et al. 1997). Apart from the simple availability of data, however, the focus on House races reflects scholars' long-standing interest in the national legislature, where the "electoral connection" between voters and government leaders (Mayhew 1974a) is an important regularity.

Unfortunately, the literature's heavy emphasis on recent congressional elections may reduce its relevance to understanding the impact of campaign spending in general. During this period, for example, incumbent members of the House won reelection at very high rates compared to other eras and other offices.[3] However, a focus on House races has certain virtues as well: they occur every two years, involve hundreds of candidates and campaigns, and cover a variety of political circumstances all across the country. So from a scientific point of view, U.S. House elections are a good subject for the systematic study of campaign spending.

As in virtually all American elections, victory goes to the congressional candidate who receives the most votes.[4] Accordingly, political scientists have typically designed their analyses to assess the impact of campaign spending on the proportion of votes received by each candidate in the race.[5] This approach allows us to address all three of the popular claims we are considering because (1) the person receiving the most ballots wins, and (2) winners can be either newly elected or reelected candidates. The ultimate target of interest in such analyses, votes received by the respective candidates, is most often measured as a percentage of the two-party (Republican plus Democratic only) ballots.[6] Although this percentage can be calculated in various ways, the measures used have had little effect on scholars' substantive findings.

Obviously the central explanatory factor in this research is campaign spending and it, too, has been measured in slightly different ways. The most common approach is to compare each candidate's spending in thousands of dollars, whether it involves Democrats versus Republicans in open-seat races (as in Table 4.1) or incumbents versus challengers otherwise (as in Table 4.2). In contrast to candidate's share of the vote, the use of different methods to calculate campaign spending sometimes *has* led researchers to reach modestly different conclusions; for example, measuring money in thousands of dollars typically shows incumbent spending to have no impact on the vote, while measuring it as a percentage of the total spending in the race shows a significant impact for incumbent spending.

A variety of other factors (or variables) also are taken into account in such analyses because they are thought to influence election outcomes directly, and scholars want to isolate their impact on voting from the effects of money. Typically these variables include the degree to which a district or state has voted Republican or Democratic in the past,[7] candidates' party affiliation, presence or absence of an incumbent in the race, and quality of the challenger (usually measured in terms of whether nonincumbents have prior experience running for office; see Jacobson 1989). The specifics vary widely from study to study, however.

A final issue faced by researchers is the choice of statistics for systematically sorting out the effects of campaign spending on the vote, taking into account the impact of other variables. The most common choice (involving a single linear equation) is to assume that the vote can be accurately predicted by simply adding up the unique contributions of the factors under consideration. Scholars generally prefer this approach because the results of statistical analyses are relatively easy to interpret; it does not, however, fully capture the complexity of the electoral process. As a result, some researchers prefer to use more complex statistical models that they believe do a better job of describing the various forces that determine which candidates win and which ones lose on election day (a point discussed in greater detail later).

For ease of presentation, I refer to the most commonly used (simple linear) approach as the "basic model," some of the best examples of which are found in the work of Gary Jacobson.[8] A few scholars have tested variations of the basic model for both House and Senate elections, while others have applied versions of it to contests below the federal level.[9] All of these investigations have arrived at roughly similar conclusions.

Nonincumbent Spending

Most tests of the basic model reach a conclusion consistent with the pattern depicted in Table 4.1: in open-seat races, both Democratic and Republican candidates' money tends to increase their own share of the vote, taking into account other explanatory factors.[10] This result is unstable from election to election, however, reflecting in part the relatively small number of races involved—as well as, perhaps, the very high levels of spending by both candidates that characterizes most open-seat races. When both candidates are extremely well funded, money may have less of an impact than other factors, such as the quality of the candidates' messages (a point I will return to momentarily).

Studies that use the basic model also confirm the finding evident in Table 4.2 that challengers' spending has a strong, positive, and significant impact on their share of the vote, taking into account incumbent spending and various other factors. Further, the impact of challenger spending appears at first glance to be much larger than that of incumbent spending. Such results suggest that a challenger's spending is often critical in determining who wins the election or, put another way, that it helps to determine how many votes the incumbent fails to receive on election day.

This point is worth elaborating. Research based on the basic model sometimes concludes that challengers tend to spend money more efficiently than do incumbents. That is, the additional return for each dollar spent is greater for the former than the latter; in other words, challengers on average get more bang for the buck. This is not really surprising, since challengers have more to gain from campaign spending: they are typically not well known to voters, and every dollar spent during the campaign can help to overcome this initial weakness. Thus, when a high-quality challenger succeeds at amassing a large enough war chest, he or she can sometimes make the race very close—and once that happens, either candidate has a legitimate chance to win. Most challengers are not high-quality (politically experienced) candidates, however, and are unable to raise enough money to make the election close even though their spending may be more efficient than that of the incumbent.

It would seem that open-seat candidates and challengers have something in common, specifically, that spending can help to overcome some of their electoral disadvantages—most notably, for open-seat candidates, the high level of spending by their opponents and, for challengers, the power of incumbency. In fact, spending appears to be helpful (though not always decisive) in overcoming many kinds of political disadvantage, such as a district predisposed toward the other party or unfavorable national trends that exist in a particular election year.[11]

Overall, the findings presented in these studies support the popular claim that money attracts votes for candidates. Yet evidence from the basic model also refines and extends such claims. Not only does the effect of money vary to some degree by candidate status, but it also varies with election circumstances. There are, for example, strong *threshold effects* for nonincumbents, with candidates needing to spend beyond a certain minimum to have any realistic chance of winning. Many challengers (but few open-seat candidates) fail to exceed the threshold and thus are not competitive. Once past the threshold, nonincumbents spend relatively efficiently, though eventually even they experience diminishing returns: as their standing with the public improves, the net effect of additional spending declines. Few challengers (but many open-seat candidates) reach this point, while incumbent candidates do so regularly. Put another way, until candidates spend adequately, only a small number of voters will receive their message; therefore, that message can, by definition, have only modest impact on voting decisions. But once candidates obtain an adequate level of spending, additional funds become less important and the content of the message communicated becomes more significant, precisely because many voters have received it.[12]

Related Evidence on the Impact of Spending

The argument outlined in the preceding section is mostly supported by evidence of the impact of spending on individual voters (see note 6). National survey data suggest, for example, that nonincumbent candidates routinely lack name recognition with the public, let alone favorable evaluations (Mann and Wolfinger 1980). Campaign spending can help to remedy such problems (Jacobson 1978, 2001), which is why challenger spending sometimes appears to have a greater impact on individual vote choice than incumbent spending does.[13] Evidence also suggests that the amount of information possessed by voters increases with higher total levels of campaign spending (Coleman and Manna 2000), and that even the much-criticized television advertising that dominates contemporary campaigns may serve, on balance, to improve voters' knowledge and their level of interest in the campaign (Freedman, Franz, and Goldstein 2004). Further, it appears that turnout rates tend to increase as total campaign spending by all candidates expands.[14] Thus, although election campaigns are hardly models of civic discourse, higher spending—especially by challengers and open-seat candidates, but perhaps by incumbents as well—may actually contribute to, rather than detract from, the overall quality of democracy in the United States.

Campaign spending by political parties (Jacobson 1999) and interest groups (Jacobson 1985) appears to operate in much the same way as spending by nonincumbents, that is, mainly by taking votes away from the incumbent candidate. And although relatively little attention has been paid to the new kinds of "outside" spending that are so prominent today, these likely have a similar impact as well. On balance, the available evidence seems to indicate that party soft money prior to 2002, so-called 527 committee spending in 2002–2004, and spending by interest groups for issue advocacy in both time periods were most effective at generating votes against incumbents rather than nonincumbents (Magleby and Monson 2004).[15] Nevertheless, outside spending may be less effective in this regard than spending by the nonincumbent candidates themselves (Herrnson and Dwyre 1999).

Incumbent Spending

The basic model of campaign spending also confirms the findings in Table 4.2 for incumbent candidates, but in a somewhat puzzling fashion. As noted earlier, the typical (though not universal) conclusion reached by scholars is that incumbent spending has at best a modest impact on the vote; some estimates even imply that the more an incumbent spends, the worse he or she is likely to do on election day (the pattern observed in Table 4.2). Yet few analysts, including some of the basic model's strongest proponents, would endorse such a counterintuitive conclusion. As Jacobson (1985, 41) pointed out,

> If incumbents really gain nothing by spending in campaigns, ironies abound. Incumbents spend defensively and reactively, but pointlessly: the doubling of their real spending over the past decades has merely compounded the waste. The unpleasant work of fundraising which members of Congress complain about so passionately is not even necessary. Most of whatever influence PACs may enjoy must be based on illusion if incumbents do not really need PAC contributions. It is not easy to believe that irrationality is so pervasive; alternative explanations need to be considered.

In fact, the search for "alternative explanations" of incumbent spending has occupied scholars since the advent of the basic model. It is worth noting two accounts that were initially advanced for the puzzling relationship between incumbent spending and the vote, one substantive and one methodological.

The substantive account follows from the logic of the impact of nonincumbent spending that was outlined earlier: Incumbents are relatively well known to voters, partly because they have already won an election and partly because they constantly make efforts to communicate with their constituents between campaigns. Consequently, because incumbents have much less to gain from high spending levels than do challengers, they begin their campaigns at something close to the point of diminishing returns. If faced with a personal scandal, unfavorable political trends, or a well-funded challenger, incumbents generally react by dramatically increasing their spending. But because they are already well known (and already in political trouble), their spending may end up having a modest impact compared to other factors in the race. Although embattled incumbents still win much more often than not, nearly every election has at least one well-publicized example of an incumbent, like Rep. Phil Crane, R-Ill., in 2004, who lost despite massive spending. Cases such as these help create the odd pattern in Table 4.2, in which higher spending is associated with a greater likelihood of defeat. At the same time, incumbents who face no adverse circumstances or serious challengers tend to spend relatively little (because there is no need) and cruise to victory by large margins.

The argument here surely contains a large dose of truth. It has been doubted, however, because of a methodological limitation associated with the simple statistics used to test the basic model. The approach in question assumes that causality flows in just one direction, in this case, that money attracts votes, and that causality does not also run in the other direction—specifically, that votes also attract money. In fact, both things undoubtedly happen in congressional (and other) campaigns. As noted earlier, if the vote is expected to be close, incumbents usually spend more money, but if the vote is expected to be lopsided in their favor they tend to spend less. This makes intuitive sense: After all, the likely outcome of an election will undoubtedly influence the decisions—including whether to run, whether to contribute, and whether to work for or endorse—of candidates, political consultants, campaign contributors, and other political elites (Jacobson and Kernell 1983). As a result, the *expected* vote may well attract money even as campaign money is simultaneously attracting votes. This "simultaneity problem" can lead analysts to underestimate the impact of incumbent spending and overstate the effect of challenger spending (Jacobson 1985, 29–30). Proponents of the basic model are fully aware of the simultaneity problem, of course, and they have sought to take it into account by using more complex statistics.[16] Their initial tests, however, seemed to confirm the basic model's findings, that incumbent spending has very little impact on the vote.

The Puzzle of Incumbent Spending

Academic scholars have offered four kinds of solutions to the puzzle of incumbent spending produced by the basic model. Each provides an alternative explanation for why incumbents engage in campaign spending that seemingly has no effect, and each has contributed to a broader understanding of the role of money in elections. However, none of these solutions change the basic pattern shown in Table 4.2. Instead, they investigate additional circumstances that influence the impact of spending on the vote.

Distortions in Spending

The first solution is to investigate possible distortions in incumbent spending that could cause a modest impact on the vote. One possibility is an *inaccurate measure* of campaign spending. Typically, spending has been defined as the total disbursements by a candidate. Many candidates, however, and especially incumbents, spend money for things other than contacting voters. Indeed, the most extensive investigation of how congressional campaign funds are spent described a "gold-plated politics" wherein some incumbents spend lavishly on activities not directly linked to the campaign at all (Fritz and Morris 1992; also see Morris and Gamache 1994).[17] Ansolabehere and Gerber (1994) used the results of this study to reestimate the basic model for the 1990 congressional elections. They found that a more precise measure of campaign spending based on communication with voters (advertising, direct contact, and so on) increased the observed impact of money on the vote, especially for challengers. But this analysis also indicated that incumbent spending had no significant influence on the vote, much as in the basic model. Nevertheless, additional refinement in measuring campaign spending may lead to the discovery of an effect for incumbent spending; in fact, Goldstein and Freedman (2000) observed just such an effect when improved measures of exposure to television advertising were used to predict citizens' voting behavior.

Another possible distortion is *strategic spending* by incumbents. For example, some scholars have argued that it is quite rational for incumbents to accumulate and spend money early on in an effort to discourage high-quality challengers from entering the race in the first place. If the basic model is correct, a quality challenger is *the* principal threat to an incumbent's reelection prospects.[18] One way to discourage quality challengers may therefore be to build a large "war chest" in advance, a pattern demonstrated by Box-Steffensmeier (1996; but see Goodliffe 2001). Along the same lines, large war chests allow incumbents to spend preemptively to undermine the viability of prospective opponents. Some incumbents also may spend inefficiently to "run up the score" in their reelection bids as a prelude to seeking higher office (Goldenberg, Traugott, and Baumgartner 1986).

All such distortions help to explain why incumbents' spending is rational but relatively inefficient compared with that of nonincumbents. In fact, Jacobson (1989, 1990) has discovered that when a large number of elections are aggregated for analysis, the basic model indicates that incumbent spending has a small, positive, and statistically significant impact on the vote after all. Taken together, these findings provide some support for the popular claim that spending helps to maintain incumbents in office.

Effectiveness Versus Efficiency

The second solution to the puzzle of incumbent spending moves beyond spending efficiency to stress its effectiveness. It may be that despite a low level of efficiency, incumbents win elections because of a high volume of expenditures. Put another way, incumbents may be able to secure the last handful of votes necessary for victory by expending an extraordinary level of money for those voters. This argument is attractive in part because it also helps explain the close wins registered by well-financed challengers and open-seat candidates. Thus the marginal effectiveness of funds (that is, the extent to which extra spending produces enough votes for a candidate to win the race, typically 50 percent of the number of ballots cast) may matter as much to winning as their marginal efficiency.

Thomas (1989) estimated a version of the basic model for the 1978 and 1980 U.S. House elections that included an additional variable: share of total spending in the campaign accounted for by the challenger. In this model, incumbent spending measured in thousands of dollars had a positive impact on the vote but challenger spending measured in the same way did not. However, challenger spending measured as a percentage of the total spending by both candidates did have a positive impact on the vote. In other words, it was the relative size of the challenger's spending compared to the incumbent's that mattered, and not the actual amount spent (which varied substantially from district to district). This result suggests that well-funded challengers can indeed attract votes at the incumbent's expense but that incumbent spending is effective at "winning back" such votes. These findings imply that incumbents can win close contests due to the sheer volume of expenditure, even if they spend less efficiently than challengers.

James Campbell (2003) took a step further the notion that the overall level of spending is important to winning, investigating the relationship between share of the vote won and share of spending accounted for by the incumbent. His results led him to describe a "stagnation of congressional elections," one important cause of which is the enormous advantage incumbents have over their challengers in terms of total funds spent. He summed up the argument as follows:

> While some claim that money does not buy elections . . . there can be no doubt that at some point it does. . . . The typical election to the House is not one in which the incumbent spends twice or three times what his or her opponent spends. . . . In the typical election to the House in recent times the incumbent spends six to twelve times what the challenger spends. (Campbell 2003, 151–152)

Many proponents of the basic model tend to agree with the substance of this conclusion, if not the rhetoric, though the pattern may result as much from insufficient challenger funds as from excessive incumbent spending (Abramowitz 1991).

Correcting Incumbent Spending

The third solution to the puzzle of incumbent spending is to develop corrected models of spending. As noted earlier, proponents of the basic model sought to address the simultaneity problem (that money attracts votes, but expectations of probable victory also attract money to a campaign) by conducting more sophisticated statistical analyses, specifically, by "correcting" incumbent spending for expectations about the likely vote. In essence, this procedure attempts to adjust the actual spending by taking into account the effects of "expected vote" (which is estimated using such factors as strength of the challenger's party in the district, challenger quality, and number of years the incumbent has been in office). Such a correction is typically applied to the spending of incumbents (but sometimes to challenger spending as well). It yields an estimate of what the incumbent would have spent if expectations about the likely vote had not played a role in the campaign. Although initial results were largely consistent with the basic model, some researchers used different factors to make the necessary corrections and, as a result, obtained stronger evidence of the impact of incumbent spending on the vote.

Green and Krasno (1988), for example, found "salvation for the spendthrift incumbent" in their corrected model of spending and the vote in the 1978 congressional elections (also see Jacobson 1990; Green and Krasno 1990).[19] This model corrected incumbent spending by taking into account the incumbent's funds in the previous election (1976) along with other political factors; it also included a more detailed measure of challenger quality. Results indicated that corrected incumbent spending had a significant and positive impact on the vote. The effect of challenger spending, on the other hand, was somewhat lower than in the basic model and subject to diminishing returns, but it was still larger than for incumbent spending.

In addition, Green and Krasno (1988, 898) found that challenger quality mattered a great deal, changing "the structure of the House vote by increasing the importance of quality and decreasing the role of previous electoral outcome." Indeed, their more accurate measure of challenger quality may be one reason why they found incumbent spending to have a significant impact on the vote. Gerber (1998) took a similar tack to investigating spending in Senate elections but used different factors (for example, challenger wealth and the particular offices previously held by challengers) to make the correction for incumbent spending. The results showed that corrected incumbent and challenger spending both mattered in determining the vote, with the former having a larger impact. These studies further specify the circumstances under which spending influences the vote.

Elaborate Models of Spending

The fourth and final solution to the puzzle of incumbent spending is to develop more elaborate models of spending that recognize the complexity of political campaigns. The key insight here is that both the vote and campaign spending are products of the same political process and that, to accurately estimate the impact of spending on the vote, all elements of the process must be taken into account simultaneously. Such analyses also correct incumbent spending for the expected vote (discussed earlier) but go a step further by performing similar corrections on challenger spending and other factors such as challenger quality. For example, Goidel and Gross (1994) estimated an elaborate model that systematically corrected both incumbent and challenger spending, as well as challenger quality, for a variety of other potential influences on the vote.[20] These corrected variables, along with a number of additional ones, were used to predict the vote in congressional elections from 1986 to 1990. Incumbent spending was found to have a positive impact on incumbent's vote—enough to make a measurable difference in winning an election. However, as in the basic model, challenger spending continued to have a much greater impact than incumbent spending. This research therefore makes a more plausible case for the conclusions of the basic model, fitting even better with popular claims about money and elections.

One of the most comprehensive treatments of spending in congressional elections was undertaken by Erikson and Palfrey (1998). They estimated a complex model that corrected both incumbent and challenger spending for the expected vote in congressional races between 1972 and 1990.[21] Specifically, their model allowed for the effect of money on attracting votes to be estimated separately from the effect of votes on attracting money. They found that corrected incumbent spending had a positive impact on the incumbent's vote. Although the overall impact of incumbent spending was smaller than for challengers, Erikson and Palfrey also concluded that the effect of campaign spending varied over an incumbent's career. The largest impact occurs when a newly elected incumbent seeks reelection for the first time—an election when such candidates are often quite vulnerable. Under these circumstances, incumbent spending appears to be more influential than challenger spending. That influence declines steadily the longer an individual is in office, however, with challenger spending eventually gaining the advantage (also see Goidel and Gross 1994). On the one hand, this result confirms the basic model's finding of diminishing returns for incumbent spending; on the other hand, it suggests that incumbent spending may have a cumulative effect that, in turn, helps to explain the high reelection rate of incumbents.

Erikson and Palfrey (2000) expanded their analysis with an even more elaborate model of what they called "campaign spending games," further illuminating the effect that expectations about an election can have on campaign spending. The authors found that expectations were least consequential in very close elections, in which incumbent and challenger spending had about the same impact once expectations were taken into account. The less competitive an election became, however, the larger the role played by expectations. For veteran incumbents, corrected spending revealed a positive impact of money on their votes but at a level below that for challengers.

Thus, the closer an incumbent-challenger race becomes, the more it resembles an open-seat race where, as we have seen, each candidate's spending has a roughly equivalent effect on the distribution of the vote. This still advantages incumbents, of course, who typically "outspend challengers and . . . achieve roughly equal effectiveness per dollar in close races, where it matters most" (Erikson and Palfrey 2000, 606). Consequently, because most races are characterized by a strong incumbent fundraising advantage to start with, the true impact of incumbent spending is often obscured in scholarly analyses. The conclusions reached by these more elaborate models generally confirm, but in a nuanced and sophisticated fashion, the popular claims about the importance of money in maintaining control of elected office.

Conclusion: The Effects of Campaign Spending

Three decades of academic research have yielded considerable support for widely shared assumptions about the role of money in electoral politics, though the findings are not always as straightforward as one might expect. Overall, three conclusions seem warranted:

- First, money is a dynamic factor in campaigns, with the capacity to change the behavior of voters; all else being equal, money has a market-like impact on the votes that candidates receive.

- Second, the impact of money varies with the context of the campaign. Because all else is rarely equal, and factors other than money influence how people vote, money matters more for some kinds of candidates than for others, and its effect varies with electoral circumstances.
- Third, money is most valuable in gaining control of elected office and less valuable (but still important) in maintaining such control.

Scholars do not agree, however, on the implications of this research for the nation's laws governing campaign finance.[22] Proponents of the basic model tend to favor reforms, such as public financing, that would put more money in the hands of challengers. They are skeptical of laws that restrict overall fundraising and spending on the grounds that it would hurt challengers (who need money the most, and tend to spend more efficiently when they have it). In contrast, researchers who find evidence of a positive impact for incumbent spending often advocate spending limits in order to reduce the advantage that is typical of well-heeled officeholders seeking reelection. The practical and legal complexity of such proposals aside, it may well be that a combination of both approaches would make elections more competitive.[23]

At least three major sets of unanswered questions confront those who wish to study the role of money in campaigns. First, an effort should be made to develop a "standard model" of campaign spending that incorporates all of the insights provided by the literature reviewed in this chapter. Once such a model is in hand, scholars can use it to investigate spending in the full range of campaigns, from the courthouse to the White House. It could also be extended to all manner of campaign activities, from outside spending by interest groups to get-out-the-vote programs by campaign volunteers.

Second, the practicality of any model might be enhanced if it estimated the number of votes received by a candidate rather than simply the proportion of the two-party vote. After all, real campaigns are dedicated to contacting and persuading actual voters. Such an approach would allow researchers to examine the effects of spending in both large and small constituencies, using the type of office sought as a variable in the analysis. It would be interesting, for example, to know whether campaign spending is more or less important in a presidential or a state legislative campaign. Furthermore, this development would allow for the integration of turnout and vote choice—both of which clearly matter on election day—into the same model.

Finally, having focused largely on total spending, we still do not know a great deal about the effectiveness of different types of campaign expenditures. What, for example, are the relative benefits of spending for television ads versus direct mail? How should campaigns allocate their funds across different areas, and how should those expenditures be distributed over time? What proportion of the budget should be devoted to overhead (in particular, maintaining and staffing a campaign headquarters) versus direct voter contact? Are political consultants worth their fees in terms of helping candidates to win elections (see chapter 10 in this volume)? By addressing such questions, scholars can further refine and expand our understanding of the relationship between money and electoral success.

The Consultants Respond About

CAMPAIGN SPENDING

Our consultants generally shared the academic view that money plays a major role in shaping election outcomes, if not always to the same degree that advocates of campaign finance reform might have us believe. Other factors often are more important, and the amount of money has less of an impact than the manner in which money is spent by candidates (and their supporters).

INDEPENDENT POLITICAL ANALYST. There are fewer and fewer races today where money matters. It's hard to sneak up on candidates anymore. In 2004, for example, there were only maybe twenty competitive U.S. House seats in the country.

Two themes dominated the discussion about campaign spending at our conference. First, there was agreement that money must be raised in a timely fashion for it to have the desired effect:

REPUBLICAN POLLSTER. Academic studies confirm a lot of political consultants' assumptions. One area that deserves more study, though, is timing because when the money comes in and is spent by a campaign is very important. Plus, now we also have early voting in many states. When the money comes in and the ads go on may be just as critical as anything else that the academics are studying.... Campaigns traditionally have wanted to be up and advertising earlier when there is less clutter. However, maybe voters don't get interested in the campaigns until there is enough clutter and ads to wake them up.

REPUBLICAN MEDIA CONSULTANT. When the money comes into a campaign is very important. If a campaign doesn't advertise early, it can be in trouble.

REPUBLICAN POLLSTER. I've been in campaigns that have more money than Midas in the last week but, unfortunately, voters made their decision about most of [those races] weeks ago. I've

continues...

been in campaigns where people give $5,000 contributions on election day, and I want to ask them, "Are you insane? What are we going to do with this? I can't go down to the TV station today and start buying ad time." But interest groups actually come with a check in hand as if somehow they're doing you a favor, and it makes you more angry than anything else.... Many campaigns live off fumes in the early stages, when they want to get their advertising up but the donors aren't there yet.

The second theme that dominated our discussion had to do with independent spending. Perhaps predictably, some consultants expressed both amazement and concern about the growing role of 527 organizations (see note 15) in campaigns today:

DEMOCRATIC MEDIA CONSULTANT. One thing that needs to be considered more closely is outside spending. Campaigns have become almost irrelevant compared to outside spending. We were involved in several races last year in [a mountain west state], and I've never seen that kind of effort and expenditure on both sides. EMILY's List was leasing five jumbo jets to fly 1,800 people in from New York and Washington to work on one of the campaigns. And that doesn't take into account the amount of ad spending that went on from the DCCC [Democratic Congressional Campaign Committee] and the NRCC [National Republican Congressional Committee].

INDEPENDENT POLITICAL ANALYST. Money by the candidates is one factor, but also by outside forces. In some cases, the incumbent may actually be outspent and still win dramatically simply because of the money that campaign committees are throwing in.

What the consultants feared more than anything else from 527s was their independence:

REPUBLICAN POLLSTER. Most of us want to get rid of 527 organizations because, from both the consultant's and candidate's point of view, they can hurt your campaign. They're so bad sometimes, and get off message even if they're trying to help you, that I think they become at best a necessary evil and something you have to deal with. You think you're controlling your own strategy, but the truth is that this third weird force out there is placing ads and their message may not be the same as yours even though you're supposedly on the same side. It would be like in a football game, and you have one team in red and one team in blue—except there's one guy in gray and sometimes he's going to be aligned with you, but sometimes with the other side. And sometimes, he'll line up with you and still do things to hurt you. I don't think that would work in football, and I don't think it's working very well in politics.

DEMOCRATIC MEDIA CONSULTANT. A campaign consultant wants to control everything, but we can't control the

527s. One problem is when a big independent-expenditures buy comes in and eats up time slots in certain types of programming that a campaign might be looking to advertise in, and also drives up the [cost] of ads.

On a more positive (primarily Republican) note:

REPUBLICAN GENERAL CONSULTANT. When we least expect it, sometimes democracy breaks out. The 527 groups are an example of that. There were so many predictions that 527s were going to be a tool of special interests, but it just didn't happen. All the individual donors found a way to say, "OK, I'm going to give my twenty bucks and it's going to help put this ad on the air." It was a way for people to make their twenty bucks count again. That's who really funded the 527s.

REPUBLICAN MEDIA CONSULTANT. Republicans need 527 groups. The left used to outspend us, and conservative groups didn't put in the money necessary to win. Now, 527 groups have leveled the playing field.

REPUBLICAN GENERAL CONSULTANT. 527s give citizens the ability to express their opinions and political views in a way not structured by Congress. It's a good thing when voters find a way around the system to express their opinions.

INDEPENDENT POLITICAL ANALYST. We made these assumptions that the new campaign financing rules would cause all these shadow groups associated with the NRCC and the DCCC to emerge. But that didn't happen.

Notes

1. Actual vote buying is not unheard of in the United States today, though it appears to be much less common than in the nineteenth century (Thayer 1973). For one thing, levels of voter turnout are substantially lower now and it is simply more efficient for campaigns to spend money to encourage turnout. What most people mean by "buying votes" is shorthand for something like "buying advertising to influence voters."

2. Interestingly, these claims are stated most clearly in the political science literature. See, for example, Jacobson (1980); Green and Krasno (1988); Erikson and Palfrey (1998).

3. There are many reasons for the "power of incumbency" in recent congressional elections, ranging from more precise redistricting to increased perquisites of office. For a brief summary of these factors, see J. Campbell (2003, 144–145).

4. This stands in obvious contrast to presidential elections, where the popular vote does not matter directly because of the electoral college.

5. The vote measure used is sometimes the challenger's, the incumbent's, or the winner's percentage of the two-party total; on other occasions, the winning candidate's margin of victory (winner's minus loser's vote percentage) is used.

6. What I am describing here and throughout most of the chapter is research done at the aggregate level. Other scholars have assessed the impact of money on individual vote choice by merging, for example, district or state spending data with survey responses (see Jacobson 1990; Kenny and McBurnett 1992). The results of these studies are discussed in greater detail, as appropriate.

7. In individual-level studies (see note 6), this would be the voter's own self-identification as a Republican, Democrat, or independent.

8. See Jacobson (1978, 1980, 1985, 1987, 1989, 1990). The preferred statistical technique used for testing the basic model is ordinary least squares (OLS) regression analysis; see Jacobson (1985) for a more detailed discussion.

9. See, for example, Glantz, Abramowitz, and Burkart (1976); Abramowitz and Segal (1986); Abramowitz (1988, 1991). For summaries, see Gross and Goidel (2003); Malbin and Gais (1998); Jacobson (1985).

10. The basic model typically shows that party strength in the district, the challenger's party, and challenger quality all have a significant impact on the vote. For a good summary, see Jacobson (2001).

11. See Jacobson (1985, 1987).

12. Although the threshold appears to vary with type of race and election year, Jacobson (1985, 43–44) estimated that congressional challengers needed to spend at least $250,000 in 1986 to be minimally competitive; in Table 4.2, that figure would be about $500,000.

13. See Jacobson (1990); Kenny and McBurnett (1992); but also see Goldstein and Freedman (2000).

14. See Copeland (1983); Caldeira, Patterson, and Markko (1985); Jackson (1996). Much of the money that candidates spend today is for negative attacks on the opposition. Although some research purports to show that negative advertising reduces turnout (Ansolabehere et al. 1994), the bulk of the evidence seems to suggest otherwise (Clinton and Lapinksi 2004; Finkel and Geer 1998; Freedman and Goldstein 1999; Goldstein and Freedman 2002a; Kahn and Kenney 1999; Lau and Pomper 2001).

15. Party soft money refers to funds spent by political parties in accordance with state rather than federal campaign finance law. Historically, these funds influenced federal elections through voter registration drives and other party-building activities, but by the mid-1990s they were being used by national party organizations for television ads aimed at influencing the election of presidential and congressional candidates. Much of the money would have otherwise been illegal under federal law because the amounts exceeded contribution limits and the checks came from prohibited sources, such as corporate and union treasuries. In response to this situation, party soft money was banned in 2003 by the so-called McCain-Feingold law. One consequence of McCain-Feingold was that some of the banned party soft money was redirected into interest-group committees formed under section 527 of the federal tax code—tax-exempt organizations that supposedly exist to express positions on issues rather than influence campaigns and are therefore not subject to the same contribution limits as interest-group political action committees. However, 527 committees are prohibited from spending money contributed by corporate or union treasuries in federal candidate campaigns within thirty days of a primary or sixty days of a general election. Such restrictions notwithstanding, both party soft money and 527 committees are examples of how political parties, interest groups, campaign contributors, and candidates are able to exploit loopholes that exist in the nation's campaign finance laws (see Malbin 2003 for more details).

16. The technique of choice here is two-stage least squares regression analysis, in which OLS regression is performed on one candidate's spending, typically the incumbent's, and the estimated results (called "instrumental variables") are entered into a second-stage OLS regression (see Jacobson 1985).

17. These might include, for example, such purely personal items as home mortgage payments, country club memberships, and family vacations. On the campaign side, candidates spend money for fundraising, overhead (for campaign headquarters), polling, contributions to other campaigns, and a variety of activities not aimed specifically at communicating with and mobilizing voters.

18. See Bond, Covington, and Fleisher (1985); Jacobson (1989).

19. These studies used two-stage least squares regression analysis and instrumental variables; see Green and Krasno (1988) for details.

20. The technique used was three-stage least squares regression analysis; see Goidel and Gross (1994) for details.

21. Erikson and Palfrey used a simultaneous equations technique with a three-equation system and uncorrelated errors solution.

22. Every major research report cited in this chapter considered campaign finance reform from the perspective of its own findings.

23. For a good summary of the issues involved here, see Goidel, Gross, and Shields (1999).

5 Political Advertising

Lynda Lee Kaid

Despite the biennial complaints of journalists and various other critics about the damage done to democracy, political advertising remains the major avenue of communication between candidates and voters in the American electoral system. Spending reports and media databases indicate that the 2004 presidential campaign marked a new high for spending on advertising, with a total in excess of $600 million ($547 million of which went to television ads; see TNS Media Intelligence 2004). These record spending levels surprised many observers who thought that the growth of the Internet and frequent expressions of public distaste for negative political advertising would result in fewer 30- and 60-second spot ads. In fact, it was the express purpose of the 2002 Bipartisan Campaign Reform Act (see chapter 4 in this volume) to eliminate the use of soft money for campaign advertising and to discourage negative attacks by requiring more stringent sponsorship and disclaimer notifications on all ads (Kaid and Jones 2004).

Candidates, political parties, and an unprecedented number of independent groups nonetheless continued to rely on political advertising in 2004, and a large body of research in political science and communication suggests that this was generally a wise choice. However, academic research does more than simply verify the overall effects of campaign ads; it also provides a road map that can assist candidates, parties, and professional consultants in their efforts to determine the most effective strategic uses of political advertising. In this chapter I summarize what has been learned thus far and discuss the implications and applications of prior research for decisions that are made in the pragmatic world of political campaigning. Such research falls basically into two categories: (1) general descriptions of the content of political advertising and (2) efforts to assess its effects on voters. Although this chapter begins with a brief discussion of content studies, my emphasis is primarily on research that examines the effects of televised political advertising.[1]

Content of Political Advertising

One of the most enduring complaints about political advertising is that it is too much about image and provides voters with too little useful information about candidates' policy stands. Yet from the earliest attempt at systematic analysis of campaign spot ads (see Joslyn 1980) to the present, this criticism has proven to be unfounded. For example, in a study that used "videostyle" (a perspective that examines candidate presentation through advertising in terms of verbal, nonverbal, and video production techniques), Kaid and Johnston (2001) documented that, beginning with the first extended use of paid ads by Eisenhower in 1952, presidential candidates have generally focused their television advertising mainly on issues—not on personal qualities or images. In fact, the percentage of issue ads in presidential campaigns (an average of 66 percent from 1952 through 1996) has increased substantially in recent years to an all-time high in 2004 of 85 percent.[2] Issue ads also are the leading content type in electoral contests below the presidential level (Joslyn 1980). Vavreck (2001), for example, analyzed the ads of 290 candidates in the 1998 elections and found that only 30 percent were predominately trait based, while 52 percent were dominated by issues and over 80 percent contained some mention of issues.

Negative or attack advertising has earned a special place in the hearts and minds of American voters, gaining a stronghold as the advertising style voters have been taught by the media to say they despise while nevertheless being regularly affected by it (see below).[3] The early years of presidential advertising on television were mixed in their negative-positive distribution, averaging roughly 38 percent negative from 1952 through 1996 (Kaid 2001). The 1980s, however, heralded new levels of negativity in ads both at the presidential level and in lower-level races (Kaid 2004). The prize for the highest proportion of negative ads in a presidential campaign so far is claimed by Bill Clinton, with 69 percent in 1992 and 68 percent in 1996; this record was almost matched in 2000 by Al Gore, with 62 percent negative ads (Kaid 2004). Elections below the presidential level also saw a sharp increase in negative advertising during the same period, led by independent and third-party groups such as the National Conservative Political Action Committee (NCPAC), which targeted Democratic congressional and senatorial candidates in many parts of the country (Kitchens and Powell 1986). More recently, negative advertising has become a recurring strategy, especially likely to be used by challengers and in highly competitive races.[4]

Of course, the percentage of negative ads *produced* is not the only measure of a campaign's overall negativity. As some researchers have suggested, the distribution of ads that actually *aired* is an important measure of the tone of a campaign as well (Goldstein and Freedman 2002b; Ridout et al. 2004). For example, Goldstein and Freedman (2002b) examined the top seventy-five market buys in 2000 and concluded that ads aired by Bush reflected a more negative tone than those aired by Gore.

Effects of Political Advertising

Academic research on the effects of political advertising has been conducted from a number of theoretical perspectives, but this chapter focuses on what we know about effects that can be applied to political campaigning. First, I identify the broad cognitive, affective, and behavioral consequences of campaign ads, and the special conditions under which these consequences are more or less likely to occur. Second, I address the specific effects of negative advertising. In the final section I summarize research regarding the impact of negative advertising on the political system as a whole.

General Effects of Exposure to Political Advertising

Voter Knowledge of Candidates and Issues. A great deal of research on political advertising has documented that exposure to political advertising can have a substantial effect in increasing voter awareness of and knowledge about candidates and campaign issues. Box 5.1 lists some of the general effects of exposure to political advertising. The fact that campaign ads often succeed at raising the profile of candidates is especially clear in races below the presidential level (Kaid 1982; West 1994). Moreover, televised ads are an important source of voter information about campaign issues and candidates' positions on those issues.[5]

The type of ad to which a voter is exposed appears to make a difference, with some research showing that image ads tend to produce greater recall of information than issue ads (Kaid and Sanders 1978), especially in the case of candidates who are less well-known to start with (Schleuder 1990). The type of information recalled also varies across individuals, with research indicating that motivational factors can lead to differential recall of issue versus image information from particular ads (Faber and Storey 1984; Garramone 1983, 1984a, 1986). Further, voters who watch ads for information-seeking reasons are more likely to be affected in their voting choices by ads that emphasize issue-related information (Christ, Thorson, and Caywood 1994).

> **Box 5.1 General Effects of Exposure to Political Advertising**
>
> **Campaign ads can:**
>
> - Increase voter knowledge about candidates and issues, with greater learning evident from political television advertising than from televised campaign news or candidate debates.
> - Have an agenda-setting effect on both voters and news media.
> - Affect evaluations of candidates (either positive or negative).
> - Shape voting behavior, increasing the likelihood of voting for or against a candidate.

Research on agenda setting has contributed to the state of our knowledge about voter recall of political advertising. Specifically, it appears that the content of ads often correlates with voters' judgments of issue salience and candidate attribute salience.[6] In other words, the issues and personal characteristics that candidates stress in their ads are often communicated successfully to voters and become the issues and attributes that voters believe to be important. The issues in political advertising can also affect the news agendas of media outlets,[7] thereby allowing candidates to use their controlled media (advertisements) to influence the issue messages distributed to voters through noncontrolled media (news).

Perhaps surprisingly, evidence indicates that voters may learn more about candidates' issue stands from campaign ads than from either television news or newspapers.[8] Even televised debates do not appear to offer a strong advantage over advertising in terms of issue learning.[9] Freedman, Franz, and Goldstein (2004) found the relationship of citizen knowledge to ad exposure in 2000 to be less clear in the presidential contest than in congressional races, though exposure to presidential ads did improve one's ability to place candidates correctly on issue scales and increased the number of likes and dislikes that a voter could recall about the candidates. However, some scholars have contested the finding that ad exposure leads to knowledge gain (Chaffee, Zhao, and Leshner 1994; D. Weaver and Drew 2001; Zhao and Chaffee 1995), partly because of doubts raised by the use of different methodologies and measurement techniques in these studies.[10]

Candidate Evaluations. Box 5.1 shows that, in addition to learning information about candidates and issues, exposure to campaign ads also can affect voters' evaluations of candidates. Both experimental and survey-based studies have provided strong evidence that exposure to television spots can result in changes in a candidate's image.[11] For instance, when respondents' attitudes about 1996 presidential nominees Bill Clinton and Bob Dole were measured before exposure to political spots and then again afterward, results demonstrated that exposure to the spots had a significant impact (Kaid 1998; Kaid and Chanslor 2004). The effects on candidate evaluation that result from advertising exposure seem to hold when voters' party affiliation, education, and gender are taken into account (West 2001); thus, it appears that television ads can sometimes affect even voters who are predisposed by their partisanship to favor one candidate over his or her opponent. This does not mean, of course, that every political spot has a positive effect on the image of the sponsoring candidate. To the contrary, other variables can (and often do) determine how voters react to candidates and their messages. Some of these conditions and their impact on candidate evaluations related to television advertising are discussed below.

Voting Behavior. While it is unrealistic to expect that all television spots will shape voters' behavior in the manner intended by their sponsors, convincing evidence indicates that such effects are at least possible. Some researchers have found a relationship at the aggregate level between the amount of money spent for campaign advertising and candidate support levels in the electorate, though spending appears to be less influential in ballot proposition races.[12] Daron Shaw (1999b) looked at advertising time-buy data and vote results for three presidential elections (1988–1996) and found that the volume of ad buys has a positive effect on candidates' percentage of the statewide vote. Personal appearances by the candidate also have an impact and can interact with ad buys to produce an additive improvement in vote totals, especially among undecided voters. Although none of this aggregate-level research proves that campaign ads persuade individual voters to support the sponsoring candidate (or, in the case of negative ads, to oppose that candidate's opponent), experimental and survey-based studies provide more direct evidence that exposure to televised political ads can have such an impact (Cundy 1986; Kaid and Sanders 1978; West 1994).

> **Box 5.2 Factors That Condition the Effects of Exposure to Political Advertising**
>
> - Political advertising overcomes partisan selective exposure.
> - Effects of political advertising are greatest when the level of voter involvement is low.
> - Effects on voting may be greatest on undecideds or late-deciders.
> - Emotional content of advertising can affect voters' feelings about candidates and their ads.
> - Issue ads are more effective than image ads, particularly when they relate to an issue over which the candidate's party is believed to have "ownership."
> - Production characteristics of ads can affect voters' responses to candidates.
> - Channels of communication interact with source variables; that is, some candidates are better on radio than on television, some are better on the Internet, and so on.
> - There are differences in advertising effects for male and female candidates.

Conditions for Political Advertising Effects

A number of conditions (that is, characteristics of the individual and of the advertising to which he or she is exposed) can influence the extent to which televised campaign ads have the desired effect on voter knowledge levels, candidate evaluations, and vote preference. Box 5.2 outlines some of these conditions.

Selective Exposure. Selective processes are considered one of the major reasons why media messages often are unsuccessful in causing opinion change. According to cognitive dissonance theory (Festinger 1957; Klapper 1960), voters are assumed to expose themselves primarily to messages that are in line with their existing partisan predispositions. As a result, the probability of opinion change occurring would seem to be rather low. Numerous studies, however, have shown that televised political advertising can sometimes overcome this barrier to persuasion. In other words, because television ads in the United States are aired as interstitial messages in between regular programming, they are likely to be seen by supporters of all political parties and ideological persuasions. Indeed, academic research confirms that television ads frequently reach a broad distribution of voters with a mix of political outlooks (Atkin et al. 1973; Surlin and Gordon 1976).

The pattern here probably needs to be reconsidered in light of new technologies, such as remote controls, video recorders, and TiVo, which give the viewer more control over the time, structure, and environment of their television viewing. These techniques are unlikely to have eliminated the ability of political television ads to reach broad voting constituencies, but the exposure potential may have been lessened for some groups. However, Iyengar, Hahn, and Prior (2001) found that when given the opportunity to expose themselves to campaign information directly from candidates or from traditional sources on CD-ROM in the 2000 presidential election, very few voters exercised selectivity in exposure to candidate messages. In fact, "attention to Gore or Bush-oriented pages tended to vary only slightly by party or ideological affiliation" (13), leading the authors to conclude that new technologies failed to activate strong selective exposure in this instance.

Nevertheless, even if television advertising lessens the likelihood of partisan selective exposure, selective perception of the message can still occur, and research has frequently verified that viewers sometimes interpret political ads through partisan bias (Ansolabehere and Iyengar 1995; Donohue 1973; Faber, Tims, and Schmitt 1993). Research has also shown, however, that political advertising can sometimes overcome partisan perceptions, as well as exposure biases. For example, Ansolabehere and Iyengar (1995) discovered that advertising can increase vote likelihood among viewers of the partisan affiliation opposite the sponsor while at the same time boosting vote preferences for the sponsor among his or her own party members. Negative ads seem to be particularly powerful in overcoming such partisan perceptual bias (Garramone 1985; Kaid and Boydston 1987).

Voter Involvement and Decision Making. Regardless of their partisan leanings, some voters simply do not consider elections to be very important. Early research on political advertising found that voters with low levels of campaign involvement were precisely the ones most likely to be affected by political spots (Cundy 1990; Rothschild and Ray 1974). It appears that low-involvement election situations allow television ads to convey a message without the voter being fully aware of its impact. Citizens with low levels of campaign and candidate awareness are similarly more likely to be influenced in their evaluations of candidates following exposure to advertising (Valentino, Hutchings, and Williams 2004).[13] Along the same lines, experimental and survey-based studies have shown that undecided voters and those who make up their minds very late in a campaign are particularly susceptible to persuasion effects in political advertising (Bowen 1994; Hofstetter and Buss 1980).

Emotional Content. The emotional aspects of a political ad can affect viewer recall (Lang 1991), with recall being more likely to occur for information that evokes an emotional response. In addition, political advertising that generates such a response (including optimism, patriotism, anger, fear, hope, and pride) can have a strong effect on candidate evaluation.[14] Fear appeals, in particular, are capable of influencing citizens' vote preferences in certain circumstances (Brader 2005). The emotional content of an ad also may interact with the motivations of viewers. For example, ad viewers who have high information-seeking needs are likely to experience higher levels of arousal and pleasure when exposed to issue ads that fulfill those needs, but only pleasure in response to image ads containing little or no issue content (Christ, Thorson, and Caywood 1994).

Issue Ads, Image Ads, and Production Characteristics. The type of television spot a viewer sees may help to shape his or her evaluation of a candidate. Issue ads seem to be more effective, on balance, than image (or character) ads at raising a candidate's overall ratings.[15] This observation holds especially when the ads focus on issues over which the candidate's party can claim "ownership," that is, on which voters generally regard the party as being better able to deal with than the opposition (see Ansolabehere and Iyengar 1994; Petrocik 1996). For instance, Democrats are often thought to do a better job of dealing with issues such as education and the environment, while Republicans tend to have the advantage on foreign affairs and national security. Recent studies have confirmed that such issue-ownership differentials for the two parties are evident in their political advertisements, with Democratic candidates airing ads that stress issues they feel the public associates with their party, and Republican candidates doing the same (Benoit 2004; Benoit and Hansen 2002).

Researchers also have validated the effectiveness of several aspects of video and audio production techniques in shaping citizens' reactions to political advertising. The structure and design of ads, for example, can affect both voter recall and candidate evaluation.[16] Geiger and Reeves (1991) found that political spots with a dynamic structure (showing the candidate in varied scenes with fast cuts and music) resulted in more positive candidate evaluation than spots with a static structure (single scene, candidate talking directly into the camera). Music can be important as well, because it sometimes enhances visual recall and increases the viewer's feelings of emotional arousal (Thorson, Christ, and Caywood 1991a, 1991b).

Channel Effects in Political Advertising. McLuhan's (1964) proclamation that the "medium is the message" seems to be particularly true in relation to candidates and their messages. Political advertising research has verified that some politicians do better on one medium (radio versus television, for instance), some on another (Andreoli and Worchel 1978; Cohen 1976). Particularly intriguing are new findings that suggest a difference in candidate evaluations depending on the use of television or Internet for advertising messages. Specifically, in the 2000 presidential campaign, voters exposed to ads on the web were likely to vote for Al Gore, whereas those watching the same ads on television leaned toward George W. Bush (Kaid 2002). Similar results were found in 2004, with ads for John Kerry eliciting more positive response in voters when viewed on the web (Kaid and Postelnicu 2005). Channel of ad exposure also seems to influence a wide range of information-seeking and voting behaviors. For instance, viewers of political ads on the Internet (which allows users to seek out other information) are significantly more likely to want to see more ads, watch more news, and read more newspaper stories about the candidates, and to express the intention to vote in the next election. In contrast, seeing political ads in the traditional television medium encourages people to volunteer to work in a campaign, to engage in an electronic chat about the candidates, and to be interested in contributing money (Kaid 2002, 2003).

Campaign Ads for Male and Female Candidates. More women are running for office today, and serving at all levels of government in the United States, than ever before. The increasing number and visibility of female candidates have led to considerable research that explores which techniques are most effective in political advertising when male and female candidates confront each other on the television screen and, ultimately, at the ballot box.

Although many political observers have assumed that female candidates would be more likely to discuss "feminine" than "masculine" issues (for example, education rather than foreign policy) and character traits (for example, compassion rather than strength), a substantial body of research suggests that few differences exist in the overall content of male and female political advertising (Bystrom and Kaid 2002). Also, from the 1980s on, few gender-based differences appear to exist in the amount and tone of campaign advertising (Kahn 1996), though men tend to use a more hard-hitting, assaultive style in their negative ads (Trent and Sabourin 1993). Nevertheless, by the 1990s women were using negative advertisements as frequently as their male counterparts.[17]

Experimental studies have provided a way to test the relative effectiveness of advertising for male and female candidates. Surprisingly, the latter seem to receive higher evaluations and greater vote likelihood scores when they appear in typical masculine settings (for example, a construction site or farm), rather than in stereotypical feminine settings such as a schoolroom surrounded by children or posing with family (Kaid et al. 1984; Wadsworth et al. 1987). Women candidates also seem to be more positively evaluated in neutral settings such as offices (Hitchon, Chang, and Harris 1997). Hitchon and Chang (1995) suggested that campaign ads for male and female candidates are often processed differently by voters, with female candidates eliciting greater recall of family and personal appearance, and recall for male candidate ads being linked more closely to political situations such as appearances at campaign rallies or formal speeches.

The content or type of issue on which political advertising is based can also influence gender differences in advertising effects. Chang and Hitchon (2004), for example, found that men are rated as significantly better able to handle "masculine" issues (such as agriculture or foreign policy) after subjects have been exposed to ads dealing with these issues, while women candidates are rated better when they are portrayed as dealing with "feminine" issues (education, health care, or family-related concerns). Perhaps even more interesting are findings about "default processing" that may occur when gender-specific issues are *not* discussed: Chang and Hitchon (also see Gordon, Shafie, and Crigler 2003) discovered that gender stereotypes regarding the handling of stereotypically feminine and masculine issues occur only when dealing with those issues not specifically addressed in the ads. Pragmatically speaking, then, a man who wants to emphasize his competence with women's issues should do so overtly in his ads, because the default processing does not work in his favor when the messages do not address these issues specifically. The same is true for women candidates, who must address positively their competence on men's issues to avoid default processing that causes voters to conclude that men are better at these issues. Thus, for example, a female candidate who does not address foreign policy issues specifically in her spots is likely to find that voters automatically consider a male opponent to be superior to her in the foreign policy arena because the latter has assumed, by default, superiority on such issues.

Overall, research on male and female political advertising suggests that women politicians are increasingly successful in competing with men on an even playing field. Winning female candidates seem to be most successful when their advertising is positive, emphasizes personal traits of toughness and strength, and capitalizes on the importance of "feminine" issues such as education and health care, while simultaneously balancing their campaign issue emphasis with "masculine" issues such as the economy and national defense or security (Bystrom et al. 2004).

Effects of Negative Advertising

The number of academic studies devoted specifically to negative advertising has skyrocketed since the mid-1970s. Research on the content of televised political advertising documents a growing usage of negative ads, at least in presidential campaigns (Kaid 2005; Kaid and Dimitrova 2005; Kaid and Johnston 2001). Scholars also have examined the impact of negative advertising, and with certain qualifications their findings show that negative ads can be effective at providing voters with knowledge and information, as well as at shaping their attitudes toward candidates and voting preferences (Kaid 2004). Box 5.3 summarizes the range of effects discussed here. As for how the American public feels about negative campaigning, the results are mixed. Because media coverage of negative advertising tends to be fairly critical (Kaid et al. 1993; Tedesco, Kaid, and McKinnon 2000), one might suspect that this would lead citizens to disapprove of the practice even though the process of comparing the pros and cons of policy positions and candidate qualifications is at the very heart of democratic politics (Geer 2006; Mayer 1996). Yet voters often end up taking both sides of this issue. In a national survey conducted after the 1996 presidential campaign, for example, Kaid, McKinney, and Tedesco (2000) found that while 70 percent of their sample said that "candidates have a right to point out weaknesses of their opponents," 43 percent indicated that "negative ads are unethical."[18]

Overall Effectiveness of Negative Ads. As with political advertising in general, negative ads have identifiable (if not always consistent) effects on audience recall, evaluation of candidates, and voting behavior. Research shows that recall of negative ads tends to be higher than for positive ads, presumably because people are more likely to remember negative information.[19] This is not always the case, however.[20] Geer and Geer (2003) tested recall of campaign ads using positive and negative candidate radio spots and found no difference between

> **Box 5.3 Effects of Exposure to Negative Advertising**
>
> - Negative ads can increase voter knowledge of issues, (sometimes) decrease the favorability of the opponent at whom the negative advertising is directed, and (sometimes) raise the likelihood of voting for the sponsoring candidate.
> - Alternatively, negative ads can sometimes have a backlash effect.
> - Negative ads are more effective when sponsored by a third party, or independent group, than when they are candidate-sponsored.
> - Negative ads are more effective if the attack is on an issue rather than on personal or image aspects of the opponent.
> - Rebuttals can blunt the effect of a negative ad.
> - Inoculation also can help defend against negative ads; that is, getting your message out first to offset the possible effects of later attacks seems to help.
> - The effectiveness of negative advertising may be related to the context or content of the television programming in which it appears.
> - Evidence is mixed as to whether negative ads decrease voter turnout or are otherwise detrimental to democratic politics.

the two, though exposure to negative ads was associated with significantly higher amounts of *inaccurate* recall.

The evidence is decidedly mixed on whether negative ads are effective at shaping voters' perceptions and evaluations of candidates. Some studies show, for example, that positive ads are better for creating favorable impressions of both lesser known and more visible candidates.[21] Others demonstrate that negative ads can be effective as well in terms of boosting evaluations of the sponsor or lowering ratings of the candidate being attacked.[22] Nevertheless, it is difficult to draw any firm conclusions from the academic literature about what type of advertising is likely to be more effective under what circumstances.[23]

A similar inconsistency characterizes research on whether negative ads help or hurt at the ballot box: A handful of studies seem to indicate that going negative can generate electoral support,[24] but these studies are countered by research that suggests otherwise.[25] In fact, candidates who sponsor negative ads may sometimes experience a backlash that lowers their standing among voters and reduces their changes of winning the election.[26] Such backlash effects are certainly not inevitable, however, and evidence suggests that these effects may be circumvented with the use of humor or less harsh negative attacks (Pfau, Parrott, and Lindquist 1992).

Sponsorship and Types of Negative Ads. Negative ads seem to be more effective when sponsored by a third party or a source independent from the campaign,[27] though most of the research on this point was done before the proliferation of independent advertising and heightened visibility of advertising sponsored by groups whose agendas are increasingly well-known. A notable exception is Borick (2005), who found that the so-called Swift Boat attack ads played a significant role in defeating Democratic nominee John Kerry's presidential bid in 2004. Nevertheless, this is an area of political advertising to which scholars should pay closer attention, especially given the skyrocketing expenditures of independent groups in recent elections (Kaid and Dimitrova 2005).

Another issue in sponsorship was raised by the Bipartisan Campaign Reform Act 2002, which requires that candidates for federal office make explicit statements about the sponsorship of their ads (popularly known as the Stand-By-Your-Ad provision). Despite concerns that the requirement might cause voters to react negatively to candidates who sponsor negative ads, research to date has detected a *positive* effect for candidates, suggesting that the explicit attribution of an ad may increase the degree of respect for and confidence in the sponsor's claim (K. Patterson et al. 2005).

Apart from sponsorship, considerable evidence indicates that the content of negative advertising is related to its effectiveness. Specifically, negative ads that deal with the issue positions of the opposing candidate are usually more effective than those that criticize the opponent's character or image.[28] But when personal attacks are nonetheless made,[29] the sponsoring candidate may have greater success by focusing on the opponent's competence or experience (Homer and Batra 1994) or, better yet, by linking the character or image attack with a substantive issue. This strategy might explain the success of the 2004 Swift Boat ads, which questioned Kerry's experience and competence to be commander-in-chief and thereby denigrated his leadership on military and terrorism issues.

Rebuttal and Inoculation. When a candidate is attacked, whether on issues or personal qualities, rebuttals are an essential aspect of campaign strategy and have sometimes been successful in blunting attacks.[30] Although there may be certain situations in which rebuttals are not possible (perhaps because the charges are true) or in which they raise other undesirable concerns, an unanswered attack could lead voters to believe that the candidate who does not protest at all must surely be guilty. Research demonstrates the effectiveness of rebutting a claim directly and forcefully (Roddy and Garramone 1988), not indirectly or by trying to establish the targeted candidate's good points on the issue or image point being contested. For instance, Michael Dukakis may have been damaged in the 1988 presidential race by attacks on his prison furlough program while governor of Massachusetts (see Diamond and Bates 1992) because his campaign's original response dealt mainly with the Democrat's successes and leadership on crime issues generally—but did not address the specific charges made by his opponent.

Although it is no substitute for a direct rebuttal when attacked in a negative ad, inoculation can help to limit or sometimes even prevent serious damage resulting from an opponent's attacks.[31] A candidate who gets out his position early and often has a better chance of deflecting attacks and convincing voters that he or she is not guilty as charged when an attack does come. The offensive approach may also discourage attacks before they surface.

Program Positioning for Negative Advertising. The context in which negative advertising occurs can be important. Political time buyers have long believed that the relationship between program content or type and commercial content or type is important. DeVries and Tarrance (1972), for example, described the strategy for a Michigan gubernatorial race in which spots with drug and crime content were purposely (and successfully) aired during programs that themselves had themes of crime and violence. In 1980 Reagan's presidential campaign developed spots with a news or press conference format for use during or adjacent to local news shows (Diamond and Bates 1992). However, although product advertisers have conducted considerable research on the compatibility of programming and advertising content,[32] this topic has received little attention from political communication scholars. One notable exception is Kaid, Chanslor, and Hovind (1992), who found that negative political ads are more likely to affect vote decisions when shown in a news environment.

Negative Advertising and Democracy. Some political observers and research scholars insist that negative advertising has harmful effects on the American political system as a whole. The best-known claims in this regard are those that suggest exposure to negative ads leads to reduced voter turnout.[33] A number of researchers, however, have used the American National Election Studies and other survey data to contest the demobilization hypothesis, finding either no discernible effect of negative advertising on turnout rates[34]—or that increased negativity causes turnout to go up rather than down,[35] especially so long as the criticisms leveled are seen by voters as being legitimate and not mudslinging (Kahn and Kenney 1999).

In a similar vein, some researchers have claimed that exposure to negative advertising has other harmful effects on the political system, most notably by contributing to higher levels of political alienation, inefficacy, and cynicism toward government and the political process.[36] Once again, though, the evidence in support of this argument is neither consistent nor altogether persuasive.[37] Some researchers have attempted to apply the techniques of meta-analysis in hopes of establishing some general findings regarding the effects of negative advertising that transcend differences in methodology and measurement.[38] In particular, meta-analyses comparing negative ads with positive ads have not found any reason to believe that the former are necessarily superior (Allen and Burrell 2002; Lau et al. 1999; Lau, Sigelman, and Brown 2005).

Unfortunately, the narrow focus of this work limits its usefulness. Not only do the authors typically fail to consider a number of important political advertising studies, but they seem interested only in the question of whether negative ads are more effective than positive ads—something that, for political advertising practitioners, is surely not the point since negative ads can be independently effective (or not) regardless of whether positive ads are being aired. In reality, campaigns often involve combinations of positive and negative messages, which may be effective or ineffective either individually or in combination. Further, the meta-analyses ignore the importance of campaign context (such as incumbent-challenger candidate status and closeness of the race), as well as the implications of third-party or independent advertising effects, which previous studies have shown to be important determinants of the effectiveness of political advertising.

Conclusion

The present chapter has provided a limited review of the vast academic literature that deals with political advertising. Beyond the space and conceptual limitations of this analysis, for example, many studies address questions of political advertising effectiveness in noncandidate contests (including referendum and initiative elections) and in the arena of policy advocacy. Looking to the future, research on political advertising still has many avenues to explore. Of particular interest would be a reexamination of the credibility and effectiveness of advertising by third-party or independent sources. As mentioned earlier, the increased visibility of independent groups as sponsors of both positive and negative ads warrants closer scrutiny of the conditions under which such advertising is most effective.

Also, the expanded role of the Internet as a channel for political advertising messages will undoubtedly attract an increasing amount of research attention (see chapter 7 in this volume). Candidates, parties, individuals, and independent groups will all vie for voters' attention and involvement through this developing channel. Especially important will be the development of new formats that allow for interactivity and thus the opportunity for greater involvement and participation by ordinary citizens. The Internet, and other new technologies such as podcasting, will offer additional opportunities for candidates and parties to target messages to voters who have specific interests and characteristics. Political advertising is not going away any time soon, but the form it takes and the channels through which it is distributed will present new challenges for both scholars and practitioners.

Notes

1. Although television advertising is the primary focus of this chapter, I also report the results of some research findings regarding print advertising when those findings inform our understanding of the broader issues. I make no attempt to summarize or analyze the laws and regulations that affect political advertising in the American political system; for more details on these issues, see Kaid and Jones (2004).

2. See A. Johnston and Kaid (2002); Kaid (2005); Kaid and Dimitrova (2005).

3. Voters routinely express negative views of negative ad campaigns (Cook 2001; Devlin 1989; Guskind and Hagstrom 1988; Johnson-Cartee and Copeland 1989; Roddy and Garramone 1988). The news media contribute to these attitudes by regularly heaping criticism and focusing "ad watches" on instances of negative advertising (Tedesco, Kaid, and McKinnon, 2000; also see chapter 6 in this volume).

4. See Goldstein et al. (2001); Hale, Fox, and Farmer (1998); Kahn and Kenney (2000); Tinkham and Weaver-Lariscy (1990, 1995); Vavreck (2001).

5. See Atkin and Heald (1976); Craig, Kane, and Gainous (2005); Martinelli and Chaffee (1995); Ridout et al. (2004); Valentino, Hutchings, and Williams (2004).

6. See Bowers (1977); Herrnson and Patterson (2000); Roberts (1992); Sulfaro (2001); West (2001); Williams, Shapiro, and Cutbirth (1983).

7. See Roberts and McCombs (1994); Schleuder, McCombs, and Wanta (1991).

8. See Brians and Wattenberg (1996); Craig, Kane, and Gainous (2005); T. Patterson and McClure (1976); Zhao and Bleske (1995).

9. See Holbert et al. (2002); Just, Crigler, and Wallach (1990).

10. Differences in how researchers have measured voters' exposure to advertising, and especially the use of survey data (self-reports) to differentiate levels of exposure, have been an ongoing concern. Similar questions can be raised about the ways in which various studies control for the exposure to other types of information (obtained from television news, newspapers, and so on).

11. See Atkin and Heald (1976); Cundy (1986, 1990); Kaid (1991, 1997, 1998, 2001); Kaid and Chanslor (1995, 2004); Tedesco and Kaid (2003).

12. On campaign spending and candidate support generally, see Ansolabehere and Gerber (1994); Goldstein and Freedman (2000); Jacobson (1975); Joslyn (1981); Daron Shaw (1999b); Wattenberg (1982); Weaver-Lariscy and Tinkham (1987, 1996); on ballot proposition races, see Bowler and Donovan (1994) and chapter 8 in this volume.

13. Alternatively, it has been suggested (for example, see Zaller 1996) that media effects generally are most likely to be evident among individuals with intermediate (rather than unusually high or unusually low) levels of exposure or involvement.

14. See Brader (2005); Kaid (1991); Kaid and Chanslor (1995, 2004); Tedesco (2002); Tedesco and Kaid (2003).

15. See Kaid, Chanslor, and Hovind (1992); Kaid and Sanders (1978); Thorson, Christ, and Caywood (1991a, 1991b).

16. See Bucy and Newhagen (1999); Geiger and Reeves (1991); Lang (1991).

17. See Bystrom and Kaid (2002); Bystrom and Miller (1999); Kahn (1996); Procter and Schenck-Hamlin (1996); Proctor, Schenck-Hamlin, and Haase (1994); Robertson et al. (1999); Williams (1998).

18. Also see chapter 11 in this volume. Findings such as these suggest that voters do not reject negative campaigning in every instance. To the contrary, attacks based on a candidate's issue stands, criminal activities, and overall public record are generally considered acceptable, while those relating to personal matters (medical history, religion, sex life, family members, marital difficulties) are seen as being off limits (Johnson-Cartee and Copeland 1989; also see Freedman et al. 1999; Just et al. 1996; Lau et al. 1999). Likewise, in a 1998 survey of Florida voters, roughly 65 percent agreed (40 percent strongly) with the statement that "there's nothing wrong with political ads in which one candidate criticizes the other, so long as the information presented in the ad is truthful" (Craig and Kane 2000).

19. See Brians and Wattenberg (1996); Chang and Hitchon (2004); Johnson-Cartee and Copeland (1989); Kahn and Kenney (2000); Lang (1991); Newhagen and Reeves (1991); Sulfaro (1998).

20. See Basil, Schooler, and Reeves (1991); Hitchon and Chang (1995).

21. On lesser known candidates, see Kahn and Geer (1994); Mathews and Dietz-Uhler (1998). On more visible candidates, see Hill (1989); Hitchon, Chang, and Harris (1997); Kaid, Chanslor, and Hovind (1992); Merritt (1984).

22. See Brader (2005); Fridkin and Kenney (2004); Jasperson and Fan (2002); Kaid (1997); Kaid and Boydston (1987); Shen and Wu (2002); Tinkham and Weaver-Lariscy (1993).

23. Complicating matters here is the fact that incumbents may be affected differently from challengers (by their own ads as well as by those of their opponents), and that some types of negative ads (for instance, issue-based versus candidate trait; see Box 5.3) may have a greater impact than others. For example, see Fridkin and Kenney (2004); Tinkham and Weaver-Lariscy (1991).

24. See Ansolabehere and Iyengar (1995); Kaid (1997); Pfau et al. (1989); Pinkleton (1998); cf. Roddy and Garramone (1988). Negative advertising is potentially dangerous to the targeted candidate in part because support for that candidate may be undermined not only among independents or members of the opposing party but also among his or her own partisans and natural consistencies (Kaid and Boydston 1987).

25. See Brader (2005); Capella and Taylor (1992); Mathews and Dietz-Uhler (1998); Nickerson and Arceneaux (2005); M. Shapiro and Rieger (1992).

26. See Garramone (1984b); Haddock and Zanna (1997); Jasperson and Fan (2002); King and McConnell (2003); Lemert, Wanta, and Lee (1999); Martinez and Delegal (1990); Shen and Wu (2002); Sonner (1998).

27. See Garramone (1984b, 1985); Garramone and Smith (1984); Pfau et al. (2002); Shen and Wu (2002).

28. See Fridkin and Kenney (2004); Johnson-Cartee and Copeland (1989); Kahn and Geer (1994); Pfau and Burgoon (1989); Roddy and Garramone (1988); Sonner (1998).

29. Strategic considerations presumably govern most decisions about whether, when, and in what manner a campaign will go negative. See, for example, Damore (2002); Hale, Fox, and Farmer (1998); Haynes and Rhine (1998); Sellers (1998); Skaperdas and Grofman (1995); Theilmann and Wilhite (1998).

30. See Garramone (1985); Roddy and Garramone (1988); Sonner (1998).

31. See Pfau and Burgoon (1988); Pfau and Kenski (1990); Pfau et al. (2001).

32. See Kennedy (1971); Murphy, Cunningham, and Wilcox (1979); Soldow and Principe (1981).

33. See Ansolabehere and Iyengar (1995); Ansolabehere, Iyengar, and Simon (1999); Ansolabehere et al. (1994). Also see Lemert, Wanta, and Lee (1999).

34. See Clinton and Lapinski (2004); Finkel and Geer (1998); Wattenberg and Brians (1999).

35. See Freedman and Goldstein (1999); Goldstein and Freedman (2002a); Martin (2004); Vavreck (2000). Some studies indicate that this effect is more evident among certain groups and in certain elections, rather than across the board.

36. See Ansolabehere et al. (1994); Craig and Kane (2000); Kaid, McKinney, and Tedesco (2000); Schenck-Hamlin, Procter, and Rumsey (2000); Thorson et al. (2000).

37. See Garramone et al. (1990); Kaid (2002); Martinez and Delegal (1990); Pinkleton, Um, and Austin (2002). Also see Sigelman and Kugler (2003).

38. Meta-analysis is an approach that uses statistical techniques to combine the results of several different studies in order to provide a quantitative evaluation or summary of the effects of variables common to the studies.

6 Free Media in Campaigns

Erika Franklin Fowler and Kenneth M. Goldstein

Part of the reason I'm going around the country, by the way, is because not everyone gets their news from the national news. In all due respect to the national Pooh-Bahs, most people get their news from the local news. And if you're trying to influence opinion, the best way to do it is to travel hard around the country and give the people their dues.

—President George W. Bush
(Froomkin 2005)

Candidates for major political office in the United States, along with their party and interest group allies, spend most of their money airing political advertisements (paid media) and most of their time trying to attract favorable press attention (free media).[1] For scholars and practitioners alike, whether and how paid and free media matter for citizen engagement, knowledge, turnout, and voting behavior—and which mode of communication matters more—are some of the most compelling questions relating to the study of political communication and elections, and the allocation of resources in elections.

President Bush made the comments quoted at the beginning of this chapter in the midst of a campaign-style swing around the country in late spring of 2005 to promote proposed reforms in the Social Security system. Although they occurred well after his successful bid for reelection and he was not campaigning for any office at the time, the president's point is a crucial one for students of political communication who wish to understand the role of the media in elections. Much sound and fury surrounds the scores of political talk shows that appear on cable outlets such as CNN, Fox, CNBC, and MSNBC, and most scholarly studies of the news media focus on national newspapers like the *New York Times* or the national broadcast networks (ABC, CBS, and NBC). President Bush was correct, however, when he pointed out that "most people get their news from the local news."

Accordingly, the empirical focus of this chapter is on how local news covered politics during the 2002 and 2004 elections. We begin, though, by summarizing what is known about the impact of political communication in general and by outlining a logical framework for when we should expect to see media effects. We then discuss how these expectations should differ depending on the type or form of media involved (paid versus free, national versus local, print versus broadcast, and so on). Finally, we present data from a large-scale research project that tracked the volume and nature of local news in the 2002 and 2004 elections.

What We Know About Media Effects

The current scholarly consensus is that the media do play a role in helping to shape voter engagement, knowledge, turnout, and behavior, even if such effects are not evident for everyone equally at all times. This was not always the predominant view, as early studies of voting behavior consistently failed to find significant media effects on individual attitudes and voting decisions (Berelson, Lazarsfeld, and McPhee 1954; A. Campbell et al. 1960; Lazarsfeld, Berelson, and Gaudet 1944). In fact, most research concluded that the media tended to reinforce people's existing predispositions rather than change their minds. T. Patterson and McClure (1976) suggested that one reason researchers failed to observe any media effects was that campaign news coverage was generally presented as entertainment and therefore provided little real information. Advertisements, they concluded, often had more serious information than news (though they found little effect of either type of media).

Undeterred by the "minimal effects" scholarly conventional wisdom, however, campaign practitioners continued to focus much of their attention on (1) disseminating information via paid advertisements and (2) earning favorable coverage in the free media. Campaign expenditures continued to rise (see chapter 4 in this volume), and campaigns became even more focused on trying to hone and control their messages in the media. Partly due to the incongruity of millions of dollars being spent and countless staff hours being continually expended on efforts that most research suggested had little impact, scholarly investigations of media effects were renewed. An example is the work of Larry Bartels, who described the state of research on this topic as "one of the most notable embarrassments of modern social science" (Bartels 1993, 267). Indeed, Bartels's findings, combined with other recent studies, have largely discredited the notion of minimal effects. Conventional wisdom today acknowledges that the news media (along with paid ads) can have a direct effect on citizens' attitudes, knowledge, and levels of political engagement, as well as an indirect effect through agenda setting (determining which issues are regarded by the public as most important; see Iyengar and Kinder 1987) and the framing of issues (shaping the symbolic meaning of those issues and thus the way they are interpreted; see Iyengar 1987). However, as we noted earlier, the media do not affect all individuals equally at all times.

Media effects depend on an individual's exposure to a particular message, his or her reception of the message (which varies both by attention level and by political sophistication), and predispositions that may affect the person's likelihood of being influenced by the message. Whereas the probability of receiving (that is, understanding and accepting) a political message increases with one's degree of political sophistication, the probability of being influenced by that message actually decreases with sophistication. Consequently the people most likely to be influenced by media are those who possess a moderate—not too high, not too low—amount of political sophistication (Zaller 1992).

Consider, for example, two individuals. The first pays very little attention to politics, rarely watches the news, and thus knows relatively little about current affairs. We will refer to this individual as a *political novice,* someone with a low level of political sophistication. The second individual (the *political sophisticate*) pays a great deal of attention to politics, consumes lots of news, and is therefore quite knowledgeable about politics and current affairs. Media messages (in this case, campaign ads and campaign news stories) are most likely to affect the novice who knows little about politics and does not have strongly formed opinions on most issues; however, because the novice consumes very little news, he or she is unlikely to be exposed to the messages in the first place. The political sophisticate, in contrast, is likely to be exposed to a wide range of media messages given his or her attentiveness to current affairs; but because the sophisticate already has a multitude of information about any particular topic, one new piece of information in the media is much less likely to have an impact on his or her opinion than it is on the novice's. As a result, people who are most likely to be influenced by media messages are those located somewhere in between the novice and the sophisticate—specifically, citizens who pay a moderate amount of attention to politics.

Many scholars maintain that the study of media effects suffers from at least two major limitations: First, effects are difficult to measure, which makes them difficult for researchers to detect (Bartels 1993; Graber 1993); and second, even when measured well, communication flows—especially in a news media environment that favors "objective" journalism—are likely to be two sided, thereby canceling each other out (Zaller 1992). On the first point, in a perfect world we would have complete information regarding the viewing habits and attention spans of each citizen, comprehensive measures of the content of all messages viewed, and knowledge of how much of that information was actually received and retained. Unfortunately the research instruments available to us are not sufficient for observing all of these things. On the second point, we know from studies of persuasion that one-sided flows of communication are most effective in changing opinions; however, since most journalists strive for objective balance, news stories generally cover both sides of the issues (two-sided communication flows). In other words, we should expect the media to have a substantial persuasive effect on voters' attitudes only in campaigns when one side's message is dominant, and when readers or viewers do not already have strong predispositions toward one candidate.

Consider an example drawn from American politics today. A listener to Rush Limbaugh's daily radio program is certain to receive a steady flow of messages from one side of the partisan divide; in fact, Democrats and their supporters contend that Limbaugh and his comrades on conservative talk radio and the Fox News Network—including, for example, Sean Hannity, Michael Savage, and Bill O'Reilly—provide the political right with a huge advantage in terms of using the media to shape people's opinions. But do such personalities actually change minds on political issues?

In considering contemporary political talk radio, there can be little doubt that it is a medium dominated by conservatives. Both during and after elections, comments in favor of Republican policies and leaders, and against Democratic policies and leaders, clearly outnumber pro-Democrat or anti-Republican messages on that medium (Rutenberg 2003). Nevertheless, it is also true that most of those who follow Limbaugh and O'Reilly, in particular, are predisposed in the conservative or Republican direction to begin with; more than three-quarters (77 percent) of Limbaugh's regular audience call themselves conservatives, as do almost as many (72 percent) of those who watch O'Reilly (Pew Center for the People and the Press 2004a). Especially in the case of nontraditional media, many people selectively expose themselves to content that is consistent with their preexisting views, either left or right. It is therefore difficult to make claims about the causal effects of exposure to the types of media that tend to have one-sided flows of information (talk radio, Internet blogs, and ideologically slanted magazines such as *Mother Jones* and *National Review*). On the other hand, those who are most susceptible to being influenced are more likely to follow mainstream media and their relatively balanced flows of information (Pew Center for the People and the Press 2004a).

Despite these difficulties of interpretation, scholars have learned a great deal about how the news media can shape the policy agenda, prime particular attitudes, and frame public debate.[2] As noted earlier, one of the most powerful ways in which the media shape individual attitudes is through agenda setting; that is, media coverage of particular issues elevates the perceived importance of these issues on the national stage.[3] The more stories a person encounters about Social Security, for example, the more likely he or she is to believe that Social Security is one of the most important issues facing the country. Hence, the classic line that the mass media may not tell us what to *think,* but they do determine what we think *about.*

Priming, which involves the ability to affect the criteria or considerations used to evaluate political objects, is another way in which the media influences voter attitudes and decisions.[4] The basic principle here is that if an individual has recently viewed news reports about one particular issue (even if those reports do not discuss the issue's implications or connections with other issues), they are more likely to take it into account when expressing an opinion or giving an evaluation. For example, if people are exposed to a story (or several stories) concerning the economy and then are asked to evaluate the president, they are more likely to use the president's performance on economic issues in their evaluation because they have been "primed" to regard the economy as an important consideration.

Framing, another type of media effect, occurs whenever the manner in which a message is packaged or presented influences people's attitudes about an issue.[5] In this way, framing helps to define the terms of political debate concerning that issue. For example, T. Nelson, Clawson, and Oxley (1997) investigated two frames of tolerance relating to a rally organized by the Ku Klux Klan: one story discussed the rally as an issue of free speech, while the other framed it as a disruption of public order. As one might expect, participants who viewed the free speech story expressed a greater degree of tolerance for the KKK.

One aspect of framing is evident in news coverage of political campaigns (and of politics generally), with its greater emphasis on the competitive "game" aspect than on matters of public policy (also see chapter 2 in this volume). Campaign strategy and "horse-race" coverage that deals with who is up and who is down in the polls, and why, have come increasingly to dominate in both broadcast and print media since the early 1970s.[6] To a large extent, this approach reflects a story selection process that stresses excitement and entertainment above all else,[7] and it relies heavily on input from "expert" political analysts and spin doctors representing the various contenders.[8] The media also have a tendency to dwell on personal characteristics such as trustworthiness, leadership ability, and compassion, not always to the benefit of the candidates being portrayed.[9]

Some media critics complain that when campaigns, not to mention the political process as a whole, are depicted (framed) in this manner, it contributes to a mass public that is cynical about politics and disaffected from its elected leaders and governmental institutions.[10] In a narrower sense, the tone of campaign news coverage (that is, positive or negative) also can affect the candidates' relative standing in the polls and, ultimately, the outcome of the election itself.[11] Further, with their tendency to focus on conflict and controversy, the news media may give voters the impression that the campaign is more negative than it actually is.[12]

Academic research has shown that audiences generally learn more and are more likely to understand events when they are covered thematically (explicit connections being made between the specific case and other similar circumstances) rather than episodically (as a stand-alone occurrence that may seem to affect only those individuals who are immediately involved; see Iyengar 1991).[13] In practice, however, news coverage of isolated campaign events tends to overshadow broader issues and societal themes, which may help to explain why many studies fail to observe large media effects on citizens' attitudes or behavior. And although newspapers are often considered to be the gold standard for policy coverage (relative to their broadcast counterparts), recent work demonstrates that they are not necessarily more likely to focus on candidate positions on issues (Just, Crigler, and Buhr 1999); in fact, evidence suggests that voters learn more about what those positions are from paid ads than they do from either newspapers or television news (Craig, Kane, and Gainous 2005).

Differences in Media

Although much ink has been spilled in an effort to document media effects (in campaigns and elsewhere), relatively little attention has been paid to differences between media. Both theoretically and empirically, academic studies often fail to distinguish between paid and free media, between print and broadcast outlets, and between reporting that occurs at the national and local levels. Yet common sense tells us that the format, message, and intended goal of the communication are likely to vary substantially from paid to free, from newspaper to television, and from national to local.

Two important distinctions between free and paid media are frequently overlooked by scholars: The two forms differ, first, in their intended objective (to inform versus persuade) and, second, in the nature of exposure by citizens to messages (intentional versus unintentional)—with each factor, in turn, affecting the probable impact of those messages. Readers and viewers generally choose to expose themselves to news content, which increases the likelihood that messages will be received and understood. Although these conditions must be met in order for persuasion to occur, the goal of free media is not to persuade but rather to inform and engage the public at large. Some reporters and some stories may be slanted, but the professional norm for news reporters and producers is to convey information in an unbiased fashion. Setting aside occasional exceptions in which the information flow becomes one sided, the most common effect of news media in campaigns may be indirect, for example, advantaging one side or another through agenda setting or the priming of issues that benefit a particular candidate or party (see Petrocik 1996).

Paid media, in contrast, is designed primarily by practitioners to engage and persuade supporters and swing voters, respectively—not to affect the behavior of the electorate as a whole. Since we know that persuasion, in particular, depends on one-way communication flows (Zaller 1992), it is not surprising that explicitly biased content is the trademark of campaign advertising. However, citizens typically do not deliberately expose themselves to specific ads; instead, exposure is a consequence of something else (tuning into a television or radio program during which an ad is being aired, living in a neighborhood that has been targeted by a campaign to receive direct mail, and the like). Although this lack of purposive exposure could impede reception, advertising messages are easily packaged and produced in such a way as to ensure that viewers understand the central argument. As a result, it seems reasonable to assume that paid media will be more persuasive and influential than free media in shaping voter decisions, and the finding that ads often have more of an effect in this regard than news is to be expected. In addition, a byproduct or indirect effect of paid media is that it may inform the public by presenting a clear, cleanly packaged message that is easy to comprehend and retain (Freedman, Franz, and Goldstein 2004).

Scholars have probably paid the most attention to differences between broadcast and print media.[14] Nevertheless, it is worth spelling out these differences in some detail. As with paid versus free media, broadcast and print differ in terms of (1) the amount of attention required of consumers and (2) the intentionality of exposure to messages. As Chaffee and Schleuder (1986) pointed out, newspapers compel audience attention (it is difficult to read while thinking about other things) to a degree that television does not. Moreover, individuals must intentionally expose themselves to articles in a newspaper, picking and choosing which ones they will read. With broadcast media, people are not afforded the same luxury. Although there is certainly more intentional exposure involved with news broadcasts than with political advertisements, once an individual turns on the television (or radio) he or she is exposed to whatever the broadcast producers have decided is the news of the day. Attention to specific stories may vary but, in general, individuals who watch a news program are exposed to the full spectrum of news regardless of whether that was their intent.

Another difference between broadcast and print media is obvious: the extent to which the former depend on visuals. As a result, some observers believe that television news is vulnerable to being manipulated by the campaigns it is covering. According to Larry Sabato, "broadcast journalists especially seem trapped by their need for good video and punchy soundbites and with regret find themselves falling into the snares set by campaign consultants, airing verbatim the manufactured message and photo clip of the day" (Sabato 1994, 195). Further, if candidates do only one or two events a day and are disciplined about staying on message, the media has little choice but to cover what they are talking about. And if it is true that even network news producers sometimes cannot avoid helping the campaign to spread its message of the day, then the broadcast journalists who arguably are most likely to air these kinds of manufactured campaign "commercials" are local news stations that lack the resources (financial, personnel, experience) of the major networks.[15]

During the 2004 presidential race between George W. Bush and John Kerry, Kornblut and Klein (2004) wrote in the *Boston Globe,*

> It is impossible to correlate a candidate's travel schedule with his ability to win votes, but it is an article of faith in politics that visiting a targeted region helps draw support, generating mostly positive local news coverage and making local residents feel valued.

Accordingly, an article in the *New York Times* (Rich 2005) explained the reasoning behind one of the tactics used by the president's campaign:

> The pre-fab "Ask President Bush" town hall-style meetings held during last year's campaign (typical question: "Mr. President, as a child, how can I help you get votes?") were carefully designed for television so that, as Kenneth R. Bazinet wrote last summer in New York's *Daily News,* "unsuspecting view-

ers" tuning in their local news might get the false impression they were "watching a completely open forum."

Yet even though broadcast television may occasionally be maneuvered into airing well-crafted campaign visuals, a big difference remains between free broadcast media and paid broadcast media. Although campaigns clearly are able to influence some of what broadcast journalists put on the air, overall coverage of the campaign on the evening news is not crafted, not packaged, and not completely controlled by the candidates and their professional consultants.[16]

Another important distinction is between local and national free media, stemming primarily from the disparity in resources and expertise between local stations and newspapers and the major networks and newspapers. Local media often rely on affiliates to provide content and video and seldom have enough money to hire dedicated political journalists. As a consequence, many scholars and politicians alike view local news—in both print and broadcast—as softer (more features, less hard news) and more positive (less critical, fewer investigative stories) than their national counterparts (Graber 2005; Just et al. 1996). In addition, local and national free media obviously differ in the focus of their coverage. Local media usually make some effort to cover major national events as well as those taking place in their local or regional area. Jeffery Mondak (1995b) discovered, however, that the absence of a local newspaper (which happened to be on strike during the period covered by his study) did not lead to diminished knowledge (or perceptions of knowledge) at the national or international level but did have a negative effect on actual and perceived knowledge locally. In other words, local media may not contribute much to voters learning about national events and issues, but they certainly play a role in shaping political knowledge and awareness in their communities.

Limitations of Current Research

Although both scholars and practitioners know a little about the ways in which free media may matter in campaigns, they rely on different types of evidence that is often less than ideal. Scholarly research tends to focus on one race in a small number of media markets and generally examines only a single source of media information (either newspapers or national news). Practitioners, on the other hand, rely on their own experience and sometimes will overstate the influence of particular strategic media decisions in shaping electoral outcomes. The average citizen is not likely to attribute his or her voting decision to a specific media strategy or message; moreover, nobody experiences one campaign isolated from all others on the ballot, nor are voters exposed to just one source of political information regarding that campaign. Understanding the effects of this barrage of political information demands, first and foremost, a comprehensive knowledge of the full array of political messages delivered to voters. Researchers and political professionals alike must be able to sort out, by market and by race, the chaotic flurry of an election campaign in which candidates for president, governor, U.S. Senate, and U.S. House simultaneously compete against their opponents as well as others above and below them on the ballot to get their voices heard and messages out.

Further, one aspect of free media is often ignored completely in the study of campaigns and elections: local television news. As noted earlier, the vast majority of scholarly work on media effects has focused on national outlets: ABC, CBS, and NBC on the television side, and the *New York Times* and *Wall Street Journal* on the print side (though the growing availability of archives has made research utilizing local newspapers more common in recent years). This overwhelming focus in free media research on national sources is problematic for two reasons. The first, and perhaps most obvious, reason has to do with changes in the media environment over the past several decades, especially with the rise of cable television and corresponding declines in both network viewership and newspaper readership. With the wide variety of options that Americans now have for getting their news, it is no wonder that network television news ratings and newspaper subscriptions have dropped (see Figures 6.1, 6.2, and 6.3).

Possibly the most important reason why a scholarly focus on national television and newspapers is problematic, however, has to do with the oft-ignored fact that most people get most of their information about politics and current events from local television news. According to recent surveys, roughly eight in ten Americans (79 percent) regularly watch television news programs, and a majority (59 percent) report that they watch local news regularly, a substantially higher proportion than for any other news source (Pew Center for the People and the Press 2004a). Similarly, almost three-quarters (74 percent) obtain their information about national and international affairs from television, and of those who use television as their primary source, more people report getting their news locally than from any one of the three national networks (Pew Center for the People and the Press 2005).[17] Approximately three-quarters of the American public (76 percent) also report getting their election information from television, and once again more of them receive this information from local news than from cable programming or any of the three net-

Figure 6.1 Cable Television News Audience Growth, 1989–2003

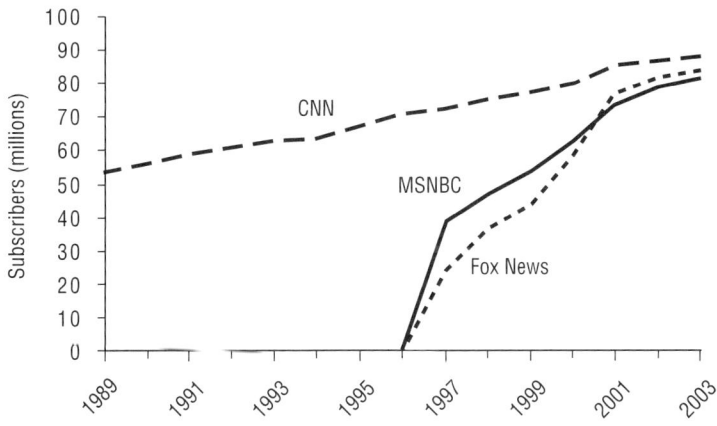

Source: Kagan Research, unpublished data, www.kagan.com (see also www.stateofthenewsmedia.org).

works (Pew Center for the People and the Press 2004b). Yet even though citizens watch local television more than any other news source and report receiving their information about political, national, and international affairs primarily from local news, few systematic studies have examined the content and effects of local broadcast news.

Studying Local News Coverage of Campaigns and Elections

Given the prevalence of local television news as a source of information for most Americans, the dearth of academic research on the topic is puzzling at best. On the other hand, although political consultants and policy makers have paid a great deal of attention to local television news and its potential (or perceived) effects, academics, consultants, and public policy makers all share a common problem: lack of appropriate data to support or refute any claims. More specifically, there has been no systematic capture and storage of local news coverage. The existence and growing accessibility of both newspaper and national news archives have proved to be a valuable resource for citizens, policy makers, and scholars alike over the years. Until recently, however, nothing comparable existed for local television news.

Figure 6.2 U.S. Daily Newspaper Circulation Versus Number of Households, 1940–2000

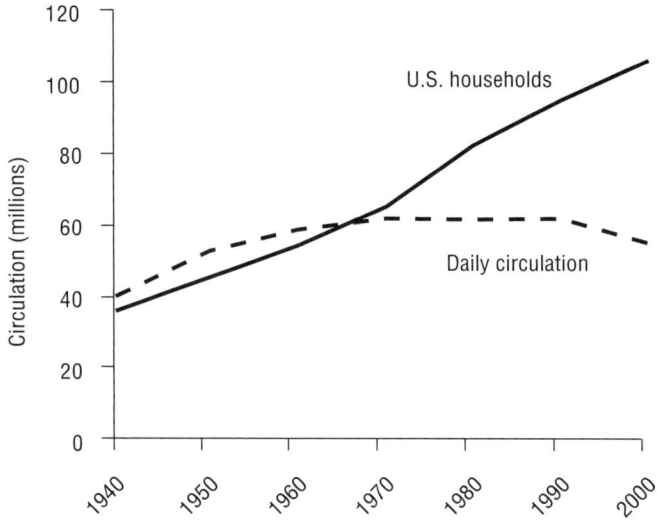

Source: Editor and Publisher Yearbook data; U.S. Census Bureau (see also www.stateofthenewsmedia.org).

The lack of good, comprehensive data on local television news across the country is a problem for scholars, practitioners, and reformers alike because little is known about the content and effectiveness of the media most often consumed by the general public. Thus, on the academic side, the absence of data has led the few researchers who study state- or market-level communication flows to focus on local news in a limited number of media markets (Graber 1993; Just et al. 1996; Just, Crigler, and Buhr 1999) or to ignore local television news information altogether in favor of newspapers or national news (Beck et al. 2002; Kahn and Kenney 1999), where data are more readily available. Results of the former, while a step in the right direction, cannot be generalized to local television across the country, and the latter solution further compounds the gap between media use and academic attention. For scholars hoping to understand how different types of political communication influence citizen engagement, knowledge, turnout, and vote choice, this lack of information on the volume and content of local news coverage of politics has presented a serious impediment to the study of media and campaign effects.

Figure 6.3 Evening News Viewership, All Networks, 1980–2004

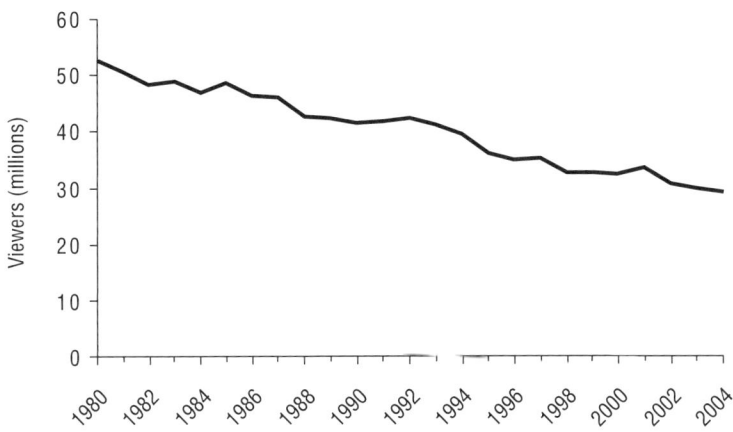

Source: Nielsen Media Research, unpublished data, www.nielsenmedia.com; ratings taken for month of November (see also www.stateofthenewsmedia.org).

Campaigns and politicians, for their part, are increasingly devoting time to garnering favorable coverage on local broadcasts, as evidenced by President Bush's comments presented at the beginning of this chapter. In fact, recent history is replete with examples of politicians going over the heads of national media outlets to tell their story to local television reporters, who are generally less critical than their national counterparts (Graber 2005; Kernell 1986). Political consultants clearly believe that free media matter (otherwise they would not devote so much time and effort to gaining favorable coverage), yet even practitioners know little about the effects of local news—a situation compounded by the lack of data similar to those available for advertising. Whereas campaigns routinely use focus groups and opinion polls to test the effectiveness of individual paid spots, and simultaneously monitor the ad buys of both friends and foes,[18] practitioners have a much harder time even tracking news coverage, let alone testing its influence.

For policy makers, a great deal of public attention has been devoted to a discussion of how to improve the quality and quantity of election coverage. In 1998 the President's Advisory Committee on Public Interest Obligations of Digital Television Broadcasters (otherwise known as the Gore Commission, a group that brought together industry leaders and various public interest representatives) sent a list of recommendations to Vice President Al Gore regarding the obligations that digital broadcasters should be expected to assume. These recommendations involved, for example, the establishment of permanent funding for public broadcasting, adoption of a voluntary code of conduct for broadcasters (one aspect of which would involve disclosure of stations' public interest programs and activities), and the volunteering of five minutes per night of free air time for use by candidates during the thirty days prior to an election. Most proposed reforms, including those made by the Gore Commission, have been based on the premise that more issue-based campaign coverage will lead to a more informed and active electorate, thereby improving the quality of democracy in America; however, policy discussions of this sort (including the more recent debate concerning media ownership) are typically based on anecdotal information and impressionistic assessments.[19] However, in the absence of systematic data on the nature of local news across the country, evidence cannot be brought to bear either supporting or refuting policy recommendations of any kind.

To understand the effect of media on citizens, the actions of political strategists in anticipation and in response to news coverage, as well as how one might improve the quality or quantity of election coverage, we first need to understand the nature, focus, and tenor of local news. For better or for worse, campaigns today are often hyper-targeted (with specific messages, from television and radio ads to direct mail, being directed to specific audiences) and that has consequences for citizens and practitioners alike. In recognition of this changed communications environment, scholars have certainly become better at identifying the dynamics of targeted political advertising. Research on the content and effectiveness of local news is, however, long overdue—not only for scholars but also for practitioners and policy makers who similarly lack evidence concerning local television, the primary source of information for most Americans. With this in mind, we now present some data from the last two election cycles regarding the content of local news across the country.

In the 2002 and 2004 elections, the NewsLab at the University of Wisconsin-Madison captured and archived a large sample of local news content.[20] For six weeks leading up to the midterm elections in 2002 (September 18 through November 4), NewsLab captured and analyzed the highest-rated early- and late-evening broadcasts from a representative sample of 122 stations in the top fifty media markets, covering 66.81 percent of the nation's television audience.[21] In 2004, NewsLab captured and analyzed 6.5 hours of programming

(5:00 to 11:30 P.M.) from every station in eleven markets (covering 23 percent of television viewers in the nation) for four weeks preceding the election (October 4 through November 1).[22]

For both studies, every captured broadcast was reviewed and election stories were analyzed on a range of variables, from office sought to type of coverage (strategy, issue, horse-race, and so on), story tone (positive, negative, balanced, or value neutral), and length of candidate sound bites. In 2004 the video of each story along with the coded data were made available on a web-based searchable archive. Together these two data sets represent the most comprehensive and systematic collection of campaign news coverage on local television stations ever gathered. Understanding and cataloguing what airs on local news is crucial for government policy makers who are responsible for regulating local news coverage, as well as for social scientists who wish to build valid measures of media exposure and to gauge the effects of this important source of political information. Such measures demand a record of what is aired at the market level and what individuals watch in these markets—information that, at least at the content level, has not previously been available.[23]

Volume of Coverage

On the 10,066 broadcasts tracked over the course of the 2002 midterm election, a total of 7,460 campaign stories aired. In 2004 NewsLab found 6,994 campaign stories on the 4,033 broadcasts analyzed. The impressive aggregate numbers notwithstanding, fewer than half (44 percent) of the local news broadcasts aired during the 2002 election in the country's fifty largest markets contained a campaign news story. Coverage in 2004 increased, however, with almost two-thirds of all broadcasts (64 percent) containing at least one such story, although most of this increase was devoted solely to presidential coverage. For the two elections combined, the average length of a campaign story was just under a minute and a half (89 seconds in 2002 and 86 seconds in 2004). Despite the increase in coverage for the 2004 election, the amount of time given to candidates to state their case in their own words did not change: fewer than three in ten stories (28 percent) showed a candidate speaking, and the average length of a candidate sound bite was a mere 12 seconds in both 2002 and 2004.

Breakdown of Coverage

In 2004 NewsLab tracked the subject of all stories (election related and otherwise) on forty-four local news stations plus the three major networks. A typ-

Table 6.1 Breakdown of Typical Hour of News Coverage in 2004

	Local News	National News
Advertising	8 minutes, 51 seconds	9 minutes, 16 seconds
Sports/Weather	6 minutes, 21 seconds	0 minutes, 55 seconds
Elections	3 minutes, 11 seconds	8 minutes, 15 seconds
Crime	2 minutes, 34 seconds	0 minutes, 37 seconds
Local Interest	1 minute, 56 seconds	0 minutes, 21 seconds
Teaser/Intro/Intro Music	1 minute, 43 seconds	1 minute, 40 seconds
Health	1 minute, 22 seconds	1 minute, 39 seconds
Unintentional Injury	0 minutes, 55 seconds	0 minutes, 10 seconds
Business/Economy	0 minutes, 47 seconds	0 minutes, 57 seconds
Political/Government (nonelection)	0 minutes, 28 seconds	0 minutes, 46 seconds
Iraq	0 minutes, 25 seconds	2 minutes, 59 seconds
Foreign Policy	0 minutes, 13 seconds	1 minute, 22 seconds
Other	1 minute, 12 seconds	1 minute, 2 seconds

Source: NewsLab, University of Wisconsin-Madison.

ical half-hour for both local and national news broke down as shown in Table 6.1. Election coverage was the most prominent type of news story for national news, and it ranked second only to sports and weather on local news. Of the three minutes and eleven seconds of election coverage on local news, however, a full two minutes of that time was filled by coverage of the presidential race, with just thirty seconds of the remaining time being devoted to other races at the local, state, and federal levels. In other words, coverage of local races on local television news was scarce.

Focus of Coverage

In both presidential and midterm elections, local news election coverage is dominated by the top-of-the-ticket race. In 2002, coverage of gubernatorial races appeared in roughly four out of every ten stories (38 percent). By contrast, U.S. Senate coverage was far less prominent (20 percent of stories), and fewer than one in ten stories (7 percent) were about candidates for the U.S. House of Representatives. In fact, reporting on all local races (including U.S. House, state legislative, other county and municipal races, and so on) made up less than 15 percent of all election coverage.

Similarly, stories about the presidential race dominated the airwaves in 2004. Over half (55 percent) of all broadcasts contained at least one such story, and presidential stories made up almost two-thirds (61 percent) of all election coverage. Although ten of the eleven markets captured in the 2004 study had a race for U.S. Senate, only 6 percent of broadcasts had a story about that race, and overall these stories accounted for only 4 percent of the total. In Los Angeles, the local news on all networks devoted less time to the Senate race in a month than they collectively gave to teasers and bumper music in a single night. The skew in coverage improved slightly in markets where the Senate race was competitive. In Denver, for example, just over one out of every ten broadcasts (12 percent) contained a story about Colorado's tightly contested open-seat contest. Even so, local television news stations in Denver devoted roughly six times more coverage to crime, and twice as much time to accidental injuries, compared with their coverage of the Senate race.

Moreover, coverage of all local races in the ten markets captured made up less than one-tenth (8 percent) of total election coverage. In fact, eight times more coverage during local news broadcasts went to stories that dealt with accidental injuries, and twelve times more coverage went to sports and weather than to stories about local political campaigns. For policy-minded individuals, however, a notable difference existed between the stations in the 2004 sample that took a public pledge to provide free air time and those that did not. The twenty stations that pledged to provide free air time to candidates aired almost twice the amount of local political coverage compared with the twenty-four stations that did not take the pledge.

Type of Coverage

Scholars and media critics alike have decried the news media's focus on campaign strategy and the horse-race at the expense of more detailed coverage of candidates' issue positions and policy proposals (Bartels 1988; Graber 2005; T. Patterson 1993). Coverage of the 2002 and 2004 election cycles lends support to the critics. The following U.S. Senate story, which aired on Denver NBC affiliate station KUSA on the evening of October 31, 2004, was fairly typical of horse-race coverage that aired across the country.

> *Anchor:* A final 9 News poll shows Colorado's race for U.S. Senate to be a toss-up. It confirms what Republican Pete Coors and Democrat Ken Salazar have been saying all campaign long, that their race would be extremely close. 9 News Reporter Adam Schrager joins us now. Adam, the statewide survey was conducted at the end of last week.
>
> *Adam Schrager:* It was, from last Thursday through yesterday. 622 likely Colorado voters were surveyed about their preference for Colorado's next U.S. senator. Their answers showed election night could be a long one for both supporters of Coors and Salazar. The likely voters who were asked by Survey USA if the election for U.S. senator from Colorado were today, who would

you vote for? 49 percent chose Salazar, the state's attorney general, 47 percent chose Coors, the head of his family brewery, 3 percent chose other candidates. The margin of error [was] 4 percent. Survey USA describes the race as a tie. Now, this rollercoaster of a race has been close for the last couple of months. Back in August when Survey USA started tracking the race, the candidates found themselves in a statistical tie. Since then, Coors has inched ahead a couple of times but each time, Salazar has pulled even, and in the case of today's results moved ahead ever so slightly just before Election Day.

As illustrated by the text of the story here, strategy and horse-race coverage generally has little to do with the issue and policy substance of the campaign. Moreover, these kinds of stories, which contain little to no relevant issue information to help citizens with their voting decisions, are far more prevalent than stories with information on the policy stances of the candidates.

Strategic or horse-race coverage of the 2002 midterm campaign was nearly twice that given to substantive issues. Almost half (47 percent) of the election stories aired in the top fifty markets during the period of the study focused on campaign strategy or the horse-race (who is winning and losing), while fewer than one in four (24 percent) dealt with issues and only 3 percent were ad-watch stories.[24] In 2004 strategy and horse-race coverage comprised nearly half (44 percent) of all election stories; issue reporting was up slightly from the midterm, however, with almost a third (32 percent) of campaign stories overall. Ad-watch coverage was nearly nonexistent in 2004, constituting less than 1 percent of the total.

Conclusion

As we noted at the outset of this chapter, the big question for both scholars and practitioners in media studies is one of effect: Do the media matter? Does political advertising or political news coverage influence voters' attitudes and behaviors and, ultimately, help to shape election outcomes? By their actions, candidates and consultants obviously believe that the money they spend on paid media and the efforts they expend trying to secure favorable free media matter quite a lot. They think that the media are a crucial way to convey messages and to prime the most appealing attributes of their candidates. Although "minimal effects" was the reigning conventional wisdom among scholars for many years, such wisdom today holds that political communication can shape the policy agenda, prime specific attitudes, frame public debate, and have the most influence on people who are neither political novices nor political sophisticates.

Still, scholars remain somewhat circumspect, realizing that selective viewer exposure and the general balance of competing messages in competitive campaigns or mainstream media are likely to dampen observed effects. As academic research goes forward in studying and analyzing the influence of media, we have made two major arguments in this chapter. On the theoretical side, we have maintained that scholars need to distinguish between paid and free media when they test for effects. On the empirical side, we have emphasized that local news is the single most important source of news for most Americans. Practitioners and politicians, from the president on down, understand this. Acknowledging the importance of local news is not enough, however. More data detailing the content and tenor of local news are needed, because only with such data can we adequately measure overall media effects in elections.

Our overview of the 2002 and 2004 elections revealed that election information on the single most frequently consumed source of media, local television news, is far from abundant. And when election stories do air, they tend to focus primarily on strategic and horse-race aspects of the campaign at the expense of substantive issue coverage. On the positive side, the overall partisan balance on local news is roughly equal in terms of both number of stories and airtime. In other words, although election coverage on local television news may be relatively scarce and superficial, it does not appear to be biased.[25] More worrisome is the fact that presidential and gubernatorial coverage dominated news coverage across the country, while candidates for Congress (especially the House of Representatives) and for lower office generally received little or no coverage on local news.

As we conclude, there is one additional point to make. It is our sense that there may be more agreement than disagreement between scholars and practitioners regarding media effects in campaigns. Both groups believe that certain fundamental factors drive political attitudes and election outcomes, most notably voters' partisan attachments and the condition of the national economy. Even with better theory and more broad and precise measures of exposure to different sorts of political communication, media (both paid and free) are likely to matter mainly at the margin, influencing perhaps 1, 2, or 3 percent of the vote in any given election. In comparison with other factors, those are minimal effects indeed. At the same time, however, political strategists can do relatively little (at least in the short term) to influence the distribution of partisanship, inflation or unemployment rates, or a variety of other issues and events both nationwide and around the world that may determine how people vote. Instead, they focus on what they *can* affect: paid and free media. The results of their efforts are usually evident only at the margin, but in a country divided fairly evenly between the two major parties, as the United States is currently, the margin matters. To paraphrase Bill Clinton, the difference between practitioner and scholarly perceptions when it comes to media effects may just depend on what you mean by *matter*.

THE CONSULTANTS RESPOND ABOUT

PAID AND FREE MEDIA

Although it has been the subject of considerable scholarly research (see especially chapter 5), campaign advertising *per se* did not inspire many comments by the consultants who attended our conference. As previously noted, a few mentioned it either as a strategic consideration (involving decisions about when and how to go negative) or, more commonly, in terms of the kinds of ads to which voters are most likely to be responsive.

Driving home a point made in chapter 3 in "The Consultants Respond" box, about issues versus character (and Republican versus Democrat):

INDEPENDENT POLITICAL ANALYST. Republican ads really focus on character early on, either defining their own candidate or basically undercutting the Democratic candidate . . . like, he hits puppies and pushes older people down the stairs. So ultimately, when the issue segment comes up the response is, "Why should I trust this senior-pushing, dog-hitting person. I don't care what he says about Social Security because he seems like a bad person over all."

DEMOCRATIC MEDIA CONSULTANT. Issues are being used to say something about a candidate. Social Security is a great example. A typical Democratic ad on Social Security talks about the program and focuses on forward-looking seniors lamenting the loss of their Social Security and looking out rainy windows and seeing lots of Social Security cards being ripped apart. But what does a good Republican ad on Social Security feature? The candidate's mother or grandmother saying, "My boy would never cut or privatize Social Security. He loves his mother." And that's the impression voters get, too: "He loves his mother, and I don't think he'll cut Social Security because his mother wouldn't go on television and say that. And more importantly, I didn't see his opponent's mother."

One consultant referred to advertising in challenging the prevailing view (see "The Consultants Respond" box in chapter 4) that early money is necessarily the best money in campaigns:

REPUBLICAN POLLSTER. A lot of people say they're going to run early media, the

continues...

logic being that they want to be on TV early when there's less clutter. They don't want to be on in the last week because they say, "Well, the sheriff has his ad on in the last week and we don't want to put our fancy U.S. Senate ad up at the same time." Sometimes my thinking is, "Wait a second here. Maybe voters really don't get interested in this process until enough ads get on and there's enough clutter that it wakes them up and they understand that there's a race going on." If you're running ads in July, it could be that they're like, "What is that? I didn't get it. I don't have my political voter hat on right now."

Most comments on this topic, however, dealt with so-called free (or earned) media. In general, the press is regarded as being potentially influential but not usually very good in its campaign coverage. As for influence:

INDEPENDENT POLITICAL ANALYST (discussing a congressional race in Chicago that involved a thirty-five-year incumbent). There was no serious presidential race going on, so the local media fell in love with this other race; the campaign actually had two or three local camera crews with them every day. Now, first of all, that doesn't happen to congressional candidates, and it certainly doesn't happen in the Chicago market. In fact, the media helped drive the campaign, this underdog candidate. Each party's campaign committee spent lots of money on ads, but that was nothing compared to the effect the local media had in propelling the challenger forward.

And as for the quality of coverage:

DEMOCRATIC MEDIA CONSULTANT. I'm highly critical of the way local media covers campaigns. The news seems to isolate campaigns that are extraordinary in one way or another, which I don't find at all unusual. That's how the media covers everything. You don't read stories every day about the 10,000 planes that landed on time and let everybody off safely, but when a plane crashes it gets all the coverage. And when you do hear a story about the planes landing, it's in the context of a story about how late they are. The media simply love conflict, they love an extraordinary story and rarely report on the normal or the routine. When the number-one basketball team in the nation loses, that's the lead story on the sports in almost every market in the country. When the number-one team wins a game, it's buried somewhere.

Saying that things have been getting worse rather than better, this same consultant continued:

DEMOCRATIC MEDIA CONSULTANT. The quality of television news coverage of campaigns has declined over time because, in my opinion, the people doing the coverage are more likely to come to it with almost no background in print journalism, and no classical training in political science. They get assigned to the beat for an assortment of other reasons, but not because they bring to it any intuitive knowledge of [for example] how Congress works and therefore they're qualified to cover congressional elections on the local level.... The quality of coverage is directly related to the backgrounds and expertise and experience of the journalists who cover it and the news directors who assign them. And that's a facet of coverage that needs more study because I think it's just hitting rock bottom, and I don't see it getting better any time soon.

A few consultants also commented, more or less respectfully, on the role of media campaign ad-watches (see chapter 5):

REPUBLICAN POLLSTER. They're impactful in the sense that when you're working in different states, you tend to be more mindful of the states that do have them. You kind of think, "OK, what is George (the guy who writes the ad-watch) going to say? What bothers George?" But that's not the same as saying they're impactful with voters. My guess is that this is so far down the food chain in respect to what most voters read.... In terms of true undecided voters, watching the ad-watches and making some kind of value judgment about whether a candidate is honest or forthright, I just don't think that [plays much of a role]. Still, even though I'm not sure why we care if we get a bad ad-watch, we do try to avoid them if we can.

DEMOCRATIC MEDIA CONSULTANT. I'll tell you why we care if we get a bad ad-watch. It's not because we think any voter will actually read it—it's because we assume the ad-watch will show up in our opponent's next ad when they go about discrediting the ad we just created. Although we don't sit around wondering what so-and-so who might write the ad-watch is going to think about this, we do think about it much harder than people in our profession thought about it fifteen or twenty years ago. While they may not do much to educate voters (because voters don't really pay much attention to them), they've served the purpose they were originally intended to serve, which is to hold media consultants' feet to the fire in terms of meeting some level of credibility on the claims they make in their advertising. So I think they serve a useful purpose, even if I disagree with some of the analysis.

Notes

1. Our friends who work as political consultants or in public relations take umbrage at the idea that there is any such thing as *free media;* instead, they prefer to use the term *earned media* when describing press coverage received by candidates during their campaigns.

2. See Entman (1989); Iyengar (1987, 1991); Iyengar and Kinder (1987); Kellstedt (2000); Krosnick and Kinder (1990); T. Patterson (1993).

3. See Entman (1989); Erbring, Goldenberg, and Miller (1980); Iyengar and Kinder (1987).

4. See Iyengar and Kinder (1987); Krosnick and Kinder (1990); Valentino (1999).

5. See Iyengar and Kinder (1987); Nelson, Clawson, and Oxley (1997); Tversky and Kahneman (1981).

6. See Bartels (1988); Goldstein, Fowler, and Rivlin (2004); Graber (2005); Just et al. (1996); T. Patterson (1993).

7. See Graber (2005). More generally, soft news (otherwise known as infotainment news) is increasingly replacing hard news on all major media outlets, though it does not yet account for a majority of coverage (T. Patterson 2000).

8. See Blumler and Kavanagh (1999); Kerbel (1999); Esser, Reinemann, and Fan (2001).

9. See Just, Crigler, and Buhr (1999); T. Patterson (1980); Robinson and Sheehan (1983). Candidates rarely speak for themselves in today's free media and, when they do, their sound bites are typically brief (Hallin 1992; Just et al. 1996; Kendall 1995). Perhaps surprisingly, newspapers are the medium that appears to afford the least amount of time or space to candidate sound bites (Just, Crigler, and Buhr 1999).

10. See Cappella and Jamieson (1997); Fallows (1996).

11. See Farnsworth and Lichter (1999); T. Patterson (1980, 1993).

12. See Just, Crigler, and Buhr (1999); Pelika and Fowler (2004).

13. An example of episodic coverage would be when a story features a few individuals who lost their jobs and the difficulties they have encountered in finding new work. In contrast, thematic coverage would be if that same story about job loss linked the individuals' predicament to rising unemployment and the difficulty of finding work in the nation as a whole.

14. See Chaffee and Schleuder (1986); Just et al. (1996); Just, Crigler, and Buhr (1999).

15. For a discussion of resource discrepancies between network and local news stations, see Graber (2005); Kaniss (1991).

16. For a discussion of how media goals differ from the goals of candidates and politicians generally, see Graber (2005).

17. In addition, Americans view local television news as more fact-oriented than any other news source, including local and national newspapers, national network news, cable outlets, morning news shows, Internet blogs, and talk radio (Pew Center for the People and the Press 2005).

18. Campaigns can purchase tracking data on political advertisements (from companies such as Campaign Media Analysis Group) that detail exactly when, where, and on what program particular ads of opponents, interest groups, and party organizations are aired. This information, along with transcripts of the ads, allows campaigns to adjust their own advertising strategies accordingly.

19. On June 2, 2003, the Federal Communications Commission (FCC) voted to relax the rules governing media ownership, allowing fewer corporations to own more television stations and newspapers in most cities. The 3–2 party-line vote was hotly contested by interest groups and a bipartisan group of lawmakers, who feared that the new rules would give a handful of media conglomerates too much control over the airwaves and shut out diverse views. In September 2003, the day before the rules were supposed to go into effect, the U.S. Court of Appeals for the 3rd Circuit in Philadelphia issued a stay, concluding that the FCC had not provided sufficient justification for its actions. In January 2005, faced with mounting opposition, the FCC along with the Bush administration abandoned plans to ask the Supreme Court to put the rules in place (see Ahrens 2005), thereby effectively putting the issue on hold.

20. For more information, see www.localnewsarchive.org.

21. Early-evening newscasts aired from 4:00 P.M. to 7:30 P.M., late-evening newscasts from 9:00 P.M. to 11:30 P.M.

22. In 2002, broadcasts in all markets were captured by stringers with DVD recorders. In 2004, however, media servers, located physically in each of the eleven markets, electronically captured television news programming from the four major affiliate stations (ABC, CBS, Fox, and NBC) from 5:00 P.M. to 11:30 P.M. every evening and divided it into thirty-minute segments of digitally recorded video. These segments from each day's captured programming (572 segments, 286 hours of news per day) were sent overnight via the Internet to the University of Wisconsin's NewsLab main servers, which have over a terabyte of storage capacity. Once the content arrived in Madison, each segment was viewed and clipped into individual news stories; election-related stories were subsequently coded and made available by the next evening on an online searchable archive similar to LexisNexis, where users could search for any type of coverage and view video from individual stories.

23. For a recent discussion of the difficulties inherent in developing these types of indicators, see Goldstein and Ridout (2004); Craig, Gainous, and Kane (2005).

24. Ad-watch stories are ones in which a newscaster analyzes the veracity of statements made in political advertisements, generally providing data that support, refute, or modify each claim. A variation on the same theme is the "debate-watch" story, which assesses candidate statements made in debates. For a discussion of the benefits of ad-watch stories, see Milburn and Brown (1995).

25. See Goldstein, Fowler, and Rivlin (2004) for a content analysis of partisan bias. As noted earlier, survey evidence indicates that Americans view local television news as more fact oriented than any other news source (Pew Center for the People and the Press 2005).

7 Campaigning on the Internet

Dennis W. Johnson

The 2004 presidential election reached a new plateau for online political campaigning and election activities. Record amounts of campaign dollars were raised over the Internet. Candidates and political parties reached millions of committed and potential voters through sustained e-mail communications. Web logging, or blogging, came into its own as a way for citizens to communicate directly with one another about politics, and campaigns created the new staff position of blogmaster to facilitate the flow of communication with supporters.[1] Outside organizations, particularly the so-called 527 groups (see chapter 4 in this volume), used blogging, e-mail, and their web sites to motivate activists and mobilize get-out-the-vote drives. More than ever before, the Internet was peppered with bombast and unfounded, caustic, and negative charges.

Months before any votes were cast, former governor Howard Dean of Vermont became the hands-down front-runner and expected Democratic nominee for president. By linking up with Meetup.com, his campaign was able to create both virtual and real communities of supporters throughout the country, and his one-time campaign manager bragged about the ability of the Internet to "overthrow everything," asserting that "this revolution will not be televised" (Trippi 2004). In the end, however, the Dean campaign famously crashed and burned, while the other Democratic candidate most heavily dependent on online communications and fundraising, Rep. Dennis Kucinich of Ohio, barely made a dent in the public's consciousness. Probably the best use of online communications came not from an insurgent candidate but from the Bush-Cheney campaign and the Republican National Committee.

Campaigning on the Internet has come a long way from its first tentative years during the early 1990s, but in comparison to television advertising, targeting, survey research, or any of the other aspects of modern campaigning, it is still the newcomer, in its formative stages. For years, proponents of online communications touted e-mail and web sites as revolutionary campaign tools that would change forever the way campaigns were conducted. Others have predicted that thanks to the Internet whole new communities of politically active people would emerge, that we could look forward to the day when online voting was commonplace, and that eventually our democratic system might cut out the middlemen of legislators and bureaucrats and go directly to the people through national electronic referenda.

Over the years, several widely publicized events have suggested that the Internet and online communications were going to play an important new role in campaigns and elections, including

- An extraordinarily successful e-mail campaign for the abolition of land mines
- Online protest movements against the World Trade Organization
- An estimated 20 million people worldwide who viewed the 1998 Starr Report over the Internet[2]
- A new online grassroots organization, Moveon.org, that sprang to life in response to President Clinton's impeachment trial
- Outsider candidate Jesse Ventura claiming the governorship of Minnesota in part because of savvy use of the Internet
- Senator John McCain's success in raising two million dollars over the Internet in a matter of days during the 2000 Republican primaries

Certainly, something was going on during this period, though it was unclear whether we were at the beginning of a major revolution in campaigns and citizen mobilization or simply being dazzled by electronic hyperbole.

There also have been critics and skeptics, among both professional consultants and social scientists. In the early years of online campaigning, many consultants acknowledged that Internet campaigning and electronic mail were important new tools but insisted that they would take their place merely as two more arrows in the quiver of campaign tools and techniques. Some social scientists, too, looked skeptically at online communications and adopted a wait-and-see attitude. But social science research remains in the preliminary rounds of investigation, with many more questions still to be addressed and researched. The 2004 campaign added a rich new layer of online campaigning experience, and gave both political consultants and social scientists many things to consider.

Research on Campaigns and the Internet

The use of online communications in political campaigns essentially began with the Clinton-Gore campaign in 1992, and the first campaign web site for a major candidate was launched in 1995 by Sen. Diane Feinstein, D-Calif. Republican presidential candidate Bob Dole made history in October 1996 by becoming the first candidate to announce his web site address during a presidential debate; even though he garbled the address, his campaign received two million visitors over the next twenty-four hours. By 1998 most congressional and gubernatorial candidates had web sites, and those running for lower-level office were beginning to catch on as well. (See the appendix to this chapter for a list of milestones of campaigning on the Internet.) Social scientists for several years had been writing about online communications, and with the Internet and e-mail now playing a role in political campaigns, they turned their attention to this interesting subject.

Early Assessments and Observations

Selnow (1994), writing during the very first days of online communications, focused on the impact that computer technology would have on targeting, polling, and database management, and gave us just a hint of how important electronic mail might be in future political campaigns. Four years later, following the 1996 campaigns, Selnow (1998, 203) noted the growing divide between politicians and voters and argued that the Internet, while not a perfect communication tool, might be our "greatest, best hope" to bridge that divide.

Corrado (1996) took a similarly expansive view of the possibilities of online communications. He argued that Internet communication could be a force in revising democratic politics by improving voter information, increasing candidate access to the political process, providing voters with a wider selection of candidates, and increasing civic participation. Corrado also saw possibilities in electronic voting, campaign fundraising, and perhaps most important, allowing citizens to participate in initiatives and referenda electronically, that could one day lead to a national referendum process.

Many social scientists were not so impressed, however, maintaining that online communication was basically an extension of established formats. Graber (1996) noted that there seemed to be surprisingly little that was new or different on this thing called the World Wide Web, suggesting that although there was bound to be an explosion of information available online, the political information diet of average Americans would probably remain rather meager. Richard Davis (1999) looked at these formative years of Internet campaigning and concluded that online campaigns would not be a force to transform or upset traditional political power. Rather, he saw that politicians, campaigns, and the media would use the Internet to reinforce their strengths in communicating ideas and advocating policy.[3]

Margolis, Resnick, and Chin-chang (1997) examined use of the World Wide Web during the 1996 primary campaigns by the presidential candidates and the national political parties. They argued that despite explosive growth, it was doubtful the Internet would fundamentally alter the nature of American electoral politics. Instead, the authors felt the Internet would reinforce the existing structure of politics. Looking at a much larger number of races, Kamarck (2002) reached a similar conclusion. After considering the state of Internet campaigns through the 2004 election, she noted that the Internet in campaigning did not yet have a single defining moment when it truly came into its own; rather it had become another medium through which campaigns conduct their business as usual. Along the same lines, Campbell and Dulio (2003, 26) observed that, in congressional campaigns, many "are using the Internet to fight the same ground war they have always fought, and if the results are not fruitful, they simply discard the Internet as somehow ineffectual."

Bimber (2003) concluded that four major lessons were to be learned from the 1998 campaigns, dealing with the interplay of online communications and elections. The first lesson was that Internet audiences are self-selective and, consequently, the principal audience for campaign web sites is supporters (of the sponsoring candidate), a few undecided voters, and journalists. The second lesson was that, although rudimentary web sites can be inexpensive, Internet sites are growing in sophistication and competition among sites is increasing. As a result, any effort to launch and sustain an effective Internet technology will require the investment of fairly substantial amounts of money. The third lesson was that, in the area of interactivity, the Internet offers real value.[4] Bimber's fourth lesson for the 1998 election cycle was that, under the right circumstances, it is indeed possible for candidates to wage a successful campaign even with little in the way of traditional organizational infrastructure. This is particularly true for smaller-scale campaigns involving candidates for city council, for example, in a community with relatively high use of online communications.

Examination of Campaign Web Sites

One of the more frequent research projects undertaken by social scientists has been the content analysis of candidate web sites. For the most part, these scholars have not been terribly impressed. Dulio, Goff, and Thurber (1999) content analyzed sixty-eight web sites of 1998 U.S. Senate candidates and sixty-five web sites of 1998 U.S. House candidates vying for open seats. This was the first election cycle in which a significant number of congressional candidates had web sites. The authors discovered that the web sites were difficult to find and that most campaigns had little experience with the medium; the approach typically was to adopt existing technologies but without adapting them to the specific requirements of the political environment, that is, to winning the election. Dulio and his colleagues concluded that candidates underutilized the full potential of web sites in their campaigns, and they found no evidence that a web site provided the winning margin in any of the congressional races examined.

Kamarck (1999) conducted a comprehensive analysis of all candidates for federal office during the 1998 election cycle, concluding that 1998 was the year in which politics came to the Internet. She observed, among other things, that candidates were still (so far) putting their best foot forward in this new medium, usually refraining from providing negative or critical information about the opposition on their web sites. Candidate web sites in 1998 were just beginning to get into interactivity (see note 4): the great majority of sites (72 percent) were only partially interactive, while a full 27 percent were passive, billboard sites. At about the same time, Margolis, Resnick, and Wolfe (1999) examined major- and minor-party web sites in the United States and the United Kingdom and found that while minor parties had a greater web presence in the United Kingdom than in the United States, in both countries the major-party web sites were more prominent and sophisticated and received more attention both online and from traditional media sources than did minor-party web sites.

Puopolo (2001) analyzed sixty campaign web sites established by 2000 U.S. Senate candidates, and provided a detailed account of the content of those sites, by issues. She noted, for example, that Republican candidates had much more to say about military and foreign policy than did Democrats, while Democrats were far more likely to discuss the issue of prescription drugs. Further, Puopolo found that female Senate candidates (six out of sixty candidates overall) disclosed more personal information on their web sites than did the male candidates. In her opinion, the best web site among those analyzed belonged to Democrat Hillary Rodham Clinton. Bimber and Davis (2002) also looked at campaign web sites in 2000 and concluded that they served mainly to reinforce the attitudes of committed voters, rather than to mobilize nonvoters or assist undecided voters in making their electoral choices.[5] They noted that both candidate and nonpartisan political web sites generally failed to provide opportunities for interactivity with citizens, or to encourage communication they could not control, such as the posting of chat-room comments.

Wicks, Souley, and Verser (2003) reviewed the content of Bush and Gore presidential web sites in the 2000 election. These scholars discovered that, in terms of textual material, the web sites were rather similar: roughly the same number of news postings (with around 75 percent of the information containing negative charges against the opponent) and relatively safe issue papers and statements on predictable themes. The big difference between the two candidates came in their use of visual images, with Gore's web site presenting seven times as many images as that of Bush. As a result, the former looked informal and folksy while the latter appeared businesslike and professional, though no clear evidence indicated that either was more effective than the other in terms of shaping voters' perceptions of the candidates. Bimber (2003) addressed the "so what?" question by asking how voters are affected by Internet campaign sites. His answer: it depends on the type of voter, but for most (including undecideds) the effects were minimal. According to Bimber, "the reality is not only that campaign sites fail to change the minds of citizens, but they also fail even to assist many undecided citizens in making up their minds" (231). Campaign web sites usually attract supporters of the sponsoring candidate, and the messages on these sites are likely, at best, to strengthen and reinforce voters' predispositions in a limited way.

Negative Advertising Over the Internet

Research on the impact of negative television advertising (and of negative campaigning in general) has become almost a cottage industry among political communication scholars. In their review of the literature, Lau and Sigelman (2000; also see Lau, Sigelman, and Brown 2005, as well as chapter 5 in this volume) considered four principal questions:

1. Are negative political ads more readily processed and remembered by voters than positive advertisements? (There was no strong evidence showing this to be the case.)

2. Are negative ads more effective than positive ads in achieving their objectives—that is, persuading people to vote for the sponsoring candidate? (Again, there is no reason to believe that this is true in most instances; in fact, negative advertising may sometimes have the opposite effect.)

3. Do citizens really dislike negative ads? (Yes. In some studies negative ads were rated as less ethical and less fair than other types of ads.)

4. Do negative ads have serious unintended consequences for the American system of government, such as lower turnout rates and diminished public trust of elected leaders? (Perhaps, but the jury is still out on this question.)

Now, researchers are turning to the impact of negative advertising over the Internet.

For the first few years of online campaigning, Kamarck (1999) found that there was little in the way of negative attacks either on web sites or through e-mail. One of the earliest negative ads (by Peter Vallone, a candidate for governor of New York in 1998, who attacked opponent George Pataki's qualifications) caused a flurry of interest on local television and newspapers precisely because it was posted on the Internet. The attack was rather mild in comparison to many televised negative ads or the frequently more adventuresome broadsides that are made via direct mail, but this particular criticism was big news because it occurred in a new medium (Johnson 2001, 143). Soon, however, e-mail and campaign web sites joined television, radio, and direct mail as vehicles for communicating negative or attack messages. Wicks and Souley (2003) reported that the majority of television ads run by the Bush (80 percent) and Gore (62 percent) presidential campaigns in 2000 were either attack or contrast ads. These authors also looked at the 487 web site news releases posted by the two campaigns and found that nearly three-quarters contained some sort of attack on the opposition. This figure closely paralleled the level of negative ads on television in 2000 and provided support for the argument that close races are likely to produce a high degree of negativism by the competing candidates and their supporters (Wicks and Souley 2003, 130).

The Use of Electronic Mail as a Campaign Device

The political use and impact of electronic mail has not received much attention from social science researchers, though it may ultimately prove to be one of the most valuable online tools that any campaign can assemble. An early study by Gibson, Margolis, Resnick, and Ward (2003) concluded that candidates were using e-mail to improve the efficiencies of familiar campaign tactics, such as contacting volunteers or getting out the vote, rather than to try new ones, like electronic fundraising. Similarly, Trammell and Williams (2004) examined eighty-nine e-mail messages sent by incumbent Jeb Bush and Democratic challenger Bill McBride during the 2002 Florida gubernatorial campaign; they concluded that neither candidate used e-mail as an effective marketing tool, especially in the sense of soliciting money from this most attentive audience of likely supporters.

Cornfield (2004, 27) considered the potential of e-mail as a campaign tool, asserting that it would outperform a campaign web site "ninety-nine days out of a hundred"; his conclusion was that e-mail is delivered (whereas web sites must be found), e-mail is read (whereas web sites are navigated), e-mail is easy to respond to (whereas web sites "engender frames within frames"), and e-mail is harder than a web site for the press and opposition to monitor. What applies in campaigning, however, does not necessarily apply in electronic lobbying and advocacy, especially when Congress is the intended recipient of online communications. Cornfield found that a great portion of the millions of e-mails arriving daily in Congress were automatically discarded by filtering devices used by member and committee offices. Further, for a number of members of Congress, e-mail still was not regarded with the same urgency and sense of priority as "regular" mail (Johnson 2004). Goldschmidt (2001) found that while congressional offices were bombarded with e-mail, many of those offices did not use e-mail filtering and correspondence software to its full advantage, failing to realize the potential management efficiencies that such software could provide.[6]

The Web Versus Television as a Communication Tool

What are the consequences of political advertising over the Internet in comparison to more traditional communication through television advertising? Kaid (2003; also see Kaid 2002) found that citizens who watched both television ads and televised candidate debates in the 2000 presidential election were less cynical about politics and government than before; but no similar positive result was found for those who were exposed to Internet campaign ads. She also discovered that the Internet was quite successful in encouraging voters to seek out additional types and sources of political information, such as links to other political web sites and news media, while television was more effective at encouraging citizens to volunteer, contribute money, and contact candidates. Ku, Kaid, and Pfau (2003) examined the impact of web site campaigning on traditional news media and the processing of information. The authors concluded that web site campaigning could be a useful tool for effective public relations, though candidates need to develop better web site strategies to reach online users while continuing as in the past to provide press releases for traditional media. Their expectation was that as electronic communications expand, the gap will be closed between citizens and politicians and there might be, as a result, a better informed citizenry.

Electronic Participation

A number of commentators, including Putnam (1995, 2000), Postman (1985), and Hart (1994), maintain that television, for a variety of reasons, has had a negative impact on citizen participation and civic engagement. More recently, several scholars have turned to online communications in an effort to determine its impact and effect on voter interest and participation: Does this new form of communication encourage citizens to participate more fully in politics? Are new communities of interest emerging? Or are we simply seeing the same political activists turning to new forms of communication, with no overall increase in the level of political involvement?

Stromer-Galley (2000) argued that characteristics of the Internet—specifically, its relatively low cost to the campaign, ability to send a high volume of messages, and speed—could make for a more democratic turn in the political realm of daily life in America, thereby moving the nation closer to Barber's (1984) notion of "strong democracy," that is, the participation of all the people in at least some aspects of self-government some of the time. Davis, Elin, and Recher (2002) asserted that the most important aspect of Internet campaigning during the 2000 presidential election was not the raising of money or the gathering of votes, but the building of online communities of like-minded individuals. Accordingly, Davis and his colleagues predicted a bright future for grassroots political action and community building over the Internet. Mack (2004, 74) also is optimistic about electronic participation, suggesting that the Internet introduces a "gateway for political community, offering real promise for a new paradigm of political discourse and governance of societies in the twenty-first century." This new paradigm will be seen in a new freedom of expression, which will be both proactive and reactive, and the Internet will open up "tremendous hope for the future" (74).

Bimber (2001), on the other hand, found little relationship between online information availability and political engagement, looking at survey data on Internet usage from 1996 to 1999. The only form of political participation that he found to be positively connected to Internet use was the donating of campaign funds. From a global perspective, A. Shapiro (1999) cautioned against those who believe that online communications would necessarily foster democracy. He argued that politicians who claim that the Internet is inherently democratizing were basing their claim on an "empty truism and a dangerous one at that" (53).

Internet Voting

Especially in the wake of the controversy surrounding the 2000 presidential election,[7] there has been considerable interest in the idea that citizens might one day be able to cast their votes electronically, either at polling stations or in their homes over the Internet. Some proponents look at the irregularities and misadventures involving paper ballots and see technology and (presumably) foolproof election software as the key ingredients to secure and reliable voting. Others are not so sure, especially when voting is conducted over the Internet in a citizen's home or office rather than at a monitored polling station. Alexander (2001), for example, cautioned against proposals that would permit remote Internet voting on the grounds that it was highly susceptible to voter fraud, could erode the right to cast secret ballots, and posed potential threats to personal privacy when trying to determine citizen identity and voter eligibility.

In 2000 the Arizona Democratic Party experimented with the first binding Internet election for public office in the United States. During this presidential primary, citizens were given the chance to vote online, by mail, or at traditional voting booths with paper ballots. Although we cannot generalize from this one instance, it does offer a starting point in examining the problems and promises of Internet voting. Solop (2001), for example, found that the Arizona contest attracted younger and better-educated voters compared with other primaries, and that it stimulated a surge in voter participation. The enthusiasm for Internet voting, however, has been tempered in recent years due to concerns about potential weaknesses in the technologies and procedures that might be used. While the Help America Vote Act passed by Congress in 2002 provided federal assistance to the states in modernizing and standardizing their voting equipment, there has been criticism of private vendors and worrisome security lapses in electronic voting software programs. A team of computer scientists found widespread failures in voting system source code that fell "far below even the most minimal security standard" applicable (Kohno et al., 4).[8]

The 2004 Presidential Campaign and Future Research

The 2004 presidential campaign attracted considerable interest from academic scholars and others who study campaigning and the Internet. That election saw the most intense use of online campaigning to date, including soaring levels of fundraising, innovative efforts at grassroots coalition-building, the first widespread appearance of blogs, and exploitation of the Internet by 527 organizations and other political groups.

As this chapter was being written, two preliminary studies had been completed on the 2004 primaries, looking at individuals who visited web sites for information about the presidential candidates and politics generally. Winneg and Jomini (2004) examined the Democratic pre-primary and primary stages of the race and found that, despite greater overall use of the Internet in 2004, the number of likely voters who were getting their information from that source in 2004 increased only modestly compared to 2000. They also found, among other things, that for the Democratic primaries, people who accessed information from campaign web sites tended to be younger, better educated, and more ideologically liberal than those who did not visit web sites for information. In a second study, Graf and Darr (2004) discovered that not only were individuals who gathered information online more politically engaged than non-Internet users, they were also "influential" (respected, listened to, and persuasive) among their friends, family, and colleagues. These "online political influentials" were more likely to be male, young, and well educated than the rest of society.

The 2004 presidential campaign saw Internet participants in action in at least three important venues: volunteering for campaigns, participating in web blogs, and giving money to candidates and causes online.

Volunteering on the Campaign Trail

Presidential campaigns typically bring out many party activists and ideologically committed volunteers. Throughout the country, from the precincts of New Hampshire to get-out-the-vote drives in early November, presidential candidates and their parties can always count on receiving help from thousands of volunteers. Yet the 2004 election was different, in that *millions* of volunteers were recruited. The Bush campaign, through its official web site, boasted of having an energetic corps of e-citizens, some six million supporters (or more; see chapter 9 in this volume) who communicated with others via the Internet, spread the Republican message, and motivated people to do what they could to help reelect the president. These activists augmented the efforts of roughly another million or so Bush volunteers on the ground (performing more traditional tasks such as voter contact via telephone or neighborhood walks). The Kerry campaign, along with labor unions and hundreds of political organizations such as Americans Coming Together and Moveon.org, also managed to recruit volunteers in unprecedented numbers. Earlier in the year, during the pre-primary stage of the race, Howard Dean moved from long shot to serious contender for the Democratic nomination by using the Internet not only to raise money but also to attract a large number of volunteers to his campaign in New Hampshire and elsewhere.

In assessing these developments, social scientists may want to consider several questions: What was so different about the 2004 presidential contest that millions of new volunteers came out to support their favored candidates? Was it simply a product of the increasing animosity and ideological cleavage that currently exists between Republicans and Democrats?[9] Or was it due to the effectiveness of a new set of techniques used by the political parties and campaign professionals to engage these volunteers? And in particular, was it because the Internet and e-mail helped to break down barriers for organizing and motivating volunteers? Can the parties and candidates sustain this kind of enthusiasm in the future, and build a more or less permanent following of like-minded people?

Blogs and Bloggers

The first blogging software was developed in 1997, and its use has grown dramatically, almost exponentially, in the years since. Perseus Development Corporation (2004) estimated that by the end of 2003 there were 5.1 million hosted blogs, with 10.3 million being forecast by the beginning of 2005. The overwhelming majority of these had very limited readership; were not linked to other sites; were meant primarily for family and friends; were hosted by teenagers; and dealt with topics such as dating, personal relationships, and music.

Nevertheless, blogs began to be used in a serious way during the 2004 elections. Howard Dean became the first presidential candidate to establish a blog (called Blog for America) and the first to employ a blogmaster for his campaign. Other Democrats followed, with the campaigns of Bob Graham, Wesley Clark, John Edwards, and John Kerry all creating blogs. The Bush-Cheney campaign web site also launched a blog, though it lacked the interactivity of other such sites and basically served as a newswire service for the campaign.[10] The Internet search site Yahoo.com compiled a list of forty-eight blogs that were dedicated to the 2004 presidential campaign; the five biggest among these attracted over half a million visitors a day—a greater readership than all but the largest metropolitan newspapers (Drezner and Farrell 2004, 33). Blogs had an impact on political journalism as well in 2004, helping, for example, to keep alive stories about the botched CBS News–Dan Rather investigation of President Bush's National Guard service.[11]

One of the core principles of modern professional electioneering is that a campaign must be controlled from the top; specifically, the candidate and his or her senior staff are responsible for developing the campaign's message, strategy, and tactics. While these individuals certainly listen to ordinary citizens, the mechanism for doing so is usually through scientifically based survey research or focus groups. The Dean campaign in 2004 went a step further, however, attempting to incorporate unfiltered (and unrepresentative) opinion coming in through its web log into the campaign's overall message and strategy.[12] The goal was to infuse the former governor's improbable bid for the presidency with some degree of bottom-up rather than top-down direction. Was Dean simply an anomaly, or is this the future of political campaigning? Only time will tell, though Rice (2003, 9; also see DeSantis 2005) concluded that blogs have the potential to become "useful communication tools" and predicted that they would soon become standard practice at the presidential, followed by state and local levels of campaigning.

Various forms of "new media" that were developed earlier, such as cable opinion shows and radio call-in, seem to be dominated by conservative voices. At least in the 2004 election, the blogs and Internet audio and video files provided by various political groups, appeared to add a higher proportion of liberal and independent voices to the mix (Graf and Darr 2004). Still, we are just beginning to get a sense of the shape and potential influence of the blogging community, that is, who bloggers are and what they can accomplish. As one example outside the electoral arena, Drezner and Farrell (2004) discovered that blogs worldwide are making an impact on international relations, particularly in countries such as Iran where freedom of expression has been largely suppressed.[13] They noted, too, that the "blogosphere" acts as "a barometer for whether a story would or should receive greater coverage by the mainstream media" (32).

On the down side, Levin (2002) observed that while blogs sometimes resemble genuine communities of citizens, in other instances they seem to embody some of the Internet's shortcomings, for example, feeling like an echo chamber, being placeless, and thriving on instant responses to the latest events. The immediacy of blogs suggests that while they clearly provide new opportunities for the expression of political opinion, for the most part that opinion is unreflective. What, then, do we make of the so-called blogging community? Social scientists may want to consider some or all of the following questions: Simply put, who are these people and what motivates them to spend hours on political blog sites? Who constitutes the audience for blogs? What are their political leanings, level of engagement, and demographics? How do bloggers impact other types of media? Do they form any kind of sustainable voice or political community (however that latter term is defined)? Are their activities a meaningful form of civic engagement? Do, or should, candidates for office and the media pay attention to them? The same questions may apply to another, somewhat different set of online communicators: those who use mobile technology, like cell phones, text messaging, or "moblogging" (publishing data from a camera-equipped cell phone to the Internet).

Fundraising on the Internet

In campaign fundraising, one of the most intriguing questions has been this: How can candidates, parties, and political causes increase the pool of citizens willing to contribute money? In looking at the 2004 presidential primary season, the Campaign Finance Institute (2004) found that major-party candidates were able to raise twice the amount raised by their counterparts four years earlier, and that smaller donations (under $100) had increased fivefold. While the intensity and competitiveness of the race undoubtedly fueled the trend, much credit also has to go to the Internet. Campaign fundraising has traditionally been a costly enterprise, conducted through telephone solicitation, direct mail, or personal appeals (Johnson 2001). Raising money over the Internet, in contrast, is relatively simple and inexpensive, and an extraordinary number of small donations came to the presidential candidates in 2004 through this medium. In 2000 presidential candidate John McCain showed the great potential of Internet fundraising, and his successors in both parties (most notably Howard Dean, John Kerry, and George W. Bush) built on that model to accrue record amounts online in 2004. From this point forward, electronic fundraising will surely be a central aspect of campaigning at all levels.

E-mail as a Campaign Tool

Electronic mail is now used widely by both candidate and issue campaigns. In July 2004, for example, John Kerry revealed his choice for the Democratic vice-presidential nomination, Sen. John Edwards of North Carolina, by sending an e-mail message to his supporters. In anticipation of this announcement, the Kerry presidential campaign reported that another 150,000 individuals e-mailed the campaign asking to be included on the campaign e-mail listserv so that they would continue to hear from the candidate periodically for the duration of the campaign. As noted earlier, the Bush-Cheney campaign claimed to have the e-mail addresses of over six million supporters, whom they dubbed their "e-activists."

The advantages of electronic mail make it an important tool for any political campaign. E-mail, which can now come with graphics, color, and attachments, just might be the dominant software application (the so-called killer app) of online communications. It is inexpensive, fast, and an extraordinarily efficient way to communicate with a large audience. E-mail also has an unique viral quality, that is, a message sent by a political campaign often encourages the recipient to pass it on to others or to use a link provided within the e-mail to connect to a web site or listserv. Electronic mail has some disadvantages as well, however. It is not as easy to harvest e-mail addresses as it is to gain access to citizens' voting records (are they registered? have they voted in past elections?). Further, e-mail addresses give no clue as to where the individual resides, no tell-tale ZIP code, and no information about their voting history. A growing business among political consultants is to match voting files with e-mail addresses; still in its formative stages, when this effort becomes more mature it will presumably make electronic mail an even more potent campaign tool. On the other hand, electronic mail still must compete with other electronic messages, including commercial spam, for the attention of recipients. Also, the potential exists for campaign e-mail overload, that is, the temptation to bombard supporters with too much information, too often, thereby diminishing its impact and importance. Scholars should monitor this simple but increasingly important form of campaign communication, in an effort to better understand its impact on the behavior of voters.

A Thousand Voices on the Internet

Traditional news sources and campaign ads have been joined by the clatter of third-party voices over the Internet. In July 2004 JibJab Media launched on its web site an animated election parody, with cut-out figures of Bush and Kerry singing "This Land Is Your Land." It was an overnight sensation, generating 65 million hits on the JibJab web site, and was featured on CBS and NBC evening news shows. Over the course of the campaign, numerous other animations, video clips, parody web sites, and amateur campaign commercials were made available on the web for political junkies to download at their leisure. Most were fairly tame, but a few were so raunchy that they could never be shown on television (Institute for Politics, Democracy, and the Internet 2004). Whereas early campaign users of the Internet shied away from negative political advertising, this medium now appears wide open to smear, invective, and all sorts of salacious materials. As a result, scholars interested in knowing the consequences of negative advertising have a new set of examples to explore. Who produced this material and what effect, if any, did it have on voters? Who accessed these third-party web sites? For those inclined to dip into normative questions, have our presidential and other campaigns been cheapened and coarsened by the no-holds-barred political material appearing on the Internet?

Should there be attempts to regulate or limit the robust, freewheeling political traffic that has emerged on the Internet?

Conclusion

Social scientists have barely scratched the surface with their research on campaigning and the Internet. Many existing studies were concluded in the earliest years of the Internet, and so much has changed since then in both technology and the use of electronic communication that their findings seem rather antiquated. Thus, while scholars continue to investigate the topic, many areas are yet to be explored. Beyond candidate campaigns, for example, there is a whole other world where political consultants ply their trade: in direct democracy (initiatives and referenda), issue advocacy, and corporate political affairs. Each of these is undoubtedly affected by the revolution in online communications, and each presents a complex and fascinating set of research issues and problems just waiting for the attention of academic researchers and students of politics.

The Consultants Respond About

CAMPAIGN TECHNOLOGY

Our consultants generally agreed that the emergence of web-based campaigning (and other technological innovations such as e-mail, TiVo, and cell phones) in recent years has altered the political landscape and, in the process, influenced the way they go about doing their jobs. As might be expected, not everyone was enthusiastic about these developments.

On the (mostly) positive side:

DEMOCRATIC MEDIA CONSULTANT. As much of an impact the Internet may or may not have had on voter behavior, it's had an extraordinary effect on the way we do our work in a campaign. It has sped up the process immensely in a variety of ways—for example, the speed at which we can advise a candidate on what to say to the press, or how to handle a question in a debate. We've had situations where candidates are in a debate and the press secretary, in a state halfway across the country, is e-mailing him about the last exchange, "How do we clean this up?" I e-mail them back a suggestion, they give it to the candidate on the station break, and it comes out during the debate. That was impossible to do before e-mail and

continues...

the Internet came along and sped things up.

It's also changed the way we make spots, and the way our candidates approve spots. And it's changed the amount of material we have available to use in spots. We used to have to spend an extraordinary amount of money transmitting video footage of opposition ads. Now I can sit and watch clips of my opponent in my e-mail every morning, if we've got good campaigns collecting those data. Sometimes, literally minutes after the news hits, I'm being e-mailed the latest statement from our opponent with a quality that's good enough to put into an ad. So, I can tell you definitively, it has fundamentally changed the way we do our business.

DEMOCRATIC POLLSTER. I've always thought that politics lags about ten years behind the business world and how they run their [marketing] campaigns. Finally, though, we're starting to be more creative in how we try to engage voters, and especially younger voters—for example, using different mediums such as the Internet, instant text messaging, and things like that.

But if technological change opens up new opportunities for consultants to ply their trade, its accessibility to voters also presents challenges:

REPUBLICAN GENERAL CONSULTANT. All consultants want campaigns to be run top-down. But now campaigns are fragmented with TiVo, e-mail, and the Internet—voters getting their information in a variety of ways. It's coming in smaller doses from more sources. There's just a lot more going on out there that you can't control.

DEMOCRATIC MEDIA CONSULTANT. Campaigns can't depend solely on television these days to win; voters now get their information from a cocktail of impressions—TV, friends, the news, in the mailbox [direct mail], and through the Internet. Most winning campaigns do a good job of blending a cocktail of impressions and reinforcing that cocktail mix through a number of different channels.

The persuasive potential of web-based campaigning is not obvious to everyone, however:

REPUBLICAN POLLSTER. Most of the people who use the Internet are the ones who've already made up their minds, and they go to different sites to try and reinforce that.

DEMOCRATIC MEDIA CONSULTANT. This idea that campaigns are going to be best run and driven by the ideas of literally thousands of people e-mailing and blogging [see note 1] goes against the fundamental nature of political communication, which is, you've got to keep it simple. You've got to keep it direct and be repetitive, because people are busy and they just don't have time. I'm not sure who these bloggers are, but they just don't think like most of the people we have to try and persuade in campaigns.

In the 2004 race for the Democratic presidential nomination, the rise and fall of former Vermont governor Howard Dean was seen as a textbook illustration of the Internet's limitations as a campaign tool. On the one hand:

INDEPENDENT POLITICAL ANALYST. The Dean campaign was able to figure out how to tap into this movement and feeling on the ground. Dean voters were excited that there was finally someone out there who understood them and was speaking up for them.

But on the other:

DEMOCRATIC POLLSTER. Even today, television is still the number-one way to communicate with voters.

DEMOCRATIC MEDIA CONSULTANT. For all their talk about the Internet and the role it played in promoting his candidacy, no one spent more early money on television than Howard Dean. And yet in the end, it was television that killed Dean. First of all, a candidate having his or her campaign run by thousands of citizens through the Internet goes against the fundamental nature of campaigns. And then later in Iowa, when Dean imploded on television after the primary . . . he had burned $41 million on TV ads, and had no money to repair his image.

One aspect of the new technology that our consultants (especially pollsters) found troubling is the proliferation of cell phones:

DEMOCRATIC POLLSTER. The number of people under age thirty-five who are using cell phones as their primary phone is growing. Unless we get legislatures to pass laws that would get those numbers for us, it's going to be an increasing problem.

REPUBLICAN POLLSTER. Luckily, it's becoming a problem with people who are the least likely to vote. If it were seniors that were going to cell phones, then we would be in real trouble. . . . Although we haven't yet seen a dramatic decrease in the accuracy of our polls, that's probably going to change. But I don't think we'll go back to door-to-door polling.

REPUBLICAN GENERAL CONSULTANT. I absolutely think consultants will go back to door-to-door polling. In some of our campaigns, we look at the polling and see blind spots because of the high penetration of cell phones.

DEMOCRATIC POLLSTER. One problem is that with voters we can't get on the phone, we also can't reach them at their door. That's what will preclude pollsters from going back to door-to-door polling.

Appendix: Selected Internet Campaign Milestones

May 1994   Edward M. Kennedy becomes the first U.S. senator to have a web site.

August 1994   Minnesota creates e-democracy.org, a web site to help organizations distribute information online.

September 1994   Dianne Feinstein hosts the first major candidate web site in her campaign for the U.S. Senate.

October 1994   Minnesota's e-democracy.org hosts the first online debates for gubernatorial and Senate candidates.

June 1995   The Democratic National Committee becomes the first major U.S. party to host a web site (www.dnc.org).

October 1996   Robert Dole, at a presidential debate, uses closing remarks to announce his campaign's web site address (two million visitors check out the site, even though the address given by Dole is incorrect).

January 1997   Frank O'Bannon of Indiana is the first governor to simulcast his inauguration via web site.

October 1997   Minnesota gubernatorial candidate Ted Mondale is the first candidate to buy political advertising on a political web site.

July 1998   PoliticsOnline is the first vendor to offer software directed at campaign fundraising.

July 1998   The Connecticut state Democratic convention is the first to be covered "live" on the Internet.

September 1998   The Starr Report is released by the Office of Independent Counsel, viewed by 24.7 million people the first day.

October 1998   Peter Vallone, running for governor of New York against George Pataki, is the first candidate to post a negative ad on the *New York Times* web site.

November 1998   The Internet aids in the successful gubernatorial race of Reform Party candidate Jesse Ventura (Minnesota), helping to organize volunteers, raise money, and control the flow of information.

March 1999   Steve Forbes becomes the first presidential candidate to announce his candidacy over the Internet.

May 1999 The first effective presidential parody site, www.gwbush.com, is created. It becomes the target of an FEC complaint from the Bush campaign.

June 1999 The FEC issues new regulations extending the presidential matching-fund system to include online credit card contributions.

November 1999 Bill Bradley is the first presidential candidate to raise $1 million (roughly 5 percent of his total contributions) from online donations.

February 2000 John McCain becomes the first candidate to collect over $500,000 in one day online, and $2 million in a week.

March 2000 Arizona is the first state to have an online binding primary (Democratic presidential); participation levels are twice what they were in 1996.

April 2000 Policast.com, the first all-politics Internet radio site, is launched.

May 2000 The first presidential online chat room permits Bill Clinton, speaking from St. Paul, Minnesota, to chat with children nationwide.

November 2000 George W. Bush is the first candidate to publish a list of campaign contributors online following the 2000 presidential campaign.

November 2000 Between October 23 and November 2, more than one million K–12 students participate in mock elections on election.com.

November 2000 The Republican National Committee (RNC) web site (www.gop.org) is hacked and temporarily shut down; it is restored as polls open on Election Day.

November 2000 The RNC becomes the first political party to collect the names and e-mail addresses of one million activists (starting from a list of 17,000 activists in 1999).

September 2001 The Internet aids in the nation's recovery from the September 11 terrorist attacks, providing an avenue for raising approximately $55 million for relief efforts.

December 2002 Internet sites publicize Senate majority leader Trent Lott's comments about Strom Thurmond (that the former segregationist should have won the presidency in 1948) on the latter's birthday; Lott resigns leadership position shortly thereafter.

February 2003 The web site Meetup.com is used to mobilize supporters of Howard Dean's presidential candidacy.

March 2003   Dean for America is the first presidential campaign to effectively use a web log, or blog.

April 2003   The Internet is used in an effort to draft former general Wesley Clark for president.

June 2003   Moveon.org gives two million members an opportunity to vote their preferences online; Howard Dean receives 44 percent of the total.

November 2003   A web site established to remove California Governor Gray Davis from office (www.RecallGrayDavis.com) collects enough signatures to place this issue before voters in a statewide election.

January 2004   Moveon.org sponsors Bush30Seconds online, with contestants submitting more than 1,000 possible television commercials; $4 million is raised to buy broadcast time during the Super Bowl, but CBS ultimately blocks the ads.

February 2004   The RNC unveils an online attack ad against John Kerry, sending it to millions of recipients via e-mail.

July 2004   JibJab Media, a private animation firm, releases an Internet parody featuring Kerry and Bush singing to the tune of "This Land Is Your Land"; with 65 million hits, this becomes the most viewed web animation in campaign history.

July 2004   John Kerry announces his running mate, John Edwards, via a personal e-mail; approximately 150,000 new e-mail addresses are gathered by the Kerry campaign in anticipation of that announcement.

Source: Adapted from Institute for Politics, Democracy, and the Internet (2004).

Notes

1. A blog (or web log) is a web page that serves as a publicly accessible personal journal or commentary.
2. U.S. Special Prosecutor Kenneth Starr released this sometimes salacious report in September 1998, detailing the allegations against President Bill Clinton in the Monica Lewinsky affair.
3. This might include, for example, using the Internet to post issue papers, cite favorable newspaper articles, and post messages from the candidate to volunteers and friends.
4. An interactive web site encourages viewers to get involved, for example, by posting their comments or participating in an online poll. This interaction is valuable be-

cause it gives campaign volunteers and supporters a much better sense of participation in the campaign.

5. These sites generally focused on messages that appealed to the candidate's and party's base of support. In other words, policy statements, communications from candidates, electronic newsletters, and other forms of online communication were targeted at the already committed and those likely to vote in the first place.

6. When utilized to its fullest potential, correspondence management software can, for example, automatically route e-mails to the congressional staffer handling the issue, insert key phrases in the text of responses, keep tallies of constituent e-mail, and maintain running accounts of correspondence with each constituent. Some software, though used only on an experimental basis in Congress, uses artificial intelligence to identify key words and phrases and to prepare automatic responses.

7. For a discussion of the 2000 presidential election, see Ceaser and Busch (2001); Toobin (2001).

8. The researchers found several potential vulnerabilities in the AccuVote-TS voting terminal: (a) by using an unauthorized electronic card, voters could cast multiple ballots without leaving a trace, (b) poll workers and others could tamper with unsecured machines, and (c) voting terminals could be compromised by downloading data over unsecured phone lines or wireless Internet connections.

9. For more on the nature of this cleavage, see Abramowitz and Saunders (2005); Fiorina (2005).

10. The Bush-Cheney blog was carefully controlled by the campaign itself, with the campaign staff determining what subjects were discussed on the blogs and when they would be open for visitors' comments.

11. In early September 2004, CBS News publicly disclosed information that was highly critical of President Bush's National Guard service. The authenticity of the reports was called into question almost immediately, and they were eventually discredited. An independent board chastised CBS for failing to follow basic journalistic principles, and the network subsequently fired three top news executives. Anchorman Dan Rather, who reported the story, retired early in March 2005.

12. Web logs are unrepresentative of public opinion because the responses are self-selective; that is, only those persons who are interested in the topic or who have a particular point of view they want to express will participate in the blog.

13. Iranian dissidents, like many across the world, were using blogs to keep each other informed of public events, provide alternative points of view to the official government sources, and develop a medium through which they could express themselves.

8 Direct Democracy and Candidate Elections
Daniel A. Smith

When casting ballots in voting booths or filling out absentee ballots at home, citizens are asked to choose from an array of candidates running for federal, state, and local offices. More often than not, voters are also asked to decide among a spate of policy questions placed on the ballot for their consideration either by fellow citizens or by lawmakers. These ballot measures may create new state laws; alter state constitutions; or amend local, municipal, or county charters. From statewide ballot initiatives, to legislative referrals, to down-ballot local referendums and advisory questions, citizens are increasingly being asked to serve as election-day lawmakers.[1] Though the process of direct democracy entails binary (yes-no) choices on sometimes complex policy questions with long-term consequences (Chambers 2001), voters are generally understood to be able to use limited information to make competent choices on ballot measures (Lupia 1994, 2001).

Although the content of these measures may be of some personal concern to the coterie of professional consultants working on local, state, and federal candidate campaigns, growing evidence indicates that the impact of ballot measures goes well beyond any substantive policy outcomes stemming from their passage. Specifically, it is growing increasingly apparent that ballot measures may alter the electoral fortunes of candidates running for office. As campaign consultant Kellyanne Conway, the president of a Washington, D.C.–based consulting and market-research firm, cautions, "A candidate [who] ignores an initiative on a ballot that shares his or her name does so to their own peril" (Fulk 2004). Conway's imperative is not generally welcomed by campaign consultants working on candidate elections. "Candidates hate ballot initiatives," longtime GOP consultant David Hill notes, "because they skew voter turnout and create competition for money, interests and votes" (Fulk 2004).

In this chapter I examine something that is largely a blind spot for political scientists: the indirect impact of ballot measures on candidate races. Indeed, little has been written thus far on the topic.[2] However, because political consultants are usually more attuned to the nuances of campaigns than are political scientists, many of these consultants are becoming quite cognizant of the potential impact that ballot measures can have on candidate races. They appreciate how measures on the ballot, even ones not highly salient to voters, can alter the contours of the electorate as well as their own campaign strategies.

Even scholars of direct democracy have been slow to recognize the impact that ballot measures may have on candidate campaigns and elections. The academic literature on state-level uses of direct democracy, and "citizen" initiatives in particular, has blossomed over the past decade, but researchers have only just begun to systematically assess the procedural byproducts (or what is sometimes called the "educative effects"; D. A. Smith and Tolbert 2004) of direct democracy on candidate races. Since the Progressive Era (see McGerr 2003), observers of the three mechanisms of direct democracy—the initiative, popular referendum, and recall—have noted that these processes have a series of indirect, attendant effects that can alter the attitudes and behaviors of citizens and political organizations at the state and local levels. The importance of ballot measures is not, however, limited to state and local politics, given that statewide ballot propositions can also affect the course of national elections.

In fact, one needs only to point to the 2004 election and the reelection of President George W. Bush to understand the potential ramifications of ballot measures on candidate elections.[3] Assessing Bush's narrow victory in Ohio, which tipped the electoral college balance in his favor, journalists and political analysts were quick to credit the mobilizing effects of Issue 1, a statewide anti-gay-marriage measure on the ballot that year.[4] According to Karl Rove, Bush's chief political advisor and architect of his reelection campaign, Ohio's ballot measure banning gay marriage was a major motivating factor in the election (Davies 2004), as it supposedly brought evangelical and rural voters to the polls in support of the measure, and also in support of the president (Rosenkrantz and Runningen 2004). Across the country, "state constitutional amendments banning same-sex marriage increased the turnout of socially conservative voters in many of the 11 states where the measures appeared on the ballot," according to James Dao of the *New York Times*; those measures "appear to have acted like magnets for thousands of socially conservative voters in rural and suburban communities who might not otherwise have voted, even in this heated campaign" (Dao 2004).

In the present chapter I consider how the dynamics of ballot-measure campaigns can affect candidate campaigns and electoral outcomes. Following a brief discussion of the growing use of the mechanisms of direct democracy—

paying close attention to statewide initiatives—I provide an overview of the recent scholarly literature on the instrumental as well as the indirect effects of citizen lawmaking, that is, respectively, how the plebiscitary mechanism provides citizens with an institutional check on the system of representative governance and how the byproducts of that process affect the attitudes and behaviors of citizens and political organizations. I then discuss three ways in which ballot measures affect candidate campaigns. First, I assess how certain propositions on the ballot may underscore campaign themes and set the agenda in candidate elections. Second, I outline how ballot measures may alter the campaign financing parameters of candidate elections. Third, I examine how such measures may affect the composition of the electorate by mobilizing certain voters to the polls. The potential impacts of ballot measures on candidate races in these three realms, which are not necessarily mutually exclusive, are attendant byproducts of the process of direct democracy. I conclude the chapter with an argument that candidates and campaign consultants (not to mention political scientists studying campaigns and elections) should be ever more attentive to the presence of propositions on the ballot, not simply for the intrinsic merit or policy substance of these measures but also for their indirect electoral effects on candidate races.

The Growing Use of (and Scholarship on) Direct Democracy

Over the course of the twentieth century, the use of direct democracy was quite cyclical; that is, the propensity for citizens and groups to place measures on the ballot in the American states ebbed and flowed over the decades.[5] Between 1911 and 1920, a period during which many states initially adopted the mechanisms of direct democracy, citizens considered 293 initiatives on statewide ballots. By the 1960s the number of initiatives qualifying for statewide ballots had fallen below 100. The downward trend reversed, however, following the 1978 passage of Proposition 13, California's property tax–slashing proposition; the landslide adoption of this measure created an explosion in ballot initiative use throughout the American states.[6] Between 1981 and 1990, citizens across the nation considered 271 statewide initiatives; in the next decade, citizens voted on 389 initiatives, including 93 statewide initiatives in 1996 alone.[7]

Although the number of initiatives on statewide ballots has tapered off slightly since the 1996 high-water mark, many states continue to have initiative fever. Nationwide in the 2004 general election, there were no fewer than 163 statewide measures on the ballots of 34 states, including 54 citizen initiatives, 107 legislative referendums, and 2 popular referendums.[8] On the ballots of all fifty states there also were hundreds more local referendums and initiatives.[9] Substantively, ballot measures cover a remarkable range of issues; some of the issues involved are complex, whereas others are relatively straightforward. Some ballot propositions make national headlines, but others remain obscure in terms of public or media attention. In some of the two dozen states that permit statewide ballot initiatives, voters have cast ballots dealing with issues as diverse as banning gay marriage, punishing negligent doctors, prohibiting the confinement of pregnant pigs, limiting the taxation and spending powers of state governments, funding stem cell research, and ending affirmative action programs and social welfare benefits to illegal aliens. Virtually no subject is off limits.

On the November 2004 ballot alone, six states featured initiatives banning same-sex marriage, while another five had legislative referrals on the same topic. Four states had measures dealing with tort reform and medical malpractice, with voters in Florida and Nevada being faced with competing proposals authored by dueling doctors and trial lawyers. Floridians and Nevadans also voted to raise the minimum wage. Coloradoans approved measures mandating utility companies to develop alternative energy sources and raising taxes on tobacco, but they rejected a proposal calling for the proportional allocation of electors for the electoral college. Voters in Montana approved legalizing marijuana use for medicinal purposes. Californians voted on sixteen statewide measures, including eleven initiatives and one popular referendum; one of the five initiated measures approved that day was a proposition authorizing the state to issue $3 billion in state bonds over ten years to finance embryonic stem cell research. As voters in Florida, Nebraska, and Oklahoma all voted to expand gambling operations in 2004, their counterparts in Michigan and California opted to rein in gambling operations by Native American tribes, and voters in Washington nixed the expansion of slot machines in current gaming establishments (Ballot Initiative Strategy Center 2004). Fickle as they may sometimes be, citizens nevertheless generally like having the plebiscitary power of the initiative.[10]

Critics of direct democracy argue that the process has spun out of control, with ordinary citizens and special interests, rather than elected officials, having too much power to shape legislation and tinker with state constitutions.[11] Writing in the late 1990s, journalist David Broder (1997) observed that "ballot measures are as copious in California as convertibles. They pop up in primaries and in general elections like Shasta daisies." The *Los Angeles Times* (2003), a longtime and persistent critic of the initiative process, recently editorialized (once again) that "direct democracy is running amok" in California. Critics in other states agree, such as the former president of the Florida Senate, Jim King, who warned of the potential "Californication" of Florida resulting from the rash of initiatives on the 2002 and 2004 statewide ballots (Ulferts 2003).

Not surprisingly, the scholarly literature on direct democracy in the American states has burgeoned, reflecting the upsurge in the usage, prominence, and criticism of ballot measures. Almost exclusively, studies have focused on the instrumental use of the initiative to achieve policy outcomes. In their endeavor to examine the instrumental effects of the initiative process, scholars have examined the role of money and special interests in determining ballot outcomes, the competence of voters in casting votes on ballot measures, the impact of direct democracy on the rights of minorities, whether or not initiative outcomes reflect public opinion and state policies, and whether ballot measures are implemented effectively.[12]

Unfortunately, this latest wave of academic work on the instrumental outcomes of direct democracy has little relevance to campaign consultants working on candidate races, as the research is largely divorced from the broader electoral context. Recently, though, some political scientists have begun to address how ballot measures can affect candidate races by taking a page from early twentieth-century writings. During the Progressive Era, a handful of scholars theorized, and reformers fantasized, about how direct democracy might have a transformative "educative value" (D. A. Smith and Tolbert 2004). In addition to any substantive changes to public policy it produced, Progressives understood how the process of voting on ballot measures could transform the electorate. Harvard political scientist William Munro (1912, 20–21), for example, highlighted the "educative value of direct legislation," arguing that "a spirit of legislative enterprise is promoted among the voters; men are encouraged to formulate political ideas of their own and to press these upon public attention with the assurance that they shall have a fair hearing." Similarly, Reinsch (1912, 158) argued that the processes of direct democracy would "assist the people, the body of the electorate, in the development of its political consciousness," making it "more familiar with legislative programs and more interested." Thus, irrespective of the policy consequences of direct democracy, these and other Progressives emphasized the educative aspects of citizen lawmaking, suggesting that the process itself could not only bolster turnout but also stimulate civic engagement, increase citizens' trust in government, and even minimize the political power of interest groups and party bosses.[13] Many Progressives, then, understood full-well how voting on ballot propositions could shape the political attitudes and political behavior of the broader electorate, which indirectly could affect candidate elections.

How Ballot Measures Can Set the Agenda in Candidate Races

One of the most obvious ways in which ballot measures can shape candidate races is by bringing into sharp relief the issues on which politicians running for office may agree or disagree. As with gay marriage in 2004, ballot measures are sometimes used strategically in an effort to control the agenda; that is, by sponsoring or speaking out on a proposal, candidates attempt to gain instant name recognition and political credibility. Then, during the campaign, the candidates tie their messages directly to an issue they are backing (or opposing), or perhaps have backed (or opposed) in a previous election. In this way, ballot measures can have a synergistic effect by connecting tangible, substantive policies to what otherwise might be vacuous or vague policy commitments floated by the various contestants. In short, by tethering themselves to ballot measures, candidates attempt to use issues to set the agenda and energize their own campaigns.

A growing amount of evidence suggests that ballot measures do help to set the agenda in candidate contests. Nicholson (2005), for example, found this to be the case and concluded that, as a result, ballot measures are yet another issue source that can provide useful information to voters at relatively low cost. While voters may not necessarily link issues on the ballot directly to specific candidates, Nicholson maintained that those issues nevertheless can have "spillover effects" that "indiscriminately" affect citizens' judgments in candidate races (128). In other words, the "indiscriminate priming effect[s]" of ballot measures may help to reinforce (rightly or wrongly) voters' partisan stereotypes of the issue positions held by candidates (71).[14] Building on research that shows candidate choice to be influenced by issue preferences, especially when information about an issue is readily accessible to voters (Nie, Verba, and Petrocik 1976; Popkin 1991), Nicholson argued that the effect of ballot measures is likely to be most pronounced in election contexts where information is relatively scarce (in particular, below the presidential level).

Putting his theory to an empirical test, Nicholson demonstrated that ballot measures—from tax-limitation, to environmental regulation, to illegal immigration, to affirmative action, to the freezing of nuclear weapons production—

can indeed influence the agenda in candidate races. For example, he found that the nuclear-freeze issue in 1982,[15] irrespective of whether it was openly discussed by candidates, was one of the most important considerations to voters in candidate races in the ten states that had such a measure on their ballot but was largely irrelevant in states that did not. According to Nicholson, the various freeze measures helped to set the agenda for candidates not only in U.S. Senate elections but also in low-information U.S. House races and even in some gubernatorial contests. Nicholson (2005, 111, 124) also showed how the indiscriminate priming effects of California's Proposition 187 (in 1994, concerning social services to illegal immigrants) and Proposition 209 (in 1996, concerning affirmative action) shaped the agenda not only in high-profile statewide races (president, governor, U.S. Senate) but also in some down-ballot contests as well.

Using ballot initiatives to advance a candidate's profile has become a refined art in California, which ranks second only behind Oregon as the leading initiative-use state in the country. Peter Schrag, an astute and longtime observer of politics in the Golden State, described in his scathing book on direct democracy, *Paradise Lost,* how the initiative process encourages the "embracing and demagoguing [of] hot-button issues" by candidates who hope to "showcase" their credentials (Schrag 1998, 226). The use of ballot propositions in California to help candidates define and differentiate themselves from the pack dates back at least to Democrat Jerry Brown's run for governor in 1974. To boost his primary campaign, Brown brought together Common Cause and a group called the People's Lobby to place Proposition 9, the California Political Reform Act, on the June ballot (Allswang 2000). The measure (which dealt with campaign finance regulations) passed easily, and Brown became his party's nominee; he continued to exploit the issue in the months that followed, while sailing through to a comfortable win in the general election (Schrag 1998).

Perhaps pushing the effort to campaign on initiatives too far, in the 1990 Democratic gubernatorial primary, Attorney General John Van De Kamp cosponsored no less than three ballot measures: Proposition 128 (dealing with the environment), Proposition 129 (a proposal to increase spending on prisons, jails, and drug education and treatment), and Proposition 131 (a measure to create legislative term limits and some public financing of campaigns; see Schrag 1998).[16] In fact, the candidate contributed $277,000 out of his own campaign fund to the political committee sponsoring Proposition 133, and another $560,000 to the committee behind Proposition 131 (Allswang 2000). Unfortunately for Van De Kamp, he faired as poorly at the polls as did his three measures, all of which went down to defeat in the June primary (Schrag 1998).

On the Republican side of the 1990 California gubernatorial primary, moderate Pete Wilson latched onto Proposition 115, a tough-on-crime initiative, in a successful effort to "beat off a group of conservative opponents" in the election (Schrag 1998, 227). In 1994, Wilson once again turned to the initiative process, this time to invigorate his flailing bid for reelection. The governor actively campaigned that year on two ballot measures having broad levels of popular support: Proposition 184 (a severe "three-strikes" measure for repeat criminal offenders) and Proposition 187 (a proposal to deny social services to illegal immigrants and their children). Serving as Proposition 187's spokesperson, Wilson was able to bolster his image of being tough on illegal immigrants and even contributed roughly $2 million from his own reelection campaign coffers to pay for campaign ads touting the measure.[17]

California's current governor, Republican Arnold Schwarzenegger, has taken campaigning via ballot initiatives to even further heights. More than a year before deciding to toss his hat into the October 2003 recall election that led to the replacement of Democratic incumbent Gray Davis,[18] Schwarzenegger sponsored a ballot measure that was placed on the 2002 general election ballot. His successful initiative, Proposition 49, required the state to direct surplus general revenue funds to pay for after-school programs in public schools. For those who are inclined to be more cynical, this policy proposal was seen as part of a broader calculus designed by Schwarzenegger's political advisors to prepare him for a gubernatorial bid in 2006 (Hasen 2005). The measure presumably would help to soften the film star's often violent and callous on-screen persona, promoting instead a portrayal of a strong supporter for educational programs to benefit the state's children; rather than voters thinking of the former bodybuilder as "Conan the Barbarian" or "the Terminator," Proposition 49 would frame him as a more congenial and children-friendly "Kindergarten Cop." When the October 2003 recall election became a reality, the foundation had already been laid and Schwarzenegger was able to accelerate his time frame for capturing the governorship.

Since becoming governor, Schwarzenegger has skillfully used the ballot process to advance his policy agenda and political clout. He officially endorsed or opposed nine of sixteen measures on the November 2004 ballot, and had the state GOP mail a slick multipage brochure—titled "Governor Arnold Schwarzenegger's Ballot Proposition Voter Guide"—to millions of registered voters (D. A. Smith 2005). In office for little more than a year, Schwarzenegger subsequently threatened to use direct democracy to circumvent the recalcitrant Democratic-controlled legislature in Sacramento if it did not place referendums on the ballot in support of his fiscal agenda, and to funnel unlimited campaign contributions from special interests to a host of ballot-measure committees that he controlled (E. Garrett 2004; Hasen 2005). Then, in 2005, he once again attempted to govern by using direct democracy, making good on his promise to take policy questions directly to the people by calling for a special election that would ask citizens to vote on several measures (none of which passed, however).[19]

Other instances of how ballot measures are used by political operatives to set the agenda and frame candidate elections abound, with some tactics being less seemly than others. In 1998, for example, Democratic and Republican party operatives in Colorado each tried to link statewide candidates from the opposing party to what they viewed as unpopular measures that were on the statewide ballot that year. Howard Gelt, a former state Democratic Party chair, formed a political committee to raise money for campaign ads linking Republican gubernatorial candidate Bill Owens, who was trying to distance himself from the social conservatives in his party, to three conservative initiatives on the ballot (including two antiabortion measures and a third dealing with school vouchers). Responding in kind, Don Bain, a former chair of the Colorado Republican Party, founded a political committee to air negative television ads depicting Democratic candidates running for statewide office as supporters of liberal ballot measures (most notably Referendum B, a statutory referral placed on the ballot by the legislature that would have allowed the state to retain excess tax revenues to pay for education and transportation projects, rather than refunding those revenues to taxpayers as required by the state constitution; see E. Garrett and Smith 2005).[20]

More recently in Florida, where there were eight measures overall (six initiatives) on the 2004 general election ballot, the rival U.S. Senate candidates attempted to craft their campaign themes accordingly. Republican nominee Mel Martinez, for example, mentioned several ballot issues in his standard stump speech and at the candidate debates. Martinez endorsed Amendment 2, a measure placed on the ballot by the GOP-controlled state legislature that required parental notification before a minor is able to obtain an abortion, but spoke out (quietly) against Amendment 3, a tort reform measure placed on the ballot by the Florida Medical Association and favored by Florida governor Jeb Bush and President George W. Bush. At the same time, Martinez, a former president of the Academy of Florida Trial Lawyers, attempted to distance himself from his barrister past by actively criticizing Amendments 7 and 8, two initiatives backed by trial lawyers that protected patients' rights and penalized wayward doctors. Martinez also strongly criticized Amendment 5, an initiative that sought to raise the minimum wage by $1 and index future increases to the rate of inflation.

While Martinez's Democratic opponent, Betty Castor, also opposed Amendment 3, she routinely spoke of her support for Amendment 5 and tried (in vain) to make it a wedge issue in the campaign (Erickson 2003). As David Hill, a Martinez consultant, said during the campaign, "There has always been a belief that when you put a measure like raising the minimum wage or anything that would help blue-collar workers on a ballot it would bring more Democrats to the polls and actually hurt Republicans" (Fulk 2004). Trying to seize on the moment, Castor's communications director endeavored to make Amendment 5 a polarizing issue of the campaign, emphasizing that, "Betty Castor supports raising [the] minimum wage, Mel Martinez does not" (Fulk 2004). But while there was considerable excitement among Democrats that the minimum wage measure would help both Castor and presidential nominee John Kerry in Florida,[21] the direct impact of Amendment 5 on the candidate races was overstated: Castor and Kerry lost to their Republican opponents, even as the minimum-wage proposal passed with over 70 percent of the vote.

Finally, initiatives placed on the ballot can be used by political operatives to divert the attention of the media and the public from a candidate's record. Dave Noble, executive director of Stonewall Democrats, a gay and lesbian group, claimed that the anti-gay-marriage measures on eleven statewide ballots in the 2004 general election were "being used as one way to distract voters from what we think should be the real issues." In particular, "Every time something goes wrong in Iraq," according to Noble, Republicans would try to "scare voters" by bringing up the subject of gay marriage (Lowy 2004). Although the GOP did not sponsor any of these ballot measures and publicly downplayed the effect they might have on the presidential vote, party leaders were privately quite excited by the prospects of their being on the ballot in several key swing states, including Michigan, Oregon, and Ohio. As the chairman of the Ohio Republican Party said after the election, "I'd be naïve if I didn't say it helped," especially "in what we refer to as the Bible Belt area of southeastern and southwestern Ohio, where we had the largest percentage increase in support for the president" (relative to the 2000 election; Dao 2004).

How Ballot Measures Can Alter the Financing of Candidate Races

Ballot measures can have a profound, if indirect, effect on the campaign financing of candidate elections, although scholarly research on this topic is fairly thin. In contrast to all federal and most state and local races for political office, where ceilings have been placed on the amount of money that can be given to a candidate, there are no limits on the size of contributions (or expenditures) in ballot campaigns. As a result, the equivalent of a "soft-money" loophole exists when it comes to ballot measures, making the sky the limit for these contests.[22] Also unlike federal and many state candidate races, corporate and labor union treasuries are permissible sources for contributions to ballot campaigns (E. Garrett and Smith 2005). In 1998, for example, nearly $400 million was spent by ballot-issue committees nationwide to support or oppose sixty-one initiatives and dozens more referendums in forty-four states (D. A. Smith 2001b). The national Republican and Democratic Parties, by way of comparison, raised *only* a total of $285 million in soft money during the 1997–1998 election cycle (D. A. Smith 2001a).

While the amount of money being channeled into ballot campaigns is noteworthy in and of itself, the indirect (strategic) use of the initiative process by crafty practitioners is a development that candidates and their campaign staffers should be concerned about. In the early 1990s, Grover Norquist, the well-connected head of Americans for Tax Reform (ATR), a conservative nonprofit organization with a primary goal of curtailing taxes and government spending, provided a detailed blueprint of how conservatives could use the initiative process to promote their agenda in the states (D. A. Smith and Tolbert 2004, 177). Writing in 1993, he correctly anticipated how ballot initiatives limiting legislative terms and cutting both taxes and government spending, as well as anticrime, victims' rights, and parental rights ballot measures could potentially bring fiscal and "social conservative Republican voters to the polls" in 1994 and 1996, while at the same time draining the resources of Democratic allies, most notably organized labor (Norquist 1993).

In October 1996 the Republican National Committee (RNC) transferred $4.6 million in soft money to Norquist's ATR to run issue ads, details about which were not publicly disclosed until formal hearings were held by the U.S. Senate in 1997 (E. Garrett and Smith 2005; D. A. Smith 2004). ATR subsequently transferred a substantial amount of RNC money to groups in California, Colorado, and Oregon that sponsored conservative ballot proposals in 1996 and 1998, including several antitax, right-to-work, and so-called paycheck-protection measures (see note 23). In the 1996 general election, ATR contributed $509,500 to the tax-slashing Oregon Taxpayers United, which amounted to nearly 60 percent of the total amount raised by the group that year (D. A. Smith 2004). Then, during the 1998 June primary in California,

ATR funneled $441,000 to Campaign Reform Initiative, the group backing Proposition 226 on "paycheck protection."[23] Even though Proposition 226 went down to defeat at the polls, Norquist is on record saying that "[e]ven when you lose, you force the other team to drain resources for no apparent reason" (D. A. Smith and Tolbert 2004, 108).

Norquist's innovative approach of using the initiative process for ulterior motives, that is, diverting campaign resources from the opposition's candidate campaigns, appears to be gaining acceptance. "Activists in both parties are also taking advantage of election laws that permit unlimited contributions to campaigns for and against ballot measures as a way to pump money into key presidential campaign states," said Kristina Wilfore, executive director of the Ballot Initiative Strategy Center, a nonprofit organization promoting progressive ballot measures (Lowy 2004). Recently, labor unions in California and Oregon have had to spend more than $40 million to defeat various ballot initiatives. "That's $40 million that didn't go into races and didn't go into other issues," Wilfore argued. According to Wilfore, over $75 million was spent between 1994 and 2000 to defeat conservative ballot measures that were intended not first and foremost for their policy outcomes but rather to drain the resources of key Democratic support groups (Lowy 2004).

Although the precise amount of money that various interests have diverted over the years into ballot campaigns is impossible to verify, the claim still resonates with a certain level of credibility. The "initiative industrial complex," as some commentators (Schrag 1998, 189) have called the process of direct democracy, is clearly fueled by money from special interests.[24] Indeed, the process has long been influenced by the role of money, with paid signature gatherers, professional consultants, and lawyers employed to write the text of the ballot language becoming a regular occurrence in ballot campaigns by the early 1900s.[25] Facilitated by recent campaign finance regulations banning soft money in candidate races,[26] however, it seems likely that contributions once invested in those races are now increasingly finding their way into ballot campaigns (E. Garrett and Smith 2005). Campaign and elections scholars are only beginning to investigate the financial nexus existing between ballot measures and candidate races.

How Ballot Measures Can Alter the Composition of the Electorate

Perhaps the most exciting academic literature concerning the indirect effects of direct democracy on candidate races has to do with how the former can help to alter the composition of the electorate. Public opinion data indicate that citizens have some degree of interest not only in the candidates who are seeking office but also in the policy proposals that happen to be on the ballot in the same year (Cronin 1989; Waters 2003). Since, as we have seen, these proposals can be used to set the agendas of candidate races,[27] adroit consultants who run candidate campaigns are increasingly looking to use them strategically in ways that tweak the electorate to their clients' advantage. Scholars are only just beginning to investigate how this process works.

With regard to the impact that ballot measures have on voter turnout, researchers have discovered that the plebiscitary process does, in fact, alter the electoral landscape. At the aggregate level, states that use the initiative process frequently are more likely to have citizens turn out to vote not only in midterm elections when presidential candidates do not compete with ballot measures for media attention, but also (though to a slightly lesser degree) in presidential elections (Tolbert, Grummel, and Smith 2001; Tolbert and Smith 2005). In municipal races, parallel evidence indicates that the use of direct democracy boosts voter turnout locally (Hajnal and Lewis 2003). These findings run counter to earlier state-level research showing minimal effects of the initiative on voter turnout (Everson 1981; Magleby 1984).[28]

At the individual level, research using survey data has shown that salient ballot measures tend to generate higher turnout in midterm elections (Lacey 2005; M. Smith 2001). Arguing that not all ballot measures are the same, Mark Smith (2001) found that the presence of "salient" initiatives and legislative referenda (defined as those with a greater amount of front-page newspaper coverage devoted to them on the day following the election) from 1972 to 1996 increased the probability of voters turning out in midterm, but not presidential, elections by roughly three percentage points. Researchers have also shown that citizens living in states that allow the initiative tend to be more knowledgeable and engaged in civic affairs,[29] and more trusting of government,[30] than those who do not.

Also at the individual level, scholars have only just begun to determine what *types* of voters are motivated to participate because of ballot measures. Recent studies indicate that initiatives and referendums tend to have a greater mobilizing effect on those who vote regularly as opposed to more episodic (including younger) voters. Partisanship appears to play a role as well, with self-identified Republicans and Democrats being more likely than independents to say they are aware of and interested in ballot measures, and to report that their decision to participate in an election was influenced by the presence of such measures on the ballot (Donovan and Smith 2004).[31]

Cognizant of the potential mobilizing effects of ballot measures, parties and candidates have tried (with varying degrees of success) to use them to mobilize their base supporters as well as episodic voters. Though this happens rarely, in a few instances more votes have been cast on a ballot measure than in the candidate races being held simultaneously. Proposition 13, for example, the tax-cutting measure in California, garnered more votes than all the gubernatorial candidates who were listed on the state's June 1978 primary ballot. More recently, in Missouri's August 2004 primary, turnout exceeded 40 percent of the eligible electorate for the first time in over a quarter-century. Most observers agreed that many voters were attracted to the polls in this election not to cast their ballots in the contested Republican and Democratic races for governor and U.S. Senate but rather to vote on a legislative referendum banning gay marriage. Roughly 137,000 and 39,000 more citizens cast ballots on the anti-gay-marriage amendment than participated in the Senate and gubernatorial contests, respectively (Donovan and Smith 2004).

Clearly, proponents of the gay-marriage bans in several swing states, most notably Ohio, had ulterior motives for placing these measures on the ballot; that is, they wanted to encourage Protestant evangelicals and ideological conservatives to turn out at the polls in support of a ban—and, at the same time, to cast a vote for Bush in the presidential race. The degree to which this mobilization strategy succeeded is open to interpretation. Turnout in Ohio, for example, was up ten points statewide in 2004, yet counties with greater numbers of evangelicals did *not,* all else being equal, experience a disproportionate jump in turnout relative to the 2000 election (D. A. Smith 2005). Indeed, across the country, turnout rates in 2004 were lower, on average, in the eleven states that had gay-marriage proposals on their general-election ballot than in the thirty-nine states that did not (Abramowitz 2004; Burden 2004). Nevertheless, as pollster Brad Bannon predicted prior to the November election, the presidential race "is going to be so close in these battleground states where there are ballot measures" that the impact of initiatives on turnout "may very well decide" the outcome (Lowy 2004). In the end, the gay-marriage proposals may have helped to tip the election in Bush's favor, especially in the battleground state of Ohio, by mobilizing some conservatives who had actively championed the issue to turn out and support the president.[32] Further, as I noted earlier, beyond merely setting the agenda in candidate races, ballot measures can prime vote choice in those races (Nicholson 2005); in other words, issues that are on the ballot sometimes become highly salient and, as a result, are given greater weight when voters decide which candidate to support. As Donovan et al. (2005) have documented using survey data, the anti-gay-marriage proposals had strong partisan priming effects on 2004 presidential vote choice in three battleground states (Arkansas, Michigan, Ohio), with supporters of the gay-marriage bans, all else being equal, more likely to vote for President Bush than for Senator Kerry.

In addition to generating turnout, candidates (and parties) have tried to use ballot measures as cross-cutting wedge issues with the intent of splintering their opposition's base constituencies.[33] Perhaps the best example of a ballot proposal serving as a wedge issue was Proposition 209, the 1996 California initiative that successfully banned the use of affirmative action guidelines by public agencies. Republicans, led by Governor Pete Wilson and U.S. House Speaker Newt Gingrich, hoped that the measure would garner support from white ethnic voters, prying them away from the Democratic Party (Chávez 1998; D. A. Smith and Tolbert 2004). In a teleconference call with Gingrich, Wilson crowed that Proposition 209 was "a partisan issue ... that works strongly to our advantage [and] has every bit the potential to make a critical difference" in helping to defeat then-President Bill Clinton (Schrag 1998, 226). Although Clinton won reelection handily, the measure produced some internal tensions within the Democratic Party's base coalition.

Although voter preferences are generally understood to be less stable in ballot campaigns relative to candidate races (with people tending to make up their minds much later in the former[34]), partisanship is increasingly important in structuring vote choice on ballot measures (D. A. Smith, Tolbert, and Donovan 2005). The framing of ballot questions, of course, remains crucial to their success,[35] but several studies indicate that parties, candidates, and other political elites have increasingly taken positions on them,[36] and that citizens rely heavily on partisan cues to inform their voting decisions.[37]

Finally, political context undoubtedly matters with respect to the magnitude of any effect that ballot measures might have on a local, statewide, or even national election. Not all such measures affect turnout to the same degree, with their mobilizing potential depending partly on how they are used to target certain voters. For example, in Nevada and Florida, two battleground states in the 2004 presidential election, progressive activists, with the blessing of the Democratic National Committee, introduced initiatives to raise the minimum wage in an effort to attract low-income voters to the polls. Based on focus groups and preelection surveys that pretested the language of a variety of different proposals, Democrats anticipated that the ones put forward would help to mobilize low-income workers who would also support Democratic candidates, including John Kerry. While both measures passed, and turnout was considerably higher in those two states than the national average, Kerry appeared to benefit only in Nevada—and not enough to tip the state in his favor even there. The impact of most of the eleven gay-marriage proposals on statewide ballots was also quite limited, given that eight of the eleven were in "red states" (Republican-leaning) to begin with. While the measures may have boosted turnout among conservative voters (though limited empirical evidence supports this claim; see D. A. Smith 2005), it is unlikely that they had a significant impact on the outcome of the presidential contest.

Conclusion

Political consultants running candidate races have become more attuned to the indirect impact that ballot measures may have on candidate campaigns. First, recognizing the strong partisan voting patterns that exist in most instances, consultants are beginning to understand how these measures can be useful in helping their clients to set the agenda and frame the issues that will be raised in their campaigns. Accordingly, there is an increasing willingness to coordinate candidate messages with issues appearing on the ballot, and a growing awareness that ballot measures can often be used to attack the policy positions of their clients' opponents. Second, because of recent regulatory changes in campaign finance law at both the federal and state levels, campaign consultants are looking for ways to use direct democracy to circumvent contribution and expenditure limits in candidate races; using ballot measures to channel prohibited soft money into candidate races may help to synergistically advantage or disadvantage those running for elective office. Finally, savvy consultants understand that ballot measures may have a positive effect on electoral turnout, mobilizing certain voters to come to the polls on election day. In turn, the priming effects of ballot measures may help to shape voting patterns in candidate elections. Although using ballot measures to tweak an electorate in order to achieve electoral gains—by bringing out the candidate's partisan base or by dividing the opponent's supporters over a cleaving issue—is far from an exact science, candidate campaign consultants will likely continue to try to "take the initiative."[38]

Broder's book *Democracy Derailed* (2000, 1) contended that direct democracy "threatens to challenge or even subvert the American system of government in the next few decades." Whether or not one agrees with the dire assessments and predictions of Broder and other critics of the process, the practice of direct democracy is not dying off anytime soon. The sooner more campaign consultants (and the political scientists studying campaigns and elections) realize the potential synergistic effects of ballot measures on candidate elections, the better off candidates (and the scholarly literature) will be. It is time for scholars of direct democracy and, more important, those studying candidate campaigns and elections to catch up to the political reality that ballot measures may have pronounced, albeit marginal, effects on candidate races.

Notes

1. See Mendelsohn and Parkin (2001); Tolbert, Lowenstein, and Donovan (1998); Waters (2003).

2. See, for example, Bailey et al. (2000); Burton and Shea (2003); DiClerico (2000); Herrnson (2001); Salmore and Salmore (1989); Semiatin (2004); Shea and Burton (2001); Thurber and Nelson (2000, 2004); Watson and Campbell (2003).

3. See Abramowitz (2004); Burden (2004); Donovan et al. (2005); Hillygus and Shields (2005); D. A. Smith (2005).

4. See Diamant (2004); Fulk (2004); Greenberger (2004); Hook (2004); C. Jones (2004); Shaffrey (2004).

5. See Magleby (1984); Tolbert (2003); Waters (2003).

6. See Schrag (1998); Sears and Citrin (1982); D. A. Smith (1998); Tolbert (2003).

7. Twenty-four states currently permit citizen initiatives, and twenty-seven allow for popular referendums. The legislatures in all fifty states have the authority to place issues on the ballot for voter approval. See Waters (2003).

8. Ballot Initiative Strategy Center (2004).

9. Use of the initiative process (whereby citizens gather signatures petitioning to place either statutes or constitutional amendments on the statewide ballot) is not evenly distributed across the twenty-four states where it is permitted. Since first adopting it, Oregon (1,902) and California (1,911) have led the pack in initiative use, averaging 6.4 and 6.2 initiatives, respectively, per general election. Other western states, most notably Colorado, North Dakota, Arizona, and Washington, have also been relatively heavy users of the initiative process since the Progressive Era. Indeed, roughly 60 percent of all initiative activity since the beginning of the twentieth century has taken place in these six states (Ballot Initiative Strategy Center 2004). At the opposite end of the spectrum, Utah, Wyoming, Illinois, and Mississippi have had very limited usage of the initiative. In addition, the popular referendum, which allows citizens in roughly half the states to challenge laws passed through the legislative process, is seldom used.

10. See Bowler and Donovan (2002); Matsusaka (2004); Waters (2003).

11. See Broder (2000); Ellis (2002); Schrag (1998); D. A. Smith (1998).

12. On the role of money and special interests, see E. Gerber (1999); Lowenstein (1982); Magleby (1984); D. A. Smith (2001a, 2001b). On the competence of voters, see Bowler and Donovan (1998); Lupia (1994). On the impact on the rights of minorities, see Bowler and Donovan (2002); Cronin (1989); Gamble (1997); Hajnal, Gerber, and Louch (2002); Matsusaka (2004); Tolbert and Hero (1996); Wenzel, Donovan, and Bowler (1998). On the reflection of public opinion and state policies, see Camobreco (1998); Craig, Kreppel, and Kane (2001); E. Gerber (1996); E. Gerber and Lupia (1995);

Hero and Tolbert (2004); Lascher, Hagen, and Rochlin (1996); D. A. Smith (2001c). And on implementation, see E. Gerber et al. (2001).

13. See Boehmke (2002, 2005); D. A. Smith and Tolbert (2001, 2004); M. Smith (2001, 2002); Tolbert, Grummel, and Smith (2001); Tolbert, McNeal, and Smith (2003); Tolbert and Smith (2005).

14. Priming occurs when ballot measures capture the attention of voters and cause them to give greater weight to certain issues than they otherwise would have; these issues may then be used as a basis for evaluating candidates. Even if a candidate does not take an official stance on the ballot measure (such as ending affirmative action programs in his or her state), the issue may nonetheless prime voters to think about the candidate in terms of stereotypical positions held by his or her party (in this instance, Democrats generally supporting affirmative action programs and Republicans generally opposing them).

15. The production and deployment of nuclear weapons is, of course, a matter of national rather than state policy; as such, nuclear-freeze ballot measures were of symbolic value only, that is, election results were not binding on elected officials in Washington or anywhere else.

16. A competing measure to Proposition 129, Proposition 133, was sponsored by Leo McCarthy, the Democratic lieutenant governor who was seeking reelection in 1990 (Allswang 2000).

17. See Chávez (1998); Schrag (1998); D. A. Smith and Tolbert (2004).

18. Davis's opponents were able to gather over 1.3 million valid signatures (far more than the 897,158 they needed) to force a special vote on whether to recall the California governor. On October 7, 2003, a majority of voters elected to remove Davis from office and replace him with Schwarzenegger.

19. During the 2003 recall campaign, Schwarzenegger controlled a ballot-issue committee called "Total Recall" (after one of his earlier films); this committee, which was not subject to contribution limits (state law at the time restricted gifts to candidate committees from individuals and political action committees to $21,100 per election cycle), raised over $4.5 million in support of the recall. After taking office, Schwarzenegger created "Governor Schwarzenegger's California Recovery Team," yet another ballot-issue committee with no caps on contributions. Recovery Team raised approximately $18.7 million in just a few months to support Proposition 57 (a bond measure) and Proposition 58 (a balanced budget measure), two successful referendums placed on the March 2004 primary ballot by the legislature that the governor said would help dig California out of debt. Prior to the November 2004 election, Schwarzenegger created several new ballot-issue committees, soliciting large contributions from individuals and corporations to help finance campaigns for or against specific initiatives on which he took positions. See E. Garrett (2004); Hasen (2005).

20. Whether revenues are considered "excess" is determined by a formula that takes into account both population growth and the rate of inflation in Colorado; this policy was itself set by a citizen initiative adopted in 1992.

21. To accomplish this, ACORN (the Association of Community Organizations for Reform Now, which had originally sponsored the minimum-wage initiative) was granted the opportunity to present its campaign strategy at a special session at the Democratic National Convention in Boston (Lowy 2004).

22. Until the 2004 election cycle, national parties were permitted to raise unlimited contributions from individuals, corporations, and labor unions for "party-building" ac-

tivities. Much of this unregulated soft money, however, was spent on issue ads, which by and large supported or attacked candidates running for office but did not explicitly urge viewers to vote for or against any of the candidates.

23. By forcing union members to regularly check off whether they wanted a portion of their dues to go to explicitly political causes (as opposed to the current practice of allowing union leaders to make those decisions), this measure would have sharply curtailed the political voice of organized labor.

24. See Broder (2000); Ellis (2002); D. A. Smith (2001c); but also see E. Gerber (1999).

25. See McCuan et al. (1998); D. A. Smith and Lubinski (2002).

26. In 2002, Congress passed and President Bush signed into law the Bipartisan Campaign Reform Act (BCRA), also known as McCain-Feingold, which among other provisions banned the national parties from collecting or spending unregulated soft money. See Malbin (2003).

27. See Donovan et al. (2005); Nicholson (2005); D. A. Smith (2005); D. A. Smith, Tolbert, and Donovan (2005).

28. Magleby (1984, 197), for example, concluded that "turnout is not increased by direct legislation, and alienated nonparticipants are not moved to the polls by the initiative and referendum." Occasionally, he conceded, highly salient measures such as California's Proposition 13 in 1978 (see above) "might encourage" higher turnout; even so, Magleby maintained that "only the educated will be able to master the complicated ballot whenever the election is held."

29. See Mendelsohn and Cutler (2000); M. Smith (2002); Tolbert, McNeal, and Smith (2003).

30. See Bowler and Donovan (2002); Hero and Tolbert (2004); D. A. Smith and Tolbert (2004).

31. In addition, research shows that partisanship is a strong predictor of the direction of vote choice in ballot measure elections (Branton 2003; Citrin, Reingold, and Walters 1990; Donovan and Snipp 1994; D. A. Smith and Tolbert 2001; D. A. Smith, Tolbert, and Donovan 2005).

32. The salience of the gay-marriage issue is, however, evident from the fact that in two Ohio counties, more votes were cast for and against the ballot measure than for all the presidential candidates combined (D. A. Smith 2005).

33. See Donovan and Smith (2004); Hasen (2000); D. A. Smith (2005); D. A. Smith and Tolbert (2001).

34. See Bowler and Donovan (1994, 1998); Magleby (1984, 1989).

35. See Magleby and Patterson (1998); Nicholson (2003); D. A. Smith (1998, 2004); D. A. Smith and Herrington (2000). Because ballot measures are issue based, consultants face relatively few constraints when determining how to define the issue and frame the debate. "A ballot measure," noted one professional who has worked on numerous initiative campaigns, "is words on a piece of paper, and they mean what the reader thinks they mean" (Magleby and Patterson, 1998, 163). The challenge for consultants, then, is to help provide that meaning. In 2004, for example, proponents of a successful statewide initiative that would allow residents of two South Florida counties (Miami-Dade and Broward) to vote on whether to place slot machines in pari-mutuel facilities, and then permit the state legislature to tax revenues from those slots with proceeds going toward public education, deftly framed the issue not as a vote to expand gambling in the state—but rather as one involving local control and much-needed funding for public schools.

36. See Karp (1998); D. A. Smith and Tolbert (2001, 2004); Hasen (2000, 2005).

37. See Bowler and Donovan (1998); Branton (2003); Donovan and Smith (2004); Donovan et al. (2005); Lupia (1994); D. A. Smith, Tolbert, and Donovan (2005).

38. The long-term effects on the parties of tying candidates to ballot measures are not clear, however. By tacitly backing gay-marriage ballot measures, for example, Republicans run the risk of alienating younger voters, many of whom (including those who support the GOP) oppose the measure or see it as a nonissue.

9 Grassroots Mobilization

Peter W. Wielhouwer

The second political lesson I learned from my first campaign came from Mrs. O'Brien, our elocution-and-drama teacher in high school, who lived across the street. The night before the election, she said to me, "Tom, I'm going to vote for you tomorrow even though you didn't ask me to."

I was shocked. "Why Mrs. O'Brien," I said, "I've lived across from you for eighteen years. I cut your grass in the summer. I shovel your walk in the winter. I didn't think I had to ask for your vote."

"Tom," she replied, "let me tell you something: people like to be asked."

—Tip O'Neill (1987)

According to the Democratic National Committee (2005), in 2004 the party "recruited over 25,000 trained precinct captains, conducted 530 Organizing Conventions across the country, mobilized 233,000 volunteers, knocked on 11 million doors and made 38 million volunteer phone calls and 56 million paid calls.... Because of the tremendous investment in ground operation, Democrats significantly increased turnout in 2004 from 2000: 2.5 million more African American voters in 2004, 2.1 million more Hispanics in 2004 and 2.2 million more young people voted in 2004. Democrats also saw a surge in 1st time voters: 13 million first time voters in 2004 with Democrats winning by four percentage points."

According to the Republican National Committee (2005), the party's "grassroots get-out-the-vote activities in 2004 surpassed all of the committee's expectations. Last year, 2.6 million Team Leaders and volunteers, and 7.5 million e-activists took action on behalf of the party and its candidates: 102,000 calls were made to talk radio shows; 411,989 letters to the editor were sent; 69,000 personal letters were sent to targeted voters; 467,000 voters were registered via the Web; 9.1 million doors were knocked on; and 27.2 million phone calls were made."

As the 2004 presidential election unfolded, it became clear that grassroots mobilization efforts would reach unprecedented levels. At least $100 million was set aside for get-out-the-vote (GOTV) efforts, and you have just read what the parties claim to have done with the money. They may be right. The 2004 American National Election Study estimated that during the campaign, nearly 44 percent of American adults were personally contacted by a party or campaign worker on behalf of a candidate—the highest proportion since the survey first began asking the question in 1952. Moreover, those numbers may *understate* 2004's mobilization efforts because many 527 organizations (see chapter 4 in this volume) and interest groups (including union, environmental, and religious organizations) also worked to generate electoral support for candidates supportive of their policy preferences. As noted by the Center for the Study of Elections and Democracy (2005) at Brigham Young University, the 2004 campaign finance laws produced an environment in which campaign funds

> purchased record amounts of television and radio advertising, phone calls, person-to-person contacts, and direct mail pieces. . . . [S]ophisticated marketing techniques helped campaigns identify voters who sometimes received more than a dozen contacts. . . . [P]olitical parties and interest groups devoted more money to the ground war than ever before . . . and targeted a hard money bonanza into ground war activities and independent expenditures.

This is heady stuff for students of elections. Grassroots politics seems to be healthy and vibrant in American politics, and both parties are pleased with their performance "on the ground" during the 2004 elections. It would appear that nearly everything candidates and parties need to know about grassroots campaigning is well in hand, wouldn't it? Answering that question is the point of this chapter. What exactly do we *know* about grassroots campaigns? How is what we know different from what we *don't know*? Is there a knowledge gap between the extraordinary claims made by the parties and by professional political consultants and the conclusions reached by academic scholars who study campaigns and elections? To answer these questions, and others, we need to understand how what we do know was ascertained. Once we have a handle on how grassroots politics has typically been studied, we will be well situated to assess the state of our knowledge on the subject.

First things first: As defined in the *Encyclopedia of American Political Parties and Elections* (Wielhouwer 2006), "Grassroots is a term that refers to mass-based political activity; that is, any political activity that involves large numbers of 'real' people, as opposed to activity that involves mainly political elites." Thus, when I refer to a grassroots campaign, or grassroots campaigning, it means campaigns, related to the electoral process, that involve many people. A grassroots campaign, for example, would include efforts to distribute political information to large numbers of people using what appear to be very personal methods. A group of campaign volunteers going from house to house in various neighborhoods would be considered a grassroots campaign, whereas phone calls made by a candidate to a relatively small number of people for the purpose of generating large donations would not.

Certain aspects of grassroots campaigns will not be reviewed here. For instance, an interest group that encourages its members to phone or e-mail their representatives in Congress is engaging in a grassroots lobbying effort that falls beyond the scope of the present discussion. I also will not consider the merits of an election campaign being labeled (either by itself or by the media) as a "grassroots" campaign. Such a label has a positive connotation that usually implies a candidate has wide-ranging popular support and is relying on the involvement and contributions of large numbers of citizens to get elected. This would be in contrast to a candidate perceived as out of touch with the public, or who is seen as the favorite of political elites (such as a party machine or some other self-serving and unrepresentative group of political actors).

Grassroots campaigning has long been part of the American political scene. Formalized procedures for conducting grassroots campaigns were articulated as early as 1840, when a Whig committee, which included Abraham Lincoln, distributed instructions to state party chairs. This strategy, sometimes referred to as the "Lincoln Four-Step," lays out fundamental principles for segmenting, targeting, and mobilizing voters. They wrote:

> Our intention is to organize the whole state, so that every Whig can be brought to the polls in the coming presidential contest. We cannot do this, however, without your co-operation; and as we do our duty, so we shall expect you to do yours. . . . 1st. To divide [each] county into small districts, and to appoint in each a sub-committee, whose duty it shall be to make a perfect list of all the voters in their respective districts, and to ascertain with certainty for whom they will vote. . . . 2nd. It will be the duty of said sub-committee to keep a constant watch on the doubtful voters, and from time to time have them talked to by those in whom they have the most confidence, and also to place in their hands such documents as will enlighten and influence them. 3d. It will also be their duty . . . on election days [to] see that every Whig is brought to the polls.[1]

This document summarizes the steps for effective grassroots campaigning: divide states (or counties, cities, and so on) into districts of manageable size; make a list of all the voters in each district and determine their underlying political preferences (now called voter identification); distribute campaign information, especially to swing or uncommitted voters; and make sure that partisans show up to vote on election day. Interestingly, in a Republican analysis of their own GOTV shortcomings in the 1990s, four of the top five identified weaknesses (including inadequate person-to-person campaigning, insufficient GOP base turnout, and the recruitment of too few new Republican voters) were directly related to failed implementation of the Whig strategy, especially compared with Democratic efforts in the same time period.[2]

The technologies for implementing these processes have obviously advanced in recent years for national, state, and local elections (Strachan 2003; Wielhouwer 2003). Lists aren't kept by pen and paper anymore; they're maintained on large voter databases. Voter identification is still accomplished with door-to-door canvassing, but records in many campaigns are updated via handheld personal digital assistants that synchronize with voter lists via satellite. Campaign materials are distributed by hand, mail, television, e-mail, and in an interesting new development, by campaign workers carrying portable DVD players with targeted messages from candidates to prospective voters (Beutler 2004).

In the remainder of this chapter I discuss various aspects of grassroots politics, with an emphasis on what social scientists have learned about them, and then compare that knowledge with what political and campaign professionals say. Central to our knowledge of grassroots campaign effects are both early and more recent research on political party organizations, individuals in the American polity, and intermediate mobilizing organizations. The chapter concludes with a summary of answered and unanswered questions facing students of election campaigns.

Early Research on Grassroots Campaigning

Three major themes are found in what might be considered the early grassroots mobilization literature. To be candid, that scholarship wasn't really focused on either grassroots or mobilization; rather, the distribution of political information and getting out the vote emerged as central political activities performed by party workers in studies of urban political machines. These activities continued, even with the degrading of the power of most of those machines during the first half of the twentieth century. Thus the first theme that emerged from the early research had to do with the activities of the *local party organizations*. A second theme emerged from experimental research on political propaganda that examined the impact of different vehicles of *campaign information delivery* on registration and voter turnout rates. These two themes cannot be separated completely, for they are inextricably entwined: the party machine's principal tactics for influencing votes revolved around the distribution of party propaganda (Key 1942).

A third avenue of inquiry emerged as the use of social science opinion surveys increased during the 1940s, and particularly as researchers from Columbia University began to study the development of *individuals' political attitudes and behaviors*. As heirs of the first two themes, these scholars examined information distribution in the electorate and the organizational activities of parties using a combination of case study and survey research. The American National Election Studies surveys also were developed during this time.

Party Organizational Activities

Historically, one of the sources of power for local party organizations was their ability to generate electoral support as a byproduct of their traditional social-service activities. In the 1930s Chicago Democratic machine, for example, precinct captains' service role included tasks such as providing food and coal and acting as a broker between residents and the local governments and courts. Their political activities involved canvassing for votes, the central purpose of which was to distribute candidate and party information, solidify voter registration lists, and deliver votes for machine candidates. Electioneering was, of course, directly related to party workers' social-service duties. According to Gosnell (1968, 81), "Precinct captains who have put themselves out in many ways to serve their constituents do not have many difficulties in trying to get a hearing when they canvass their districts for votes."

The power of the local machines degraded with the incorporation of political reforms and the assumption by both national and state governments of the kinds of social services that had traditionally been converted by the machines into political power. These changes, combined with an expansion of the American electorate between the 1860s and 1950s and the advent of radio (and, later, television), brought about important changes in the electoral role of the machine and in the responsibilities of political parties generally. Key (1942, 570–571) described the effect of the transition from machine-dominated campaigning to the new reality of a vastly expanded electorate as follows:

> At one time word of mouth, personal influence, and parlor caucuses were probably of greater importance as methods of carrying a campaign to the voters than they are now.... The party organization remains, with workers in almost every precinct who seek to build up person-to-person relationships with the electors in their bailiwicks; but the radio, the newspaper, and the mass meeting are more important channels for the dissemination of appeals calculated to manipulate the attitudes of the electorate.

Thus, Key observed that it still fell to local party organizations to get out the vote on election day on the theory that proximity to voters made personal and machine-based appeals more practical in that process, as compared with the far-removed context of the national party organizations. However, knowledge about the relative effectiveness of party workers compared with the mass media was, at that time, slender. What had emerged regarding the art of campaigning was a set of "common-sense" rules for campaigning that Key (1942, 582–583) characterized as "superstition" and "the folklore of the trade."

Experiments on Campaign Information Distribution

Central to the parties' campaigning techniques was propaganda, "the management of collective attitudes by the manipulation of significant symbols" (Lasswell 1927, 627), which bypassed "deliberative" processes of opinion manipulation in favor of simple competition among culturally defined political symbols. Propaganda distribution efforts were concentrated where they did the most good, usually in closely contested and marginal areas. Messages were conveyed through both mass and partisan media; political rallies and campaign tours; and a variety of leaflets, pamphlets, and circulars. In confirmation of Key's observations, however, local party organizations still provided the structure through which campaign information was distributed and votes were delivered. In fact, research to the current day continues to trace candidate performance at the polls to the organizational activities of party and campaign operatives, even as personal party attachments of individuals in the American electorate have weakened.[3]

Beginning in the 1920s, experimental research on campaign propaganda distribution emerged to assess effects on the political behavior of prospective voters. Gosnell, for example, conducted a field experiment in the 1920s to examine the effect of a nonpartisan mail canvass on voter registration and turnout in Chicago (Gosnell 1926, 1927). After obtaining lists of residents who were registered and those who were not registered to vote, he mailed three sets of nonpartisan materials to half of the unregistered group. The first mailing contained a factual notice of the registration requirement for voting. The second mailing (sent to those who had not promptly registered following the initial contact) took two forms: one simply reiterated the original message, while the other showed a cartoon picturing the nonvoter as a "slacker." The registration rates of individuals who received the cards were substantially higher than those of citizens who did not receive them. A second experiment involved sending postcards to registered voters containing "a cartoon notice picturing the honest but apathetic citizen as the friend of the corrupt politician" (Gosnell 1926, 870). This time, voter turnout (as opposed to registration) rates were higher among citizens who received mailers. As might be expected in those golden days of the Chicago machine, context was important: Where local party organizations were strongest, the mailer had less of an effect (because turnout was already relatively high in those areas), whereas weaker organizations were associated with larger effects.

Twenty years later, Gosnell still believed that voters were influenced by the campaign information they received, and that this information informed their vote choices—not simply the decision to register and vote. He characterized the nature of the appeals made by party canvassers as "not always highly rational. Some party workers appeal for votes, not on the basis of the merits of their party candidates, but on the basis of sympathy for themselves or the potential services which their party may render locally" (Gosnell 1948, 280). Nevertheless, Gosnell remained optimistic about the powers of discrimination and good judgment that voters ultimately would show when making their vote decisions.

In the 1950s Eldersveld and his colleagues conducted experiments using their political science classes to assess various campaign influences.[4] In a municipal election (revising a city charter), Ann Arbor, Michigan, residents indifferent or hostile to the revisions were selected either for personal contact by college students arguing in favor of the revision, or for mailed "propaganda" in support of the revision. The results suggested that opinions and voter turnout were positively influenced by both types of influence. A second experiment assessed the ability of different types of personal contact techniques and mailers to influence the turnout of citizens who had never voted in municipal elections. Mobilization effects of the experiment were rather large, though residents recalled the personal contacts at a much greater rate than the mailed propaganda. In short, personal contacts and, to a lesser extent, mail appeals yielded higher voter registration rates, voter turnout, and support for ballot propositions.[5]

Individuals and Survey Research

By the 1950s the experimental approach gave way to a new technique for studying political behavior and public opinion—the use of surveys—a technique that has since come to dominate academic work on this topic. By enabling researchers to collect information about, and assess the attitudes and behavior of, large and representative numbers of citizens, surveys vastly improved our knowledge about, for example, the mechanisms of political mobilization, the effects of campaigns on individuals and groups, and the orientations of people to their social and political contexts. In particular, two sets of researchers, one based at Columbia University and the other at the University of Michigan, were instrumental in these developments.

In a groundbreaking analysis of voting decisions in Erie County, Ohio, during the 1940 presidential election, Columbia sociologists Lazarsfeld, Berelson, and Gaudet (1944) assessed the process by which people developed their opinions and candidate preferences. With regard to campaign effects, their research (like that discussed above) was focused mainly on propaganda distribution and mass media information flows. Three important effects were identified. First, the most prominent and important consequence of information provided by the parties was to *reinforce* previously held partisan preferences. A second effect involved the *activation of* people's interest in the campaign beyond their latent political predispositions. Finally, a few people (but not many) were genuinely *converted* to a new political position through the information they received from the campaigns. Of critical importance to the conclusions of Lazarsfeld and his colleagues was the role of informal personal contacts and channels of influence that existed among personal friends. While outlining the advantages of these influences,[6] the authors emphasized their unstructured, informal nature and their distinct lack of connection to formal campaigning.

However, in the subsequent analysis by Berelson, Lazarsfeld, and McPhee (1954) of voting in the 1948 presidential election, the political party reemerged as a significant object for research in the formation of individual opinions and behaviors. This study examined personal-contact campaigning, focusing on the patterns of information distribution by party workers who served as a link between the local party organization on the one hand, and local activists and ordinary voters on the other. Although the local organization was largely ineffective at connecting "real" people with national party leaders, it acted as a cog in the administrative machinery of the national party to make the process work. Specifically, local party leadership sought to mobilize not only voters of their own political stripe but also "problem voters" who needed extra stimulation to get out to the polls on election day. The latter group included aged citizens who needed rides to polling places; absentee and new voters; wives "who must be brought to the polls by husbands who take the family responsibility in such things"; and "the 'vote-if-induced' people, who in some districts have come to expect a little extra compensation (in the way of a few dollars or a drink) to exercise their franchise" (Berelson, Lazarsfeld, and McPhee 1954, 172). The small number of changes in candidate preference that occurred were related to personal relationships that some voters had with activists in the opposite party.

During this same time period, the American National Election Studies were being developed and implemented through the Center for Political Studies at the University of Michigan. These national-level surveys asked a broad range of questions relating to political opinions and behavior and, in the process, revolutionized research on public opinion and political participation. Having inherited the body of knowledge we are discussing, the National Election Studies in 1956 began asking respondents whether they had been contacted during the election campaign. The question was, "Did anybody from either one of the parties call you up or come around and talk to you during the campaign?"[7] Early analysis of this item uncovered variation in contacting by political context, with competitive areas having relatively greater incidences of canvassing than party strongholds (including the one-party South). While nonvoting was prevalent among citizens who had not been contacted by the parties, and mobilization was inferred, the effects of the canvass on presidential vote choice was weak (Janowitz and Marvick 1964).

Modern Grassroots Campaign Research

Modern research on grassroots campaigning has continued to study party organization, propaganda, and the behavior of individual voters, yielding a body of knowledge that musicians might call variations on a theme. It is clear, for example, that the central role of party organizations has diminished somewhat, undermined by changes in election and campaign finance laws.[8] Those laws have produced what some observers describe as a "candidate-centered" process (Wattenberg 1991), in which candidates and their advisers are the driving force behind campaign organization and funding. Accordingly, expertise in campaign conduct is no longer limited to party operatives but increasingly resides with professional consultants, and each new election cycle sees a wide range of interest groups undertake massive voter education and mobilization drives, some of them nonpartisan and others supportive of specific candidates. Nevertheless, the parties-as-organizations have not withered away altogether; they continue to serve as clearinghouses for expertise, strategy, innovation, and, importantly, the coordination of mass-level campaign activities.

On the academic front, the number of survey-based studies that look at national-level mobilization efforts has mushroomed, while direct evidence concerning the effects of campaign communications such as campaign advertising, direct mail, and literature drops is growing as well. Analyses of media information flows (including campaign information provided through network and cable television, radio, and the Internet) are ubiquitous, though this research is related only indirectly to grassroots campaigning. Finally, experimental research on the impact of GOTV efforts has witnessed a resurgence since 1998, with important implications for our understanding of the efficacy of various methods of grassroots campaigning.

Survey Research

Our principal source of knowledge about national-level grassroots campaign activities over an extended period of time is the American National Election Study series, which allows us to track long-term trends in mobilization efforts and outcomes. Figure 9.1 shows the percentage of National Election Studies respondents (who more or less represent the American adult population) between 1956 and 2004 who reported that they were contacted in person or by phone by a worker from a political party on behalf of a candidate.[9] The top line in the figure shows that the overall personal campaign contact rates have generally increased over time, though the late 1980s and early 1990s saw lower rates. Recently, the revived energy of the campaign "ground wars" in each party has pushed mass mobilization efforts to levels unseen in the post–World War II era.

In 2004, for example, 43.5 percent of adults reported a major-party candidate campaign contact. With an estimated 217.8 million adults in the United States, that rate represents some 97.4 million people contacted personally, either in person or by phone. Both of the major parties contributed substantially to this total: In 2004, Democratic candidates and party workers contacted about 33 percent of all voting-age adults (72.7 million), while their Republican counterparts contacted roughly 26 percent (56.4 million). Although the numbers here should be interpreted with a bit of caution (as respondents may be recalling one of several types of campaign contact as coming from party

Figure 9.1 Personal Contacting Rates, 1956–2004

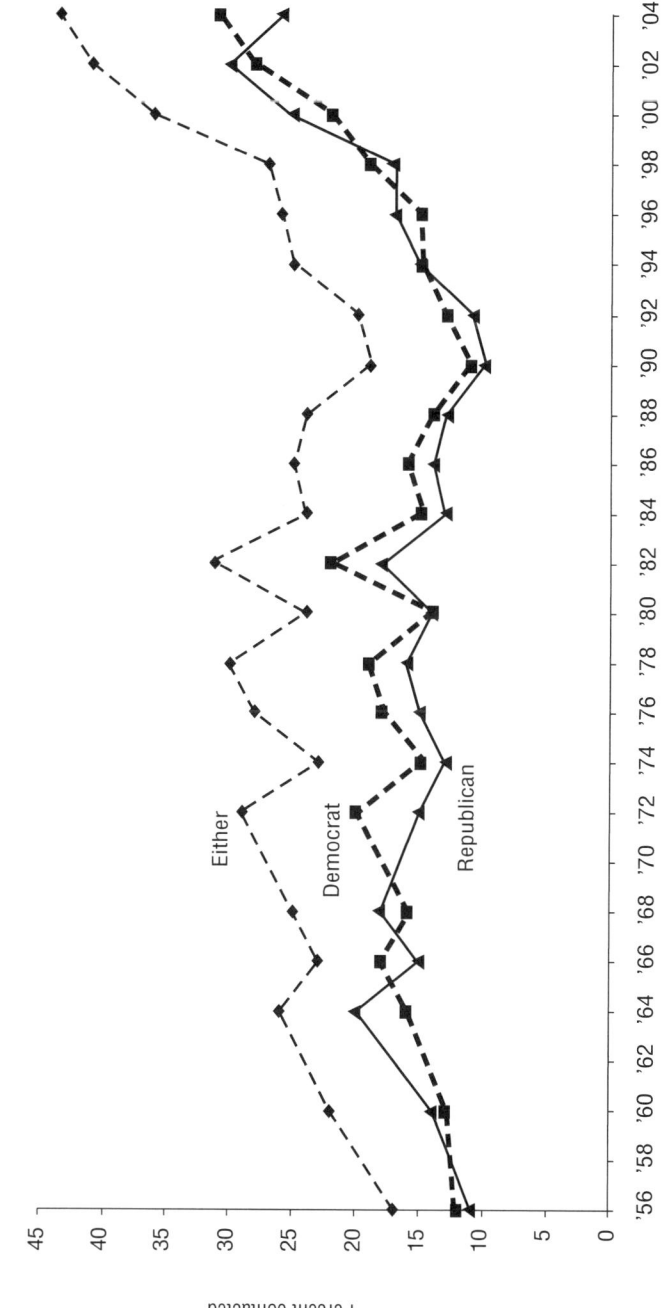

Source: American National Election Study series.

sources), at a minimum we can probably assume that they were spoken to by some campaign worker on behalf of a candidate.

Research shows that the parties' grassroots contacting efforts are not random but rather are strategically targeted toward specific segments of the population. The rationale for this approach is straightforward: the likelihood of victory hinges on *who* shows up to vote, not on whether *more* people show up. Campaigns therefore work to shape the electorate in ways that give them a higher likelihood of winning. Taking into account a host of individual and contextual factors, the people most likely to be contacted are those already predisposed to participate (that is, those with high socioeconomic status, those who are registered to vote, and those who are socially connected to their communities) and to vote for a particular party's candidates (that is, Democrats mainly contact Democrats, Republicans mainly contact Republicans).[10]

The effects of such contacts are well documented: People who are personally contacted by campaigns are significantly more likely to become politically active, even taking into account their participation predispositions. They are more likely to vote, to work for campaigns, to display campaign paraphernalia (such as buttons, bumper stickers, and yard signs), and to contribute financially to campaigns.[11] Moreover, a major survey (the Citizen Participation Study, or CPS) conducted in 1989–1990 showed that (1) of those who are asked to work for a campaign, about half say yes, and (2) of those who are asked to contribute financially, about one-quarter say yes (Verba, Schlozman, and Brady 1995, 137). The success of requests for political participation frequently hinges on who does the asking, with personal acquaintance continuing to play a key role. As with voters in the Columbia studies back in the 1940s and 1950s, CPS respondents reported that more than half of requests to work on a campaign came from someone known personally to them; another 28 percent came from people with just one relationship removed from the respondent.

Research dating back to the early Columbia studies has shown that the social context within which people live also influences their political preferences and behaviors. It appears, for example, that the educational level of one's neighborhood can affect an individual's likelihood of engaging in such activities as voting and registering people to vote. Moreover, political activity (such as party canvassing and displaying of yard signs) in a neighborhood helps to shape both the candidate preferences and participatory choices of people living there. In this way, the effects of an action (here, the original canvass) can have what are called "cascading consequences," that is, consequences that spill over to other people, whether in a household, neighborhood, or social organization

(Huckfeldt 1986; Huckfeldt and Sprague 1992). And to the extent that our political attitudes and behaviors are indeed influenced by the people with whom we have close personal relations, and with whom we discuss matters of importance to us (our "discussion network"), academic studies of voter mobilization efforts may tend to underestimate their total impact.[12]

Experimental Studies

Political scientists Donald Green and Alan Gerber recently spearheaded what has been a resurgence of experimental approaches to analyzing the impact of nonpartisan and campaign mobilization efforts. Their numerous studies examining door-to-door canvassing and literature distribution, direct mail, phone calls, and e-mail have provided new levels of specificity regarding the effects and costs of grassroots campaigning. Asserting the superiority of their methods over survey research, and in contrast to the "war stories" often told by campaign professionals, D. Green and Gerber (2004, chapters 1–2) highlight the strengths of social experimentation's well-defined control groups and parsimonious models.[13]

The historical record highlights the importance of face-to-face contacts for campaign information distribution and getting out the vote. (Recall the Lincoln Four-Step and the anecdote by Tip O'Neill that began this chapter.) Similarly, experimental studies strongly suggest that face-to-face canvassing is relatively effective at generating more voters, though it is unclear whether partisan canvassing increases votes for the contacting campaign's candidate, which is, after all, its main purpose. A mobilizing effect is present not only for individuals who are contacted but also among members of their households.[14] Distributing campaign leaflets to people's homes, another staple of grassroots campaign tactics, generates additional votes, but to a much lesser degree than face-to-face contacts (Nickerson 2005).

Substantial evidence has begun to accumulate on the efficacy of campaign phone calls. The most effective phone-based method of generating votes uses a script delivered in a slow, casual, and conversational manner. Volunteers do this best, though professional phone banking callers can be trained to do the same thing. Prerecorded phone calls delivering taped messages from candidates or their surrogates (known as "robocalls") have been found to be ineffective. The timing of calls matters, too. According to D. Green and Gerber (2004, 78), "[c]alls are most effective during the last week prior to the election," but multiple phone calls do not appear to increase the impact of a single, well-timed call on turnout.[15]

While scholars have studied GOTV tactics using experimental designs with some degree of success, so have the parties themselves. In a prominent example, the Republican National Committee in 2001 sponsored a series of pseudo-experiments in state and local elections.[16] They found that by making modest organizational changes and undertaking certain GOTV efforts, their party performance in these elections improved enough to justify future application of the methods. Specifically they found that (1) having a full-time staff member working the district for at least one month, then mobilizing (or "flushing") known Republicans on the Monday before election day and on election day itself, and (2) using volunteer (as opposed to paid) GOTV phone calls, each increased turnout in a district by between two and three percentage points. A five-week program for mobilizing social and religious conservatives in two counties improved those constituencies' as well as overall GOP performance in the areas involved, compared with counties where the program was not implemented. And a relatively well-controlled campaign communication experiment with newly registered Republicans in Pennsylvania found that contacting by the party increased turnout by about six percentage points.[17] These and other results also were used by the GOP to form "72-Hour Task Forces" (teams armed with detailed strategic plans for the three days prior to election day) across the nation for the 2002 and 2004 elections.

More Than Just the Parties

Historically, party organizations at the national, state, and local levels were the principal source of expertise for running campaigns (Key 1942). That simply is no longer true today. Political consultants (such as professional campaign managers and, in the modern era, pollsters, media advisers, fundraisers, opposition researchers, grassroots organizers, and others) have been present in American politics for many years, of course, but since the 1960s both the number of people for whom campaigning is a profession and the degree of specialization in the services they offer have increased greatly. Further, the campaign professionalization that we usually associate with presidential, gubernatorial, and U.S. Senate campaigns has now trickled down to state legislative and even local elections (Medvic 2000; Strachan 2003).

Although some scholars once suggested that consultants and political parties stood in opposition to one another (Sabato 1981), recent research reveals widespread collaboration and coordination between party organizations and independent campaign professionals (Dulio and Thurber 2003; Kolodny 2000; also see chapter 10 in this volume). The national and state parties today work closely with consultants, retaining some directly while simultaneously maintaining lists of preferred consultants to whom they refer candidates. There even are some areas where party leaders believe (correctly or not) that they do a better job than consultants, including fundraising, getting out the vote, candidate research—and grassroots organization (Kolodny 2000). Whatever the truth may be, however, parties and consultants now work together to coordinate campaign activities designed to maximize their candidates' chances of winning on election day.

As for grassroots mobilization, many intermediary organizations undertake such activities as well. Labor unions, for example, have long been a critical component of the Democratic Party's ground war, though as the number of union members in the United States has declined, so has the mobilization capacity of this segment of the coalition.[18] Other interest groups also provide important resources, human as well as fiscal, for candidates of both parties. The success of religious conservative organizations at mobilizing their adherents since the 1970s is well-documented, though their effects vary across national, state, and local elections. Nevertheless, groups such as the Christian Coalition America and others are effective fundraisers and resources for conducting the ground war, especially on behalf of conservative GOP candidates (J. Green, Rozell, and Wilcox 2003).

In 2004 significant resources were spent by organized interests, and especially by Democratic-leaning groups, on grassroots mobilization efforts. For example, America Coming Together, a so-called 527 organization (see above and chapter 4 in this volume) that was financed and run by longtime Democratic activists, spent almost $85 million—much of it involving grassroots organizing in battleground states—on behalf of presidential nominee John Kerry. In addition, the League of Conservation Voters committed 75 percent of its 2004 budget on grassroots (about $4 million), seeking to mobilize 25,000 volunteers for GOTV work and to organize activists on nearly 100 college campuses around the country.[19] A report by the Center for the Study of Elections and Democracy (2005) pointed out, however, that the numerous Democratic-leaning groups failed "to coordinate message and effort with the candidate and party, [which put] the overall Democratic ground effort at a disadvantage compared to the Republicans who communicated with the candidate and delivered a 'Vote Bush' message because their ground operation was run almost entirely by the RNC."

Summary: What We Know and Don't Know

As things stand, what do we know about grassroots campaigning and its effects in U.S. elections? Most conventional forms of mobilization are at least somewhat effective at encouraging people to participate in politics who might not otherwise have done so. People personally contacted by campaigns (or whose family, friends, and other discussion partners are contacted) will vote, take part in campaign activities, and make a financial contribution at significantly higher rates than those who are not so contacted. If this were not the case, then the energy of millions of volunteers and hundreds of millions of dollars spent over the last few election cycles would have been wasted. Thus, what Key (1942) characterized as "common-sense," "superstition," and "the folklore of the trade" is largely confirmed in modern times, though evidence has raised doubts about the alleged impact of phone banks in delivering votes. Yet volunteer phone calling does seem to be somewhat successful at getting people to the polls (A. Gerber and Green 2005), depending on the quality of the contacts made (that is, impersonal efforts such as robocalls are less effective mobilizers than high-quality mailers and personal contacts).[20] We do, however, need a better understanding of the varying effects of *partisan* messages, since most experimental research assesses nonpartisan GOTV efforts (Levine and Lopez 2005).

African-American mobilization has received substantial attention from scholars, largely in case studies of municipal elections or as a function of the organizing capacity of predominantly black churches.[21] Blacks have long been well integrated into the Democratic Party's mobilization efforts, while being largely excluded from GOP contacting efforts through 1996 (though in the years since then, Republican outreach at the grassroots level has increased appreciably). African Americans tend to respond to mobilization efforts with higher rates of participation, even taking into account existing predispositions to vote and varying political contexts (Leighley 2001; Wielhouwer 2000). In contrast, D. Green (2004) found little mobilization among blacks as a consequence of interest-group advocacy phone calls or personal contacts, though direct mail had modest effects.

Evidence on the impact of mobilization efforts among other minority groups comes from a small but growing literature. Leighley (2001), for example, concluded that Latinos were mobilized into political activities predominantly by friends and acquaintances; that being recruited was largely a function of the individual's education, income, and sociopolitical context; and that political participation was affected by interactions between context and mobilization efforts. The messenger also matters; that is, knowing the mobilizer personally or having an ethnic "match" (with a Latino being recruited by another Latino) influences whether mobilization is likely to be successful. Overall, the effect of mobilization on Latino turnout can be quite large (see also Michelson 2003, 2005; Michelson and Villa 2003). Similar results are obtained for Asian American voters (Wong 2005).

One area in which our knowledge is limited has to do with the effects of particular kinds of messages on the people who receive them. Some experimental evidence suggests that simply reminding people about election day, encouraging them to perform their civic duty, and not being too negative will help get them to the polls (D. Green and Gerber 2004). In fundraising, appeals to emotions such as fear and anger apparently motivate people to contribute money (Godwin 1988), and it is therefore assumed—without much supporting evidence—that a similar approach works for mobilization to other activities as well. We also know relatively little about the role of message repetition, though campaign professionals assume that repetition is good, and that free repetition (with coverage by the media, especially television) is even better than the original ad buy. Do multiple messages from the same group have a cumulative impact on voters? What are the consequences of conflicting messages? Do partisan and nonpartisan messages have similar effects? Further research regarding the full range of campaign communications (and their impact on vote choice and participation) is needed.

At the individual level, scholars lack a well-formed body of knowledge about people's responses when they are contacted. For example, when someone receives a piece of political literature amidst other mail, what does he or she do with it? When someone comes home from work and campaign literature is on the door, what happens to it? Is it read and consciously considered, or simply thrown out? Phone calls appear to have modest effects, but what happens after the call? We assume that the message prompts some level of conscious thought and perhaps conversation, producing cascading consequences—but what is the process by which this sort of thing occurs? Thinking along the same lines, we don't know much about the effects of different campaign messages on different recipients. What, for example, are the consequences of GOP campaign contacts on strong Democrats, weak Democrats, and independents? We know that campaigns are generally advised to avoid the opposition, and that demobilization efforts (much accused but little used) are difficult to make work, but there isn't much empirical evidence to tell us what happens when opposition contact is made. These effects, if extensive enough, could have significant implications for coalition building and expansion, as opposed to mere coalition maintenance and getting the base out.

A high level of uncertainty is found in any GOTV effort directed toward groups perceived as traditionally part of the opposition. Much was made of Republican efforts in 2004 to win Latino and African American votes and thus to expand the GOP coalition. But whereas George W. Bush earned as much as 44 percent of Latino votes, exit polls also revealed that his showing among blacks was about the same as other Republican presidential candidates since the 1970s (roughly 11 percent).[22] As I talk to GOP consultants and officials, they are mostly receptive to including (as opposed to excluding) blacks in their mobilization strategies, but they are perplexed about how to do so. Some complain about blunders committed by "the old guard" (an example would be Senate majority leader Trent Lott's praise of Strom Thurmond's 1948 presidential campaign, which was founded on opposition to racial desegregation),[23] while others feel locked out of black social networks and don't know how to get in. Parallel questions can be asked about the Democrats and conservative Christians. One effort to resolve this problem involved the party bringing in liberal Christians like *Sojourners*'s Jim Wallis to provide advice on how to use religious language to frame its policy messages.[24] Still, with Democrats and Republicans alike having (relatively) limited resources and time, campaigns are most likely to revert to well-known and default campaign mobilization targets.

Conclusion

The involvement of large numbers of people in the American political process may be seen as a measure of the nation's democratic health. Grassroots campaigns have been essential to elections at least since the development of the mass parties in the 1820s, and broader participation lends greater legitimacy to electoral outcomes. Political parties have historically been the major vehicles for mobilizing voters, and they changed into being service providers as our elections became more candidate centered. Now, working in concert with political consultants and a broad range of organized interests, the parties continue to be clearinghouses of expertise, fundraising, and data for the candidates running under their labels. The 2004 cycle, in particular, saw major changes in the ways in which campaigns generated grassroots activism. Howard Dean's campaign for the Democratic presidential nomination, for example, applied innovative techniques such as using text messaging to generate spontaneous "meet-ups," along with unprecedented levels of Internet-based fundraising. Dean's subsequent election as Democratic National Committee chair would seem to have positioned the party for a more technologically progressive approach to networking the grassroots, though significant advances were made in database management and exploitation even before he came aboard.

Decades of research involving case studies, surveys, and social experiments have given us a substantial body of knowledge about what works and what doesn't. Nevertheless, our grasp of the processes through which individuals respond to grassroots mobilization efforts is not as well developed from empirical observation as it should be. Then again, it may be something as simple as people liking to be asked.

Notes

Portions of this chapter originally appeared in Wielhouwer (2001).

1. This document is from *The Collected Works of Abraham Lincoln,* www.hti.umich.edu/l/lincoln, September 19, 2005.
2. These shortcomings were identified in a 2002 PowerPoint presentation ("72-Hour Task Force") prepared by the Republican National Committee (personal copy).
3. For recent research on party organizations and their capabilities for mobilization, see Gershtenson (2003); McClurg (2004); Wielhouwer (1999); Wielhouwer and Lockerbie (1994). On the erosion of mass partisanship, see Fiorina (2002); Wattenberg (1998).
4. In particular, see Eldersveld (1956); Eldersveld and Dodge (1954).
5. In an interesting twist, Eldersveld eventually parlayed his understanding of campaign dynamics to get elected mayor of Ann Arbor.
6. For example, the ability of personal relationships to convey information informally and casually made that information more credible and influential; informal networks also facilitated information flow from political elites to undecided voters via trusted and intimate relationships (see Lazarsfeld, Berelson, and Gaudet 1948, chapter 16).
7. A more candidate-centered question was asked in the 1952 American National Election Study. The validity of this now-standard question has been criticized (for example, by Teixeira 1992); for a response, see Wielhouwer (1999).
8. These changes include the introduction of the Australian ballot (which was designed to reduce election fraud perpetrated by local party machines) at the turn of the twentieth century, the expansion of primary elections to determine nominees for a wide range of offices (making it more difficult for party bosses to control the process), and campaign finance reforms passed by Congress in the 1970s (which forced candidates for national office to raise money with appeals that were geographically diverse rather than predominantly local). See Hershey and Beck (2004); Ladd with Hadley (1978); Reichley (1992).
9. See the *NES Guide to Political Behavior,* available at www.umich.edu/~nes. While the percentage contacted in 2004 is not strictly comparable to other years in a statistical sense (due to data weighting differences), its value stands as an accurate estimate for that year.

10. See Huckfeldt and Sprague (1992); Rosenstone and Hansen (1993); Verba, Schlozman, and Brady (1995); Wielhouwer (1999). The basic approach involves "attempts to elevate gross turnout within certain definable groups where the candidate has overwhelming strength . . . [and] to identify and selectively increase participation among voter subgroups where strength exists but is not dominant" (Tyson 1999, 133). From paper-and-pencil targeting plans to high-performance computer applications, the goal is to segment the electorate and avoid the opposition (Kim 2004; Shea and Burton 2001).

11. See Rosenstone and Hansen (1993); Wielhouwer and Lockerbie (1994).

12. Organizations, especially churches, have been used quite effectively as mobilizing institutions throughout American history (Ahlstrom 1972). The remarkable strength of African-American churches (Frazier 1963; Harris 1999) in this regard has been matched in recent years by socially conservative evangelical churches (J. Green et al. 1996; J. Green, Rozell, and Wilcox 2003). More generally, churches of all stripes are contexts in which political discussions can be influential because the people with whom those discussions take place are more important to us than other casual acquaintances (Huckfeldt, Plutzer, and Sprague 1993; Huckfeldt and Sprague 1991; Kenny 1992).

13. While research by Donald Green, Alan Gerber, and their colleagues has been published widely in academic journals (for example, A. Gerber and Green 2000a, 2000b, 2001), their book *Get Out the Vote!* (D. Green and Gerber 2004) cogently summarizes and synthesizes the results. I have relied heavily on that work for the present discussion.

14. This result seems to hold in races with varying levels of electoral competitiveness.

15. Also see Cardy (2005); A. Gerber and Green (2005); McNulty (2005); Nickerson (2005).

16. See note 2. By *pseudo*-experiments, I refer to efforts to assess the effects of various GOTV and organizational methods without using the rigorous controls and measurements required by true experimentation.

17. In one suburban Philadelphia county, the Republican National Committee divided all registrants into two groups: a test group and a control group. The former was sent a variety of communications motivating them to vote and explaining the mechanics of voting, while the latter received nothing from the party. In the ensuing election, 19 percent of contacted registrants voted, compared with 13 percent of those not contacted. These results are drawn from the "72-Hour Task Force" presentation cited in note 2.

18. This declining capacity (of unions to mobilize) is true despite the fact that union members and their families continue to have above-average turnout rates.

19. See League of Conservation Voters (2004).

20. There also are doubts about the mobilizing effectiveness of partisan direct mail; see A. Gerber, Green, and Green (2003).

21. For example, see Brown and Wolford (1994); Browning, Marshall, and Tabb (1994); Calhoun-Brown (1996); Dawson, Brown, and Allen (1990); Harris (1999); Pinderhughes (1992); Preston, Henderson, and Puryear (1982); Walton (1994).

22. For example, see "Exit polls—President" (2004).

23. See Mercurio (2002).

24. According to its web site, Sojourners is "a Christian ministry whose mission is to proclaim and practice the biblical call to integrate spiritual renewal and social justice." See www.sojo.net.

10 The Effects of Political Consultants

David A. Dulio

In his victory speech on November 3, 2004, newly reelected President George W. Bush recited the customary litany of postelection acknowledgements. He thanked his wife, his daughters, and the rest of his family; he also thanked his running mate, and complimented his opponent for having waged a spirited campaign. In addition, Bush went on to say, "I want to thank my superb campaign team," a key part of which was "the architect, Karl Rove" (*New York Times* 2004).

One need look no further than the 2004 presidential race to see the impact that political consultants can have in modern American elections. Karl Rove initially served as President Bush's chief political adviser in the White House, where he headed the Office of Strategic Initiatives, before being elevated to Deputy Chief of Staff for the president's second term. More important, Rove, who had been a successful political consultant specializing in direct-mail persuasion pieces before joining the 2000 Bush campaign, was the acknowledged mastermind behind the winning strategy used by the Bush-Cheney reelection team.

As the political media frequently reported during Campaign 2004, it was Rove who was largely responsible for crafting the strategy of turning out a larger share of the Republican base, including millions of evangelical Christians, to drive up Bush's vote total relative to what he had received in 2000 (Allen 2004). It also was Rove who, during the summer of 2001, began holding clinics for White House officials to lay out his game plan for reelecting the president (Allen 2004). Yet Bush's successful bid for a second term was ably assisted by a number of other advisers besides Rove, including pollster Matthew Dowd, media guru Mark McKinnon, and campaign manager Ken Mehlman. Michael Barone of *U.S. News & World Report* noted, for example, that, "If Karl Rove was the architect of George W. Bush's thumping reelection victory, Mehlman was the structural engineer who turned the plans into reality" (quoted in Pierce 2004, A5).

The Bush-Cheney campaign was not the only one to hire campaign professionals in 2004, of course, nor was 2004 the first election cycle in which candidates for public office hired consultants to assist them in achieving their electoral ambitions. Senator John Kerry had several professionals as part of his team, including veteran presidential campaign consultant Bob Shrum, his media firm partners Michael Donilon and Tad Devine, as well as pollsters Mark Mellman and Tom Kiley, and campaign manager Mary Beth Cahill. Moreover, scores of candidates at all levels hire consultants during each election cycle. In campaigns today, no serious contender for a seat in the U.S. House of Representatives, the U.S. Senate, or a governor's mansion goes into battle without help from political professionals—a trend that is rapidly extending into state legislative races and local contests for mayor, county commissioner, and even school board (Herrnson 2004; Johnson 2001; Medvic 2001). Moreover, consultants have played an active part in elections for quite some time, dating back at least to 1933.[1]

Before going any further, I want to make clear exactly what it means to be a political consultant. This is easier said than done, however, because "[u]nlike those that apply to other professionals such as attorneys, physicians, or even cosmetologists, there are no barriers to entry, no certification procedures, and no training requirements to become a political consultant" (Dulio 2004, 43). Anyone who would like to be a political consultant need only hang out a shingle and find a client. This makes it difficult to differentiate between the true professional who offers advice to candidates for a living and the college professor who conducts a poll for a friend who is running for state legislature. Only after consultants were associated with the public relations field for many years did Sabato (1981, 8) offer the first real definition of a political consultant as "a campaign professional who is engaged primarily in the provision of advice and services (such as polling, media creation and production, and direct-mail fundraising) to candidates, their campaigns, and other political committees." Even though this helped to clarify who consultants are, the definition was still too vague. As Sabato (1981, 8) himself noted, his definition can apply to "almost any paid staffer on even the most minor of campaigns." In addition, some individuals in campaigns provide services that are strategic in nature while others provide services that are more technical. This distinction is similar to the one made by Johnson (2000, 2001) between "strategists" and "vendors." True consultants are those who provide strategic advice and services that are central to the execution of a campaign.

Why do candidates hire political consultants? Do candidates, who often pay consultants a great deal of money, get a fair return on their investment? In the present chapter I provide an overview of research that has been done to assess the impact of political consultants in modern American elections. Central to this question are the effects that consultants have in candidates' campaigns on election day; that is, by hiring consultants do candidates tend to receive more votes than they otherwise would? More narrowly, do consultants help candidates with their fundraising efforts (an important consideration given the influence that money can have in shaping election outcomes; see chapter 4)? Further, the impact of political consultants in today's elections may extend into other areas that are broader than just one candidate's campaign. After consultants came onto the electioneering scene in the United States, for example, some critics worried about the negative consequences they allegedly were having on political parties, voters, and the electoral process as a whole. In this chapter I also review the literature that examines consultants' effects in these less tangible areas.[2]

The study of consultants in the academic literature is in its infancy compared to more traditional areas of inquiry in the field of campaigns and elections. Many of the first works devoted to the study of consultants were focused on describing the phenomenon and providing basic information about what consultants do. My purpose here, however, is not to review the growth of the consulting industry in the United States, nor to describe the job of a consultant in great detail. Rather, it is to understand what consultants bring to our elections as we move forward into twenty-first-century campaigns. I begin by considering the impact of consultants on political parties and the general public because, in many ways, this can help us to better understand their more clear-cut and distinguishable campaign effects in the form of fundraising and vote totals, which are the next topics considered. Finally, I briefly examine future possibilities for the study of political consultants.[3]

Consultants' Effects on Political Parties

Initial assessments of the impact of political consultants on the parties were consistently negative. This view was summed up nicely in Sabato's *The Rise of Political Consultants* (1981, 286):

> The "personality cult" campaign and the general deterioration of the party system are perfectly acceptable to most political consultants. In fact, they themselves, along with their electoral wares, have played a moderate part in personalizing and glamorizing American politics and in the continuing decline of party organization. While certainly not initiating the party's decline, they have nonetheless aided and abetted the slide, sometimes with malice

aforethought.... The services provided by consultants, their new campaign technologies, have undoubtedly supplanted party activities and influence.

An interwoven set of criticisms relating to consultants' negative effects on parties is contained in Sabato's statement, including that consultants have (1) contributed to the parties' decline, (2) willingly and knowingly aided this decline, and (3) commandeered areas of electioneering once dominated by parties. Also embedded in this argument is the notion that consultants and the parties are locked in a competition for modern candidates' loyalties.

Consultants supposedly have contributed to the parties' decline by becoming the main service providers to candidates; this, in turn, leads to candidates severing ties with their party and, ultimately, to parties no longer playing a meaningful role in elections. According to Sabato (1981, 286), "Party leaders used to be the ones thought to have the keys to success, *the* secrets to winning elections. Now political consultants ... are the new experts, and their advice and support are considered to be more valuable publicly and privately than almost any party leader's." Much of this transformation occurred during a time of great technological innovation that included the development of radio and then television as channels of communication with voters, and the shift was noticed by scholars and journalists alike. Farrell (1996) described it as a transition from campaigns that were labor intensive to ones that were capital intensive. Not long after the preeminence of television became evident, Broder (1971, 239) argued that consultants were usurping the parties' dominance in communicating campaign messages and that television was making "one of the party's old functions irrelevant—that of serving as a bridge between the candidate or officeholder and the public." Nimmo (2001, 9) concurred, suggesting that because consultants came in and took over the provision of campaign services from the parties, they were responsible for "displacing the full-time [pols] of party machines."

According to Sabato (1981, 289), "A natural consequence of the consultant's antagonism toward the party is his willingness to run his candidates apart from, or even against, their party label." Nimmo (2001, 10) agreed and claimed that the growth of the consulting industry had brought forth "the means for candidates to secure office regardless of the wishes of the party leaders, indeed over the heads of those leaders; what was replaced was party control of candidate recruitment, selection, and election." As one of the most severe critics of consultants and their impact on political parties, Sabato (1988, 21; also see Crotty and Jacobson 1980) argued that consultants had become "the main institutional rivals of the parties, luring candidates away from their party moorings and using the campaign technologies to supplant parties as the intermediaries between candidates and the voters."

Making matters worse, in this view, was that consultants generally did not have the same degree of ideological or broad programmatic commitment as did the parties. Broder (1971, 237), for example, complained that "the professional campaign managers tend to be as anti-party as they are nonideological," and recounted that by 1971, "all of the major states—California, New York, Illinois, Pennsylvania, Ohio, Florida—[had] seen wealthy or well-financed men, with little background in party activity, little support among the party cadre, and little allegiance to the party or its programs, come in and beat the formally or informally designated organization favorite with expensive campaigns managed by outside political consultants" (238). Thus, lacking ideological principles themselves, consultants were accused of encouraging candidates to wage campaigns outside the traditional party structure and (in the process) to take positions that sometimes were inconsistent with basic party principles.

The most damaging critique of consultants in this regard is that they pushed parties to the side of electioneering on purpose and as a power grab. Such characterizations of the relationship between consultants and parties have been challenged by more recent work, however, which takes the position that rather than displacing parties knowingly, consultants came in to fill a void created by changes in the electoral environment (Dulio 2004). Among these changes are reforms instituted during the Progressive movement of the early 1900s (including the direct primary, initiatives and referendums, and the Australian ballot) and, more recently, the great technological advancements that ushered in the era of campaigns conducting scientific public opinion research, communicating with voters over the airwaves through television, and carefully targeting citizens to receive direct-mail pieces (Dulio 2004; Farrell 1996). As campaigning moved from a system based mainly on candidates canvassing and shaking hands to one dominated by television and the mass media, parties found that they could no longer either help their entire slate of candidates or campaign the way they once had. Moreover, candidates started to behave like any consumers would as they increasingly demanded services that were part of the technological revolution. In short, many contemporary inquiries have concluded that consultants were not a reason for the decline of parties, but rather that they were a reaction to what had already happened and that they came in to fill a void left by that decline (Dulio 2004; Dulio and Nelson 2005).

One last point about the effects that consultants have had on parties is that the early work examining the relationship viewed it as a competitive one.

O'Shaughnessy (1990, 136), for example, argued that "party and consultants are in competition and see each other as rivals: to some extent they duplicate each other's functions." Today, it is recognized that this is not always the case. Kolodny and Logan (1998) were among the first to systematically examine the question of whether consultants and political parties are adversaries or allies. "According to the adversarial view," they wrote, "consultants do not complement parties and act as little more than advertising agencies"; campaign professionals tend to see parties and candidates as clients whose main purpose is to increase their revenues (155). Under the allied view, however, consultants "value party goals," and, more important, "do for candidates what political parties simply cannot: they offer targeted technical assistance and personal advice to the candidate who hires them" (155).

Kolodny and Logan (1998), in a study that examined consultants' attitudes toward parties, found evidence for the allied view. Specifically, rather than pushing parties into decline or being a detriment to their cause, these scholars learned that consultants see themselves as assisting parties in achieving the goal of electing candidates to public office. Other recent work also has been consistent with the allied view of the consultant-party relationship. In particular, studies that survey campaign professionals and party elites generally find agreement among both groups that consultants have replaced parties in providing some services to candidates, and that there are some things consultants can do that parties simply cannot (Dulio and Thurber 2003; Dulio and Nelson 2005). However, this is not a negative consequence because, according to consultants and party leaders alike, the parties continue to play a meaningful role in campaigns. If anything, a fairly clear division of labor has emerged between the two groups that allows each to focus on its own areas of efficiency and expertise (Dulio 2004); that is, a cooperative and symbiotic relationship has developed in which consultants are the main providers of campaign services that center on message creation and delivery (for example, strategic advice and management, survey research, television advertising) while parties are looked to for services that require large amounts of staff and time (for example, opposition research, fundraising, get-out-the-vote efforts), which the parties have in greater supply than do individual consulting firms.

Additional evidence of this alliance or partnership is provided by the fact that parties frequently looked to consultants for assistance during the time of the parties' so-called resurgence or revitalization in the 1980s and 1990s.[4] According to Kolodny (2000, 112), "As some were predicting the death of political parties, the parties instead found that forming alliances with consultants was a rational solution to the upheavals of modern campaigning." In other words, parties began to hire consultants to help with their fundraising efforts and to provide some of the other services demanded by candidates and utilized directly by the parties themselves[5]—a trend that continues today, as both Republican and Democratic party organizations pay a great deal of money directly to outside consultants and recommend consultants that candidates might choose to hire on their own.[6] The overall picture is one of cooperation more than of conflict or competition.

In sum, whereas it was once believed that consultants had a decidedly negative effect on political parties, the truth may be just the opposite; that is, by working for individual candidates as well as the party apparatus itself, consultants have helped the parties to become more efficient in seeking their primary goal: to elect more of their candidates to public office. In the process, the parties have learned "that today's skilled professional consultants are essential to modern electioneering, and moreover, that the campaign techniques they provide have not destroyed the parties but have strengthened them" (Luntz 1988, 144).

Consultants' Effects on Citizens

Research dealing with the effects of political consultants on the individuals who are on the receiving end of their work is nearly as divided as that exploring the consultant-party relationship. Once again, we can see a division between more dated work (which generally portrays the consequences as being harmful) and recent studies (some of which come to a rather different conclusion). Even contemporary scholars, however, are not agreed as to whether the impact of consultants on ordinary citizens is positive or negative.

The notion that consultants are likely to have some effect on citizens is based on three considerations. First, as already noted, members of the electorate are the targets of what most modern political campaigns produce, that is, messages designed either to persuade or to reinforce beliefs already held by prospective voters.[7] Second, these messages are delivered principally through television and radio ads, or direct-mail pieces, which then become a candidate's public face and have the potential to shape how people think about the campaign. Third, a number of academic studies make it clear that campaign communications can and do have an impact on viewers and readers. For instance, the literature leaves little doubt that citizens' evaluations of candidates are subject to influence from effects such as agenda setting, priming, and framing that result from strategic messages delivered either directly (by candidates) or indirectly (through earned, or free, media).[8]

Nevertheless, no real consensus exists among scholars about the effects of television commercials, radio ads, and direct-mail pieces—in other words, the very communications that are often the end product of consultants' work in a campaign. In the eyes of some critics, the impact is dastardly and devious. As O'Shaughnessy (1990, 135) pointed out, "Consultants have been regarded by some as the agents of corruption, the mercenary pimps and whores of the political waterfront." This corruption allegedly comes in a variety of forms, including through the use of campaign ads that distort the records of candidates, selective reporting of results from an opinion survey, and the fostering of ambiguity and symbolism in campaign rhetoric.[9] Because of their actions, consultants are accused of engaging in "manipulation" (Johnson-Cartee and Copeland 1997b; O'Shaughnessy 1990), saturation of "the mass electorate with partisan and image propaganda" (Nimmo 2001, 222; also see Kelley 1956; Sabato 1981), and the use of "mercantilist metaphors" (Johnson-Cartee and Copeland 1997a). In short, a crucial impact that consultants supposedly have is to deceive and manipulate the public through their use of sophisticated campaign techniques such as polling and television ads. In a related vein, consultants are frequently criticized for relying too heavily on the so-called negative advertising that is believed by some to undermine campaign learning, turn people off to the electoral process, and even drive down voter turnout (see Lau and Pomper 2004; Lau and Sigelman 2000, 2005).

The argument here deserves closer scrutiny. First, there certainly are cases throughout the history of American elections in which campaigns have distorted the truth. One might argue, however, that such incidents do not reflect a problem with advertising per se but rather with the unethical nature of a specific message or communication (see chapter 11 in this volume for a more extended discussion of campaign ethics). Yet for some people there is no difference, and all advertising is suspect. According to Johnson-Cartee and Copeland (1997b, xxii), "Political advertising as a science and an art is a manipulative business" and, therefore, due to the ads that pollsters and media consultants create, "millions of voters are manipulated each campaign season." This assessment is not new. As far back as Kelley's (1956, 214) writing about "the public relations man," it was noted that the consultant (who represented an outgrowth of the public relations field) "strives to determine vote by controlling attitudes." Petracca (1989, 13) described this type of manipulation using the words of one of the first modern political professionals, Joe Napolitan, who advised, "Decide what you want the voter to feel or how you want him to *re*act. Decide what you must do to make him react the way you want. Do it."

Petracca's contention was that consultants do not always strive to create clear distinctions between candidates. Nimmo (2001, 221), writing originally in the 1960s, agreed, claiming that in situations in which consultants have a strong presence, "[e]lections are approached neither as conflicts between parties nor as confrontations of principle. They are viewed instead as contests of personalities and, even more basically, they offer a choice between the sophisticated engineers working on behalf of those personalities." And while politicians may argue that they would never fall victim to the perils of using a consultant, "the fact remains that these technicians can make a candidate appear to be what he is not" (221). Reflecting this, political professionals have been called "image merchants" (Hiebert et al. 1971) and are said to be in the business of "impression management" (Johnson-Cartee and Copeland 1997b) and "product management" (O'Shaughnessy 1990)—labels that clearly come with a negative connotation attached. Beyond the shaping of candidate images, there is the fact that consultants are able to place new issues on the agenda. This is supposedly a cause for concern because, first, issues are chosen based on what is wrong with the opponent rather than on whether the issues are genuinely important to voters (O'Shaughnessy 1990; Peele 1982), and second, being able to set the agenda gives unelected consultants more power than they should have in democratic politics (O'Shaughnessy 1990).

To some critics, then, the work of political consultants amounts to nothing more than selling candidates as more traditional marketers would sell laundry detergent. Sabato (1981, 321) argued, for example, that "the ad man's selling instinct among political consultants is the most degrading and repulsive aspect of their profession." Accordingly, Sabato endorsed Adlai Stevenson's observation that the merchandising of "candidates for high office like breakfast cereal is the ultimate indignity to the democratic process."[10] Nimmo (2001, 219) expressed concern that the consequences of consultant activity may extend beyond a simple vote choice on election day; such activity, he said, hits at the heart of the democratic nature of elections and "introduces not only the possibility but indeed the likelihood of systematic deception in electoral politics."

In contrast, some newer research on consultants does not characterize their impact on the public as being duplicitous at all. To the contrary, rather than reflecting efforts at manipulation that cause problems for democratic politics, the work of consultants today is more likely to be seen as activating citizens' previously held beliefs and, along the way, perhaps even raising the level of debate within the electorate.[11] This new interpretation is rooted in a closer consideration of the process that consultants usually engage in when they design the strategy and message of a campaign. Earlier research simply looked at the content of the most visible outputs produced by consultants—that is, television and radio ads, and direct-mail pieces—and assumed a dastardly motive. Examining the process leading to those outputs can shed light on their effects because it can help to reveal motive.

Although the literature dealing with political consultants generally lacks theory (see Thurber 1998), some recent developments speak to the effects that consultants may have on the electorate. Specifically, Medvic's (2001) theory of *deliberate priming* brings together ideas from various strands of research to identify what consultants actually do when they develop a strategy and message for a campaign. Central to Medvic's argument, as noted before, is an understanding of the process that consultants go through to develop a message that they wish to communicate to potential voters. At the heart of this process is public opinion research. Critics would argue that a reliance on polling is in and of itself dangerous because consultants simply end up using the data to tell candidates what position they should take on issues. The process described by Medvic, however, is different and more subtle. Instead of using polling to take the pulse of the electorate in the sense of finding out what policy positions most citizens hold, consultants seek "to determine which issues are most salient, both actually and potentially to voters" (Medvic 2001, 49). Note that Medvic stops short of the problematic aspects of critics' claims and contends that the central goal of polling is simply to identify issues that are salient, not modal issue positions. Specifically, "consultants in the early stages of a campaign help candidates understand how, but not where, to position themselves" on an imaginary opinion spectrum in the electorate (50).

Ideally, the results of early research conducted by a campaign "should have identified the most salient issues in the election, as well as issues of potential salience, and should have uncovered the effects of the various ways that those issues could be framed. In addition, the best (and worst) characteristics of the candidate should have been explored and the weaknesses of the opponent pinpointed" (Medvic 2001, 51). This information is then used by the campaign in deciding the best way for the candidate to communicate with the public. In other words, specific messages are tested through survey research to identify how a candidate can best talk about the position(s) he or she already holds.

Candidates obviously cannot talk about every issue they might like to over the course of a campaign; the public simply does not have sufficient time for, or interest in, that kind of detailed policy discussion. Rather, candidates must choose a subset of issues on which to focus in their communications, and consultants are hired to help them with this task. The crux of the theory of deliberate priming is that "campaigns emphasize certain topics with the intention of altering the criteria that voters use for candidate evaluation" (Medvic 2001, 51). It is critical to keep in mind that this is usually done before any television ads or direct-mail pieces have been developed. Consequently, those who maintain that consultants have a manipulative effect on the public begin their critique too late in the process, by focusing on the point at which electronic and print communications are created. The missing piece of the puzzle is the *process* that consultants go through to determine the content of their ads and mail pieces. Medvic (2001, 62) summarizes his theory as follows:

> Campaigns attempt to disseminate a theme by using various messages to appeal to distinct groups of voters. The theme and its messages have one goal, and that is to prime voters to evaluate the candidate on his/her terms; that is, certain issues (whether of a character or policy nature) play to the advantage of some candidates while other issues benefit other candidates. Campaign consultants are brought in to determine which issues their client should emphasize and how those issues should be framed.

In a sense, then, consultants are indeed the "issue choosers" (O'Shaughnessy 1990) that their critics describe. Nevertheless, the process should not automatically be assumed to have negative consequences for the electorate. As the theory of deliberate priming suggests, consultants help candidates pick issues on which to campaign that will give them a competitive advantage over their opponent; in doing so they naturally try to choose issues that will give their candidate the best chance to win on election day (for exceptions, see Damore 2004).

One might still believe, of course, that it is misleading or somehow detrimental to the public when candidates' campaigns merely pick and choose from the full set of issues that could potentially be important to voters. Yet I have argued elsewhere (Dulio 2004) that the process by which consultants help candidates identify issues and then discuss those issues in a certain way is beneficial to the public for two reasons. First, it forces candidates and campaigns to focus on issues that are important to the members of the electorate. It would do no one any good if a candidate for office talked about issues that the public did not care about or was not interested in. For instance, assume a candidate has deeply held opinions about issues such as the environment, taxes, Social Security reform, homeland security and the war on terror, and abortion. Also assume that, through polling, it is learned that the public cares or is interested mainly in homeland security, Social Security reform, and taxes. The electorate would not be well-served if the candidate spent a large amount of time talking about abortion and the environment. Conducting research that allows candidates to focus on issues that the public cares about only serves to further the overall public interest.

A second advantage of deliberate priming is that, by focusing on issues the public cares about, campaigns (with the help of consultants) can elevate the level of debate and give potential voters more of what they are looking for. If, for example, the candidates in a race learn through their polling that the electorate is focused primarily on the issues noted above—homeland security, Social Security reform, and taxes—it is likely that the Democrat will focus on Social Security reform (or other entitlement programs) because that is an issue that traditionally gives Democrats an advantage over their Republican rivals. By the same token, it is likely that the Republican will stress the remaining two issues (for similar reasons of competitive advantage). However, because the two sides are talking about different issues, there may be pressure either from the press or from voters themselves to address issues that each would prefer to avoid.[12]

As Medvic (2001) explained, each candidate will make an effort to define the turf on which the campaign will be waged; specifically, they will talk primarily about issues that benefit them (or perhaps their party; see note 12). However, even candidates who manage to win the turf war cannot simply ignore issues that are part of the larger terrain. For example, during the 2004 presidential contest, the Bush-Cheney team clearly wanted the campaign to be about homeland security and the general war on terror, while the Kerry/Edwards campaign wanted the race to be about missteps in the war in Iraq as well as the decision-making process leading up to the decision to go to war in the first place.[13] These are two sides of the same coin, but each candidate was driven by the other to address issues that he would have preferred to avoid. George W. Bush had to talk about Iraq because that is what Kerry stressed, while Kerry was challenged by the president to justify some of his votes in the U.S. Senate that were seemingly more dovish than the positions he took during the campaign. In other words, each candidate had to address issues that he would have liked to stay away from. The strategic aspect of this lies in the fact that the campaign that does the best job of having the campaign waged on its turf is often the one that ends up winning on election day.

Consultants' Effects on Campaigns

While studies that explore the effects of consultants on parties, voters, or the electoral process as a whole lack a clear consensus, the academic literature leaves little doubt about the tangible impact that consultants can have on campaigns. There are two broad streams of research focusing on two of the mainstays of any campaign: candidate success (1) in fundraising and (2) at the ballot box on election day. Every study that has examined the question of consultants' effects on fundraising and vote share has reached the same conclusion, specifically, that campaigns run by professionals tend to raise more money and garner more votes than do campaigns run by amateurs.

Efforts to investigate such questions are a fairly recent development in the political science literature, largely because the empirical data needed for serious hypothesis testing have been difficult to come by. This was certainly true in the days prior to the explosive growth of professional consulting, when Kelley (1956, 205) observed that "there are few data for evaluating, with anything like scientific accuracy, particular propaganda techniques, and certainly not for the assessment of the effectiveness of 'public relations' in general." In fact, many interesting hypotheses in political science were originally difficult to test because of a lack of reliable data sources at the time. Yet even as matters improved (often dramatically) in other areas of the discipline, the same was not true for those who wished to explore the consequences of consultant activity in campaigns. As recently as the late 1980s, Petracca (1989, 11) described the situation as follows:

> Despite the meteoric rise to prominence of political consultants in American political campaigns, political scientists have devoted surprisingly little attention to their analysis. . . . This analytic silence may be attributed to a number of factors. First, compared to voters, PACs [political action committees], or interest groups, consultants are far more difficult to study. There are no readily available data sources to either identify consultants or document their activities. Second, the considerable variation in what it means to "consult" and in the activities of professional consultants makes it difficult to identify the essence of consultancy. Finally, many scholars who study elections do so by studying voters. As a result our attention has moved away

from the analysis of electoral institutions in which consultants now play such a commanding role.

Petracca's observations remained accurate until scholars in the field began to develop new data sets more appropriate to the task at hand. The first systematic attempts to understand the role of consultants in campaigns were limited, however, by the fact that they frequently relied on opinion surveys of consultants themselves.[14] While these studies certainly were of value in that they allowed us to know more about the attitudes and beliefs of campaign professionals, they still were unable to test directly hypotheses regarding consultants' effectiveness. Subsequent research has gone further, especially by centering on congressional races in which hundreds of candidates run in each election cycle—and for which at least some requisite data are available. In particular, the *dependent* variables for the two lines of inquiry noted above (money raised and votes received) can be measured using data compiled by the Federal Election Commission (FEC) in all federal races.

Unfortunately, it remains difficult to capture the *independent* (or explanatory) variable of greatest interest: the level of consultant involvement in a campaign. One might reasonably assume that the FEC reports filed by federal candidates, in which they detail how their money was spent during the campaign, would provide the kind of information researchers need to measure consultant activity. The problem is that the FEC's reporting requirements are rather limited. When listing fees paid to consultants, candidates' campaigns typically enter "consulting" or some other vague description that tells us little or nothing about actual work performed; as a result, the data are unreliable for discerning precisely what consultants have provided in terms of strategic advice or campaign services. This limitation, coupled with the fact that each report for each candidate can be hundreds of pages long, means that the FEC is not an ideal source of data for empirical research.

Scholars have therefore had to find other ways of measuring the presence of consultants in campaigns. This concept is described in the literature as "campaign professionalization," and those who study its effects on candidates' fundraising and vote share have used a number of different indicators. Whatever their approach, however, they all reach essentially the same conclusion, which is that professionalized campaigns fare better than campaigns that do not use professional consultants. For instance, as one of the first to tackle the question of consultants' effects on candidate fundraising, Herrnson (1992) used data from questionnaires administered to congressional candidates to determine the functions performed by consultants in individual races; in other words, Herrnson asked candidates to report the number and type of services provided to their campaign by consultants. Another approach to measuring professionalization is to rely on a neutral source for information about whether candidates hired consultants in their campaigns. For example, Medvic (1998, 2000, 2001; also see Medvic and Lenart 1997) employed this method by using the "Consultant Scorecard" (a biennial listing of consultants and their reported list of clients for the election cycle) from *Campaigns & Elections* magazine, the trade publication for the consulting industry. I followed a similar strategy in my examination of the impact of consultants on congressional candidates' fundraising and electoral success (Dulio 2004). This information allows researchers to identify the specific consultants or firms (as well as the number and types) hired by individual campaign organizations.

Studies that look specifically at fundraising find that consultants have a positive and sometimes dramatic effect on the ability of candidates to raise money. According to Herrnson (1992, 866), "campaign professionalism influences the resource allocations of political parties, PACs, and individuals, and increases the campaign receipts of congressional candidates" (also see Medvic 2001). While this particular analysis showed that both incumbents and nonincumbents running for the U.S. House in 1984 increased their take from parties and PACs by hiring more professionals, individual contributors seemed to respond favorably only to a higher level of professionalism in incumbent campaigns. In a later study of House races in 1992, however, Herrnson (2000) found that professionalized campaigns, for incumbents and challengers alike, raised larger amounts of money from individuals.[15] Put simply, the presence of consultants signals to potential donors that one's race is likely to be competitive. As a result,

> deciding whether to hire professional political consultants or to field an amateur campaign organization can have a major impact on a House candidate's fundraising prospects. The implications . . . are clear: it is important to put together a high-quality professional campaign organization and let party committees, PACs, and individuals know about it. A professional campaign organization can greatly enhance a candidate's ability to raise money. This, in turn, can improve the candidate's prospects for electoral success. (Herrnson 1992, 867)

Testing the latter proposition, Medvic and Lenart (1997) discovered that the presence as well as the actual number of consultants had a significant and positive impact on share of the vote received by challenger and open-seat candidates in 1992 U.S. House races (incumbents were excluded from their analysis); this basic result is consistent through a number of other studies as well (for example, Herrnson 2000; Medvic 2000, 2001). Interestingly, though, and contrary to the pattern for fundraising reported in the preceding paragraph, it appears that incumbents do *not* invariably benefit from hiring political consultants. As the professionalism of challenger campaigns increases, the chances of winning grows accordingly. But with incumbents, candidates "who are involved in the most competitive elections usually put together the most professional campaign organizations, raise the most money"—and, typically, compile win-loss records that "are not as good as those of incumbents who face lower levels of competition and who do not feel the need to wage costly, highly professional campaigns" (Herrnson 2000, 85).[16]

Our understanding of this dynamic is enhanced further by research that examines the importance of different *types* of consultants on candidates' election day totals. That is, "What effect do pollsters, media handlers, voter contact specialists, and generalists have? Do pollsters matter most, as [the theory of deliberate priming] would suggest? Or does another type of consultant appear to be more useful to candidates?" (Medvic 2001, 104). Medvic's results show that pollsters are the most valuable type of consultant for challengers but not for incumbents, perhaps for the same reason that incumbents seem to benefit less from using consultants in the first place (because those who do so are often facing a more spirited challenge than are those who do not).[17]

Studies such as these make an important contribution to the way we think about the role of consultants in campaigns. According to Medvic and Lenart (1997, 74), they have "quantified the influence of political professionals on election outcomes and have, therefore, avoided an anecdotal analysis of the question at hand," which was a limitation of the earlier research that reached its conclusions based on speculation and conjecture. Yet the initial work done in any field is likely to spur further investigations that ask similar questions in different ways, or attempt to challenge assumptions made by the researchers who came before. The topic of consultant influence is no different in this regard.

In my own study of consultants, I have challenged the belief expressed by both Medvic and Herrnson that consultants should be considered in the same light as any other campaign resource, and that differentiating among the consultants that candidates hire is unimportant. Medvic (2000, 93), for example, concluded that "a candidate's decision about whether or not to hire a consultant is more important than the decision about whether to hire Consultant A or Consultant B." Indeed, "[j]ust as artistic talent cannot be quantified, one cannot begin to quantify savvy on the part of a consultant. It is an unusual talent. . . ." (Johnson-Cartee and Copeland 1997a, 1). I have argued, though, that distinctions can and should be made among the individual consultants hired by candidates' campaigns. Specifically, consultants who are better known in political circles should have a greater impact on candidate fundraising than will those who are less well known, and consultants who are at the top of their profession (that is, who are most effective at what they do) should deliver more votes on election day than will those with fewer skills (Dulio 2004).[18] In other words, we must keep in mind that political consulting is an art at least as much as it is a science.

My own research indicates that differences do exist among consultants, and that those differences have implications for fundraising and vote share. First, candidates who hire well-known consultants are able, on average, to attract more party and PAC money than are those who do not; that is, having a professional campaign organization assist with fundraising helps by confirming the viability of a campaign, but hiring the "right" consultants helps even more. In addition, I found that challengers who employ the most capable consultants (as determined by their peers) tend to receive more votes on election day—a finding that implies some consultants really do perform their jobs better than others. Interestingly, the opposite relationship was found for incumbents; when incumbents hire consultants who are identified as some of the best in the business, they tend to do worse than when they are assisted by either no consultants at all or consultants with a less stellar reputation.

At first glance, this finding would seem to reinforce the idea that incumbents do not benefit in any systematic way from using consultants (Herrnson 2000; Medvic 2000, 2001; but see note 15), even when those they use are, arguably, the best available. It is worth noting, however, that incumbents facing races that are expected to be extremely competitive are the ones who usually hire the most highly regarded consultants precisely because they realize that they need the best help they can find. As I have written elsewhere,

> [w]hen facing a tough challenge, [incumbents] need, more than ever, to develop a strong strategy, theme, and message, and to deliver that message effectively and efficiently. They turn to the best consultants to help them do one thing—return to the House as a member of the next Congress. Although other incumbents may be trying to increase their share of the vote to scare off potential challengers two years down the road, embattled incumbents

worry only about winning. For those who are almost guaranteed a victory, it does not really matter who they hire (as Medvic [2001] suggests). However, for those who are in a difficult race, they need the best and they hire the best. Therefore, the impact of the most effective consultants may not be measurable in terms of vote percentage. It may be better measured in terms of simple victory. (Dulio 2004, 162)

In sum, although the evidence is clear that consultants make a difference in candidates' campaigns by delivering more fundraising dollars and more votes on election day, consultants are not all-powerful and they cannot get just any candidate elected. Simply hiring a consultant does not guarantee victory. One has only to examine the star-studded team of consultants assembled by the Kerry-Edwards presidential campaign in 2004. Some of the best consultants in the industry were advising the Democrats, and yet they did not win. In fact, the Kerry campaign experienced problems because it had too many advisers on board (Russakoff and VandeHei 2004; Weissman 2004). The presence of consultants, then, is not a magic potion that can turn any candidate who hires them into an elected public official.

New Directions for Research on Consultants

Scholars have hit only the tip of the iceberg with their work on professional consultants, and there are several important and interesting directions in which they might choose to take their research in the future. The relationships between campaign professionalism and both fundraising and electoral success seem clear: consultants, on average, help candidates raise more money and garner more votes. What is less understood is *how* consultants do this. More research is needed on the ways in which consultants make decisions, especially in terms of how strategies are developed within the context of an individual campaign. In other words, we know that the services provided by consultants (polling, television and radio ads, direct mail, grassroots mobilization, and the like) do matter in campaigns. What we know less about is how consultants make those services matter. A few case studies have attempted to capture this process (Thurber 2002), and some research has begun to investigate systematically how consultants make decisions in campaigns (R. Garrett 2005; Waismel-Manor 2005), but more is needed. We also would benefit from knowing how different consultants approach their craft, and from seeking to understand how consultants adapt to changes in the electoral context.

Notes

1. Although some disagreement exists over who the first political consultants were, many observers identify Clem Whitaker and Leone Baxter as the trailblazers who established the consulting industry with their formation of Campaigns, Inc., in 1933 (see Mitchell 1992). Others point as far back as ancient Rome and Greece, where individuals such as Quintus Cicero were found to be providing advice to office seekers about canvassing voters and other tactics (DeVries 1989; Medvic 1997). Still others, focusing only on the United States, contend that the Federalists and Anti-Federalists could be considered the first consultants, given the types of tactics they used during the battle over ratification of the Constitution, such as placement of advertisements in newspapers and get-out-the-vote efforts (Dulio 2004).

2. There are, of course, other areas in which consultants have been purported to have an impact on campaigns in the United States. Some of these claims are critiques of professional consultants that argue they are behind many of the ills supposedly plaguing U.S. elections, including increasing campaigns costs, negative advertising and campaigning, and wrestling control of campaigns away from candidates. I believe each of these claims to be easily refuted and have argued as much elsewhere (Dulio 2004; Dulio and Nelson 2005). I limit my review of the literature on consultants' effects in campaigns to areas that are less clear-cut and more important to the foundations of elections.

3. Two topics *not* covered here are the internationalization of consulting and the impact of consultants in initiative and referenda campaigns, both of which have grown a great deal in recent years. For excellent work on the internationalization of consulting, see Bowler and Farrell (1992, 2000); Farrell (1998); Plasser (2000); Swanson and Mancini (1996). For insights into the role of consultants in initiative and referenda campaigns, see Bowler, Donovan, and Fernandez (1996); Magleby and Patterson (1998, 2000); McCuan and Stambough (2005). Some of the work that I review also discusses the consulting industry in general and how it has grown over time; for more on these topics, see Dulio (2004); Johnson (2000, 2001); Kelley (1956); Nimmo (1970, 2001); Rosenbloom (1973); Sabato (1981); Thurber, Nelson and Dulio (2000b).

4. For more on party resurgence, see Aldrich (1995); Menefee-Libey (2000).

5. See Herrnson (1988); Kolodny and Logan (1998).

6. See Dulio (2004); Dulio and Nelson (2005); Dulio and Thurber (2003); Kolodny and Dulio (2003).

7. I want to emphasize again that not all consultants who work in campaigns, and who produce or provide services to candidates, engage in this sort of activity. Professional consultants can be divided into several categories, for example, (1) strategist, (2) specialist, and (3) vendor (see Johnson 2000)—only some of whom participate in spreading campaign messages. The ones who do perform these duties are most often the pollster (helping to design the message that will be communicated), as well as the media consultant and direct-mail specialist. Others (fundraisers, for instance) are not engaged in communication, and it would therefore be a stretch to assume that they are in a position to have a direct effect on potential voters.

8. See Druckman, Jacobs, and Ostermeier (2004); Iyengar (1987); Iyengar and Kinder (1987); Krosnick and Brannon (1993); Jacobs and Shapiro (1994); Valentino, Hutchings, and White (2002); Zaller (1992). Not surprisingly, these messages can have different effects on different people (Zaller 1992).

9. For example, see Johnson-Cartee and Copeland (1997b); Petracca (1989); Sabato (1981).

10. Even so, Stevenson could not resist the idea of using television ads during his 1952 presidential campaign (though he did refuse to appear in them).

11. This is not to say that one cannot find examples of campaign communications that were designed to manipulate, deceive, or confuse. In my experience, however, these examples are the exception rather than the rule. Unfortunately, the "routine" (nonduplicitous) work done by the vast majority of political consultants receives less attention than the relatively few instances that so trouble their critics.

12. This sort of thing seems to happen fairly often, at least in presidential races (Sigelman and Buell 2004). On the subject of party images and "issue ownership," see Damore (2004); Petrocik (1996); Petrocik, Benoit, and Hansen (2003).

13. These were not the only issues raised during the campaign. Both candidates also discussed, for example, the state of the economy, Social Security, health care, the environment, and a number of other (especially domestic) concerns.

14. Many research projects have used surveys to provide enlightening information about how consultants view themselves and their role within the system of campaigning in the United States. These questions, however, are not the topic of the discussion here. Interested readers are encouraged to see, for example, Dulio (2004); Dulio and Nelson (2005); Kolodny (2000); Kolodny and Logan (1998); Luntz (1988); Petracca (1989); Petracca and Wierioch (1988); Swint (1998); Thurber, Nelson, and Dulio (2000b).

15. This particular study was essentially descriptive and did not involve the sort of careful multivariate analysis used in Herrnson (1992).

16. Also see Medvic (2000, 2001); chapter 4 in this volume. Further complicating matters, Medvic (2001) found that the presence of consultants generally helped Democratic incumbents but not Republicans.

17. Also see Medvic and Lenart (1997), who found that "only pollsters significantly affected challengers' vote totals while open-seat candidates gained votes by using media and mail consultants as well" (74).

18. Visibility and effectiveness were peer determined, based on a questionnaire administered to consultants themselves. For details regarding measurement, operationalization, and the general design of this study, see chapter 6 in Dulio (2004).

11 Perspectives on Campaign Ethics

R. Sam Garrett, Paul S. Herrnson, and James A. Thurber

February 8, 2005, was a busy day in the world of campaign ethics as news reports buzzed with stories about two prominent scandals. One of these took place in Baltimore, Maryland, where months of rumors about Mayor Martin O'Malley's marriage finally came to a head—though not in the way many expected. That morning, the *Washington Post* reported that allegations of the Democratic mayor cheating on his wife and fathering an illegitimate child were not only false but that a senior aide to Republican governor Robert L. Ehrlich Jr. was the one who had planted them on a conservative web site. O'Malley, who later entered the race to challenge Ehrlich in 2006, alleged that the rumors were part of an "organized effort" to discredit him before the impending governor's race (Mosk 2005). Later that same day, Ehrlich fired longtime aide Joseph Steffen, who in an interview with the *Post* admitted that he was responsible for the "[online] postings. When asked if he was part of an organized effort to disseminate the rumors, he said, 'No comment.' " During the same interview, Steffen "acknowledged that he has a reputation for hardball politics," proclaiming, "They call me the Prince of Darkness" (Mosk 2005). Observers agreed that the episode could have major ramifications for the governor's race for both candidates, not to mention a third, Montgomery County Executive Douglas M. Duncan, a Democrat, who "remained quietly offstage as the ugly drama unfolded" (Wagner 2005).

The same day in New Hampshire, a federal judge sentenced political consultant Allen Raymond to five months in prison and fined him $15,000 for "jamming Democratic Party telephone lines in several New Hampshire cities during the 2002 general election" (McCahill 2005). The consultant's intent was allegedly to suppress Democrats' election day voter-mobilization efforts. Although Democrats and Republicans throughout the state condemned the entire incident, Raymond's lawyer argued that his client had simply followed orders from James Tobin, then a regional director for the National Republican Senatorial Committee (Jansen 2005). In 2004, Tobin resigned as New England regional chairman for George W. Bush's reelection campaign after being indicted in the phone-jamming case (Finer 2005); as this is written, Tobin maintains his innocence and is awaiting trial (Finer 2005; Jansen 2005; McCahill 2005).

The events of February 8, 2005, are by no means representative. Not all campaigns are ethically challenged, and this particular day just happened to be a bad one for Republicans. Democrats are surely not immune to ethical conflicts. Throughout the 2004 campaign, for example, so-called 527 organizations (named after the section of the IRS code defining them) that were tacitly aligned with one party or the other were widely criticized for allegedly circumventing campaign finance laws (see Thurber and Nelson 2004). Critics contend that 527s are really shadow party organizations that funnel otherwise illegal contributions into campaign politics. Following the 2004 elections, the Minnesota Campaign Finance and Public Disclosure Board levied its largest fine ever ($320,000) against the 527 group 21st Century Minnesota and its parent national organization, 21st Century Democrats, determining that neither group had properly disclosed its campaign finance activities in the state. Republicans charged that the groups tried to conceal large donations from Minnesota Democrat-Farmer-Labor Party state House minority leader Matt Entenza. Democrats countered that the case arose from simple accounting mistakes. Although the board acknowledged that the violations appeared to be "inadvertent," Republicans disagreed and pushed for a wider investigation (D. Smith 2004).

The aforementioned examples provide a reminder of how prominent ethics charges are in modern campaigns, and of how little we truly know about campaign ethics. The existing work on campaign ethics is largely compartmentalized, focusing on consultants, candidates, or voters.[1] In this chapter we review the literature on campaign ethics and draw together these streams of research; we do so by relying on political elite and voter survey data to provide a more complete picture of how consultants, party officials, candidates, and voters feel about campaign ethics. Based on our analysis, we attempt to identify what political professionals, candidates, and voters believe constitutes a "fair fight" in campaign politics. We also offer a research agenda for continuing to improve the study of campaign ethics.

Existing Research on Campaign Ethics

At least four approaches have been used to examine campaign ethics. The first consists of case studies that briefly consider ethical dilemmas within the context of broader inquiries involving campaign behavior in general.[2] These case studies typically describe the who, what, where, when, how, and why of negative attacks made by candidates, political parties, and interest groups. They often conclude with normative lessons learned about ethics in public life (Thurber 1998).

The second approach explores candidate, consultant, or voter beliefs about campaign ethics using interviews, focus groups, or surveys.[3] Research has shown, for example, that candidates often draw distinctions among different types of negative campaigning. On the one hand, roughly two-thirds of all candidates believe it is appropriate to attack an opponent on campaign issues involving criminal behavior, such as failure to pay child support, nonpayment of property taxes, a documented case of sexual harassment in the workplace, or a conviction for driving while under the influence. In contrast, only one-fifth to one-quarter consider it appropriate to attack an opponent on issues involving personal matters that have not landed in the courts, such as marital infidelity, an undisclosed homosexual relationship, or youthful experimentation with marijuana (Faucheux and Herrnson 2001, 2002).

Early academic work on campaign consulting (Petracca 1989; Sabato 1981) warned that consultants might pose a threat to democratic governance—a charge raised partly because of stereotypical images of consultants as "hired guns" who are more concerned with turning a profit than with conducting responsible campaigns (C. Nelson, Medvic, and Dulio 2002). Party officials suffer from particularly poor, if perhaps undeserved, ethical reputations (Kolodny 2002). D. Miller and Medvic (2002) introduced the ideas of "civic responsibility" and "self interest" into this genre of campaign studies. A series of works by, or about, political professionals offered their response to academic views on campaign ethics, although often only in passing.[4]

A third approach examines the impact of ethical "scandals" on politicians' successes at the ballot box. In these empirical studies, "scandal" serves as an independent variable, while impact is measured in terms of voluntary retirement, challenger entry, vote loss, or fundraising.[5] One consistent finding is that, unlike many campaign-related activities, scandals sometimes have the potential to bring about the defeat of entrenched incumbents; this is especially the case when a campaign is not prepared for the crisis management needed in response to a scandal (R. Garrett 2005). Collectively, these works suggest that campaign ethics matter to both voters and campaign strategists. They do not, however, fully address the question of the impact of ethically questionable behavior on voters and election outcomes. Such behavior might include, for example, violating campaign finance laws, lying about a candidate's political record or professional accomplishments, or attacking a candidate for some previously undisclosed aspect of his or her private personal life that has little bearing on the job that candidate is seeking.

The fourth, and least developed, approach considers the development of ethics in campaigning and governance. Fowler (2004) offered a historical account of the evolution of ethics charges as a campaign tool, while others have explored the development of ethics regimes within Congress (Thompson 1995; Whaley 2003), between campaign consultants and lobbyists (Thurber 2002), or in government more generally (J. Smith 2002; Thompson 1987). Along these lines, R. Sam Garrett and colleagues (2006) found that career civil servants believe that "bureaucracy-bashing" during election campaigns is inherently unethical and that it has a negative impact on federal workers, their organizations, and their public image. Yet little is known about whether ethically questionable tactics have a significant effect on election outcomes. Only the work dealing with campaign advertising comes close to addressing whether ethically questionable tactics change voters' minds, and only then with respect to negative advertising.[6]

How and why political professionals resolve ethical campaign dilemmas remains largely a mystery as well. Theilmann and Wilhite (1998) and Waismel-Manor (2005) are among the rare exceptions, offering insights provided through experimental campaign simulations involving political consultants. And R. Sam Garrett's (2005) examination of how political professionals manage campaign crises, which often involve ethical dilemmas, demonstrated that although political professionals are fierce competitors, they often defer to their clients' ethical wishes—but only if the latter do not violate their own ethical standards.

Exploring Voter and Political Elite Attitudes

The inquiry that follows is based on four national surveys covering the attitudes of political professionals, candidates, party officials, and ordinary citizens regarding campaign ethics. Information on professionals is derived from a national survey of campaign consultants holding the position of "principal" or a similar rank in their firm. Candidates' views about campaign ethics are captured using a national survey of individuals who ran for congressional and state legislative office between 1998 and 2000. The perspective of party officials is provided by an in-depth elite survey of the executive directors and other senior officials from the Democratic and Republican parties in all 50 states and the parties' national campaign committees. Finally, we use a national survey of voting-age adults to examine how the general public thinks about campaign ethics. (Additional information about each of these surveys is provided in the chapter appendix.)

Are Campaigns Really That Bad?

Popular folklore frequently describes election campaigns as corrupt and asserts that candidates, consultants, political parties, and lobbyists will do almost anything to win.[7] But are campaign politics really "that bad"? The answer depends on whom one asks. Political professionals and the public tend to see the issue very differently: When asked how often unethical practices occur in campaigns, most consultants stated that they happen only occasionally, though independents were more likely than their major-party counterparts to see unethical campaigning as a common occurrence (see Table 11.1); specifically, roughly 74 percent of all Democratic consultants and 82 percent of all Republican consultants considered most campaigns to be ethical, whereas just 61 percent of all independents shared this view.[8] Responses for party officials were similar to those of partisan consultants, with Republicans slightly more likely than Democrats to report unethical campaign practices. Voters, however, perceive campaigns very differently from either group of political elites. Indeed, an astonishing 70 percent of all voters indicated that unethical campaign practices occur "very often" or "fairly often." As is the case with consultants, independent voters regard the world of campaign politics as being far more Hobbesian than do Democratic or Republican identifiers.

One explanation for these results is that voters, candidates, political consultants, and party officials have different things in mind when they think about campaign ethics. We suspect, for example, that voters consider almost exclusively those aspects of the campaign they can see directly, most notably, television, radio, and direct-mail advertisements; for them, campaign "ethics" probably involves attacks that candidates, parties, and interest groups lodge against each other, including mudslinging and both comparative and contrast ads. Candidates presumably share voters' concerns about attack politics, since they are usually the object of attacks leveled by the opposition. However, candidates may also be concerned about the business side of campaign ethics, including the question of whether they are receiving the services consultants have been hired to provide. Likewise, anecdotal evidence suggests that many consultants (as well as party officials) are more concerned with the business side of politics when they consider ethical behavior on the campaign trail.[9]

Candidates typically view campaign ethics from two perspectives: what they do unto others, and what others do unto them. Not surprisingly, they are inclined to believe that they themselves ran mostly positive campaigns. Less than 3 percent in our survey, for example, acknowledged waging mostly negative campaigns, while relatively few reported that their campaigns sought to compare and contrast them with their opponents. Equally unsurprising, respondents tended to provide less favorable assessments of the other side's electioneering efforts—though a clear difference exists between incumbents and challengers. As shown in Table 11.2, almost all incumbents (89 percent) and a majority of challengers (55 percent) agreed that incumbents ran positive campaigns; in contrast, a substantial number of challengers (46 percent) and an even larger number of incumbents (69 percent) maintained that the former ran either negative or comparative campaigns. These discrepancies occur because most incumbents do run predominantly positive campaigns based on their performance in office and the popular images they seek to project. Challengers, on the other hand, must provide voters with a reason to replace the current officeholder, and this often involves painting the incumbent in a negative light (Herrnson 2004). Candidates for open seats are somewhat more willing than incumbents, and less willing than challengers, to admit to negative or comparative campaigning (23 percent); they, too, tend to describe their own campaigns as having been more positive than those waged by the opposition.

Reflecting the greater success rate of incumbents, winners overwhelmingly described their campaigns as positive and their opponents' campaigns as mostly negative or comparative. On the other hand, Democratic and Republican candidates' self-reports about their campaigns and appraisals of their opponents' campaigns were virtually identical. Thus, despite differences in ideologies, policy preferences, professional backgrounds, and the constituents they claim to represent, candidates from both parties have similar perceptions of what takes place on campaign battlegrounds.

Attitudes on Questionable Campaign Practices

What specific activities are regarded as unethical in the quest for elective office? We asked candidates, political consultants, party officials, and voters for their opinions about various campaign practices that some observers might consider to be ethically questionable. Recognizing that few of these individuals would state that they approved of a campaign making outright falsehoods (Faucheux and Herrnson 2001, 132), we inquired as to whether they felt it was acceptable to manipulate the truth by making factually true statements out of context. Candidates are the least likely of our four groups to approve of this practice. According to the figures displayed in Table 11.3, approximately 3 percent consider it acceptable, 30 percent questionable, and 67 percent indicated that it is clearly unethical. Voters are only slightly more tolerant, with about 8 percent approving of making truthful statements out of context. Roughly 10 percent of the consultants who the candidates employ to run their campaigns also consider this an acceptable practice, as do 17 percent of the party officials who, among other things, attempt to influence the strategic and tactical decisions of both candidates and consultants. Partisanship makes little difference here, as Democrats and Republicans respond in a similar fashion. The only distinction worth noting is that independent consultants tend to be less accepting of out-of-context statements than are partisan consultants (that is, Democrats and Republicans who work only for candidates from their own party).

The pattern of results in Table 11.3 suggests that when one considers campaign practices concerned with manipulating the truth from the perspectives of those who are the major players in elections, they may be envisioned as three concentric circles: The further one gets from the central public face of the campaign (referring to the candidates whose names appear on ballots, and in television advertisements and other campaign communications), the more willing people are to cross ethical boundaries. Voters, by contrast, are fairly close to sharing the views of those who seek to represent them in office.

A second practice asked about in our surveys is at the core of what is widely considered to be political mudslinging, that is, focusing on an opponent's negative personal characteristics. Once again, it is evident from Table 11.4 that candidates are less likely to approve of this practice than are others who are actively involved in the campaign process. Comparing all three groups of political elites, we see that party officials are more approving of personal attacks than are candidates, and that political consultants are more approving than party officials (Magleby, Patterson, and Thurber 2002). Voters are, however, by far the least tolerant, probably because they are observers rather than players in democracy's most contentious process. As such, they do not feel personally the heat generated in a hard-fought campaign or have to make pragmatic decisions about what must be done in order to win an election. Also unlike candidates, consultants, and party officials, voters' professional reputations and livelihoods are not directly affected by election outcomes. Having less involvement and less to lose than these other groups, voters can afford to be judgmental and hold political elites to higher standards.

Table 11.1 Reported Frequency of Unethical Campaigning

	Political Consultants			Party Officials		Voters		
	Democrat	Republican	Independent	Democrat	Republican	Democrat	Republican	Independent
Very often	9.5%	4.4%	4.3%	2.3%	—%	38.7%	35.3%	41.3%
Fairly often	16.2	13.2	34.8	6.8	8.2	30.7	35.6	35.0
Sometimes	45.7	42.6	47.8	29.5	40.8	22.2	20.7	17.5
Rarely	28.6	36.8	13.0	45.5	40.8	5.2	5.2	3.9
Not at all	—	2.9	—	6.8	6.1	1.8	1.2	1.5
N	105	68	23	40	47	382	336	204

Source: CCPS Improving Campaign Conduct 2002 surveys of political consultants, party officials, and voting-age adults (see chapter appendix for further details and question wording).
Note: "—" means that less than 0.5 percent offered a particular response.

Table 11.2 Candidates' Characterizations of Latest Campaign

A. Characterization of Own Campaign

	Incumbents	Challengers	Open seat	Lost primary	Won primary, lost general	Won general	Democrat	Republican
Mostly positive	88.5%	54.3%	77.4%	71.6%	55.9%	87.2%	73.4%	74.1%
Mostly negative	1.7	3.3	2.7	3.2	3.5	1.6	2.4	2.7
Mostly comparative	9.8	42.3	20.0	25.2	40.6	11.2	24.2	23.3
N	957	784	411	250	907	1,231	1,236	1,169

Table 11.2 (continued)

B. Characterization of Opponent's Campaign

	Incumbents	Challengers	Open seat	Lost primary	Won primary, lost general	Won general	Democrat	Republican
Mostly positive	30.9%	54.6%	49.9%	49.2%	54.4%	34.9%	45.5%	42.9%
Mostly negative	51.7	28.0	33.2	32.4	28.9	47.3	37.2	39.6
Mostly comparative	17.4	17.4	17.0	18.4	16.7	17.8	17.3	17.5
N	851	764	395	244	882	1,116	1,099	1,158

Source: CAPC Campaign Assessment and Candidate Outreach 2001 survey of candidates for office (see chapter appendix for further details and question wording).

Table 11.3 Acceptability of Making Factually True Statements Taken Out of Context

	Political Consultants			Party Officials		Candidates		Voters		
	Democrat	Republican	Independent	Democrat	Republican	Democrat	Republican	Democrat	Republican	Independent
Acceptable	8.6%	9.7%	13.0%	18.2%	16.3%	3.3%	3.6%	9.8%	7.6%	7.8%
Questionable	67.6	62.5	39.1	56.8	61.2	29.2	29.6	32.6	34.7	37.9
Clearly unethical	23.8	27.8	47.8	25.0	22.4	67.5	66.8	56.1	56.3	52.9
N	105	72	23	44	49	1,260	1,181	387	343	206

Source: CCPS Improving Campaign Conduct 2002 surveys of political consultants, party officials, and voting-age adults; CAPC Campaign Assessment and Candidate Outreach 2001 survey of candidates for office (see chapter appendix for further details and question wording).

There are, by the way, some notable partisan differences on the issue of personal attacks. Compared with their Democratic counterparts, higher proportions of Republican candidates, party officials, and voters, respectively, consider it acceptable to raise personal issues in the midst of a campaign. These differences may reflect deeper divisions between Democrats and Republicans on morality issues; that is, Democrats tend to be more accepting of nontraditional lifestyles, which provide the basis for many personal attacks, while Republicans are more likely to favor traditional family values and to consider an opponent's nontraditional lifestyle as a legitimate area for public criticism (Layman and Carmines 1997). Even if this is true, however, the same partisan divisions do not extend to the political consulting community. Indeed, more Republican and independent consultants oppose attacking an opponent on the basis of negative personal characteristics than do their Democratic colleagues.

Finally, we consider respondents' attitudes toward so-called push-polls, which are not true surveys but rather mass telephone calls made by individuals posing as legitimate pollsters in an effort to spread negative or false information about an opponent.[10] Because few voters are familiar with this tactic, we limit our analysis to candidates, political consultants, and party officials (see Table 11.5). As was the case with the previous two campaign activities, candidates are substantially less approving of push-polls than are party officials or consultants. Although similarly small percentages of each group consider push-polling to be an acceptable campaign tool, it falls into the gray zone of being a questionable tactic for more party officials (roughly 60 percent, compared with 43 percent of candidates) and into the black zone of being clearly unethical for more candidates (approximately 41 percent, compared with just 23 percent of party officials). This finding is consistent across parties, with no substantial differences evident for Democratic and Republican candidates or party officials. There are, however, some rather stark partisan differences among consultants. Specifically, Democratic consultants tend to hold views about push-polls that are fairly similar to those of the candidates for whom they work, while Republican consultants are much more likely than either Republican *or* Democratic candidates to identify push-polls as an acceptable campaign practice. It may be that the 34 percent of Republican consultants who endorse using push-polls believe that Democratic turnout, which is generally less consistent from one election to the next than Republican turnout (Brady et al. 1996), is often the decisive factor in determining who comes out on top. With an election outcome at stake, then, these individuals may condone taking whatever steps are needed to demobilize an opponent's base, a strategy strongly associated with GOP political operative

Table 11.4 Acceptability of Focusing on Opponents' Negative Personal Characteristics

	Political Consultants			Party Officials		Candidates		Voters		
	Democrat	Republican	Independent	Democrat	Republican	Democrat	Republican	Democrat	Republican	Independent
Acceptable	41.0%	39.4%	26.1%	27.3%	38.8%	24.7%	32.7%	5.2%	9.0%	3.9%
Questionable	49.5	43.7	43.5	56.8	49.0	47.1	41.8	20.2	22.9	18.8
Clearly unethical	9.5	16.9	30.4	9.1	8.2	28.2	25.6	73.8	67.8	76.8
N	105	71	23	44	49	1,263	1,173	386	345	207

Source: CCPS Improving Campaign Conduct 2002 surveys of political consultants, party officials, and voting-age adults; CAPC Campaign Assessment and Candidate Outreach 2001 survey of candidates for office (see chapter appendix for further details and question wording).

Table 11.5 Acceptability of Using Push-Polls

	Political Consultants			Party Officials		Candidates	
	Democrat	Republican	Independent	Democrat	Republican	Democrat	Republican
Acceptable	17.3%	34.3%	15.0%	18.2%	16.3%	13.7%	16.5%
Questionable	33.7	32.8	30.0	56.8	61.2	45.2	41.2
Clearly unethical	49.0	32.8	55.0	25.0	22.4	41.1	42.3
N	98	67	20	44	49	1,196	1,120

Source: CCPS Improving Campaign Conduct 2002 surveys of political consultants and party officials; CAPC Campaign Assessment and Candidate Outreach 2001 survey of candidates for office (see chapter appendix for further details and question wording).

Ed Rollins (see, for example, Meyerson 2004). Overall, despite professional norms (such as the American Association of Political Consultants Code of Ethics) that reject push-polling as inherently unethical, only about one-third of the Republican consultants in our survey, along with roughly half of Democratic and independent consultants, agree with that assessment.

Shaping the Campaign Environment

The previous section established that candidates, consultants, party officials, and voters draw distinctions about the ethics of various campaign tactics. In all likelihood, these distinctions reflect the different roles played by each group in campaign politics. Candidates are the public face of the campaign, and although they may become involved in strategic decision-making, they typically concentrate on outreach (most notably, fundraising and communicating the campaign's message and theme).[11] Political consultants are primarily responsible for strategic decision-making, including using tactics to attack an opponent or respond to ethically charged campaign attacks.[12] Parties focus on providing campaign support in the form of money; technical expertise; in-depth research; and assistance in forming relationships with potential donors, political consultants, interest groups, and others who possess some of the resources needed to conduct a viable campaign (Herrnson 1988, 2004). Parties and interest groups also wage coordinated, parallel, and independent efforts related to voter mobilization and campaign communications (Herrnson 2004). It is in the latter area, referring specifically to negative television, radio, direct-mail, and Internet communications, that party organizations and advocacy groups have been labeled the "attack dogs" of campaign politics.

However, just because consultants assume strategic leadership roles in most campaigns,[13] does not mean that they disregard candidates' wishes.[14] Nor does it mean that they ignore the suggestions made by party officials. To be sure, some consultants are keenly aware that their being hired by a specific campaign was a precondition for the campaign's receiving financial support from the party.[15] Still, according to Dulio and Nelson (2005), consultants feel that more than any other group they are responsible for setting the ethical tone of campaign politics.

Most consultants consider their colleagues to be competent professionals, but this does not mean that they are willing to empower those colleagues with oversight authority on issues pertaining to campaign ethics. For example, almost 70 percent of all consultants in our survey expressed approval of a code of ethics for their profession, yet roughly 80 percent stated that the American Association of Political Consultants Code of Ethics has little or no influence on industry members' actual behavior. Consultants also exhibit suspicion toward political parties, though the latter's ability to directly hire consultants and to influence some consultant-candidate contracts gives them a measure of control over the types of campaign practices that consultants employ.[16]

Campaign Ethics, Media Coverage, and Voter Cynicism

Are voters getting the campaigns they deserve? Are political campaigns a primary cause of today's widespread political cynicism among the body politic? These questions underlie much of the research that has been done on candidate, consultant, party official, and voter perspectives related to campaign ethics. Another likely source of voter cynicism, however, is the nature of the coverage that campaigns receive in the mass media. Studies show that voters do not hold the media in very high regard (Cappella and Jamieson 1997; Graber 2005), and most of the consultants whom we interviewed shared that view: 93 percent of Democratic and Republican consultants, along with virtually all independent consultants, maintained that media coverage causes "a great deal" or "a fair amount" of voter cynicism. Moreover, approximately 60 percent of all consultants indicated that the quality of broadcast journalism has gotten either "somewhat" or "a lot" worse over the course of their careers.

The press, however, is not the entire story. Despite a generally high regard for their clients, almost 80 percent of the consultants in our survey blamed voter cynicism on politicians' poor performance in office; about one-half reported that they have helped to elect candidates whose subsequent performance was so poor that they eventually came to regret that the person was holding public office. Roughly one-fourth of all party officials expressed similar views, including 31 percent of Republican Party officials and 18 percent of Democrats (see Dulio and Nelson 2005; Thurber and Nelson 2000).

Candidates, too, feel that campaign quality has fallen in recent years, though they tend to cast blame for this state of affairs somewhat more broadly than do others in our surveys. Specifically, more than 80 percent said that their opponents, the parties, interest groups, political consultants, and the mass media were "very" or "moderately" responsible for the declining quality of campaigns. The picture that emerges from our research is one in which many candidates, consultants, party officials, and voters take strong issue with some of the strategies and tactics used in contemporary campaigns. Yet considerable disagreement exists over (1) what, if anything, can be done to improve campaign ethics, (2) who, if anyone, should shoulder the responsibility for making that happen, and (3) what, if any, sanctions should be put at their disposal.

The Need for More Research

In this chapter we have demonstrated that some general agreement exists among candidates, political consultants, and party officials about campaign ethics and what constitutes a "fair fight" in contemporary elections. At the same time, however, we have uncovered some perplexing questions that have yet to be answered. First and foremost, voters perceive of campaigns much more negatively than do those inside campaigns, that is, the candidates, consultants, and party elites. What accounts for such different images of campaign ethics? Is it that most voters possess so little interest or information about specific campaigns that all they remember are a few nasty attack ads they saw on television? If voters who have a thorough knowledge of the candidates, the issues, and the strategies involved hold the same views as less informed fellow citizens, this may imply something else. Perhaps, for example, members of the body politic embrace higher standards of behavior in conflict situations than do individuals whose livelihoods depend largely on emerging victorious from campaign battlegrounds.

Second, the findings suggest that candidates embrace higher ethical standards than do consultants and party officials. Are candidates really inclined to behave more ethically than the professionals they rely on to wage their campaigns and to provide election assistance, or are candidates simply more protective of their public reputations and thus inclined to offer more socially acceptable responses to survey questions concerned with ethics? The fact that most candidates, particularly incumbents, describe the tenor of their last campaign as being mostly positive, while at the same time characterizing their opponent's last campaign as mostly negative or comparative, suggests that candidates do indeed feel pressure to give socially acceptable answers even in an anonymous mail questionnaire. If so, skeptical voters and journalists may be forgiven for asserting that many politicians are untrustworthy hypocrites.

Third, given that candidates, consultants, and party elites often hold different views about various campaign practices, it would be helpful to learn who plays the leadership role in campaigns when ethical dilemmas arise. Case studies and in-depth interviews with campaign decision-makers provide some insights into this question, indicating that although consultants are the key strategic players overall (Faucheux and Herrnson 2001; R. Garrett 2004; Thurber and Nelson 2000), they usually defer to candidates when ethical dilemmas arise (R. Garrett 2005).

Fourth, with interest groups (including those that are closely allied with a political party as well as others that are largely independent) having assumed increasingly important roles in campaigns, we need to learn more about campaign ethics from their perspective. Given that these organizations' names appear nowhere on the ballot, that they can operate under assumed names, that they often have tremendous amounts of resources to expend, and that few regulatory statutes effectively constrain their efforts, it would be useful to monitor their activities, to determine how candidate campaigns respond to them, and to assess their impact on elections. An additional area of inquiry would be to determine whether such organizations behave differently in initiative and referenda campaigns than they do in candidate elections.

Finally, and perhaps most important: Do candidates, political consultants, party officials, and voters believe that engaging in negative campaigning or unethical tactics improves candidates' chances for victory? How malleable are candidates' views on this subject? That is, once candidates who have used questionable tactics in the past are elected—say, to a safe seat in Congress or in a state legislature—are they willing to "clean up their act" in subsequent races? And does their previous approach to political conflict influence their performance in the legislature or other policymaking arenas?

Conclusion

During the heat of a political campaign, candidates, consultants, and party officials rarely have an opportunity to consider campaign ethics in the abstract. They need to make numerous decisions with ethical implications that have a real-world impact on winning and losing. When given the opportunity to consider a variety of questionable campaign practices, most of these individuals express sentiments implying that they would take the high road in campaign politics. The instinct to win often drives decisions, however, thereby creating important distinctions among the central actors in a campaign. The results of our surveys suggest that party officials and consultants are more willing than candidates to cut ethical corners, though evidence regarding candidates is somewhat contradictory in that they tend to view their opponent's election efforts more harshly than their own. Voters, for their part, have rather low expectations and negative impressions of campaign conduct across the board.

The differences that exist among those who actively contest elections are relatively minor compared with the gap between them and those individuals who report on them or whose participation is limited to casting a vote. Many journalists and academics believe that campaign politics is indeed a dirty business and that ethical lapses are common.[17] These sentiments inform what is often referred to as "watch-dog" or "attack-dog" journalism (Sabato 1991). Voters also frequently voice negative opinions about campaign conduct, and about the political process more generally. The inevitability of such views was probably one of the worries of the framers of the U.S. Constitution, many of whom expressed strong reservations about political parties and popular contests for political power.

Disagreements over what constitutes a fair fight and what is good (or at least acceptable) conduct are bound to arise from people who play different roles and have different responsibilities in campaign politics. In this chapter we have sought to explore some of the most important sources of disagreement and to raise a number of related questions concerning campaign ethics. Considering the centrality of campaigns to elections, and of elections to American democracy, these questions are worthy of further consideration and research.

THE CONSULTANTS RESPOND ABOUT

CAMPAIGN ETHICS

Although our consultants agreed that ethical considerations were important in campaigns, they had difficulty articulating exactly what those considerations were. They acknowledged that an ethical lapse could be (but was not always) costly for candidates—and sometimes for consultants themselves, whose professional reputations are on the line in every election cycle—but were able to identify few specific examples of where this had occurred. Some mentioned instances of negative ads or questionable fundraising practices, while a few cited breaches of professional ethics that did not involve their candidates directly. Nevertheless, most insisted that they are at least as committed to running ethical campaigns as their clients, and perhaps even more so.

To begin the conversation, consultants made a careful distinction between ethics and legality:

DEMOCRATIC POLLSTER. Ethical questions can place a candidate on the front page of the newspaper, while legal ques-

continues...

tions can put a candidate in handcuffs. There's a difference.

Democratic Media Consultant. Even the perception that a candidate is skirting the law, like filing a campaign report late, can hurt.

Republican Pollster. But the law deals very little with ethics. Following the law often has nothing to do with running an ethical campaign and vice versa.

Once illegality is ruled out, however, where does that leave us? What does "campaign ethics" mean? What kinds of behaviors by candidates and their supporters are seen as crossing the ethical line? These experienced political professionals had a hard time providing clear answers to these questions:

Democratic Media Consultant. Campaign ethics are about whether a candidate can look at himself in the mirror the next morning.

Republican Pollster. It's also about the crassness of a candidate's behavior, like getting someone to be civil when they lose and give a concession speech.

Republican General Consultant. Ethics has to be about more than whether you want to see it on the front page or not the next morning. There are things that happen in campaigns that are unethical that wouldn't necessarily make the front page.

Consultants provided few concrete examples of unethical behavior they had witnessed, and most of the ones they mentioned dealt with business practices and professional ethics rather than the actions of candidates:

Democratic Pollster. One problem is in not fulfilling your obligations to clients, not getting interviews done. For example, you can take 350 interviews and weight them up to 400. This seems to me like a pretty clear case of fraud, but apparently it's happened more than a few times.

Republican General Consultant. Most of [the formal complaints that are filed with the American Association of Political Consultants] boil down to he said/she said issues. They usually have to do with misrepresentation or a breach of contract, but even that is relatively rare.

Democratic Pollster. The biggest problem I've seen is the illegal sharing of information, or pressure on me to share that information. Occasionally I get a call from a campaign manager saying that I should run specific [polling results] and give them to someone else's campaign. No, I can't do that.

Democratic Media Consultant. We were involved in a campaign recently where we did the advertising for a candidate who had employed his current opponent's advertising people in an earlier race. That firm ended up using some footage for a spot that they had attained, but never aired, when our candidate was their client—footage that our client had paid for. We were furious because that's clearly a breach of professional ethics and something we would never do.

In some cases, what might appear to be unethical behavior at first glance is really not:

DEMOCRATIC MEDIA CONSULTANT. When George Washington campaigned, he would ride from town to town in a carriage with horses and a large group of people, with usually four or five people actually in his carriage with him. Then about a half a mile outside of a town, he would hop out, unchain one of the horses, and mount that horse and ride well ahead through the town because he knew that image of him was central to his image as a war leader and head of the army. Image manipulation has been a part of politics since the day it started. If consultants weren't here to do it, candidates would do it themselves. We're just here to do it better.

REPUBLICAN GENERAL CONSULTANT. There are many examples in campaigns of opponents filing complaints with the state elections board or the Federal Election Commission, just to raise the question of impropriety. It means nothing if you file your report late by four days, except that they can now say the FEC is investigating it or a complaint has been filed against you. It just takes another bite out of your credibility. In most cases, though, the report is late because they're meticulously going through and making sure everything is accounted for.

INDEPENDENT POLITICAL ANALYST. All of us hear the anecdotal stories of, "There are phone calls going around that say this horrible thing about our candidate, and we don't know where they came from or where they started." We hear those stories every year. . . . No one quite understands this whole idea of push-polling [see note 10], and the media needs to be better educated about it. There's a difference between doing a poll and reading [a candidate's] record, and then saying, "If you knew that so-and-so did this wouldn't you hate them?"—there's a very big difference between a benchmark poll that simply asks questions with negative statements and a push-poll.

Whatever ethics may be, to the extent that anyone truly cares about them it seemingly is the consultants more than their clients:

DEMOCRATIC POLLSTER. In my sixteen years in this business, I've never had a prospective client ask about ethics in any pitch or meeting.

DEMOCRATIC MEDIA CONSULTANT. We're constantly having arguments with candidates about responding to negative ads. But we do a ton of work with the national and state parties, and we've never been asked about ethics.

REPUBLICAN POLLSTER. I think it's very blurry in most candidates' minds. I've never been asked a question about my ethics.

INDEPENDENT POLITICAL ANALYST. When you're a candidate in the heat of the campaign battle, it's hard to step back sometimes and look at things from an ethical standpoint.

And what is the appropriate response when a violation of ethical standards does occur?

REPUBLICAN POLLSTER. It's not my job to be the cop in the campaign, but it is my job to separate myself from any unethical behavior in a campaign and graciously get out.

DEMOCRATIC MEDIA CONSULTANT. We've given up a couple campaigns over [ethical] differences.

In the end, there is only so much you can do:

REPUBLICAN GENERAL CONSULTANT. We are in an industry that cannot accept the sort of restraints that are put on commercial speech. That would destroy what the First Amendment is all about. As a result, the standards that cannot be imposed from people outside have to be formulated by those who are in the business. In fact, I think they do a pretty good job for the most part. I had a race last year where there were some rumors and other things about both candidates that just didn't belong in a campaign, and so we made sure they didn't get there. It was a rough, tough campaign but there were lines [we chose not to cross].

Methodological Appendix

The data for political consultants, party officials, and voters were collected by the Center for Congressional and Presidential Studies (CCPS) at American University as part of the Improving Campaign Conduct project funded by a grant (from 1998 to 2004) from the Pew Charitable Trusts. The consultant survey was conducted in November 2002 with 200 individuals who held the title of "principal" or a similar rank in their firms. The data for party elites, also obtained in 2002, are based on responses from 108 executive directors and other senior officials from Democratic and Republican state party committees, plus others associated with various national campaign committees. Voter attitudes were measured in a 2002 nationwide sample survey of 1,163 voting-age adults in the lower forty-eight states. All three of the CCPS surveys were conducted by telephone by Yankelovich Partners, Inc.; for an expanded discussion, see Thurber and Nelson (2000); Dulio and Nelson (2005).

Data for candidates were collected by the Center for American Politics and Citizenship (CAPC) at the University of Maryland, in conjunction with *Cam-*

paigns & Elections magazine as part of the Campaign Assessment and Candidate Outreach project, also funded by the Pew Charitable Trusts. This survey, administered by mail in 2001, collected information from a national sample of congressional, statewide, state legislative, local, county, municipal, and judicial candidates who ran for office between 1998 and 2000. Results from 2,469 congressional and state legislative candidates were included in the analysis presented here; additional information about the survey appears in Abbe and Herrnson (2003); Francia and Herrnson (2003); Herrnson (2004).

Questions from the Campaign Assessment and Candidate Outreach Project

1. Do you believe the following campaign practices are acceptable, questionable, or clearly unethical?
    - Using negative advertising to decrease voter turnout.
    - Making factually true statements out of context.
    - Focusing on your opponent's negative characteristics.
    - Using push-polls.

2. Positive campaigning is usually defined as campaigning that does not mention or criticize an opponent, negative campaigning as campaigning that directly criticizes an opponent but does not explicitly compare the candidates, and comparative campaigning as campaigning that contrasts the candidates and their positions. Using these definitions, would you say your major opponent's campaign was mostly positive, mostly negative, or mostly comparative?

3. Using the same definitions, how would you describe your campaign?

Questions from the Improving Campaign Conduct Project

1. (Political consultants and party officials) In your view, how common were unethical practices in the political consulting business for this election cycle? Do unethical practices happen very often, fairly often, sometimes, rarely, or not at all?

2. (Voters) In your view, how common are unethical practices in campaigns? Do unethical practices happen very often, fairly often, sometimes, rarely, or not at all?

3. (Voters) I'm going to read you several practices that sometimes occur during the course of a campaign. As I read each, please tell me whether you believe that practice is acceptable, questionable, or unacceptable.
    - Making statements that are factually true, but are taken out of context.

- Focusing primarily on the negative personal characteristics of an opponent, rather than on issues.
- Using push-polls.

Notes

The authors gratefully acknowledge financial support from the Pew Charitable Trusts, the Center for Congressional and Presidential Studies at American University, and the Center for American Politics and Citizenship at the University of Maryland. Paul Herrnson also wishes to thank the Department of Political Science at Arizona State University for graciously providing him with an office and library privileges while he worked on this paper. The views expressed here are solely those of the authors and do not necessarily represent the views of the Congressional Research Service, the Library of Congress, or any other institution with which the authors are affiliated.

1. See Nelson, Dulio, and Medvic (2002); Thurber and Nelson (2004).
2. See Faucheux and Herrnson (2001, 2002); Maisel and West (2004); Thurber (2001).
3. See Dulio and Nelson (2005); Faucheux and Herrnson (2001, 2002); R. Garrett (2005); Nelson, Dulio, and Medvic (2002); Thurber, Nelson, and Dulio (2000a).
4. See Dulio (2004); Fowler (2004); R. Garrett (2005); Johnson (2001); Luntz (1988); Napolitan (1972); Nimmo (1970); Sabato (1981); Siegel (2002); Strother (2003); Thurber and Nelson (2000); Whitney (2002, 2004).
5. See Dimock and Jacobson (1995); Herrnson (2004); Jacobson and Dimock (1995); McCurley and Mondak (1995); Mondak (1995a); Peters and Welch (1980); Welch and Hibbing (1997).
6. See Ansolabehere et al. (1994); Brians and Wattenberg (1996); Finkel and Geer (1998); Freedman and Goldstein (1999); Kahn and Kenney (2000); Thurber, Nelson, and Dulio (2000); Lau and Pomper (2001); Wattenberg and Brians (1999); also see Dulio and Nelson (2005), on the connection between advertising and ethics.
7. See Kamber (1997); Sabato (1991).
8. These percentages refer to responses indicating that unethical campaign practices occur "sometimes," "rarely," or "not at all."
9. This refers to consultants' personal guidelines governing responsible provision of services. Issues related to billing clients, transparency in client relationships, the acceptability of finder fees for client referrals, overall attentiveness to clients, and payment method (salary/fee vs. commission) are what consultants and party officials often have in mind when they discuss campaign ethics.
10. More formally, Sabato and Simpson (1996, 245) define a push-poll as "a survey instrument containing questions which attempt to change the opinion of contacted voters, generally by divulging negative [and sometimes false] information about the opponent which is designed to *push* the voter away from him or her and *pull* the voter toward the candidate paying for the polling" (emphasis in original).

11. For additional information on relationships between parties and political consultants, see Dulio and Thurber (2003); Herrnson (2004); Kolodny (1998, 2000). For survey data on the strategic relationship between candidates and consultants, see Thurber and Nelson (2000, especially page 18).

12. See R. Garrett (2004); Thurber and Nelson (2000).

13. See Faucheux and Herrnson (2001); Thurber and Nelson (2000).

14. See R. Garrett (2005).

15. See Herrnson (2004); Salmore and Salmore (1996).

16. See Dulio and Nelson (2005); R. Garrett (2004); Thurber and Nelson (2000).

17. See Blumental (1982); Greider (1992); Jamieson (1992); Kamber (1997); Sabato and Simpson (1996); Wayne (2001).

12 Two Views From the Trenches:

Looking At Versus Looking Along
David B. Hill

Connecting the Study and Practice of Politics
David Beattie and Sheryl Lovelady

Editor's Note: At various points throughout this book, we have presented some of the reactions by professional campaign consultants to papers presented at the conference hosted by the University of Florida Graduate Program in Political Campaigning in February 2005 (see preface). Since the main purpose of that conference was to foster a dialogue between academics and practitioners, it seems only fair that our consultants be given an opportunity to describe in greater detail the kind of research they think scholars should be doing, and why. In the first of the two essays that follow, Republican pollster David B. Hill urges, among other things, that political scientists rely more heavily on qualitative approaches (including in-depth interviews) that would give them a better sense of the reality they are seeking to understand. In the second essay, Democratic pollsters David Beattie and Sheryl Lovelady recommend that academics look more closely at races below the presidential level, and that they pay closer attention to the formal rules (governing fundraising, ballot structure, and the like) that can have a tremendous impact on how the political game is played. Just as professional consultants can benefit from an awareness of the scholarly work being done on campaigns and elections, the academic community would be well advised to heed the insights that can come only from experience. Both groups have some interesting things to say about the nature of electoral politics in the United States.

Looking At Versus Looking Along

David B. Hill

C. S. Lewis, the Oxford don and Christian man of letters, once wrote an essay, "Meditation in a Tool Shed," that distinguished between "looking at" and "looking along" something. He offered a simple example to illustrate his meaning:

> A young man meets a girl. The whole world looks different when he sees her. Her voice reminds him of something he has been trying to remember all his life, and ten minutes casual chat with her is more precious than all the favours that all other women in the world could grant. He is, as they say, "in love." Now comes a scientist and describes this young man's experience from the outside. For him it is all an affair of the young man's genes and a recognized biological stimulus. That is the difference between looking *along* the sexual impulse and looking *at* it.
>
> When you have got into the habit of making this distinction you will find examples of it all day long. The mathematician sits thinking, and to him it seems that he is contemplating timeless and spaceless truths about quantity. But the cerebral physiologist, if he could look inside the mathematician's head, would find nothing timeless and spaceless there—only tiny movements in the grey matter. The savage dances in ecstasy at midnight before Nyonga and feels with every muscle that his dance is helping to bring the new green crops and the spring rain and the babies. The anthropologist, observing that savage, records that he is performing a fertility ritual of the type so-and-so....
>
> As soon as you have grasped this simple distinction, it raises a question. You get one experience of a thing when you look along it and another when you look at it. Which is the "true" or "valid" experience? Which tells you most about the thing? (Lewis 1970, 212–213; emphasis in original)

Lewis's distinction seems to have some relevance to modern-day political science in its quest to better understand the electoral process. Most academics seem to be merely looking *at* campaigns and elections. Yet by looking *along* the object of their analysis, they might make unexpected progress in theory building and relationship discovery. I am not sure that either approach, by itself, gives us a superior insight into campaigns or how they work. But unless political scientists can add looking *along* to their repertoire, their understanding will necessarily remain incomplete.

The question, then, is how can one look along campaigns and elections? I would suggest several strategies. My first admonition is to move beyond the safe confines of the academy to the trenches of political conflict. In research parlance, more political scientists should become participant observers. Fortunately, in this day and age, that's not hard to do. Scholars would seldom need to take a leave of absence to see, hear, and experience the insides of a campaign. To the contrary, narcissistic political consultants have allowed their "insider" and "secret" deliberations about politics to be portrayed in theaters (as in *The War Room* or *Primary Colors*), in books (as in Strother's 2003 memoir, *Falling Up: How a Redneck Helped Invent Political Consulting*, or most anything by James Carville), on the Sunday television talk shows (*Meet the Press, This Week*, or *Face the Nation*), and more recently in blogs and other web-based forums.

Some skeptics might wonder whether these open, public forums provide any meaningful insight into real campaign decision-making and strategy. I can enthusiastically say they do. Most consultants (more so than candidates) act pretty much the same in private as they do in public. Sure, a consultant knows that there are certain politically incorrect things you can't say on television, but, for the most part, what you see is what you get.

In this regard, let me raise a topic that, while at the heart of political campaigning, is seldom rigorously investigated by political scientists. What I refer to are "talking points," the public embodiment of campaign message development and discipline.[1] The most effective campaigns are those that consistently apply their chosen talking points from start to finish. Accordingly, many hours are spent pouring over polls and focus groups to find the best talking points, with numerous criteria being applied to assess their possible value. For example,

- Do they energize the base of core supporters?
- Do they persuade undecided voters?
- Do they cross-pressure the opposition's supporters?
- Are they easy to understand?
- Do they build an unassailable wall of logic?
- Are they credible and believable?
- Can they be easily learned and repeated by surrogates?

I have had more than one consultant tell me that they think of elections as being like a courtroom, where voters are the jury. The campaign's talking points are analogous to the opening statement, presentation of evidence, and closing statements—and if these elements can persuade a jury, they can win an election. Some consultants believe, then, that there is a logical foundation to winning campaigns, and exploring that logic through an analysis of talking points would be something best undertaken by participant observers. Academics might worry that such an approach would produce little more than a series of idiosyncratic, qualitative case studies that could not be generalized to anything larger—a concern that obviously would have merit if the participant observer didn't use these studies as a fertile field for the propagation of new theories that could be tested through larger and more comprehensive empirical research projects of broader generalizability. However, it is just this sort of propagation that I expect to occur.

Another possible avenue for advancing campaign research is also qualitative in nature: the in-depth interview. Following almost every election cycle, I receive one or two mail or web-based surveys from academics asking me about some aspect of the campaign process. Unfortunately, most of these surveys seem to have been written by people who never spent any time working inside real politics or campaigns. The words chosen to describe things, the syntax, the colloquialisms, and nearly everything else screams of being academic rather than political. I sometimes find that the questions are so far off the mark that it is nearly impossible to fashion a response. On occasion, I have tried and tried to answer a question, only to chuck the survey into the trash because I assume that anyone who would write a question like that could never understand my answer anyway.

Rather than writing surveys, or at least prior to writing surveys, it might be useful for a researcher to do some in-depth interviews; these could even be done by telephone, if necessary. Each interview might consist of five or six general questions that could be posed during the course of interviews of perhaps thirty to forty-five minutes in length. The advantages of this format would be that the researcher would encounter the natural language of the campaign participant (candidate, manager, consultant, donor, or volunteer) while having an opportunity to hear his or her questions parsed and reworded to fit the reality that he or she seeks to understand.

As with case studies, a by-product of in-depth interview encounters might be the discovery of new, testable notions about how politics works. When I changed careers from political science to political consulting, I was surprised to find a fairly robust sense of the science of politics outside the academic arena. As a junior university professor, I was frequently struck by the almost impossible nature of quantifying a true knowledge and understanding of politics. In the consulting trade, however, I routinely encountered other consultants who had rendered in their minds a coherent and often detailed scientific theory of how campaigns work. Further, most of these consultants have continued to refine and validate their theories as they moved along through their professional careers.

One consultant with whom I have worked maintains that everything in an election is about likeability. Nothing else matters—not party, not money, and not issues. (I am simplifying somewhat here, obviously.) What is truly important is which candidate is most likeable. Now, you may not think winning elections could be that simple, but someone who makes his living doing campaigns believes that. It is an elegant and testable notion about politics, and, as such, it is worth examining and refining. What constitutes likeability? Are there limits to inducing competitive likeability? How does likeability trump (or reinforce) other voting factors? The questions surrounding this small theory of campaigns and election outcomes could consume a researcher's lifetime.

Skeptics may wonder whether a consultant's "science of politics" is not merely anecdotal and lacking in systematic explanatory power across time and geography. My own experiences lead me to believe that more than a little truth can be found in much of what passes for conventional wisdom inside the campaigner community. There are axioms about the bloc voting of African Americans, for example, that invariably are confirmed from one campaign to the next. There are assumptions about the role of money that are proven anew in each electoral cycle. And there are rules of thumb about analyses of polls that I have seen validated time and again.

Let me share a few of the rules of thumb about polling that seem to find support in the real world. There is, for example, the "what you see is what you get" rule, which has several variants. The first time I encountered it was in the South twenty-five years ago. The rule postulated that Republicans would get none of the undecided vote from preelection polls. So if the final poll showed a Republican leading 46 percent to 42 percent, with 12 percent undecided, the Republican would lose by approximately 46 percent to 54 percent. The logic here was that if historically Democratic-leaning southern voters had not decided to vote Republican a week before the election, the prospects for an eleventh-hour conversion were remote. As the South has become more Republican in its long-term partisanship, things have changed substantially. Nevertheless, the "what you see is what you get" rule has several contemporary corollaries. One of these postulates is that, in issue referenda, the final poll's yes vote typically is what the yes side gets on election day; in other words, the undecided vote in the final poll typically ends up voting no by an overwhelming margin. A similar rule holds for incumbents. That is, entrenched officeholders running for reelection seldom get much of the undecided vote. If you have not decided to reelect an incumbent a week before the election, chances are that you'll end up supporting the challenger.

Another pollster rule of thumb is that preelection polls exaggerate crossover voting. For example, preelection surveys frequently show the Republican candidate getting a larger share of African American votes (often 15–20 percent) than they achieve on election day. I've learned to expect 95 percent of African Americans to vote for the Democrat, no matter what the preelection polls say. This is referred to as the "coming home" principle, whereby voters who lean toward defection for a time eventually return to their own partisan preference.

There are both obvious and elusive explanations for familiar informal rules like these, yet little systematic work has been done to find empirical support for those explanations. Regarding the African-American vote, we know that the early poll defectors are younger, better educated, and more affluent than Democrats who remain loyal to their party's candidate all along. Yet after some early dalliance with possibly voting Republican, why do these young, high-status blacks return to their Democratic roots? This is just one of numerous phenomena routinely observed by consultants that could benefit from the analysis of political scientists.

In general, the "looking along" research strategies I am suggesting are more qualitative than quantitative. Qualitative studies are more likely than their number-crunching counterparts to yield theory-building insights and perspectives on the nature of electoral politics. This is not to say that quantitative studies aren't useful. But until political scientists formulate smarter and more elegant theories of how campaigns and elections work, the progress of quantitative research will be limited accordingly. And where quantitative studies *are* used, they would benefit from a more direct approach to the discovery process. It seems that political scientists are trained to prefer inference and deduction over direct inquiry. For example, if an investigator seeks to understand why candidates or their consultants do certain things, they could look at their actions and infer or deduce certain conclusions; thus, if I want to know whether consultants think that early advertising is useful, I could study patterns of spending over the course of a campaign. Alternatively, and more directly, I could ask campaign decision-makers when they spend their money, and why. It is just so simple, yet some researchers undoubtedly would have trouble trusting the result—perhaps because of a suspicion that they will be misled by their research subjects. Whatever the source of their misgivings, they should not be afraid of asking a direct question and getting a direct answer.

A final shortcoming of academic campaign research is that it draws so deeply on the electoral behavior literature that approaches campaigns from a voter perspective. Although it is useful to examine campaigns and elections through the prism of voter behavior, that is not always how practitioners approach the topic. It may be useful to consider an example from the world of sports to make the point here: There are numerous occasions when a losing college or professional sports program hires a new coach to turn things around. Sometimes the new coach is able to win with the same players his predecessor lost with, and sometimes he induces fans to attend games and wear certain colors when his predecessor couldn't even fill the seats, much less influence wardrobe. That is how many consultants see political campaigns. Just because Consultant A couldn't get a minority-party candidate elected in a state does not mean that Consultant B cannot do so. Even though Consultant A and Consultant B may have the same knowledge and understanding of voter behavior in a state, that doesn't mean their strategies and tactics will be identical, even for the same candidate. Coaching matters. Consultants matter, even when voters and players remain the same. So merely understanding elections from a voter perspective leaves half of the equation blank.

Connecting the Study and Practice of Politics
David Beattie and Sheryl Lovelady

This book examines many of the key elements of political campaigns from the point of view of leading academic scholars and, in the process, provides a broad overview of what we know and don't know—or, more accurately, what researchers *think* we know and don't know—about campaigns and elections in the United States. It is our intent to explore further the apparent disconnect between how academics and political consultants think about campaigns. To a large degree, we believe that the different perspectives held by these two groups reflect the difference between studying the average (or norm) and studying the exception. As noted in chapter 2, academics look for patterns, developing "highly structured frameworks to help map the forest without becoming spellbound by the trees." Do campaigns really matter? According to Michael John Burton and Daniel M. Shea, "[t]he truth of the matter, when viewed from on high, is that most elections, most of the time, are decided long before the race begins. Incumbents usually win. Candidates allied with the president in times of prosperity—they win, too. So do those with experience, and who fit with the demographic, partisan, and basic attitudinal makeup of their constituency."

Consultants know the averages and patterns as well as academics do, but they also seek ways of winning the close ones and pulling off the occasional upset because that is how professional reputations, and successful careers, are made. They try to accomplish this by looking first at the district (what is its overall character and partisan balance?), next at potential weaknesses of the opposition (an incumbent, say, who is out of step with his or her district, or embroiled in some sort of scandal or personal embarrassment), then at their candidate's strengths (someone with charisma, a forceful personality, or unusual dedication can be worth a few extra points in a close race)—and, taking all of these things into account, making the correct strategic and tactical choices that combine to produce an unexpected result on election day. "If strategy does not matter," suggest Burton and Shea, "then the consultant has lost all reason for being: Why would any candidate hire someone whose actions had little or no effect on the final outcome?" Conversely, consultants who appear capable of making the exception come true are in considerable demand.

In fact, little outright disagreement exists between those who study elections and those who manage them as to whether campaigns matter at some level. Clearly, they do. There is, however, a tension between academics and practitioners—a tension rooted, first, in the natural desire by scholars to develop a unifying theory of politics, and, second, in the failure of political practitioners operating "on the ground" to recognize how their campaign fits into the broader context as they go about making discreet spending, communication, and targeting decisions on a daily basis, hoping (based on experience and intuition, and too rarely on systematic analysis) that these decisions are the correct ones. The difference here is a little like that between physicist Stephen W. Hawking's efforts to succinctly explain the workings of the universe in his book *A Brief History of Time* (1988) and journalist Malcolm Gladwell's ruminations in *The Tipping Point* (2000) on the small moments that lead to changes in perceptions and the rise of fads. The difficulty with achieving a unifying theory of political campaigns is that the rules governing them vary to some extent by location, and by level of race, and those rules change over time. For example, even if it could be agreed upon (and it hasn't yet), an overarching theory that explains election outcomes at the federal level would appear narrow and shortsighted when one is faced with the expensive and pressing decisions that must be made regularly in contests for governor, attorney general, state representative, mayor, and county commissioner.

This is one reason why the academic literature on elections is of limited relevance to campaign professionals. In part because of the ease and accessibility of data, most notably the American National Election Study (ANES) surveys,[2] presidential (and, especially since the late 1970s, congressional) studies have dominated that literature. As Thomas M. Holbrook points out in chapter 1, one must distinguish between the relative predictability of the vote for these offices and the substantial impact that campaigns frequently have at other levels—specifically, in races for roughly 500,000 state, county, municipal, judicial, and special district positions scattered throughout the United States. With academic research focused mainly at the federal level, the bulk of our understanding of campaigns is based on a small fraction of all elections. In fairness, this overemphasis on the presidency and Congress has historical roots, as the Columbia studies of the 1940s (Lazarsfeld, Berelson, and Gaudet 1944; Berelson, Lazarsfeld, and McPhee 1954) and the path-breaking work by A. Campbell, Converse, Miller, and Stokes (1960, 1966) provided a theoretical framework for subsequent generations of political scientists to review, revise, and challenge. Nevertheless, the usefulness of scholarly research to thousands of consultants (and candidates) is diminished when the bulk of it is based on campaigns that are fundamentally dissimilar to their own.

We also believe that academics should look more closely at the impact of formal rules on electoral outcomes. These rules, which (among other things) help to set the tone and determine the content of campaigns, are generally devised by those already in power to maximize their chances of remaining in power, just as our market economy tends to generate the greatest wealth for those who possess wealth in the first place. Some of the rules in question are alluded to in this book. In chapter 3, for example, Thomas E. Patterson discusses how such structural factors as multi-candidate primaries (which expanded dramatically, partly as an outgrowth of the reforms following Watergate) and legislative gerrymandering (hardly a recent development, but one that reached new levels of sophistication with the information available in commercial databases and through the use of mapping software) can affect campaigns, while John C. Green describes in chapter 4 the importance of money in determining popular support for candidates. Considering money, it is our view that the arrival of new campaign finance laws in the mid-1970s contributed to campaigns becoming much more individualized and signaled the movement of professional political consultants to the center of strategic campaign decision-making.

The 1974 U.S. Senate investigation of President Richard Nixon revealed truths about the process of political campaigning that were known internally to political professionals but had up until then been largely invisible to the general public—including in this case a number of large and illegal contributions made by individual and corporate donors to the 1972 Nixon reelection campaign. Faced with a politically charged environment, the public's fatigue after nearly two years of Watergate-related revelations (see Olson 2003), and the impending 1976 presidential election, Congress enacted sweeping reforms that limited both contributions and expenditures in campaigns for federal office. Although this legislation was challenged by free-speech advocates, the Supreme Court acted quickly to decide the case (upholding many of its key provisions) in the months preceding the 1976 presidential election.

With the Court's ruling in *Buckley vs. Valeo,* a new and very different playing field was established for federal campaigns. The law now provided for disclosure of campaign money raised; limits on contributions to candidates, political parties, and multi-candidate political action committees (PACs); and establishment of the Federal Election Commission to ensure that the rules were enforced. For the first time, presidential and congressional campaigns were required to play by the same set of rules (at least in terms of financing and reporting), and the existence of these rules set a precedent for states to follow suit with their own guidelines governing down-ballot contests (see Corrado et al. 2005; Schultz 2002). During roughly the same period, societal changes such as heightened residential mobility and the growing preeminence of television magnified the cost of campaign communications. Thus, rather than money being rendered less important, it became even more so as the need for candidates to reach voters elevated the fundraising component of campaigns to dramatic new heights.[3] Over time, fundraising began to dominate a candidate's schedule and became central to every strategic decision made by a campaign; hours of call time (asking for donations), for example, squeezed out events and face-to-face contact with voters. Consultants and campaign staff whose efforts are devoted exclusively to the money quest are now central to campaigns at all levels. With limited resources available, budget considerations drive almost every decision and effectively place the fundraising operation at the heart of the modern campaign.

Academics would do well to study this process more closely (above and beyond simply demonstrating that money influences elections) and, in general, to seek a better understanding of the tactical and strategic decisions made by campaigns on a daily basis. Some of the research reviewed in earlier chapters represents a step in the right direction, including, for example, recent studies cited by Burton and Shea (in chapter 2) and Lynda Lee Kaid (in chapter 5) that try to identify whether and when campaigns will go negative. This growing body of work—along with numerous studies described by Erika Franklin Fowler and Kenneth M. Goldstein (regarding the role of free and earned media in campaigns; see chapter 6), Dennis W. Johnson (who notes the rise of campaigning on the Internet; see chapter 7), Peter W. Wielhouwer (on the impact of grassroots organization; see chapter 9), and others—suggest that the gap between academics and practitioners may be narrowing. The good news for up-and-coming scholars is that the countless strategic and tactical decisions made in campaigns can and should be examined in a systematic way, both to deepen the academic community's understanding of politics and, ultimately, to help political professionals make better decisions.

If more scholars used qualitative research designs as recommended by David Hill, they might also gain a greater appreciation for one factor that often shapes campaign decision-making, that is, the fact that the consequences of being wrong are considerably more dire than is true on the academic side. Campaigns are truly hard work, with coldly measurable results. They begin against a backdrop where (looking at the nation as a whole) partisan loyalties lead roughly one-third of the electorate to either love or hate candidates depending on whether there is a "D" or an "R" next to their name. Further, the time constraints of politics are unlike those found in any other industry, with a full year often being spent preparing for just a few weeks of actual communication with voters. Then on election day, you either win or you lose. When a candidate loses, his or her consultants may find themselves unable to get work in that particular state for a number of years. Compare this with an academic who publishes a theory that is eventually rejected, but who is nevertheless viewed as having made a positive contribution; although a compilation of competing theories obviously cannot all be "right," they may constitute important parts of the overall debate. In contrast, a political consultant who is wrong (at least one who is wrong with any regularity) is summarily tarred, feathered, and run out of town. An academic with tenure does not lose his job for having developed a questionable theory, whereas even the most experienced political consultant is always in danger of losing hers.

The stakes are so high, of course, because consultants work in a field that is centered on a single goal: the acquisition of power. Winning office is one path to obtaining influence over the making of public policy decisions, and, as a result, electoral politics tends to attract talented and ambitious people who are driven to seek power as a means of changing society. This is true not only for candidates but also for consultants, who typically are partisans by choice rather than business necessity. They certainly want to earn a living, but they also want to make the world a better place by assisting candidates and causes in line with their personal views. Academics need to recognize the level of personal commitment involved in order to understand fully the motivations that go into making critical strategic and tactical choices in the midst of a heated campaign. This applies, in particular, to issues involving ethics. In American politics, with its First Amendment guarantee of free speech, there inevitably will be some individuals who are prepared to exaggerate, lie, or otherwise shade the truth in an effort to gain or maintain power. Some of the earliest published work regarding consultants emphasized the mercenary, nefarious, and implied unethical nature of the services and advice they provided (Sabato 1981, 1991; also see chapters 10 and 11 in this book). Although the discussion of ethics in the public arena is important, that discussion should not ignore the penchant in our society for rewarding winning over fair play, as well as the presence of a news media that prefers covering conflict over consensus (Fallows 1996; also see chapters 2 and 6). Under the circumstances, occasional violations of ethical standards are inevitable and are a valid topic for academic and journalistic inquiry (when are they most likely to occur? what impact do they have on election outcomes?). At the same time, such violations should be recognized as the exception rather than the rule in campaign politics.

A final point concerns the relative importance of candidates and consultants in the modern era. Although candidates themselves remain the principal drivers of their campaigns, professional consultants are now at the strategic center of the decision-making process because they provide both the information and the technical skills necessary to win in today's complicated, cluttered, and overcommunicated political marketplace. Even so, scholars and citizens alike should be aware that consultants make all of their decisions within a framework determined by their clients. Further, we should keep in mind that candidates are the ones who choose to risk their careers and sometimes their reputations by running, who are willing to stand trial in the public square and be prosecuted (or persecuted) by their opponents and by the "he said–she said" pack journalism that sometimes eschews facts and the merits of policy positions for a blind repetition of each side's exaggerated charges against one another, and who—at the end of the day—are the ones who win or lose elections.

At some level academics know these things, and a substantial body of scholarly research attempts to assess the role played by candidate factors in shaping voter behavior and election outcomes.[4] An excellent example is Fenno's *Homestyle: House Members in Their Districts* (1978; also see Fenno 1996), which illustrates how much can be learned by an in-depth examination of individual candidates—while exemplifying the extreme difficulty and time commitment involved in collecting detailed information about those candidates. On a smaller scale, a recent study published in *Science* (Todorov et al. 2005) looked simply at candidates' physical appearance as a predictor of citizens' vote choice. Such efforts to identify, quantify, and evaluate the impact of candidates' actions and personal traits must continue, and they must do so at levels other than the presidency, in order to provide a clear understanding of the electoral process for academics and practitioners alike.

To sum up, we believe that the study of campaigns (or "applied political science") is a valid area of scholarly inquiry much like the study of business within the field of economics. To bring the academic and practical sides closer together, we recommend that researchers expand their focus to include more nonfederal races, investigate more closely the causes and consequences of campaign decision-making (strategic and tactical), reevaluate the importance of candidates in their models of voting behavior—and, to the extent that they want to understand why some campaigns are different from others (even now, when access to new technology and professional services has been "democratized" and the once prohibitively expensive tools of elite campaigns are used in many thousands of down-ballot contests), pay greater attention to the importance of the formal rules under which electoral competition takes place. Our discussion dealt mainly with the rules governing campaign finance, but many others (partisan versus nonpartisan election, open versus closed primary, presence or absence of a runoff primary, length of time between primary and general elections, ease and cost of acquiring voter registration records, whether information such as voter race or party is recorded, ease of ballot access for third-party or independent candidates and ballot propositions, on-year versus off-year election calendar, and so on) can profoundly affect campaign strategy and resource allocation decisions as well. Rules determine how the game is played. Rules determine what decisions candidates are required to make and how they make them. Rules determine the candidate's schedule. In short, rules shape the nature and direction of the campaign, and they have a great deal to say about which candidate wins and which one loses on election day. Until academics begin to take the rules more fully into account in their research on campaigns, their understanding of the process will be incomplete.

Notes

1. I would be remiss if I failed to acknowledge that my longtime friend at Stanford University, Shanto Iyengar, is beginning to take a closer look at talking points in his study of "framing" in politics; see Iyengar (2005). In this essay, Iyengar draws on Lakoff's *Don't Think of an Elephant!* (2004) to explore the possibilities and limitations related to a candidate's and party's ability to frame messages for voters.

2. See www.umich.edu/~nes. As any journalist, political consultant, or academic knows, the presidency, in particular, is an exception to the normal rules of politics: The media cover presidential elections differently, voters pay more attention, information channels about the campaign are different (Zaller 1996; also see chapter 1), and popular expectations concerning the office and assessment of candidate qualifications are different as well.

3. In addition, independent spending by 527 organizations operating on their own (see chapter 4) has grown in both size and influence, and is beginning to overshadow the expenditures made by the campaign itself.

4. A small sampling of this literature would include work by Cain, Ferejohn, and Fiorina (1987); Funk (1999); Jacobson (1993); Jacobson and Kernell (1983); Kinder et al. (1980); Lavine (2001); Marcus (1988); McGraw, Best, and Timpone (1995); Miller, Wattenberg, and Malanchuk (1986); Rosenberg et al. (1986); Stoker (1993); D. Sullivan and Masters (1988); J. Sullivan et al. (1990).

References

Abbe, Owen G., Jay Goodliffe, Paul S. Herrnson, and Kelly D. Patterson. 2003. "Agenda setting in congressional elections: The impact of issues and campaigns on voting behavior." *Political Research Quarterly* 56: 419–430.

Abbe, Owen G., and Paul S. Herrnson. 2003. "Public financing for judicial elections? A judicious perspective on the ABA's proposal for campaign finance reform." *Polity* 35: 535–554.

Abramowitz, Alan I. 1988. "Explaining Senate election outcomes." *American Political Science Review* 82: 385–403.

———. 1991. "Incumbency, campaign spending, and the decline of competition in U.S. House elections." *Journal of Politics* 53: 34–56.

———. 2004. "Terrorism, gay marriage, and incumbency: Explaining the Republican victory in the 2004 presidential election." *The Forum* 2(4), article 3. www.bepress.com/forum/.

Abramowitz, Alan, and Kyle Saunders. 2005. "Why can't we just get along? The reality of a polarized America." *The Forum* 3(2), article 1. www.bepress.com/forum/.

Abramowitz, Alan I., and Jeffrey A. Segal. 1986. "Determinants of the outcomes of U.S. Senate elections." *Journal of Politics* 48: 433–439.

Abramson, Paul R., and William Claggett. 2001. "Recruitment and political participation." *Political Research Quarterly* 54: 905–916.

Ahlstrom, Sydney E. 1972. *A religious history of the American people.* New Haven: Yale University Press.

Ahrens, Frank. 2005. "FCC drops bid to relax media rules: Agency sought fewer limits on ownership." *Washington Post*, January 28, A1.

Aldrich, John A. 1995. *Why parties? The origin and transformation of political parties in America.* Chicago: University of Chicago Press.

Alexander, Kim. 2001. "Ten things I want people to know about voting technology." Paper presented to the Democracy Online Project's National Task Force, National Press Club, Washington, D.C. www.calvoter.org/issues/votingtech/pub/0101KAtenthings.html.

Allen, Mike. 2004. "Rove trims sails but steers for victory." *Washington Post*, October 17, A1.

Allen, Mike, and Nancy Burrell. 2002. "The negativity effect in political advertising: A meta-analysis." In *The persuasion handbook: Developments in theory and practice*, ed. James Price Dillard and Michael Pfau, 83–96. Thousand Oaks, Calif.: Sage.

Allsop, Dee, and Herbert F. Weisberg. 1988. "Measuring change in party identification in an election campaign." *American Journal of Political Science* 32: 996–1017.

Allswang, John M. 2000. *The initiative and referendum in California, 1898–1998.* Stanford: Stanford University Press.

Althaus, Scott L. 2003. *Collective preferences in democratic politics: Opinion surveys and the will of the people.* New York: Cambridge University Press.

American Political Science Association. 2005. "Symposium on the 2004 presidential vote forecasts." *PS: Political Science & Politics* 38: 23–40.

Andreoli, Virginia, and Stephen Worchel. 1978. "Effects of media, communicator, and message position on attitude change." *Public Opinion Quarterly* 42: 59–70.

Ansolabehere, Stephen, and Alan Gerber. 1994. "The mismeasure of campaign spending: Evidence from the 1990 U.S. House elections." *Journal of Politics* 56: 1106–1118.

Ansolabehere, Stephen, and Shanto Iyengar. 1994. "Riding the wave and claiming ownership over issues: The joint effects of advertising and news coverage in campaigns." *Public Opinion Quarterly* 58: 335–357.

———. 1995. *Going negative: How political advertisements shrink and polarize the electorate.* New York: Free Press.

Ansolabehere, Stephen D., Shanto Iyengar, and Adam Simon. 1999. "Replicating experiments using aggregate and survey data: The case of negative advertising and turnout." *American Political Science Review* 93: 901–909.

Ansolabehere, Stephen, Shanto Iyengar, Adam Simon, and Nicholas Valentino. 1994. "Does attack advertising demobilize the electorate?" *American Political Science Review* 88: 829–838.

Atkin, Charles K., Lawrence Bowen, Oguz B. Nayman, and Kenneth G. Sheinkopf. 1973. "Quality versus quantity in televised political ads." *Public Opinion Quarterly* 37: 209–224.

Atkin, Charles, and Gary Heald. 1976. "Effects of political advertising." *Public Opinion Quarterly* 40: 216–228.

Bailey, Michael A., Ronald Faucheux, Paul S. Herrnson, and Clyde Wilcox, eds. 2000. *Campaigns and elections: Contemporary case studies.* Washington, D.C.: CQ Press.

Ballot Initiative Strategy Center. 2004. "2004 Election results: Ballot initiative & referendum," November. www.ballot.org.

Barber, Benjamin R. 1984. *Strong democracy: Participatory politics for a new age.* Berkeley: University of California Press.

Bartels, Larry M. 1988. *Presidential primaries and the dynamics of public choice.* Princeton: Princeton University Press.

———. 1993. "Messages received: The political impact of media exposure." *American Political Science Review* 87: 267–285.

———. 2000. "Partisanship and voting behavior, 1952–1996." *American Journal of Political Science* 44: 35–50.

Basil, Michael, Caroline Schooler, and Byron Reeves. 1991. "Positive and negative political advertising: Effectiveness of ads and perceptions of candidates." In *Television and political advertising,* Vol. 1: *Psychological processes,* ed. Frank A. Biocca, 245–262. Hillsdale, N.J.: Lawrence Erlbaum.

Beck, Paul Allen, Russell J. Dalton, Steven Greene, and Robert Huckfeldt. 2002. "The social calculus of voting: Interpersonal, media, and organizational influences on presidential choices." *American Political Science Review* 96: 57–73.

Benoit, William L. 2004. "Political party affiliation and presidential campaign discourse." *Communication Quarterly* 52: 81–97.

Benoit, William L., and Glenn J. Hansen. 2002. "Issue adaptation of presidential television spots and debates to primary and general audiences." *Communication Research Reports* 19: 138–145.

Benoit, William L., Glenn J. Hansen, and Rebecca M. Verser. 2003. "A meta-analysis of the effects of viewing U.S. presidential debates." *Communication Monographs* 70: 335–350.

Berelson, Bernard R., Paul F. Lazarsfeld, and William N. McPhee. 1954. *Voting: A study of opinion formation in a presidential campaign.* Chicago: University of Chicago Press.

Bernstein, Carl, and Bob Woodward. 1974. *All the president's men.* New York: Simon and Schuster.

Beutler, William. 2004. "Now on DVD... The next step in grassroots campaigns is here." *Weekly Standard Online,* July 14, www.weeklystandard.com/Content/Public/Articles/000/000/004/320gdwkn.asp?pg=1.

Bimber, Bruce A. 2001. "Information and political engagement in America: The search for effects of information technology at the individual level." *Political Research Quarterly* 54: 53–67.

———. 2003. *Information and American democracy: Technology in the evolution of political power.* New York: Cambridge University Press.

Bimber, Bruce A., and Richard Davis. 2002. "The Internet in Campaign 2000: How political web sites reinforce partisan engagement." Unpublished paper prepared for the Center for Information Technology and Society, University of

California, Santa Barbara. repositories. cdlib.org/cgi/viewcontent.cgi?article=1004&context=isber/cits.

———. 2003. *Campaigning online: The Internet in U.S. elections.* New York: Oxford University Press.

Bishop, George F., Robert W. Oldendick, and Alfred J. Tuchfarber. 1978. "The presidential debates as a device for increasing the 'rationality' of electoral behavior." In *The presidential debates: Media, electoral, and policy perspectives,* ed. George F. Bishop, Robert G. Meadow, and Marilyn Jackson-Beeck, 179–196. New York: Praeger.

Blondheim, Menahem. 1994. *News over the wires: The telegraph and the flow of public information in America, 1844–1897.* Cambridge, Mass.: Harvard University Press.

Blumenthal, Sidney. 1982. *The permanent campaign,* revised ed. New York: Simon and Schuster.

Blumler, Jay G., and Dennis Kavanagh. 1999. "The third age of political communication: Influences and features." *Political Communication* 16: 209–230.

Boehmke, Frederick J. 2002. "The effect of direct democracy on the size and diversity of state interest group populations." *Journal of Politics* 64: 827–844.

———. 2005. "The initiative process and interest group attention to legislative activity." Paper presented at the 2005 University of California Center for the Study of Democracy/USC-Caltech Center for the Study of Law and Politics/Initiative and Referendum Institute conference, Newport Beach, Calif.

Bond, Jon R., Cary Covington, and Richard Fleisher. 1985. "Explaining challenger quality in congressional elections." *Journal of Politics* 47: 510–529.

Borick, Christopher P. 2005. "Up the river: An empirical analysis of the effectiveness of the Swift Boat commercials." Paper presented at the 2005 annual meeting of the American Political Science Association, Washington, D.C.

Bowen, Lawrence. 1994. "Time of voting decision and use of political advertising: The Slade Gorton-Brock Adams senatorial campaign." *Journalism Quarterly* 71: 665–675.

Bowers, Thomas A. 1977. "Candidate advertising: The agenda is the message." In *The emergence of American political issues: The agenda-setting function of the press,* ed. Donald L. Shaw and Maxwell E. McCombs, 53–67. St. Paul, Minn.: West Publishing.

Bowler, Shaun, and Todd Donovan. 1994. "Information and opinion change on ballot propositions." *Political Behavior* 16: 411–435.

———. 1998. *Demanding choices: Opinion, voting, and direct democracy.* Ann Arbor: University of Michigan Press.

———. 2002. "Democracy, institutions and attitudes about citizen influence on government." *British Journal of Political Science* 32: 371–390.

Bowler, Shaun, Todd Donovan, and Ken Fernandez. 1996. "The growth of the political marketing industry and the California initiative process." *European Journal of Marketing* 30: 173–185.

Bowler, Shaun, Todd Donovan, and Trudi Happ. 1992. "Ballot propositions and information costs: Direct democracy and the fatigued voter." *Western Political Quarterly* 45: 559–568.

Bowler, Shaun, and David M. Farrell. 1992. *Electoral strategies and political marketing.* New York: St. Martin's.

———. 2000. "The internationalization of campaign consultancy." In *Campaign warriors: Political consultants in elections,* ed. James A. Thurber and Candice J. Nelson, 153–174. Washington, D.C.: Brookings Institution Press.

Box-Steffensmeier, Janet M. 1996. "A dynamic analysis of the role of war chests in campaign strategy." *American Journal of Political Science* 40: 352–371.

Brader, Ted. 2005. "Striking a responsive chord: How political ads motivate and persuade voters by appealing to emotions." *American Journal of Political Science* 49: 388–405.

Brady, David W., John F. Cogan, Brian J. Gaines, and Douglas Rivers. 1996. "The perils of presidential support: How the Republicans took the House in the 1994 midterm elections." *Political Behavior* 18: 345–367.

Branton, Regina P. 2003. "Examining individual level voting behavior on state ballot propositions." *Political Research Quarterly* 56: 367–377.

Brians, Craig Leonard, and Martin P. Wattenberg. 1996. "Campaign issue knowledge and salience: Comparing reception from TV commercials, TV news, and newspapers." *American Journal of Political Science* 40: 172–193.

Broder, David S. 1971. *The party's over: The failure of politics in America.* New York: Harper and Row.

___. 1997. "Initiative fever still grips California." *Denver Post,* August 15, B7.

___. 2000. *Democracy derailed: Initiative campaigns and the power of money.* New York: Harcourt.

Brown, Ronald E., and Monica L. Wolford. 1994. "Religious resources and African-American political action." *National Political Science Review* 4: 30–48.

Browning, Rufus P., Dale Rogers Marshall, and David H. Tabb, eds. 1997. *Racial politics in American cities,* 2d ed. New York: Longman.

Bucy, Eric P., and John E. Newhagen. 1999. "The micro- and macrodrama of politics on television: Effects of media format on candidate evaluations." *Journal of Broadcasting and Electronic Media* 43: 193–210.

Burden, Barry C. 2004. "An alternative account of the 2004 presidential election." *The Forum,* 2(4), article 2. www.bepress.com/forum/.

___. 2005. "Ralph Nader's campaign strategy in the 2000 U.S. presidential election." *American Politics Research* 33: 672–699.

Burnham, Walter Dean. 1970. *Critical elections and the mainsprings of American politics.* New York: Norton.

Burton, Michael John, and Daniel M. Shea. 2003. *Campaign mode: Strategic vision in congressional elections.* Lanham, Md.: Rowman and Littlefield.

Bystrom, Dianne G., Mary Christine Banwart, Lynda Lee Kaid, and Terry Robertson. 2004. *Gender and candidate communication: Videostyle, webstyle, newstyle.* New York: Routledge.

Bystrom, Dianne G., and Lynda Lee Kaid. 2002. "Are women candidates transforming campaign communication? A comparison of advertising videostyles in the 1990s." In *Women transforming Congress,* ed. Cindy Simon Rosenthal, 146–169. Norman: University of Oklahoma Press.

Bystrom, Dianne G., and Jerry L. Miller. 1999. "Gendered communication styles and strategies in Campaign 1996: The videostyles of women and men candidates." In *The electronic election: Perspectives on the 1996 campaign communication,* ed. Lynda Lee Kaid and Dianne G. Bystrom, 293–302. Mahwah, N.J.: Lawrence Erlbaum.

Cain, Bruce, John Ferejohn, and Morris Fiorina. 1987. *The personal vote: Constituency service and electoral independence.* Cambridge, Mass.: Harvard University Press.

Caldeira, Gregory A., Samuel C. Patterson, and Gregory A. Markko. 1985. "The mobilization of voters in congressional elections." *Journal of Politics* 47: 490–509.

Calhoun-Brown, Allison. 1996. "African American churches and political mobilization: The psychological impact of organizational resources." *Journal of Politics* 58: 935–953.

Camobreco, John F. 1998. "Preferences, fiscal policies, and the initiative process." *Journal of Politics* 60: 819–829.

Campaign Finance Institute. 2004. "Funds doubled, small donations quadrupled—but mostly after nominations decided," October 4 (press release). www.cfinst.org/pr/100404.html.

Campbell, Angus, Philip E. Converse, Warren E. Miller, and Donald E. Stokes. 1960. *The American voter.* New York: Wiley.

___. 1966. *Elections and the Political Order.* New York: Wiley.

Campbell, Colton C., and David A. Dulio. 2003. "Campaigning along the information highway." In *Congress and the Internet,* ed. James A. Thurber and Colton C. Campbell, 11–30. Upper Saddle River, N.J.: Prentice Hall.

Campbell, James E. 2000. *The American campaign: U.S. presidential campaigns and the national vote.* College Station: Texas A&M University Press.

———. 2001. "When have presidential campaigns decided election outcomes?" *American Politics Research* 29: 437–460.

———. 2003. "The stagnation of congressional elections." In *Life after reform: When the Bipartisan Campaign Reform Act meets politics,* ed. Michael J. Malbin, 141–158. Lanham, Md.: Rowman and Littlefield.

Campbell James E., Lynna L. Cherry, and Kenneth A. Wink. 1992. "The convention bump." *American Politics Quarterly* 20: 287–307.

Campbell, James E., and James C. Garand, eds. 2000. *Before the vote: Forecasting American national elections.* Thousand Oaks, Calif.: Sage.

Capella, Louis, and Ronald D. Taylor 1992. "An analysis of the effectiveness of negative political campaigning." *Business and Public Affairs* 18: 10–17.

Cappella, Joseph N., and Kathleen Hall Jamieson. 1997. *Spiral of cynicism: The press and the public good.* Oxford: Oxford University Press.

Cardy, Emily Arthur. 2005. "An experimental field study of the GOTV and persuasion effects of partisan direct mail and phone calls." *Annals of the American Academy of Political and Social Science* 601: 28–40.

Carey, John M., Richard G. Niemi, and Lynda W. Powell. 2000. "Incumbency and the probability of reelection in state legislative elections." *Journal of Politics* 62: 671–700.

Carsey, Thomas M. 2000. *Campaign dynamics: The race for governor.* Ann Arbor: University of Michigan Press.

Ceaser, James W. and Andrew E. Busch. 2001. *The perfect tie: The true story of the 2000 presidential election.* Lanham, Md.: Rowman and Littlefield.

Center for the Study of Elections and Democracy. 2005. "New campaign finance law (BCRA) pushed parties, candidates to raise dramatically more money from individuals in 2004: Changes the way money is raised and spent," February 7 (press release). csed.byu.edu/Index/ PRESS%20RELEASE%20BYUCSED %202%207%2005.doc.

Chaffee, Steven H., and Jack Dennis. 1979. "Presidential debates: An assessment." In *The past and future of presidential debates,* ed. Austin Ranney, 75–101. Washington, D.C.: American Enterprise Institute.

Chaffee, Steven H., and Joan Schleuder. 1986. "Measurement and effects of attention to media news." *Human Communication Research* 13: 76–107.

Chaffee, Steven H., Xinshu Zhao, and Glenn Leshner. 1994. "Political knowledge and the campaign media of 1992." *Communication Research* 21: 305–324.

Chambers, Simone. 2001. "Constitutional referendums and democratic deliberation." In *Referendum democracy: Citizens, elites and deliberation in referendum campaigns,* ed. Matthew Mendelsohn and Andrew Parkin, 231–255. New York: Palgrave Macmillan.

Chang, Chingching, and Jacqueline C. Bush Hitchon. 2004. "When does gender count? Further insights into gender schematic processing of female candidates' political advertisements." *Sex Roles* 51: 197–208.

Chávez, Lydia. 1998. *The color bind: California's battle to end affirmative action.* Berkeley: University of California Press.

Christ, William G., Esther Thorson, and Clarke Caywood. 1994. "Do attitudes toward political advertising affect information processing of televised political commercials?" *Journal of Broadcasting and Electronic Media* 38: 251–270.

Citrin, Jack, Beth Reingold, and Evelyn Walters. 1990. "The 'official English' movement and the symbolic politics of language in the United States." *Western Political Quarterly* 43: 535–559.

Clinton, Joshua D., and John S. Lapinski. 2004. " 'Targeted' advertising and voter turnout: An experimental study of the 2000 presidential election." *Journal of Politics* 66: 69–96.

Cohen, Akiba A. 1976. "Radio vs. TV: The effect of the medium." *Journal of Communication* 26: 29–35.

Coleman, John J., and Paul F. Manna. 2000. "Congressional campaign spending and the quality of democracy." *Journal of Politics* 62: 757–789.

Converse, Philip E. 1975. "Public opinion and voting behavior." In *Handbook of*

Cook, Charlie. 2001. "The 'pot roast' election." *Cook Political Report,* November 6. www.cookpolitical.com/column/2001/110601.php.

Copeland, Gary W. 1983. "Activating voters in congressional elections." *Political Behavior* 5: 391–401.

Cornfield, Michael. 2003. "Starting to click: Online campaigning in the 2002 elections." In *Midterm madness: The elections of 2002,* ed. Larry J. Sabato, 57–67. Lanham, Md.: Rowman and Littlefield.

———. 2004. *Politics moves online: Campaigning and the Internet.* New York: Century Foundation Press.

Corrado, Anthony. 1996. "Elections in cyberspace: Prospects and problems." In *Elections in cyberspace: Toward a new era in American politics,* ed. Anthony Corrado and Charles M. Firestone, 1–31. Washington, D.C.: Aspen Institute.

Corrado, Anthony, Thomas E. Mann, Daniel R. Ortiz, and Trevor Potter, eds. 2005. *The new campaign finance sourcebook.* Washington, D.C.: Brookings Institution Press.

Corrado, Anthony, Thomas E. Mann, Daniel R. Ortiz, Trevor Potter, and Frank J. Sorauf, eds. 1997. *Campaign finance reform: A sourcebook.* Washington, D.C.: Brookings Institution Press.

Craig, Stephen C., and James G. Kane. 2000. "Winning and losing, sour grapes, and negative ads: The impact of election campaigns on political support." Paper presented at the 2000 annual meeting of the Midwest Political Science Association, Chicago.

Craig, Stephen C., James G. Kane, and Jason Gainous. 2005. "Issue-related learning in a gubernatorial campaign: A panel study." *Political Communication* 22: 483–503.

Craig, Stephen C., James G. Kane, and Jason Gainous. 2005. "Learning to build a better mousetrap." *Political Communication* 22: 523–526.

Craig, Stephen C., Amie Kreppel, and James G. Kane. 2001. "Public opinion and support for direct democracy: A grassroots perspective." In *Referendum democracy: Citizens, elites and deliberation in referendum campaigns,* ed. Matthew Mendelsohn and Andrew Parkin, 25–46. New York: Palgrave Macmillan.

Cronin, Thomas E. 1989. *Direct democracy: The politics of initiative, referendum, and recall.* Cambridge, Mass.: Harvard University Press.

Crotty, William J., and Gary C. Jacobson. 1980. *American parties in decline.* Boston: Little, Brown.

Cundy, Donald T. 1986. "Political commercials and candidate image: The effect can be substantial." In *New perspectives on political advertising,* ed. Lynda Lee Kaid, Dan Nimmo, and Keith R. Sanders, 210–234. Carbondale: Southern Illinois University Press.

———. 1990. "Image formation, the low involvement voter, and televised political advertising." *Political Communication and Persuasion* 7: 41–59.

Currinder, Marian. 2005. "Campaign finance: Funding the presidential and congressional elections." In *The elections of 2004,* ed. Michael Nelson, 108–132. Washington, D.C.: CQ Press.

D'Alessio, Dave, and Mike Allen. 2000. "Media bias in presidential elections: A meta-analysis." *Journal of Communication* 50: 133–156.

Damore, David F. 2002. "Candidate strategy and the decision to go negative." *Political Research Quarterly* 55: 669–685.

———. 2004. "The dynamics of issue ownership in presidential campaigns." *Political Research Quarterly* 57: 391–397.

Dao, James. 2004. "Same-sex marriage issue key to some GOP races." *New York Times,* November 4, A4.

Davies, Frank. 2004. "Bush's clear vision aided reelection bid, Rove says." *Miami Herald,* November 10, A6.

Davis, Richard. 1999. *The web of politics: The Internet's impact on the American political system.* New York: Oxford University Press.

Davis, Steve, Larry Elin, and Grant Reeher. 2002. *Click on democracy: The Internet's power to change political apathy into civic action.* Boulder: Westview.

Dawson, Michael C., Ronald E. Brown, and Richard L. Allen. 1990. "Racial belief systems, religious guidance, and African-American political participation." *National Political Science Review* 2. 22–44.

Delli Carpini, Michael X., and Scott Keeter. 1996. *What Americans know about politics and why it matters.* New Haven: Yale University Press.

Democratic National Committee. 2005. "DNC 2001–2005: Mobilizing, modernizing and building the Democratic Party," February. www.gwu.edu/~action/2004/parties/dnc05facts.html.

DeSantis, Joseph. 2005. *The politics of blogs.* Unpublished M.A. thesis, George Washington University.

Devlin, L. Patrick. 1989. "Contrasts in presidential campaign commercials of 1988." *American Behavioral Scientist* 32: 389–414.

DeVries, Walter. 1989. "American campaign consulting: Trends and concerns." *PS: Political Science & Politics* 22: 21–25.

DeVries, Walter, and Lance Tarrance Jr. 1972. *The ticket-splitter: A new force in American politics.* Grand Rapids, Mich.: William B. Eerdmans.

Diamant, Jeff. 2004. "Gay marriage issue could tip some black votes to Bush." Newhouse News Service, August 3. www.newhouse.com/archive/diamant080304.html.

Diamond, Edwin, and Stephen Bates. 1992. *The spot: The rise of political advertising on television,* 3d ed. Cambridge, Mass.: MIT Press.

DiClerico, Robert E. 2000. *Political parties, campaigns, and elections.* Upper Saddle River, N.J.: Prentice Hall.

Dimock, Michael A., and Gary C. Jacobson. 1995. "Checks and choices: The House bank scandal's impact on voters in 1992." *Journal of Politics* 57: 1143–1159.

Djupe, Paul A., and David A. M. Peterson. 2002. "The impact of negative campaigning: Evidence from the 1998 senatorial primaries. *Political Research Quarterly* 55: 845–860.

Donohue, Thomas R. 1973. "Impact of viewer predispositions on political TV commercials." *Journal of Broadcasting* 18: 3–15.

Donovan, Todd, and Daniel A. Smith. 2004. "Turning on and turning out: Assessing the indirect effects of ballot measures on voter participation." Paper presented at the fourth annual Conference on State Politics and Policy, Kent State University, Ohio, April 30–May 2.

Donovan, Todd, and Joseph R. Snipp. 1994. "Support for legislative term limitations in California: Group representation, partisanship, and campaign information." *Journal of Politics* 56: 492–501.

Donovan, Todd, Caroline J. Tolbert, Daniel A. Smith, and Janine Parry. 2005. "Did gay marriage elect George W. Bush?" Paper presented at the 2005 annual meeting of the Western Political Science Association, Oakland, Calif.

Downs, Anthony. 1957. *An economic theory of democracy.* New York: Harper.

Drezner, Daniel W., and Henry Farrell. 2004. "Web of influence." *Foreign Policy* (November/December): 32–40.

Druckman, James N., Lawrence R. Jacobs, and Eric Ostermeier. 2004. "Candidate strategies to prime issues and image." *Journal of Politics* 66: 1180–1202.

Dulio, David A. 2004. *For better or worse? How political consultants are changing elections in America.* Albany: State University of New York Press.

Dulio, David A., Donald L. Goff, and James A. Thurber. 1999. "Untangled web: Internet use during the 1998 election." *PS: Political Science & Politics* 32: 53–59.

Dulio, David A., and Candice J. Nelson. 2005. *The health of American campaigning.* Washington, D.C.: Brookings Institution Press.

Dulio, David A., and James A. Thurber. 2003. "The symbiotic relationship between political parties and political consultants: Partners past, present, and future." In *The state of the parties: The changing role of contemporary American parties,* 4th ed., ed. John C. Green and Rick Farmer, 215–224. Lanham, Md.: Rowman and Littlefield.

Eldersveld, Samuel J. 1956. "Experimental propaganda techniques and voting behavior." *American Political Science Review* 50: 154–165.

Eldersveld, Samuel J., and Richard W. Dodge. 1954. "Personal contact or mail propaganda? An experiment in voting turnout and attitude changes." In *Public opinion and propaganda: A book of readings,* ed. Daniel Katz, Dorwin Cartwright, Samuel Eldersveld, and Alfred M. Lee, 532–542. New York: Dryden.

Ellis, Richard J. 2002. *Democratic delusions: The initiative process in America.* Lawrence: University of Kansas Press.

Entman, Robert M. 1989. *Democracy without citizens: Media and the decay of American politics.* New York: Oxford University Press.

Erbring, Lutz, Edie N. Goldenberg, and Arthur H. Miller. 1980. "Front-page news and real-world cues: A new look at agenda-setting by the media." *American Journal of Political Science* 24: 16–49.

Erickson, Stephanie. 2003. "Wage issue could shape vote." *Orlando Sentinel,* September 22, B1.

Erikson, Robert S., and Thomas R. Palfrey. 1998. "Campaign spending and incumbency: An alternative simultaneous equations approach." *Journal of Politics* 60: 355–373.

———. 2000. "Equilibria in campaign spending games: Theory and data." *American Political Science Review* 94: 595–609.

Esser, Frank, Carsten Reinemann, and David Fan. 2001. "Spin doctors in the United States, Great Britain, and Germany: Metacommunication about media manipulation." *Harvard International Journal of Press/Politics* 6: 16–45.

Everson, David H. 1981. "The effects of initiatives on voter turnout: A comparative state analysis." *Western Political Quarterly* 34: 415–425.

"Exit polls—President." 2004. www.msnbc.msn.com/id/5297138/.

Faber, Ronald J., and M. Claire Storey. 1984. "Recall of information from political advertising." *Journal of Advertising* 13: 39–44.

Faber, Ronald J., Albert R. Tims, and Kay G. Schmitt. 1993. "Negative political advertising and voting intent: The role of involvement and alternative information sources." *Journal of Advertising* 22: 67–76.

Fallows, James. 1996. *Breaking the news: How the media undermine American democracy.* New York: Pantheon.

Farnsworth, Stephen J., and S. Robert Lichter. 1999. "No small-town poll: Public attention to network coverage of the 1992 New Hampshire primary." *Harvard International Journal of Press/Politics* 4: 51–61.

———. 2005. "The nightly news nightmare revisited: Network television's coverage of the 2004 presidential election." Paper presented at the 2005 annual meeting of the American Political Science Association, Washington, D.C.

Farrell, David M. 1996. "Campaign strategies and tactics." In *Comparing democracies: Elections and voting in global perspective,* ed. Lawrence LeDuc, Richard G. Niemi, and Pippa Norris, 158–181. Thousand Oaks, Calif.: Sage.

———. 1998. "Political consultancy overseas: The internationalization of campaign consultancy." *PS: Political Science & Politics* 31: 171–178.

Faucheux, Ronald A., and Paul S. Herrnson. 2001. *The good fight: How political candidates struggle to win elections without losing their souls.* Washington, D.C.: Campaigns and Elections.

———, eds. 2002. *Campaign battle lines: The practical consequences of crossing the line between what's right and what's not in political campaigning.* Washington, D.C.: Campaigns and Elections.

Fenno, Richard F. Jr. 1978. *Home style: House members in their districts.* Boston: Little, Brown.

———. 1996. *Senators on the campaign trail: The politics of representation.* Norman: University of Oklahoma Press.

Festinger, Leon. 1957. *A theory of cognitive dissonance.* Palo Alto, Calif.: Stanford University Press.

Finer, Jonathan. 2005. "Former GOP consultant sentenced to prison: Va. man pleaded guilty to making harassing phone calls to N.H. Democrats." *Washington Post,* February 9, A12.

Finkel, Steven E. 1993. "Reexamining the 'minimal effects' model in recent presidential campaigns." *Journal of Politics* 55: 1–21.

Finkel, Steven E., and John G. Geer. 1998. "A spot check: Casting doubt on the demobilizing effect of attack advertising."

American Journal of Political Science 42: 573–595.

Fiorina, Morris P. 1981. *Retrospective voting in American national elections.* New Haven: Yale University Press.

———. 2002. "Parties and partisanship: A 40-year retrospective." *Political Behavior* 24: 93–115.

Fiorina, Morris P., with Samuel J. Adams and Jeremy C. Pope. 2005. *Culture war? The myth of a polarized America.* New York: Pearson Longman.

Fishkin, James S. 1991. *Democracy and deliberation: New directions for democratic reform.* New Haven: Yale University Press.

Fouhy, Ed. 1995. "Some editors are saying 'no.'" *Civic Catalyst* (newsletter of the Pew Center for Civic Journalism), summer 1995.

Fowler, Linda. 2004. "Campaign ethics and the politics of personal destruction." In *campaigns and elections American style,* 2d ed., ed. James A. Thurber and Candice J. Nelson, 205–222. Boulder: Westview.

Francia, Peter L., and Paul S. Herrnson. 2003. "The impact of public finance laws on fundraising in state legislative elections." *American Politics Research* 31: 520–539.

Frazier, E. Franklin. 1963. *The Negro church in America.* New York: Shocken Books.

Freedman, Paul, Michael Franz, and Kenneth Goldstein. 2004. "Campaign advertising and democratic citizenship." *American Journal of Political Science* 48: 723–741.

Freedman, Paul, and Ken Goldstein. 1999. "Measuring media exposure and the effects of negative campaign ads." *American Journal of Political Science* 43: 1189–1208.

Freedman, Paul, William Wood, and Dale Lawton. 1999. "Do's and don'ts of negative ads: What voters say." *Campaigns & Elections* 20 (October/November): 20–25.

Fridkin, Kim Leslie, and Patrick J. Kenney. 2004. "Do negative messages work? The impact of negativity on citizens' evaluations of candidates." *American Politics Research* 32: 570–605.

Fritz, Sara, and Dwight Morris. 1992. *Handbook of campaign spending: Money in the 1990 congressional races.* Washington, D.C.: CQ Press.

Froomkin, Dan. 2005. "Bush, Deep Throat and the press." *Washington Post,* June 3. www.washingtonpost.com/wp-dyn/content/blog/2005/06/03/BL2005060300818_pf.html.

Fulk, Elizabeth. 2004. "State ballot initiatives may play large role in '04 elections; candidates ignore them 'at their own peril,' pollster says." *The Hill,* September 23. www.hillnews.com/news/092304/ballot.aspx.

Funk, Carolyn L. 1999. "Bringing the candidate into models of candidate evaluation." *Journal of Politics* 61: 700–720.

Gamble, Barbara S. 1997. "Putting civil rights to a popular vote." *American Journal of Political Science* 41: 245–269.

Garramone, Gina M. 1983. "Image versus issue orientation and effects of political advertising." *Communication Research* 10: 59–76.

———. 1984a. "Motivational models: Replication across media for political campaign content." *Journalism Quarterly* 61: 537–541, 691.

———. 1984b. "Voter responses to negative political ads." *Journalism Quarterly* 61: 250–259.

———. 1985. "Effects of negative political advertising: The roles of sponsor and rebuttal." *Journal of Broadcasting and Electronic Media* 29: 147–159.

———. 1986. "Candidate image formation: The role of information processing." In *New perspectives on political advertising,* ed. Lynda Lee Kaid, Dan Nimmo, and Keith R. Sanders, 235–247. Carbondale: Southern Illinois University Press.

Garramone, Gina, Charles K. Atkin, Bruce E. Pinkleton, and Richard T. Cole. 1990. "Effects of negative political advertising on the political process." *Journal of Broadcasting and Electronic Media* 34: 299–311.

Garramone, Gina M., and Sandra J. Smith. 1984. "Reactions to political advertising: Clarifying sponsor effects." *Journalism Quarterly* 61: 771–775.

Garrett, Elizabeth. 2004. "Democracy in the wake of the California recall." *University of Pennsylvania Law Review* 153: 239–284.

Garrett, Elizabeth, and Daniel A. Smith. 2005. "Veiled political actors and campaign disclosure laws in direct democracy." *Election Law Journal* 4: 295–328.

Garrett, R. Sam. 2004. "Congressional campaign crises and the candidate-centered campaign." Paper presented at the 2004 annual meeting of the Southern Political Science Association, New Orleans, La.

———. 2005. *Campaigns, crises, and communication: Crisis management in congressional campaigns.* Unpublished dissertation, American University.

Garrett, R. Sam, James A. Thurber, A. Lee Fritschler, and David H. Rosenbloom. 2006. "Assessing the impact of 'bureaucracy-bashing' from electoral campaigns." *Public Administration Review* (forthcoming).

Geer, John G. 1988. "The effects of presidential debates on the electorate's preferences for candidates." *American Politics Quarterly* 16: 486–501.

———. 2006. *In defense of negativity: Attack ads in presidential campaigns.* Chicago: University of Chicago Press.

Geer, John G., and James H. Geer. 2003. "Remembering attack ads: An experimental investigation of radio." *Political Behavior* 25: 69–95.

Geiger, Seth F., and Byron Reeves. 1991. "The effects of visual structure and content emphasis on the evaluation and memory for political candidates." In *Television and political advertising,* Vol. 1: *Psychological processes,* ed. Frank Biocca, 125–143. Hillsdale, N.J.: Lawrence Erlbaum.

Gelman, Andrew, and Gary King. 1993. "Why are American presidential election campaign polls so variable when votes are so predictable?" *British Journal of Political Science* 23: 409–451.

Gerber, Alan. 1998. "Estimating the effect of campaign spending on Senate election outcomes using instrumental variables." *American Political Science Review* 92: 401–411.

Gerber, Alan S., and Donald P. Green. 2000a. "The effect of a nonpartisan get-out-the-vote drive: An experimental study of leafletting." *Journal of Politics* 62: 846–857.

———. 2000b. "The effects of canvassing, telephone calls, and direct mail on voter turnout: A field experiment." *American Political Science Review* 94: 653–663.

———. 2001. "Do phone calls increase voter turnout? A field experiment." *Public Opinion Quarterly* 65: 75–85.

———. 2005. "Do phone calls increase voter turnout? An update." *Annals of the American Academy of Political and Social Science* 601: 142–154.

Gerber, Alan S., Donald P. Green, and Matthew N. Green. 2003. "Partisan mail and voter turnout: Results from randomized field experiments." *Electoral Studies* 22: 563–579.

Gerber, Elisabeth R. 1996. "Legislative response to the threat of popular initiatives." *American Journal of Political Science* 40: 99–128.

———. 1999. *The populist paradox: Interest group influence and the promise of direct legislation.* Princeton: Princeton University Press.

Gerber, Elisabeth R., and Arthur Lupia. 1995. "Campaign competition and policy responsiveness in direct legislation elections." *Political Behavior* 17: 287–306.

Gerber, Elisabeth R., Arthur Lupia, Mathew D. McCubbins, and D. Roderick Kiewiet. 2001. *Stealing the initiative: How state government responds to direct democracy.* Upper Saddle River, N.J.: Prentice Hall.

Gershtenson, Joseph. 2003. "Mobilization strategies of the Democrats and Republicans, 1956–2000." *Political Research Quarterly* 56: 293–308.

Gibson, Rachel K., Michael Margolis, David Resnick, and Stephen J. Ward. 2003. "Election campaigning on the WWW in the USA and UK: A comparative analysis. *Party Politics* 9: 47–75.

Gierzynski, Anthony, and David A. Breaux. 1993. "Money and the party vote in state House elections." *Legislative Studies Quarterly* 18: 515–533.

Gierzynski, Anthony, Paul Kleppner, and James Lewis. 1998. "Money or the machine: Money and votes in Chicago aldermanic elections." *American Politics Quarterly* 26: 160–173.

Gladwell, Malcolm. 2000. *The tipping point: How little things can make a big difference.* New York: Little, Brown.

Glantz, Stanton A., Alan I. Abramowitz, and Michael P. Burkart. 1976. "Elections outcomes: Whose money matters?" *Journal of Politics* 38: 1033–1038.

Godwin, R. Kenneth. 1988. *One billion dollars of influence: The direct marketing of politics.* Chatham, N.J.: Chatham House.

Goidel, Robert K., and Donald A. Gross. 1994. "A systems approach to campaign finance in U.S. House elections." *American Politics Quarterly* 22: 125–153.

Goidel, Robert K., Donald A. Gross, and Todd G. Shields. 1999. *Money matters: Consequences of campaign finance reform in U.S. House elections.* Lanham, Md.: Rowman and Littlefield.

Goldenberg, Edie N., Michael W. Traugott, and Frank R. Baumgartner. 1986. "Preemptive and reactive spending in U.S. House races." *Political Behavior* 8: 3–20.

Goldschmidt, Kathy B. 2001. "E-mail overload in Congress: Managing a communications crisis." Report prepared for the Congressional Management Foundation's Congress Online Project. www.congressonlineproject.org.

Goldstein, Ken, and Paul Freedman. 2000. "New evidence for new arguments: Money and advertising in the 1996 Senate elections." *Journal of Politics* 62: 1087–1108.

———. 2002a. "Campaign advertising and voter turnout: New evidence for a stimulation effect." *Journal of Politics* 64: 721–740.

———. 2002b. "Lessons learned: Campaign advertising in the 2000 elections." *Political Communication* 19: 5–28.

Goldstein, Kenneth M., Erika Franklin Fowler, and Joel Rivlin. 2004. "Media flows in the 2002 election." Paper presented at the 2004 annual meeting of the Southern Political Science Association, New Orleans, La.

Goldstein, Kenneth M., Jonathan S. Krasno, Lee Bradford, and Daniel E. Seltz. 2001. "Going negative: Attack advertising in the 1998 elections." In *Playing hardball: Campaigning for the U.S. Congress,* ed. Paul S. Herrnson, 92–107. Saddle River, N.J.: Prentice Hall.

Goldstein, Kenneth M., and Travis N. Ridout. 2002. "The politics of participation: Mobilization and turnout over time." *Political Behavior* 24: 3–29.

———. 2004. "Measuring the effects of televised political advertising in the United States." *Annual Review of Political Science* 7: 205–226.

Goodliffe, Jay. 2001. "The effect of war chests on challenger entry in U.S. House elections." *American Journal of Political Science* 45: 830–844.

Gordon, Ann, David M. Shafie, and Ann N. Crigler. 2003. "Is negative advertising effective for female candidates? An experiment in voters' uses of gender stereotypes." *Harvard International Journal of Press/Politics* 8: 35–53.

Gosnell, Harold F. 1926. "An experiment in the stimulation of voting." *American Political Science Review* 20: 869–874.

———. 1927. *Getting out the vote: An experiment in the stimulation of voting.* Chicago: University of Chicago Press.

———. 1948. *Democracy: The threshold of freedom.* New York: Ronald Press.

———. 1950. "Does campaigning make a difference?" *Public Opinion Quarterly* 14: 413–418.

———. 1968 [1938]. *Machine politics: Chicago model.* Chicago: University of Chicago Press.

Graber, Doris A. 1993. "Making campaign news user friendly: The lessons of 1992 and beyond." *American Behavioral Scientist* 37: 328–336.

———. 1996. "The 'new' media and politics: What does the future hold?" *PS: Political Science & Politics* 29: 33–36.

———. 2005. *Mass media and American politics,* 7th ed. Washington, D.C.: CQ Press.

Graf, Joseph and Carol Darr. 2004. "Political influentials online in the 2004 presidential campaign." Unpublished report prepared for the Institute for Politics, Democracy, and the Internet, Graduate School of Political Management, George Washington University. www.ipdi.org/UploadedFiles/political%20influentials.pdf.

Green, Donald P. 2004. "Mobilizing African-American voters using direct mail and commercial phone banks: A field experiment." *Political Research Quarterly* 57: 245–255.

Green, Donald P., and Alan S. Gerber. 2004. *Get out the vote! How to increase voter turnout.* Washington, D.C.: Brookings Institution Press.

Green, Donald Philip, and Jonathan S. Krasno. 1988. "Salvation for the spendthrift incumbent: Reestimating the effects of campaign spending in House elections." *American Journal of Political Science* 32: 884–907.

———. 1990. "Rebuttal to Jacobson's 'New evidence for old arguments.'" *American Journal of Political Science* 34: 363–372.

Green, Donald, Bradley Palmquist, and Eric Schickler. 2002. *Partisan hearts and minds: Political parties and the social identities of voters.* New Haven: Yale University Press.

Green, John C., James L. Guth, Corwin E. Smidt, and Lyman A. Kellstedt. 1996. *Religion and the culture wars: Dispatches from the front.* New York: Rowman and Littlefield.

Green, John C., Mark J. Rozell, and Clyde Wilcox, eds. 2003. *The Christian right in American politics: Marching to the millennium.* Washington, D.C.: Georgetown University Press.

Greenberger, Scott. 2004. "Gay-marriage ruling pushed voters." *Boston Globe,* November 7, www.boston.com/news/local/massachusetts/articles/2004/11/07/gay_marriage_ruling_pushed_voters/.

Greider, William. 1992. *Who will tell the people? The betrayal of American democracy.* New York: Simon and Schuster.

Grey, Lawrence. 1999. *How to win a local election: A complete step-by-step guide,* revised ed. New York: M. Evans.

Gross, Donald A., and Robert K. Goidel. 2003. *The states of campaign finance reform.* Columbus: Ohio State University Press.

Guskind, Robert, and Jerry Hagstrom. 1988. "In the gutter." *National Journal* 20: 2782–2790.

Haddock, Geoffrey, and Mark P. Zanna. 1997. "Impact of negative advertising on evaluations of political candidates: The 1993 Canadian federal election." *Basic and Applied Social Psychology* 19: 204–223.

Hadwiger, David. 1992. "Money, turnout, and ballot measure success in California cities." *Western Political Quarterly* 45: 539–547.

Hajnal, Zoltan L., Elisabeth R. Gerber, and Hugh Louch. 2002. "Minorities and direct legislation: Evidence from California ballot proposition elections." *Journal of Politics* 64: 154–177.

Hajnal, Zoltan L., and Paul G. Lewis. 2003. "Municipal institutions and voter turnout in local elections." *Urban Affairs Review* 38: 645–668.

Hale, Jon F., Jeffrey C. Fox, and Rick Farmer. 1998. "Negative advertisements in U.S. Senate campaigns: The influence of campaign context." *Social Science Quarterly* 77: 329–343.

Hallin, Daniel C. 1992. "Sound bite news: Television coverage of elections, 1968–1988." *Journal of Communication* 42: 5–24.

Harris, Frederick C. 1999. *Something within: Religion in African-American political activism.* New York: Oxford University Press.

Hart, Roderick P. 1994. *Seducing America: How television charms the modern voter.* New York: Oxford University Press.

———. 2000. *Campaign talk: Why elections are good for us.* Princeton: Princeton University Press.

Hasen, Richard L. 2000. "Parties take the initiative (and vice versa)." *Columbia Law Review* 100: 731–752.

———. 2005. "Rethinking the unconstitutionality of contribution and expenditure limits in ballot measure campaigns." *Southern California Law Review* 78: 885–925.

Hawking, Stephen W. 1988. *A brief history of time: From the big bang to black holes.* New York: Bantam Books.

Haynes, Audrey A., and Staci L. Rhine. 1998. "Attack politics in presidential nomination campaigns: An examination of the frequency and determinants of intermediated negative messages against opponents." *Political Research Quarterly* 51: 691–721.

Hero, Rodney E., and Caroline J. Tolbert. 2004. "Minority voices and citizen attitudes about government responsiveness in the American states: Do social and institutional context matter?" *British Journal of Political Science* 34: 109–121.

Herr, J. Paul. 2002. "The impact of campaign appearances in the 1996 election." *Journal of Politics* 64: 904–913.

Herrnson, Paul S. 1988. *Party campaigning in the 1980s.* Cambridge, Mass.: Harvard University Press.

———. 1992. "Campaign professionalism and fundraising in congressional elections." *Journal of Politics* 54: 859–870.

———. 2000. "Hired guns and House races: Campaign professionals in House elections." In *Campaign warriors: Political consultants in elections,* ed. James A. Thurber and Candice J. Nelson, 65–90. Washington, D.C.: Brookings Institution Press.

———. 2001. *Playing hardball: Campaigning for the U.S. Congress.* Upper Saddle River, N.J.: Prentice Hall.

———. 2004. *Congressional elections: Campaigning at home and in Washington,* 4th ed. Washington, D.C.: CQ Press.

Herrnson, Paul S., and Diana Dwyre. 1999. "Party issue advocacy in congressional election campaigns." In *The state of the parties: The changing role of contemporary American parties,* 3d ed., ed. John C. Green and Daniel M. Shea, 86–104. Lanham, Md.: Rowman and Littlefield.

Herrnson, Paul S., and Kelly D. Patterson. 2000. "Agenda setting and campaign advertising in congressional elections." In *Crowded airwaves: Campaign advertising in elections,* ed. James A. Thurber, Candice J. Nelson, and David A. Dulio, 96–112. Washington, D.C.: Brookings Institution Press.

Hershey, Marjorie Randon, and Paul Allen Beck. 2004. *Party politics in America,* 11th ed. New York: Longman.

Hetherington, Marc J. 2001. "Resurgent mass partisanship: The role of elite polarization." *American Political Science Review* 95: 619–631.

Hibbing, John R., and Elizabeth Theiss-Morse. 1995. *Congress as public enemy: Public attitudes toward American political institutions.* Cambridge: Cambridge University Press.

Hiebert, Ray, Robert Jones, Ernest Lotito, and John Lorenz, eds. 1971. *The political image merchants: Strategies in the new politics.* Washington, D.C.: Acropolis Books.

Hill, Ronald Paul. 1989. "An exploration of voter responses to political advertisements." *Journal of Advertising* 18: 14–22.

Hillygus, D. Sunshine, and Simon Jackman. 2003. "Voter decision making in Election 2000: Campaign effects, partisan activation, and the Clinton legacy." *American Journal of Political Science* 47: 583–596.

Hillygus, D. Sunshine and Todd G. Shields. 2005. "Moral issues and voter decision making in the 2004 presidential election." *PS: Political Science & Politics* 38: 201–209.

Hitchon, Jacqueline C., and Chingching Chang. 1995. "Effects of gender schematic processing on the reception of political commercials for men and women candidates." *Communication Research* 22: 430–458.

Hitchon, Jacqueline C., Chingching Chang, and Rhonda Harris. 1997. "Should women emote? Perceptual bias and opinion change in response to political ads for candidates of different genders." *Political Communication* 14: 49–69.

Hofstetter, C. Richard, and Timothy F. Buss. 1980. "Politics and last-minute political television." *Western Political Quarterly* 33: 24–37.

Hogan, Robert E. 1999. "Campaign and contextual influences on voter participation in state legislative elections." *American Politics Quarterly* 27: 403–433.

———. 2004. "Challenger emergence, incumbent success, and electoral accountability in state legislative elections." *Journal of Politics* 66: 1283–1303.

Holbert, R. Lance, William L. Benoit, Glenn J. Hansen, and Wei-Chun Wen. 2002. "The role of communication in the formation of an issue-based citizenry." *Communication Monographs* 69: 296–310.

Holbrook, Thomas M. 1994. "Campaigns, national conditions, and U.S. presidential elections." *American Journal of Political Science* 38: 973–998.

———. 1996. *Do campaigns matter?* Thousand Oaks, Calif.: Sage.

———. 1999. "Political learning from presidential debates." *Political Behavior* 21: 67–89.

———. 2002a. "Did the whistle-stop campaign matter?" *PS: Political Science & Politics* 35: 59–66.

———. 2002b. "Presidential campaigns and the knowledge gap." *Political Communication* 19: 437–454.

Holbrook, Thomas M., and Scott D. McClurg. 2005. "The mobilization of core supporters: Campaigns, turnout, and electoral composition in United States presidential elections." *American Journal of Political Science* 49: 689–703.

Homer, Pamela M., and Rajeev Batra. 1994. "Attitudinal effects of character-based versus competence-based negative political communication." *Journal of Consumer Psychology* 3: 163–185.

Hook, Janet. 2004. "Initiatives to ban gay marriage could help Bush in key states." *Los Angeles Times,* July 12, A1.

Huckfeldt, Robert. 1986. *Politics in context: Assimilation and conflict in urban neighborhoods.* New York: Agathon Press.

Huckfeldt, Robert, Eric Plutzer, and John Sprague. 1993. "Alternative contexts of political behavior: Churches, neighborhoods, and individuals." *Journal of Politics* 55: 365–381.

Huckfeldt, Robert, and John Sprague. 1991. "Discussant effects on vote choice: Intimacy, structure, and interdependence." *Journal of Politics* 53: 122–158.

———. 1992. "Political parties and electoral mobilization: Political structure, social structure, and the party canvass." *American Political Science Review* 86: 70–86.

Institute for Politics, Democracy, and the Internet. 2004. "Under the radar and over the top: Online political videos in the 2004 election." Unpublished report prepared for the Graduate School of Political Management, George Washington University. www.ipdi.org/UploadedFiles/web_videos.pdf.

Institute of Politics, John F. Kennedy School of Government, and Harvard University, eds. 2005. *Campaign for president:*

The managers look at 2004. Lanham, Md.: Rowman and Littlefield.

Iyengar, Shanto. 1987. "Television news and citizens' explanations of national affairs." *American Political Science Review* 81: 815–831.

———. 1991. *Is anyone responsible? How television frames political issues.* Chicago: University of Chicago Press.

———. 2005. "Speaking of values: The framing of American politics." *The Forum* 3(3), article 7. www.bepress.com/forum/.

Iyengar, Shanto, Kyu Hahn, and Markus Prior. 2001. "Has technology made attention to political campaigns more selective?" Paper presented at the 2001 annual meeting of the American Political Science Convention, San Francisco.

Iyengar, Shanto, and Donald R. Kinder. 1987. *News that matters: Television and American opinion.* Chicago: University of Chicago Press.

Iyengar, Shanto, Helmut Norpoth, and Kyu S. Hahn. 2004. "Consumer demand for election news: The horserace sells." *Journal of Politics* 66: 157–175.

Jackson, Robert A. 1996. "The mobilization of congressional electorates." *Legislative Studies Quarterly* 21: 425–445.

———. 1997. "The mobilization of U.S. state electorates in the 1988 and 1990 elections." *Journal of Politics* 59: 520–537.

———. 2002. "Gubernatorial and senatorial campaign mobilization of voters." *Political Research Quarterly* 55: 825–844.

Jacobs, Lawrence R., and Robert Y. Shapiro. 1994. "Issues, candidate image, and priming: The use of private polls in Kennedy's 1960 presidential campaign." *American Political Science Review* 88: 527–540.

Jacobson, Gary C. 1975. "The impact of broadcast campaigning on electoral outcomes." *Journal of Politics* 37: 769–793.

———. 1978. "The effects of campaign spending in congressional elections." *American Political Science Review* 72: 469–491.

———. 1980. *Money in congressional elections.* New Haven: Yale University Press.

———. 1985. "Money and votes reconsidered: Congressional elections, 1972–1982." *Public Choice* 47: 7–62.

___. 1987. "Enough is too much: Money and competition in House elections, 1972–1984." In *Elections in America*, ed. Kay Lehman Schlozman, 173–195. Winchester, Mass.: Allen and Unwin.

___. 1989. "Strategic politicians and the dynamics of U.S. House elections, 1946–86." *American Political Science Review* 83: 773–793.

___. 1990. "The effects of campaign spending in House elections: New evidence for old arguments." *American Journal of Political Science* 34: 334–362.

___. 1993. "You can't beat somebody with nobody: Trends in partisan opposition." In *Controversies in voting behavior*, 3d ed., ed. Richard G. Niemi and Herbert F. Weisberg, 241–267. Washington, D.C.: CQ Press.

___. 1999. "The effect of the AFL-CIO's 'voter education' campaigns on the 1996 House elections." *Journal of Politics* 61: 185–194.

___. 2001. *The politics of congressional elections*, 5th ed. New York: Longman.

___. 2004. *The politics of congressional elections*, 6th ed. New York: Longman.

Jacobson, Gary C., and Michael A. Dimock. 1994. "Checking out: The effects of bank overdrafts on the 1992 House elections." *American Journal of Political Science* 38: 601–624.

Jacobson, Gary C., and Samuel Kernell. 1983. *Strategy and choice in congressional elections,* 2d ed. New Haven: Yale University Press.

Jamieson, Kathleen Hall. 1992. *Dirty politics: Deception, distraction, and democracy.* New York: Oxford University Press.

Janowitz, Morris, and Dwaine Marvick. 1964 [1956]. *Competitive pressure and democratic consent: An interpretation of the 1952 presidential election,* 2d ed. Chicago: Quadrangle Books.

Jansen, Bart. 2005. "June trial planned for former Bush staffer." *Portland Press Herald,* February 6. pressherald.mainetoday.com/news/state/050206tobin.shtml.

Jasperson, Amy E., and David P. Fan. 2002. "An aggregate examination of the backlash effect in political advertising: The case of the 1996 U.S. Senate race in Minnesota." *Journal of Advertising* 31: 1–12.

Johnson, Dennis W. 2000. "The business of political consulting." In *Campaign warriors: Political consultants in elections*, ed. James A. Thurber and Candice J. Nelson, 37–52. Washington, D.C.: Brookings Institution Press.

___. 2001. *No place for amateurs: How political consultants are reshaping American democracy.* London: Routledge.

___. 2004. *Congress online: Bridging the gap between citizens and their representatives.* New York: Routledge.

Johnson-Cartee, Karen S., and Gary Copeland. 1989. "Southern voters' reaction to negative political ads in the 1986 election." *Journalism Quarterly* 66: 888–893, 986.

___. 1997a. *Inside political campaigns: Theory and practice.* Westport, Conn.: Praeger.

___. 1997b. *Manipulation of the American voter: Political campaign commercials.* Westport, Conn.: Praeger.

Johnston, Anne, and Lynda Lee Kaid. 2002. "Image ads and issue ads in U.S. presidential advertising: Using videostyle to explore stylistic differences in televised political ads from 1952 to 2000." *Journal of Communication* 52: 281–300.

Johnston, Richard, Michael G. Hagen, and Kathleen Hall Jamieson. 2004. *The 2000 presidential election and the foundations of party politics.* Cambridge: Cambridge University Press.

Jones, Charisse. 2004. "Gay marriage on the ballot in 11 states." *USA Today,* October 15, 3A.

Jones, Jeffrey M. 1998. "Does bringing out the candidate bring out the votes? The effects of nominee campaigning in presidential elections." *American Politics Quarterly* 26: 395–419.

Joslyn, Richard A. 1980. "The content of political spot ads." *Journalism Quarterly* 57: 92–98.

___. 1981. "The impact of campaign spot advertising on voting defections." *Human Communication Research* 7: 347–360.

Just, Marion R., Ann N. Crigler, Dean E. Alger, Timothy E. Cook, Montague Kern, and Darrell M. West. 1996. *Crosstalk: Citizens, candidates, and the media in a presidential campaign.* Chicago: University of Chicago Press.

Just, Marion R., Ann N. Crigler, and Tami Buhr. 1999. "Voice, substance, and cynicism in presidential campaign media." *Political Communication* 16: 25–44.

Just, Marion, Ann N. Crigler, and Lori Wallach. 1990. "Thirty seconds or thirty minutes: What viewers learn from spot advertisements and candidate debates." *Journal of Communication* 40: 120–133.

Kahn, Kim Fridkin. 1996. *The political consequences of being a woman: How stereotypes influence the conduct and consequences of political campaigns.* New York: Columbia University Press.

Kahn, Kim Fridkin, and John G. Geer. 1994. "Creating impressions: An experimental investigation of political advertising on television." *Political Behavior* 16: 93–116.

Kahn, Kim Fridkin, and Patrick J. Kenney. 1999. "Do negative campaigns mobilize or suppress turnout? Clarifying the relationship between negativity and participation." *American Political Science Review* 93: 877–889.

———. 2000. "How negative campaigning enhances knowledge of Senate elections." In *Crowded airwaves: Campaign advertising in elections*, ed. James A. Thurber, Candice J. Nelson, and David A. Dulio, 65–95. Washington, D.C.: Brookings Institution Press.

Kaid, Lynda Lee. 1982. "Paid television advertising and candidate name identification." *Campaigns & Elections* 3 (spring): 34–36.

———. 1991. "The effects of television broadcasts on perceptions of presidential candidates in the United States and France." In *Mediated politics in two cultures: Presidential campaigning in the United States and France*, ed. Lynda Lee Kaid, Jacques Gerstlé, and Keith R. Sanders, 247–260. New York: Praeger.

———. 1997. "Effects of the television spots on images of Dole and Clinton." *American Behavioral Scientist* 40: 1085–1094.

———. 1998. "Videostyle and the effects of the 1996 presidential campaign advertising." In *The 1996 presidential campaign: A communication perspective*, ed. Robert E. Denton Jr., 143–159. Westport, Conn.: Praeger.

———. 2001. "Technodistortions and effects of the 2000 political advertising." *American Behavioral Scientist* 44: 2370–2378.

———. 2002. "Political advertising and information seeking: Comparing exposure via traditional and Internet channels." *Journal of Advertising* 31: 27–35.

———. 2003. "Effects of political information in the 2000 presidential campaign: Comparing traditional television and Internet exposure." *American Behavioral Scientist* 46: 677–691.

———. 2004. "Political advertising." In *Handbook of political communication research*, ed. Lynda Lee Kaid, 155–202. Mahwah, N.J.: Lawrence Erlbaum.

———. 2005. "Videostyle in the 2004 political advertising." In *The 2004 presidential campaign: A communication perspective*, ed. Robert E. Denton Jr., 283–299. Lanham, Md.: Rowman and Littlefield.

Kaid, Lynda Lee, and John Boydston. 1987. "An experimental study of the effectiveness of negative political advertisements." *Communication Quarterly* 35: 193–201.

Kaid, Lynda Lee, and Mike Chanslor. 1995. "Changing candidate images: The effects of political advertising." In *Candidate images in presidential elections*, ed. Kenneth L. Hacker, 83–97. New York: Praeger.

———. 2004. "The effects of political advertising on candidate images." In *Presidential candidate images*, ed. Kenneth L. Hacker, 133–150. Westport, Conn.: Praeger.

Kaid, Lynda Lee, Mike Chanslor, and Mark Hovind. 1992. "The influence of program and commercial type on political advertising effectiveness." *Journal of Broadcasting and Electronic Media* 36: 303–320.

Kaid, Lynda Lee, and Daniela V. Dimitrova. 2005. "The television advertising battleground in the 2004 presidential election." *Journalism Studies* 6: 165–175.

Kaid, Lynda L., Robert H. Gobetz, Jane Garner, Chris M. Leland, and David K. Scott. 1993. "Television news and presidential campaigns: The legitimization of televised political advertising." *Social Science Quarterly* 74: 274–285.

Kaid, Lynda Lee, and Anne Johnston. 2001. *Videostyle in presidential campaigns: Style and content of televised political advertising.* Westport, Conn.: Praeger.

Kaid, Lynda Lee, and Clifford A. Jones. 2004. "Media and elections in the U.S.A." In *The media and elections: A handbook and comparative study,* ed. Bernd-Peter Lange and David Ward, 25–57. Mahwah, N.J.: Lawrence Erlbaum.

Kaid, Lynda Lee, Mitchell S. McKinney, and John C. Tedesco. 2000. *Civic dialogue in the 1996 presidential campaign: Candidate, media, and public voices.* Cresskill, N.J.: Hampton Press.

Kaid, Lynda Lee, Sandra L. Myers, Valerie Pipps, and Jan Hunter. 1984. "Sex role perceptions and televised political advertising: Comparing male and female candidates." *Women and Politics* 4: 41–53.

Kaid, Lynda Lee, and Monica Postelnicu. 2005. "Political advertising in the 2004 campaign: Comparison of traditional television and Internet messages." *American Behavioral Scientist* 49: 265–278.

Kaid, Lynda Lee, and Keith R. Sanders. 1978. "Political television commercials: An experimental study of type and length." *Communication Research* 5: 57–70.

Kamarck, Elaine Ciulla. 1999. "Campaigning on the Internet in the elections of 1998." In *Democracy.com?: Governance in a networked world,* ed. Elaine Ciulla Kamarck and Joseph S. Nye Jr., 99–123. Hollis, N.H.: Hollis Publishing.

———. 2002. "Political campaigning on the Internet: Business as usual?" In *Governance.com: Democracy in the information age,* ed. Elaine Ciulla Kamarck and Joseph S. Nye Jr., 81–103. Washington, D.C.: Brookings Institution Press.

Kamber, Victor. 1997. *Poison politics: Are negative campaigns destroying democracy?* New York: Insight Books.

Kaniss, Phyllis C. 1991. *Making local news.* Chicago: University of Chicago Press.

Karp, Jeffrey A. 1998. "The influence of elite endorsements in initiative campaigns." In *Citizens as legislators: Direct democracy in the United States,* ed. Shaun Bowler, Todd Donovan, and Caroline J. Tolbert, 149–165. Columbus: Ohio State University Press.

Karabell, Zachary. 2000. *The last campaign: How Harry Truman won the 1948 election.* New York: Knopf.

Kelley, Stanley, Jr. 1956. *Professional public relations and political power.* Baltimore: Johns Hopkins University Press.

Kellstedt, Paul M. 2000. "Media framing and the dynamics of racial policy preferences." *American Journal of Political Science* 44: 245–260.

Kendall, Kathleen E. 1995. *Presidential campaign discourse: Strategic communication problems.* Albany: State University of New York Press.

Kennedy, John R. 1971. "How program environment affects TV commercials." *Journal of Advertising Research* 11: 33–38.

Kenny, Christopher B. 1992. "Political participation and effects from the social environment." *American Journal of Political Science* 36: 259–267.

Kenny, Christopher, and Michael McBurnett. 1992. "A dynamic model of the effect of campaign spending on congressional vote choice." *American Journal of Political Science* 36: 923–937.

Kerbel, Matthew Robert. 1999. *Remote and controlled: Media politics in a cynical age,* 2d ed. Boulder: Westview.

Kernell, Samuel. 1986. *Going public: New strategies of presidential leadership.* Washington, D.C.: CQ Press.

Key, V. O., Jr. 1942. *Politics, parties, and pressure groups.* New York: Crowell.

———. 1966. *The responsible electorate: Rationality in presidential voting, 1936–1960.* Cambridge, Mass.: Belknap Press of Harvard University Press.

Kiewiet, D. Roderick. 1983. *Macroeconomics and micropolitics: The electoral effects of economic issues.* Chicago: University of Chicago Press.

Kim, Hak Ryang. 2004. *Winning campaign strategies: Methodologies and in-depth guide.* Columbus, Ohio: Camst.

Kimball, David C., and Samuel C. Patterson. 1997. "Living up to expectations: Public attitudes toward Congress." *Journal of Politics* 59: 701–728.

Kinder, Donald R., Mark D. Peters, Robert P. Abelson, and Susan T. Fiske. 1980. "Presidential prototypes." *Political Behavior* 2: 315–337.

Kinder, Donald R., and Lynn M. Sanders. 1996. *Divided by color: Racial politics and democratic ideals*. Chicago: University of Chicago Press.

King, James D. 2001. "Incumbent popularity and vote choice in gubernatorial elections." *Journal of Politics* 63: 585–597.

King, James D., and James B. McConnell. 2003. "The effect of negative campaign advertising on vote choice: The mediating influence of gender." *Social Science Quarterly* 84: 843–857.

Kitchens, James T., and Larry Powell. 1986. "A critical analysis of NCPAC's strategies in key 1980 races: A third party negative campaign." *Southern Speech Communication Journal* 51: 208–228.

Klapper, Joseph T. 1960. *The effects of mass communication*. New York: Free Press.

Kohno, Tadayoshi, Adam Stubblefield, Aviel D. Rubin, and Dan S. Wallach. 2003. "Analysis of an electronic voting system." Technical report prepared for Johns Hopkins University Information Security Institute. www.avirubin.com/vote.pdf.

Kolodny, Robin. 1998. *Pursuing majorities: Congressional campaign committees in American politics*. Norman: University of Oklahoma Press.

___. 2000. "Electoral partnerships: Political consultants and political parties." In *Campaign warriors: Political consultants in elections*, ed. James A. Thurber and Candice J. Nelson, 110–132. Washington, D.C.: Brookings Institution Press.

___. 2002. "It's the system, stupid!" In *Shades of gray: Perspectives on campaign ethics*, ed. Candice J. Nelson, David A. Dulio, and Stephen K. Medvic, 110–127. Washington, D.C.: Brookings Institution Press.

Kolodny, Robin, and David A. Dulio. 2003. "Political party adaptation in U.S. congressional elections: Why political parties use coordinated expenditures to hire political consultants." *Party Politics* 9: 729–746.

Kolodny, Robin, and Angela Logan. 1998. "Political consultants and the extension of party goals." *PS: Political Science & Politics* 31: 155–159.

Kornblut, Anne E., and Rick Klein. 2004. "On the stump, Bush slows pace to his liking." *Boston Globe*, October 22, A1.

Kramer, Gerald H. 1970. "The effects of precinct-level canvassing on voter behavior." *Public Opinion Quarterly* 34: 560–572.

___. 1971. "Short-term fluctuations in U.S. voting behavior, 1896–1964." *American Political Science Review* 65: 131–143.

Krebs, Timothy B. 1998. "The determinants of candidates' vote share and the advantages of incumbency in city council elections." *American Journal of Political Science* 42: 921–935.

Krosnick, Jon A., and Laura A. Brannon. 1993. "The impact of the Gulf War on the ingredients of presidential evaluations: Multidimensional effects of political involvement." *American Political Science Review* 87: 963–975.

Krosnick, Jon A., and Donald R. Kinder. 1990. "Altering the foundations of support for the president through priming." *American Political Science Review* 84: 497–512.

Krugman, Herbert E. 1965. "The impact of television advertising: Learning without involvement." *Public Opinion Quarterly* 29: 349–356.

Ku, Gyotae, Lynda Lee Kaid, and Michael Pfau. 2003. "The impact of web site campaigning on traditional news media and public information processing." *Journalism and Mass Communication Quarterly* 80: 528–547.

Lacey, Robert J. 2005. "The electoral allure of direct democracy: The effect of initiative salience on voting, 1990–1996." *State Politics and Policy Quarterly* 5: 168–181.

Ladd, Everett Carll, Jr., with Charles D. Hadley. 1978. *Transformations of the American party system: Political coalitions from the New Deal to the 1970s*, 2d ed. New York: Norton.

Lakoff, George. 2004. *Don't think of an elephant! Know your values and frame the debate*. White River Junction, Vt.: Chelsea Green Publishing.

Lang, Annie. 1991. "Emotion, formal features, and memory for televised political advertisements." In *Television and political advertising,* Vol. 1: *Psychological processes,* ed. Frank Biocca, 221–243. Hillsdale, N.J.: Lawrence Erlbaum.

Lasch, Christopher. 1995. "Journalism, publicity, and the lost art of argument." *Kettering Review* spring (Item #R1084): 38–44.

Lascher, Edward L., Jr., Michael G. Hagen, and Steven A. Rochlin. 1996. "Gun behind the door? Ballot initiatives, state policies and public opinion." *Journal of Politics* 58: 760–775.

Lasswell, Harold D. 1927. "The theory of political propaganda." *American Political Science Review* 21: 627–631.

Lau, Richard R., and Gerald M. Pomper. 2001. "Effects of negative campaigning on turnout in U.S. Senate elections, 1988–1998." *Journal of Politics* 63: 804–819.

———. 2004. *Negative campaigning: An analysis of U.S. Senate elections.* Lanham, Md.: Rowman and Littlefield.

Lau, Richard R., and Lee Sigelman. 2000. "Effectiveness of political advertising." In *Crowded airwaves: Campaign advertising in elections,* ed. James A. Thurber, Candice J. Nelson, and David A. Dulio, 10–43. Washington, D.C.: Brookings Institution Press.

Lau, Richard R., Lee Sigelman, and Ivy Brown. 2005. "The effects of negative political campaigns: A meta-analytic reassessment." Paper presented at the 2005 annual meeting of the American Political Science Association, Washington, D.C.

Lau, Richard R., Lee Sigelman, Caroline Heldman, and Paul Babbitt. 1999. "The effects of negative political advertisements: A meta-analytic assessment." *American Political Science Review* 93: 851–875.

Lavine, Howard. 2001. "The electoral consequences of ambivalence toward presidential candidates." *American Journal of Political Science* 45: 915–929.

Layman, Geoffrey C., and Edward G. Carmines. 1997. "Cultural conflict in American politics: Religious traditionalism, postmaterialism, and U.S. political behavior." *Journal of Politics* 59: 751–777.

Lazarsfeld, Paul F. 1944. "The election is over." *Public Opinion Quarterly* 8: 317–330.

Lazarsfeld, Paul F., Bernard Berelson, and Hazel Gaudet. 1944. *The people's choice: How the voter makes up his mind in a presidential campaign.* New York: Duell, Sloan and Pearce.

League of Conservation Voters. 2004. "2004 Election cycle," www.opensecrets.org/527s/527events.asp?orgid=46.

Leighley, Jan E. 2001. *Strength in numbers? The political mobilization of racial and ethnic minorities.* Princeton: Princeton University Press.

Lemert, James B. 1993. "Do televised presidential debates help inform voters?" *Journal of Broadcasting & Electronic Media* 37: 83–94.

Lemert, James B., Wayne Wanta, and Tien-Tsung Lee. 1999. "Party identification and negative advertising in a U.S. Senate election." *Journal of Communication* 49: 123–134.

Levin, Yuval. 2002. "Politics after the Internet." *The Public Interest* (fall): 80–94.

Levine, Peter, and Mark Hugo Lopez. 2005. "What we should know about the effectiveness of campaigns but don't." *Annals of the American Academy of Political and Social Science* 601: 180–191.

Lewis, C. S. 1970. "Meditation in a toolshed." In *God in the dock: Essays on theology and ethics,* by C. S. Lewis, ed. Walter Hooper, 212–215. Grand Rapids, Mich.: William B. Eerdmans. Originally published in *The Coventry Evening Telegraph,* July 17, 1945, 4.

Lewis-Beck, Michael S. 1988. "Economics and the American voter: Past, present, and future." *Political Behavior* 10: 5–21.

Lewis-Beck, Michael S., and Tom W. Rice. 1992. *Forecasting elections.* Washington, D.C.: CQ Press.

Lichter, S. Robert. 2001. "A plague on both parties: Substance and fairness in TV election news." *Harvard International Journal of Press/Politics* 6: 8–30.

Lipset, Seymour Martin. 1996. *American exceptionalism: A double-edged sword.* New York: Norton.

Los Angeles Times. 2003. "Democracy run amok, or running smoothly?" *Los Angeles Times,* July 29, B14.

Lowenstein, Daniel H. 1982. "Campaign spending and ballot propositions: Recent experience, public choice theory and the First Amendment." *UCLA Law Review* 29: 505–641.

Lowy, Joan. 2004. "DNC: Dems, GOP push ballot measures to influence voters." *Naples News,* July 29. www.naplesnews.com/npdn/news/article/0,2071,NPDN_14940_3071424,00.html.

Luntz, Frank I. 1988. *Candidates, consultants, and campaigns: The style and substance of American electioneering.* New York: Basil Blackwell.

Lupia, Arthur. 1994. "Shortcuts versus encyclopedias: Information and voting behavior in California insurance reform elections." *American Political Science Review* 88: 63–76.

———. 2001. "Dumber than chimps? An assessment of direct democracy voters." In *Dangerous democracy? The battle over ballot initiatives in America,* ed. Larry J. Sabato, Howard R. Ernst, and Bruce A. Larson, 66–70. Lanham, Md.: Rowman and Littlefield.

Lupia, Arthur, and Mathew D. McCubbins. 1998. *The democratic dilemma: Can citizens learn what they need to know?* New York: Cambridge University Press.

Mack, Timothy C. 2004. "Internet communities: The future of politics?" *Futures Research Quarterly* 20: 61–77.

Magleby, David B. 1984. *Direct legislation: Voting on ballot propositions in the United States.* Baltimore: Johns Hopkins University Press.

———. 1989. "Opinion formation and opinion change in ballot proposition campaigns." In *Manipulating public opinion: Essays on public opinion as a dependent variable,* ed. Michael Margolis and Gary A. Mauser, 95–115. Pacific Grove, Calif.: Brooks/Cole.

Magleby, David B., and J. Quin Monson, eds. 2004. *The last hurrah? Soft money and issue advocacy in the 2002 congressional elections.* Washington, D.C.: Brookings Institution Press.

Magleby, David B., and Kelly D. Patterson. 1998. "Consultants and direct democracy." *PS: Political Science & Politics* 31: 160–169.

———. 2000. "Campaign consultants and direct democracy: Politics of citizen control." In *Campaign warriors: Political consultants in elections,* ed. James A. Thurber and Candice J. Nelson, 133–152. Washington, D.C.: Brookings Institution Press.

Magleby, David B., Kelly D. Patterson, and James A. Thurber. 2002. "Campaign consultants and responsible party government." In *Responsible partisanship? The evolution of American political parties since 1950,* ed. John C. Green and Paul S. Herrnson, 101–120. Lawrence: University of Kansas Press.

Maisel, L. Sandy, and Darrell M. West, eds. 2004. *Running on empty? Political discourse in congressional elections.* Lanham, Md.: Rowman and Littlefield.

Malbin, Michael J., ed. 2003. *Life After Reform: When the Bipartisan Campaign Reform Act meets politics.* Lanham, Md.: Rowman and Littlefield.

Malbin, Michael J., and Thomas L. Gais. 1998. *The day after reform: Sobering campaign finance lessons from the American states.* Albany, N.Y.: Rockefeller Institute Press.

Mann, Thomas E., and Raymond E. Wolfinger. 1980. "Candidates and parties in congressional elections." *American Political Science Review* 74: 617–632.

Marcus, George E. 1988. "The structure of emotional response: 1984 presidential candidates." *American Political Science Review* 82: 737–761.

Margolis, Michael, David Resnick, and Chin-chang Tu. 1997. "Campaigning on the Internet: Parties and candidates on the world wide web in the 1996 primary season." *Harvard International Journal of Press/Politics* 2: 59–78.

Margolis, Michael, David Resnick, and Joel D. Wolfe. 1999. "Party competition on the Internet in the United States and Britain." *Harvard International Journal of Press/Politics* 4: 24–47.

Marks, Peter. 2000. "The forgotten state: Dearth of ads makes race in Kansas a snooze." *New York Times,* October 27, A26.

Markus, Gregory B. 1988. "The impact of personal and national economic conditions on the presidential vote: A pooled cross-sectional analysis." *American Journal of Political Science* 32: 137–154.

Markus, Gregory B., and Philip E. Converse. 1979. "A dynamic simultaneous equation model of electoral choice." *American Political Science Review* 73: 1055–1070.

Martin, Paul S. 2004. "Inside the black box of negative campaign effects: Three reasons why negative campaigns mobilize." *Political Psychology* 25: 545–562.

Martinelli, Kathleen A., and Steven H. Chaffee. 1995. "Measuring new-voter learning via three channels of political information." *Journalism and Mass Communication Quarterly* 72: 18–32.

Martinez, Michael D., and Tad Delegal. 1990. "The irrelevance of negative campaigns to political trust: Experimental and survey results." *Political Communication and Persuasion* 7: 25–40.

Mathews, Douglas, and Beth Dietz-Uhler. 1998. "The black-sheep effect: How positive and negative advertisements affect voters' perceptions of the sponsor of the advertisement." *Journal of Applied Social Psychology* 28: 1903–1915.

Matsusaka, John G. 2004. *For the many or the few: The initiative, public policy, and American democracy.* Chicago: University of Chicago Press.

Mayer, William G. 1996. "In defense of negative campaigning." *Political Science Quarterly* 111 (fall): 437–455.

Mayhew, David R. 1974a. *Congress: The electoral connection.* New Haven: Yale University Press.

———. 1974b. "Congressional elections: The case of the vanishing marginals." *Polity* 6: 295–317.

McCahill, Tim. 2005. "5-Month sentence in phone-jamming case." *Union Leader*, February 9. www.theunionleader.com/Articles_show.html?article=50630&archive=1.

McClurg, Scott D. 2004. "Indirect mobilization: The social consequences of party contacts in an election campaign." *American Politics Research* 32: 406–443.

McCuan, David, Shaun Bowler, Todd Donovan, and Ken Fernandez. 1998. "California's political warriors: Campaign professionals and the initiative process." In *Citizens as legislators: Direct democracy in the United States,* ed. Shaun Bowler, Todd Donovan, and Caroline J. Tolbert, 55–79. Columbus: Ohio State University Press.

McCuan, David, and Stephen Stambough. 2005. *Initiative-centered politics: The new politics of direct democracy.* Durham, N.C.: Carolina Academic Press.

McCurley, Carl, and Jeffrey J. Mondak. 1995. "Inspected by #1184063113: The influence of incumbents' competence and integrity in U.S. House elections." *American Journal of Political Science* 39: 864–885.

McGerr, Michael E. 2003. *A fierce discontent: The rise and fall of the Progressive Movement in America, 1870–1920.* New York: Free Press.

McGinniss, Joe. 1969. *The selling of the president, 1968.* New York: Trident.

McGraw, Kathleen M., Samuel Best, and Richard Timpone. 1995. "'What they say or what they do?' The impact of elite explanation and policy outcomes on public opinion." *American Journal of Political Science* 39: 53–74.

McLuhan, Marshall. 1964. *Understanding media: The extensions of man.* New York: McGraw Hill.

McNulty, John E. 2005. "Phone-based GOTV—What's on the line? Field experiments with varied partisan components, 2002–2003." *Annals of the American Academy of Political and Social Science* 601: 41–65.

Media Monitor. 1996. "The bad news campaign: TV news coverage of the GOP primaries," March/April, 3–6.

Medvic, Stephen K. 1997. *Is there a spin doctor in the House? The impact of political consultants in congressional campaigns.* Ph.D. dissertation, Purdue University.

———. 1998. "The effectiveness of political consultants as a campaign resource." *PS: Political Science & Politics* 31: 150–154.

———. 2000. "Professionalization in congressional campaigns." In *Campaign warriors: Political consultants in elections,* ed. James A. Thurber and Candice J. Nelson, 91–109. Washington, D.C.: Brookings Institution Press.

———. 2001. *Political consultants in U.S. congressional elections.* Columbus: Ohio State University Press.

Medvic, Stephen K., and Silvo Lenart. 1997. "The influence of political consultants in the 1992 congressional elections." *Legislative Studies Quarterly* 22: 61–77.

Mendelsohn, Matthew, and Fred Cutler. 2000. "The effect of referendums on democratic citizens: Information, politicization, efficacy and tolerance." *British Journal of Political Science* 30: 685–701.

Mendelsohn, Matthew, and Andrew Parkin, eds. 2001. *Referendum democracy: Citizens, elites and deliberation in referendum campaigns.* New York: Palgrave Macmillan.

Menefee-Libey, David B. 2000. *The triumph of campaign-centered politics.* New York: Chatham House.

Mercurio, John. 2002. "Lott apologizes for Thurmond comment." cnn.com, December 10. archives.cnn.com/2002/ALLPOLITICS/12/09/lott.comment.

Merritt, Sharyne. 1984. "Negative political advertising: Some empirical findings." *Journal of Advertising* 13: 27–38.

Meyerson, Harold. 2004. "The GOP's shameful vote strategy." *Washington Post,* October 27, A25.

Michelson, Melissa R. 2003. "Getting out the Latino vote: How door-to-door canvassing influences voter turnout in rural central California." *Political Behavior* 25: 247–263.

———. 2005. "Meeting the challenge of Latino voter mobilization." *Annals of the American Academy of Political and Social Science* 601: 85–101.

Michelson, Melissa R., and Herbert Villa Jr. 2003. "Mobilizing the Latino youth vote." Presented at the 2003 Annual meeting of the Western Political Science Association, Denver.

Milburn, Michael A. and Justin Brown. 1995. "Busted by the ad police: Journalists' coverage of political campaign ads in the 1992 presidential campaign." Research paper prepared for the Joan Shorenstein Center on the Press, Politics, and Public Policy. www.ksg.harvard.edu/presspol/Research_Publications/Papers/Research_Papers/R15.pdf.

Miller, Arthur H., and Michael MacKuen. 1979. "Informing the electorate: A national study." In *The great debates: Carter vs. Ford, 1976,* ed. Sidney Kraus, 269–297. Bloomington: Indiana University Press.

Miller, Arthur H., Martin P. Wattenberg, and Oksana Malanchuk. 1986. "Schematic assessments of presidential candidates." *American Political Science Review* 80: 521–540.

Miller, Dale E., and Stephen K. Medvic. 2002. "Civic responsibility or self interest?" In *Shades of gray: Perspectives on campaign ethics,* ed. Candice J. Nelson, David A. Dulio, and Stephen K. Medvic, 18–38. Washington, D.C.: Brookings Institution Press.

Mitchell, Greg. 1992. *The campaign of the century: Upton Sinclair's race for governor of California and the birth of media politics.* New York: Random House.

Mondak, Jeffrey J. 1995a. "Competence, integrity, and the electoral success of congressional incumbents." *Journal of Politics* 57: 1043–1069.

———. 1995b. "Media exposure and political discussion in U.S. elections." *Journal of Politics* 57: 62–85.

Morris, Dwight, and Murielle E. Gamache. 1994. *Gold-plated politics: The 1992 congressional races.* Washington, D.C.: CQ Press.

Mosk, Matthew. 2005. "Aide ousted over O'Malley rumors: Web postings, e-mail spread affair gossip." *Washington Post,* February 9, A1.

Munro, William Bennett, ed. 1912. *The initiative, referendum and recall.* New York: Appleton.

Murphy, John H., Isabella C. M. Cunningham, and Gary B. Wilcox. 1979. "The impact of program environment on recall of humorous television commercials." *Journal of Advertising* 8: 17–21.

Napolitan, Joseph. 1972. *The election game and how to win it.* Garden City, N.Y.: Doubleday.

Nelson, Candice J., David A. Dulio, and Stephen K. Medvic, eds. 2002. *Shades of gray: Perspectives on campaign ethics.* Washington, D.C.: Brookings Institution Press.

Nelson, Candice J., Stephen K. Medvic, and David A. Dulio. 2002. "Hired guns or gatekeepers of democracy?" In *Shades of gray: Perspectives on campaign ethics,* ed. Candice J. Nelson, David A. Dulio, and Stephen K. Medvic, 75–97. Washington, D.C.: Brookings Institution Press.

Nelson, Thomas E., Rosalee A. Clawson, and Zoe M. Oxley. 1997. "Media framing of a civil liberties conflict and its effect on tolerance." *American Political Science Review* 91: 567–583.

New York Times. 2004. "Transcript of President Bush's speech." www.nytimes.com/2004/11/03/politics/campaign/03cnd-bush-text.html.

Newhagen, John E., and Byron Reeves. 1991. "Emotion and memory responses for negative political advertising: A study of television commercials used in the 1988 presidential election." In *Television and political advertising,* Vol. 1: *Psychological processes,* ed. Frank Biocca, 197–220. Hillsdale, N.J.: Lawrence Erlbaum.

Nicholson, Stephen P. 2003. "The political environment and ballot proposition awareness." *American Journal of Political Science* 47: 403–410.

___. 2005. *Voting the agenda: Candidates, elections, and ballot propositions.* Princeton: Princeton University Press.

Nickerson, David W. 2005. "Partisan mobilization using volunteer phone banks and door hangers." *Annals of the American Academy of Political and Social Science* 601: 10–27.

Nickerson, David, and Kevin Arceneaux. 2005. "A field experiment testing negative campaign tactics." Paper presented at the 2005 annual meeting of the American Political Science Association, Washington, D.C.

Nie, Norman H., Sidney Verba, and John R. Petrocik. 1976. *The changing American voter.* Cambridge, Mass.: Harvard University Press.

Nimmo, Dan. 1970. *The political persuaders: The techniques of modern election campaigns.* Englewood Cliffs, N.J.: Prentice Hall.

___. 2001. *The political persuaders: The techniques of modern election campaigns,* 2d ed. New Brunswick, N.J.: Transaction Publishers.

Niven, David. 2001. "The limits of mobilization: Turnout evidence from state House primaries." *Political Behavior* 23: 335–350.

Norquist, Grover. 1993. "Prelude to a landslide: How Republicans will sweep the Congress." *Policy Review* (fall): 30–36.

Olson, Keith W. 2003. *Watergate: The presidential scandal that shook America.* Lawrence: University Press of Kansas.

O'Neill, Tip, with William Novak. 1987. *Man of the House: The life and political memoirs of Speaker Tip O'Neill.* New York: Random House.

O'Shaughnessy, Nicholas J. 1990. *The phenomenon of political marketing.* New York: St. Martin's.

Page, Benjamin I., and Calvin C. Jones. 1979. "Reciprocal effects of policy preferences, party loyalties and the vote." *American Political Science Review* 73: 1071–1089.

Partin, Randall W. 2001. "Campaign intensity and voter information: A look at gubernatorial contests." *American Politics Research* 29: 115–140.

___. 2002. "Assessing the impact of campaign spending in governors' races." *Political Research Quarterly* 55: 213–233.

Patterson, Kelly, Kristina Gale, Betsey Gimbel Hawkins, and Richard Hawkins. 2005. "I approved this message: A study of political disclaimers." *Campaigns & Elections* 26 (May): 39–40.

Patterson, Samuel C., and Gregory A. Caldeira. 1983. "Getting out the vote: Participation in gubernatorial elections." *American Political Science Review* 77: 675–689.

Patterson, Thomas E. 1980. *The mass media election: How Americans choose their president.* New York: Praeger.

___. 1993. *Out of order.* New York: Knopf.

___. 2000. "Doing well and doing good: How soft news and critical journalism are shrinking the news audience and weakening democracy—and what news outlets can do about it." Report prepared for the Joan Shorenstein Center on the Press, Politics, and Public Policy. www.ksg.harvard.edu/presspol/Research_Publications/Reports/softnews.pdf.

___. 2002. *The vanishing voter: Public involvement in an age of uncertainty.* New York: Knopf.

___. 2005. "Young voters and the 2004 election," February. Report of the Joan Shorenstein Center on the Press, Politics, and Public Policy, John F. Kennedy School of Government, Harvard University. www.vanishingvoter.org/Releases/Vanishing_Voter_Final_Report_2004_Election.pdf.

Patterson, Thomas E., and Robert D. McClure. 1976. *The unseeing eye: The myth of television power in national politics.* New York: Putnam's.

Peele, Gillian. 1982. "Campaign consultants." *Electoral Studies* 1: 355–362.

Pelika, Stacey L., and Erika Franklin Fowler. 2004. "A multidimensional approach to campaign media analysis: Information flows in the 2002 elections." Paper presented at the 2004 annual meeting of the Midwest Political Science Association, Chicago.

Perseus Development Corporation. 2004. "The blogging iceberg." www.perseus.com/blogsurvey/iceberg.html.

Peters, John G., and Susan Welch. 1980. "The effects of charges of corruption on voting behavior in congressional elections." *American Political Science Review* 74: 697–708.

Petracca, Mark P. 1989. "Political consultants and democratic governance." *PS: Political Science & Politics* 22: 11–14.

Petracca, Mark P., and Courtney Wierioch. 1989. "Consultant democracy: The activities and attitudes of American political consultants." Paper presented at the 1989 annual meeting of the American Political Science Association, Chicago.

Petrocik, John R. 1996. "Issue ownership in presidential elections, with a 1980 case study." *American Journal of Political Science* 40: 825–850.

Petrocik, John R., William L. Benoit, and Glenn J. Hansen. 2003. "Issue ownership and presidential campaigning, 1952–2000." *Political Science Quarterly* 118: 599–626.

Pew Center for the People and the Press. 2004a. "News audiences increasingly politicized: Online news audience larger, more diverse." people-press.org/reports/pdf/215.pdf.

___. 2004b. "Voters impressed with campaign: But news coverage gets lukewarm ratings." people-press.org/reports/print.php3?PageID=902.

___. 2005. "Public more critical of press, but goodwill persists: Online newspaper readership countering print losses." people-press.org/reports/print.php3?PageID=972.

Pfau, Michael, and Michael Burgoon. 1988. "Inoculation in political campaign communication." *Human Communication Research* 15: 91–111.

___. 1989. "The efficacy of issue and character attack message strategies in political campaign communication." *Communication Reports* 2: 53–61.

Pfau, Michael, R. Lance Holbert, Erin Alison Szabo, and Kelly Kaminski. 2002. "Issue-advocacy versus candidate advertising: Effects on candidate preferences and democratic process." *Journal of Communication* 52: 301–315.

Pfau, Michael, and Henry C. Kenski. 1990. *Attack politics: Strategy and defense.* New York: Praeger.

Pfau, Michael, Henry C. Kenski, Michael Nitz, and John Sorenson. 1989. "Use of the attack message strategy in political campaign communication." Paper presented at the 1989 annual meeting of the Speech Communication Association, San Francisco.

Pfau, Michael, David Park, R. Lance Holbert, and Jaeho Cho. 2001. "The effects of party- and PAC-sponsored issue advertising and the potential of inoculation to combat its impact on the democratic process." *American Behavioral Scientist* 44: 2379–2397.

Pfau, Michael, Roxanne Parrott, and Briget Lindquist. 1992. "An expectancy theory explanation of the effectiveness of political attack television spots: A case study." *Journal of Applied Communication Research* 20: 235–253.

Pierce, Greg. 2004. "Mehlman's job." *Washington Times*, November 22, A5.

Pinderhughes, Dianne M. 1992. "The role of African American political organizations in the mobilization of voters." In

From exclusion to inclusion: The long struggle for African American political power, ed. Ralph C. Gomes and Linda Faye Williams, 35–52. New York: Greenwood.

Pinkleton, Bruce E. 1998. "Effects of print comparative political advertising on political decision-making and participation." *Journal of Communication* 48: 24–36.

Pinkleton, Bruce E., Nam-Hyun Um, and Erica Weintraub Austin. 2002. "An exploration of the effects of negative political advertising on political decision making." *Journal of Advertising* 31: 13–25.

Plasser, Fritz. 2000. "American campaign techniques worldwide." *Harvard International Journal of Press/Politics* 5: 33–54.

Popkin, Samuel L. 1991. *The reasoning voter: Communication and persuasion in presidential campaigns.* Chicago: University of Chicago Press.

Postman, Neil. 1985. *Amusing ourselves to death: Public discourse in the age of show business.* New York: Viking.

Preston, Michael B., Lenneal J. Henderson Jr., and Paul Puryear, eds. 1982. *The new black politics: The search for political power.* New York: Longman.

Procter, David E., and William J. Schenck-Hamlin. 1996. "Form and variations in negative political advertising." *Communication Research Reports* 13: 147–156.

Procter, David E., William J. Schenck-Hamlin, and Karen A. Haase. 1994. "Exploring the role of gender in the development of negative political advertisements." *Women & Politics* 14: 1–22.

Project for Excellence in Journalism. 2005. "ePolitics 2004: A study of the presidential campaign on the Internet." www.journalism.org/resources/research/reports/campaign2004/epolitics/stories.asp.

Puopolo, Sonia. 2001. "The web and U.S. senatorial campaigns 2000." *American Behavioral Scientist* 44: 2030–2047.

Putnam, Robert D. 1995. "Bowling alone: America's declining social capital." *Journal of Democracy* 6: 65–78.

———. 2000. *Bowling Alone: The collapse and revival of American community.* New York: Simon and Schuster.

Reichley, A. James. 1992. *The life of the parties: A history of American political parties.* New York: Free Press.

Reinsch, Paul. 1912. "The initiative and referendum." *Proceedings of the Academy of Political Science in the City of New York* 3: 155–161.

Republican National Committee. 2005. *Rising tide: The magazine of the Republican National Committee.* www.rnc.org/News/RisingTideRead.aspx?ID=89.

Rice, Alexis. 2003. "The use of blogs in the 2004 presidential election." Johns Hopkins University, Department of Communication in the Contemporary Society. www.campaignsonline.org/reports/blog.pdf.

Rich, Frank. 2005. "The White House stages its 'Daily Show.'" *New York Times,* February 20, Sect. 2, 1.

Ridout, Travis N., Dhavan V. Shaw, Kenneth M. Goldstein, and Michael M. Franz. 2004. "Evaluating measures of campaign advertising exposure on political learning." *Political Behavior* 26: 201–225.

Roberts, Marilyn S. 1992. "Predicting voting behavior via the agenda-setting tradition." *Journalism Quarterly* 69: 878–892.

Roberts, Marilyn, and Maxwell McCombs. 1994. "Agenda setting and political advertising: Origins of the news agenda." *Political Communication* 11: 249–262.

Robertson, Terry, Kristin Froemling, Scott Wells, and Shannon McCraw. 1999. "Sex, lives, and videotape: An analysis of gender in campaign advertisements." *Communication Quarterly* 47: 333–341.

Robinson, Michael J., and Margaret A. Sheehan. 1983. *Over the wire and on TV: CBS and UPI in Campaign '80.* New York: Russell Sage Foundation.

Roddy, Brian L., and Gina M. Garramone. 1988. "Appeals and strategies of negative political advertising." *Journal of Broadcasting and Electronic Media* 32: 415–427.

Rosenberg, Shawn W., Lisa Bohan, Patrick McCafferty, and Kevin Harris. 1986. "The image and the vote: The effect of candidate presentation on voter preference." *American Journal of Political Science* 30: 108–127.

Rosenbloom, David Lee. 1973. *The election men: Professional campaign managers and American democracy.* New York: Quadrangle Books.

Rosenkrantz, Holly, and Roger Runningen. 2004. "Rove, Bush's campaign 'architect,' cultivated Christian base." *Bloomberg.com,* November 4. www.bloomberg.com/apps/news?pid=10000103&sid=aRubzbcnB2Z4&refer=us.

Rosenstone, Steven J., and John Mark Hansen. 1993. *Mobilization, participation, and democracy in America.* New York: Macmillan.

Rothschild, Michael L., and Michael L. Ray. 1974. "Involvement and political advertising effect: An exploratory experiment." *Communication Research* 1: 264–285.

Russakoff, Dale, and Jim VandeHei. 2004. "Lifelong collector of data can bog down his staffs." *Washington Post,* October 13, A1.

Rutenberg, Jim. 2003. "Outflanked Democrats wonder how to catch up in media wars." *New York Times,* January 1, A12. www.commondreams.org/headlines03/0101-08.htm.

Sabato, Larry J. 1981. *The rise of political consultants: New ways of winning elections.* New York: Basic Books.

———. 1988. *The party's just begun: Shaping political parties for America's future.* Glenview, Ill.: Scott, Foresman.

———. 1991. *Feeding frenzy: How attack journalism has transformed American politics.* New York: Free Press.

———. 1994. "Open season: How the news media cover presidential campaigns in the age of attack journalism." In *Media power in politics,* 3d ed., ed. Doris A. Graber, 193–203. Washington, D.C.: CQ Press.

Sabato, Larry J., and Glenn R. Simpson. 1996. *Dirty little secrets: The persistence of corruption in American politics.* New York: Times Books.

Salmore, Barbara G., and Stephen A. Salmore. 1989. *Candidates, parties, and campaigns: Electoral politics in America,* 2d ed. Washington, D.C.: CQ Press.

Salmore, Stephen A., and Barbara G. Salmore. 1996. "The transformation of state electoral politics." In *The state of the states,* 3d ed., ed. Carl E. Van Horn, 51–76. Washington, D.C.: CQ Press.

Schattschneider, E. E. 1960. *The semisovereign people: A realist's view of democracy in America.* Hinsdale, Ill.: Dryden Press.

Schenck-Hamlin, William J., David E. Procter, and Deborah J. Rumsey. 2000. "The influence of negative advertising frames on political cynicism and politician accountability." *Human Communication Research* 26: 53–74.

Schleuder, Joan. 1990. "Effects of commercial complexity, party affiliation and issue vs. image strategies in political ads." *Advances in Consumer Research* 17: 159–168.

Schleuder, Joan, Maxwell McCombs, and Wayne Wanta. 1991. "Inside the agenda-setting process: How political advertising and TV news prime viewers to think about issues and candidates." In *Television and political advertising,* Vol. 1: *Psychological processes,* ed. Frank Biocca, 265–309. Hillsdale, N.J.: Lawrence Erlbaum.

Schrag, Peter. 1998. *Paradise lost: California's experience, America's future.* New York: New Press.

Schultz, David. 2002. *Money, politics, and campaign finance reform law in the states.* Durham, N.C.: Carolina Academic Press.

Sears, David O., and Jack Citrin. 1982. *Tax revolt: Something for nothing in California.* Cambridge, Mass.: Harvard University Press.

Sellers, Patrick J. 1998. "Strategy and background in congressional campaigns." *American Political Science Review* 92: 159–171.

Selnow, Gary W. 1994. *High-tech campaigns: Computer technology in political communication.* Westport, Conn.: Praeger.

———. 1998. *Electronic whistle-stops: The impact of the Internet on American politics.* Westport, Conn.: Praeger.

Semiatin, Richard. 2004. *Campaigns in the 21st century.* Boston: McGraw Hill.

Shaffrey, Mary M. 2004. "Marriage referendum could boost Bush." Media General

Shapiro, Andrew L. 1999. "The Internet." *Foreign Policy* (summer): 14–27.

Shapiro, Michael A., and Robert H. Rieger. 1992. "Comparing positive and negative political advertising on radio." *Journalism Quarterly* 69: 135–145.

Shaw, Catherine M. 2000. *The campaign manager: Running and winning local elections,* 2d ed. Boulder: Westview.

Shaw, Daron R. 1999a. "A study of presidential campaign event effects from 1952 to 1992." *Journal of Politics* 61: 387–422.

———. 1999b. "The effect of TV ads and candidate appearances on statewide presidential votes, 1988–96." *American Political Science Review* 93: 345–361.

———. 1999c. "The impact of news media favorability and candidate events in presidential campaigns." *Political Communication* 16: 183–202.

———. 1999d. "The methods behind the madness: Presidential electoral college strategies, 1988–96." *Journal of Politics* 61: 893–913.

Shaw, David. 1996. "On the campaign trail, bad news wins out." *Los Angeles Times,* April 18, A22.

Shea, Daniel M., and Michael John Burton. 2001. *Campaign craft: The strategies, tactics, and art of political campaign management,* revised and updated ed. Westport, Conn.: Praeger.

Shen, Fuyuan, and H. Denis Wu. 2002. "Effects of soft-money issue advertisements on candidate evaluation and voting preference: An exploration." *Mass Communication and Society* 5: 395–410.

Siegel, Mark A. 2002. "Conduct, codes, and common sense." In *Shades of gray: Perspectives on campaign ethics,* ed. Candice J. Nelson, David A. Dulio, and Stephen K. Medvic, 128–150. Washington, D.C.: Brookings Institution Press.

Sigelman, Lee, and Emmett H. Buell Jr. 2003. "You take the high road and I'll take the low road? The interplay of attack strategies and tactics in presidential campaigns." *Journal of Politics* 65: 518–531.

———. 2004. "Avoidance or engagement? Issue convergence in U.S. presidential campaigns, 1960–2000." *American Journal of Political Science* 48: 650–661.

Sigelman, Lee, and Mark Kugler. 2003. "Why is research on the effects of negative campaigning so inconclusive? Understanding citizens' perceptions of negativity." *Journal of Politics* 65: 142–160.

Skaperdas, Stergios, and Bernard Grofman. 1995. "Modeling negative campaigning." *American Political Science Review* 89: 49–61.

Smith, Dane. 2004. "Democratic '527' group is hit with record fine." *Minneapolis Star Tribune,* December 22, 1B.

Smith, Daniel A. 1998. *Tax crusaders and the politics of direct democracy.* New York: Routledge.

———. 2001a. "Campaign financing of ballot initiatives in the American states." In *Dangerous democracy: The battle over ballot initiatives in America,* ed. Larry J. Sabato, Howard R. Ernst, and Bruce A. Larson, 71–90. Lanham, Md.: Rowman and Littlefield.

———. 2001b. "Special interests and direct democracy: An historical glance." In *The battle over citizen lawmaking: A collection of essays,* ed. M. Dane Waters, 59–72. Durham, N.C.: Carolina Academic Press.

———. 2001c. "Homeward bound? Micro-level legislative responsiveness to ballot initiatives." *State Politics and Policy Quarterly* 1: 50–61.

———. 2004. "Peeling away the populist rhetoric: Toward a taxonomy of anti-tax ballot initiatives." *Public Budgeting and Finance* 24: 88–110.

———. 2005. "Was Rove right? The partisan wedge and turnout effects of Issue 1, Ohio's 2004 ballot initiative to ban gay marriage." Paper presented at the 2005 University of California Center for the Study of Democracy/USC-Caltech Center for the Study of Law and Politics/Initiative and Referendum Institute conference, Newport Beach, Calif.

Smith, Daniel A., and Robert J. Herrington. 2000. "The process of direct democracy:

Colorado's 1996 parental rights amendment." *Social Science Journal* 37: 179–194.

Smith, Daniel A., and Joseph Lubinski. 2002. "Direct democracy during the Progressive Era: A crack in the populist veneer?" *Journal of Policy History* 14: 349–383.

Smith, Daniel A., and Caroline J. Tolbert. 2001. "The initiative to party: Partisanship and ballot initiatives in California." *Party Politics* 7: 738–757.

———. 2004. *Educated by initiative: The effects of direct democracy on citizens and political organizations in the American states.* Ann Arbor: University of Michigan Press.

Smith, Daniel A., Caroline J. Tolbert, and Todd Donovan. 2005. "Partisanship, direct democracy, and candidate choice." Paper presented at the 2005 annual meeting of the Midwest Political Science Association, Chicago.

Smith, James T. 2002. *The institutionalization of politics by scandal and the effect on the American view of government.* Unpublished dissertation, University of Nebraska.

Smith, Mark A. 2001. "The contingent effects of ballot initiatives and candidate races on turnout." *American Journal of Political Science* 45: 700–706.

———. 2002. "Ballot initiatives and the democratic citizen." *Journal of Politics* 64: 892–903.

Sniderman, Paul M., Richard A. Brody, and Philip E. Tetlock. 1991. *Reasoning and choice: Explorations in political psychology.* New York: Cambridge University Press.

Soldow, Gary F., and Victor Principe. 1981. "Responses to commercials as a function of program context." *Journal of Advertising Research* 21: 59–65.

Solop, Frederic I. 2001. "Digital democracy comes of age: Internet voting and the 2000 Arizona Democratic primary election." *PS: Political Science & Politics* 34: 289–293.

Sonner, Brenda S. 1998. "The effectiveness of negative political advertising: A case study." *Journal of Advertising Research* 38: 37–42.

Squire, Peverill. 1992. "Challenger profile and gubernatorial elections." *Western Political Quarterly* 45: 125–142.

Stimson, James A. 2004. *Tides of consent: How public opinion shapes American politics.* Cambridge: Cambridge University Press.

Stoker, Laura. 1993. "Judging presidential character: The demise of Gary Hart." *Political Behavior* 15: 193–223.

Strachan, J. Cherie. 2003. *High-tech grass roots: The professionalization of local elections.* Lanham, Md.: Rowman and Littlefield.

Stromer-Galley, Jennifer. 2000. "Democratizing democracy: Strong democracy, US political campaigns and the Internet." *Democratization* 7: 36–58.

Strother, Raymond D. 2003. *Falling up: How a redneck helped invent political consulting.* Baton Rouge: Louisiana State University Press.

Sulfaro, Valerie A. 1998. "Political sophistication and the presidential campaign: Citizen reactions to campaign advertisements." Paper presented at the 1998 annual meeting of the Midwest Political Science Association, Chicago.

———. 2001. "Political advertisements and decision-making shortcuts in the 2000 election." *Contemporary Argumentation and Debate* 22: 80–99.

Sullivan, Denis G., and Roger D. Masters. 1988. " 'Happy warriors': Leaders' facial displays, viewers' emotions, and political support." American Journal of Political Science 32: 345–368.

Sullivan, John L., John H. Aldrich, Eugine Borgida, and Wendy Rahn. 1990. "Candidate appraisal and human nature: Man and superman in the 1984 election." *Political Psychology* 11: 459–484.

Surlin, Stuart H., and Thomas F. Gordon. 1976. "Selective exposure and retention of political advertising." *Journal of Advertising Research* 5: 32–44.

Swanson, David L., and Paolo Mancini, eds. 1996. *Politics, media, and modern democracy: An international study of innovations in electoral campaigning and their consequences.* Westport, Conn.: Praeger.

Swint, Kerwin C. 1998. *Political consultants and negative campaigning: The secrets of the pros.* Lanham, Md.: University Press of America.

Tedesco, John C. 2002. "Televised political advertising effects: Evaluating responses during the 2000 Robb-Allen senatorial election." *Journal of Advertising* 31: 37–48.

Tedesco, John C., and Lynda Lee Kaid. 2003. "Style and effects of the Bush and Gore spots." In *The Millennium Election: Communication in the 2000 Campaigns,* ed. Lynda Lee Kaid, John C. Tedesco, Dianne G. Bystrom, and Mitchell S. McKinney, 5–16. Lanham, Md.: Rowman and Littlefield.

Tedesco, John C., Lynda Lee Kaid, and Lori M. McKinnon. 2000. "Network adwatches: Policing the 1996 primary and general election presidential ads." *Journal of Broadcasting and Electronic Media* 44: 541–555.

Teixeira, Ruy A. 1992. *The disappearing American voter.* Washington, D.C.: Brookings Institution Press.

Thayer, George. 1973. *Who shakes the money tree? American campaign financing practices from 1789 to the present.* New York: Simon and Schuster.

Theilmann, John, and Allen Wilhite. 1998. "Campaign tactics and the decision to attack." *Journal of Politics* 60: 1050–1062.

Thomas, Scott J. 1989. "Do incumbent expenditures matter?" *Journal of Politics* 51: 965–976.

Thompson, Dennis F. 1987. *Political ethics and public office.* Cambridge, Mass.: Harvard University Press.

___. 1995. *Ethics in Congress: From individual to institutional corruption.* Washington, D.C.: Brookings Institution Press.

Thorson, Esther, William G. Christ, and Clarke Caywood. 1991a. "Effects of issue-image strategies, attack and support appeals, music, and visual content in political commercials." *Journal of Broadcasting and Electronic Media* 35: 465–486.

___. 1991b. "Selling candidates like tubes of toothpaste: Is the comparison apt?" In *Television and political advertising,* Vol. 1: *Psychological processes,* ed. Frank Biocca, 145–172. Hillsdale, N.J.: Lawrence Erlbaum.

Thorson, Esther, Ekaterina Ognianova, James Coyle, and Frank Denton. 2000. "Negative political ads and negative citizen orientations toward politics." *Journal of Current Issues and Research in Advertising* 22: 13–40.

Thurber, James A. 1998. "The study of campaign consultants: A subfield in search of theory." *PS: Political Science & Politics* 31: 145–149.

___, ed. 2001. *The battle for Congress: Consultants, candidates, and voters.* Washington, D.C.: Brookings Institution Press.

___. 2002. "From campaigning to lobbying." In *Shades of gray: Perspectives on campaign ethics,* ed. Candice J. Nelson, David A. Dulio, and Stephen K. Medvic, 151–170. Washington, D.C.: Brookings Institution Press.

Thurber, James A., and Candice J. Nelson, eds. 2000. *Campaign warriors: Political consultants in elections.* Washington, D.C.: Brookings Institution Press.

___. 2004. *Campaigns and elections American style,* 2d ed. Boulder: Westview.

Thurber, James A., Candice J. Nelson, and David A. Dulio, eds. 2000a. *Crowded airwaves: Campaign advertising in elections.* Washington, D.C.: Brookings Institution Press.

___. 2000b. "Portrait of campaign consultants." In *Campaign warriors: Political consultants in elections,* ed. James A. Thurber and Candice J. Nelson, 10–36. Washington, D.C.: Brookings Institution Press.

Tinkham, Spencer F., and Ruth Ann Weaver-Lariscy. 1990. "Advertising message strategy in U.S. congressional campaigns: Its impact on election outcome." *Current Issues and Research in Advertising* 13: 207–226.

___. 1991. "Advertising message strategy in U.S. congressional campaigns: Its impact on election outcome." *Current Issues and Research in Advertising* 13: 207–226.

___. 1993. "A diagnostic approach to assessing the impact of negative political television commercials." *Journal of Broadcasting and Electronic Media* 37: 377–400.

———. 1995. "Incumbency and its perceived advantage: A comparison of 1982 and 1990 congressional advertising strategies." *Political Communication* 12: 291–304.

TNS Media Intelligence. 2004. "U.S. political advertising spending reaches $1.45 billion," November 1 (press release). www.tns-mi.com/news/11012004.htm.

Todorov, Alexander, Anesu N. Mandisodza, Amir Goren, and Crystal C. Hall. 2005. "Inferences of competence from faces predict election outcomes." *Science* 308 (June 10): 1623–1626.

Tolbert, Caroline J. 2003. "Direct democracy and institutional realignment in the American states." *Political Science Quarterly* 118: 467–489.

Tolbert, Caroline J., John A. Grummel, and Daniel A. Smith. 2001. "The effects of ballot initiatives on voter turnout in the American states." *American Politics Research* 29: 625–648.

Tolbert, Caroline J., and Rodney E. Hero. 1996. "Race/ethnicity and direct democracy: An analysis of California's illegal immigration initiative." *Journal of Politics* 58: 806–818.

Tolbert, Caroline J., Daniel H. Lowenstein, and Todd Donovan. 1998. "Election law and rules for using initiatives." In *Citizens as legislators: Direct democracy in the United States*, ed. Shaun Bowler, Todd Donovan, and Caroline J. Tolbert, 27–54. Columbus: Ohio State University Press.

Tolbert, Caroline J., Ramona S. McNeal, and Daniel A. Smith. 2003. "Enhancing civic engagement: The effect of direct democracy on political participation and knowledge." *State Politics and Policy Quarterly* 3: 23–41.

Tolbert, Caroline J. and Daniel A. Smith. 2005. "The educative effects of ballot initiatives on voter turnout." *American Politics Research* 33: 283–309.

Toobin, Jeffrey. 2001. *Too close to call: The thirty-six-day-battle to decide the 2000 election*. New York: Random House.

Trammell, Kaye D., and Andrew Paul Williams. 2004. "Beyond direct mail: Evaluating candidate e-mail messages in the 2002 Florida gubernatorial campaign." *Journal of E-Government* 1: 105–122.

Trent, Judith S., and Teresa Sabourin. 1993. "Sex still counts: Women's use of televised advertising during the decade of the 80s." *Journal of Applied Communication Research* 21: 21–40.

Trippi, Joe. 2004. *The revolution will not be televised: Democracy, the Internet, and the overthrow of everything*. New York: Regan Books.

Troy, Gil. 1996. *See how they ran: The changing role of the presidential candidate*, revised and expanded ed. Cambridge, Mass.: Harvard University Press.

Tufte, Edward R. 1975. "Determinants of the outcomes of midterm congressional elections." *American Political Science Review* 69: 812–826.

———. 1978. *Political control of the economy*. Princeton: Princeton University Press.

Tversky, Amos, and Daniel Kahneman. 1981. "The framing of decisions and the psychology of choice." *Science* 211: 453–458.

Tyson, Gerald S. 1999. "GOTV: Get out the vote." In *The Manship School guide to political communication*, ed. David T. Perlmutter, 131–136. Baton Rouge: Louisiana State University Press.

Ulferts, Alisa. 2003. "Lawmakers want hard road for initiatives." *St. Petersburg Times*, December 9. www.sptimes.com/2003/12/09/State/Lawmakers_want_hard_r.shtml.

Valentino, Nicholas A. 1999. "Crime news and the priming of racial attitudes during evaluations of the president." *Public Opinion Quarterly* 63: 293–320.

Valentino, Nicholas A., Vincent L. Hutchings, and Ismail K. White. 2002. "Cues that matter: How political ads prime racial attitudes during campaigns." *American Political Science Review* 96: 75–90.

Valentino, Nicholas A., Vincent L. Hutchings, and Dmitri Williams. 2004. "The impact of political advertising on knowledge, internet information seeking, and candidate preference." *Journal of Communication* 54: 337–354.

Van Dunk, Emily. 1997. "Challenger quality in state legislative elections." *Political Research Quarterly* 50: 793–807.

Vavreck, Lynn. 2000. "How does it all 'turnout'? Exposure to attack advertising, campaign interest, and participation in American presidential elections." In *Campaign Reform: Insights and Evidence*, ed. Larry M. Bartels and Lynn Vavreck, 79–105. Ann Arbor: University of Michigan Press.

———. 2001. "The reasoning voter meets the strategic candidate: Signals and specificity in campaign advertising, 1998." *American Politics Research* 29: 507–529.

Verba, Sidney, Kay Lehman Schlozman, and Henry E. Brady. 1995. *Voice and equality: Civic voluntarism in American politics*. Cambridge, Mass.: Harvard University Press.

Wadsworth, Anne Johnston, Philip Patterson, Lynda Lee Kaid, Ginger Cullers, Drew Malcomb, and Linda Lamirand. 1987. " 'Masculine' vs. 'feminine' strategies in political ads: Implications for female candidates." *Journal of Applied Communication Research* 15: 77–94.

Wagner, John. 2005. "O'Malley flap enters the governor's race: Fallout could affect 3 likely candidates." *Washington Post*, February 13, C1.

Waismel-Manor, Israel Sergio. 2005. *Making up their minds: Knowledge, learning and decision-making among campaign consultants*. Unpublished dissertation, Cornell University.

Walton, Hanes, Jr., ed. 1994. *Black politics and black political behavior: A linkage analysis*. Westport, Conn.: Praeger.

Waters, M. Dane. 2003. *Initiative and referendum almanac*. Durham, N.C.: Carolina Academic Press.

Watson, Robert P., and Colton C. Campbell, eds. 2003. *Campaigns and elections: Issues, concepts, cases*. Boulder: Lynne Rienner.

Wattenberg, Martin P. 1982. "From parties to candidates: Examining the role of the media." *Public Opinion Quarterly* 46: 216–227.

———. 1991. *The rise of candidate centered politics: Presidential elections of the 1980s*. Cambridge, Mass.: Harvard University Press.

———. 1998. *The decline of American political parties, 1952–1996*. Cambridge, Mass.: Harvard University Press.

Wattenberg, Martin P., and Craig Leonard Brians. 1999. "Negative campaign advertising: Demobilizer or mobilizer?" *American Political Science Review* 93: 891–899.

Wayne, Stephen J. 2001. *Is this any way to run a democratic election? Debating American electoral politics*. Boston: Houghton Mifflin.

Weaver, David, and Dan Drew. 2001. "Voter learning and interest in the 2000 presidential election: Did the media matter?" *Journalism and Mass Communication Quarterly* 78: 787–798.

Weaver, Paul. 1973. "Is television news biased?" *The Public Interest* 26: 57–74.

Weaver-Lariscy, Ruth Ann, and Spencer F. Tinkham. 1987. "The influence of media expenditure and allocation strategies in congressional advertising campaigns." *Journal of Advertising* 16: 13–21.

———. 1996. "Advertising message strategies in U.S. congressional campaigns: 1982, 1990." *Journal of Current Issues and Research in Advertising* 18: 53–66.

Weissman, Jonathan. 2004. "Kerry's inner circle expands." *Washington Post*, July 14, A1.

Welch, Susan, and John R. Hibbing. 1997. "The effects of charges of corruption on voting behavior in congressional elections, 1982–1990." *Journal of Politics* 59: 226–239.

Wenzel, James, Todd Donovan, and Shaun Bowler. 1998. "Direct democracy and minorities: Changing attitudes about minorities targeted by initiatives." In *Citizens as legislators: direct democracy in the United States*, ed. Shaun Bowler, Todd Donovan, and Caroline J. Tolbert, 228–248. Columbus: Ohio State University Press.

West, Darrell M. 1994. "Political advertising and news coverage in the 1992 California U.S. Senate campaigns." *Journal of Politics* 56: 1053–1075.

———. 2001. *Air wars: Television advertising in election campaigns, 1952–2000*, 3d ed. Washington, D.C.: CQ Press.

Whaley, John. 2003. *The evolution and maintenance of ethics regimes in Congress*. Unpublished dissertation, American University.

White, John Kenneth, and Daniel M. Shea. 2004. *New party politics: From Jefferson and Hamilton to the information age,* 2d ed. Belmont, Calif.: Wadsworth.

Whitney, Carol. 2002. "Wolves or watchdogs?" In *Shades of gray: Perspectives on campaign ethics,* ed. Candice J. Nelson, David A. Dulio, and Stephen K. Medvic, 98–109. Washington, D.C.: Brookings Institution Press.

———. 2004. "Campaign ethics: Public perception, reality, and the need to win." In *Campaigns and elections American style,* 2d ed., ed. James A. Thurber and Candice J. Nelson, 195–204. Boulder: Westview.

Wicks, Robert H., and Boubacar Souley. 2003. "Going negative: Candidate usage of Internet web sites during the 2000 presidential campaign." *Journalism and Mass Communication Quarterly* 80: 128–144.

Wicks, Robert H., Boubacar Souley, and Rebecca M. Verser. 2003. "Differences and similarities in use of campaign web sites during the 2000 presidential election." In *The millennium election: Communication in the 2000 campaign,* ed. Lynda Lee Kaid, John C. Tedesco, Dianne G. Bystrom, and Mitchell S. McKinney, 189–199. Lanham, Md.: Rowman and Littlefield.

Wielhouwer, Peter W. 1999. "The mobilization of campaign activists by the party canvass." *American Politics Quarterly* 27: 177–200.

———. 2000. "Releasing the fetters: Parties and the mobilization of the African-American electorate." *Journal of Politics* 62: 206–222.

———. 2001. "The relevance of classic readings on GOTV." Paper presented at the 2001 annual meeting of the Southwestern Political Science Association, Dallas.

———. 2003. "In search of Lincoln's perfect list: Targeting in grassroots campaigns." *American Politics Research* 31: 632–669.

———. 2006. "Get out the vote (GOTV)." In *Encyclopedia of American political parties and elections,* ed. Larry J. Sabato and Howard Ernst. New York: Facts on File, Inc. (forthcoming).

Wielhouwer, Peter W., and Brad Lockerbie. 1994. "Party contacting and political participation, 1952–90." *American Journal of Political Science* 38: 211–229.

Williams, Leonard. 1998. "Gender, political advertising, and the 'air wars.' " in *Women and elective office: Past, present, and future,* ed. Sue Thomas and Clyde Wilcox, 38–55. New York: Oxford University Press.

Williams, Wenmouth, Jr., Michael Shapiro, and Craig Cutbirth. 1983. "The impact of campaign agendas on perception of issues in the 1980 campaign." *Journalism Quarterly* 60: 226–231.

Winneg, Kenneth, and Talia Jomini. 2004. "The Internet as a source of campaign information: An analysis of its use in the 2004 Democratic presidential primary campaign." Paper presented at the 2004 annual meeting of the American Association for Public Opinion Research, Phoenix.

Wlezien, Christopher, and Robert S. Erikson. 2002. "The timeline of presidential election campaigns." *Journal of Politics* 64: 969–993.

Wong, Janelle S. 2005. "Mobilizing Asian American voters: A field experiment." *Annals of the American Academy of Political and Social Science* 601: 102–114.

Zaller, John R. 1992. *The nature and origins of mass opinion.* Cambridge: Cambridge University Press.

———. 1996. "The myth of massive media impact revived: New support for a discredited idea." In *Political persuasion and attitude change,* ed. Diana C. Mutz, Paul M. Sniderman, and Richard A. Brody, 17–78. Ann Arbor: University of Michigan Press.

Zhao, Xinshu, and Glen L. Bleske. 1995. "Measurement effects in comparing voter learning from television news and campaign advertisements." *Journalism and Mass Communication Quarterly* 72: 72–83.

Zhao, Xinshu, and Steven H. Chaffee. 1995. "Campaign advertisements versus television news as sources of political issue information." *Public Opinion Quarterly* 59: 41–65.